SENECA

II

MORAL ESSAYS

II

SENECA

IN TEN VOLUMES

II

MORAL ESSAYS

WITH AN ENGLISH TRANSLATION BY

JOHN W. BASORE, Ph.D.

PRINCETON UNIVERSITY

IN THREE VOLUMES

II

CAMBRIDGE, MASSACHUSETTS
HARVARD UNIVERSITY PRESS
LONDON
WILLIAM HEINEMANN LTD
MCMLXXIX

American
ISBN 0-674-99280-6

British
ISBN 0 434 99254 2

First printed 1932
Reprinted 1935, 1951, 1958, 1965, 1970, 1979

Printed in Great Britain

CONTENTS OF VOLUME II

INTRODUCTION

Of the essays contained in this volume, the three *Consolationes* are outstanding as interesting survivals in Latin prose[a] of a literary *genre* that was better known to the Greeks—a heritage from the philosophers that had fallen into the hands of the rhetoricians. These rather late specimens from Seneca, consequently, show little spontaneity, and abound in stock arguments, rhetorical commonplaces, and declamatory catalogues of examples from history.[b]

The origin of the type is to be associated with most of the ancient schools of philosophy,[c] but it remained for Crantor, an Academic philosopher of the fourth century B.C., to give it definite form in his famous letter to his friend Hippocles on the death of his children. Cicero by his praise[d] and by his use of the work in the *Tusculans* and in his own *Consolatio*[e] testifies to its ancient prestige.

The earliest Latin examples of the type are supplied

---

[a] Examples of the poetic *consolatio* are more common : *e.g.*, Statius, *Silvae*, ii. 6, iii. 3 ; Juvenal, xiii. and the *Ad Liviam* ascribed to Ovid.

[b] Favez, Introduction to *Ad Marciam*, p. xxvii.

[c] Buresch has collected the material in *Leipz. Stud.* **ix.** 1-164.

[d] *Academ.* ii. 135.   [e] Pliny, *Nat. Hist.* Praef. 22.

by the corpus of Cicero's correspondence—notably by his own letter to Titius [a] and that of Servius Sulpicius [b] to Cicero upon the loss of his daughter Tullia. Of Cicero's own *Consolatio* devised for self-comfort in this crisis only a few fragments remain.

Seneca's experiments with the *genre* include examples of the epistolary form [c] and the three more studied dialogues that appear here. Of these, the *Ad Marciam* and the *Ad Polybium*, with their theme of death, are marked by the stock arguments that belong to the type [d]—all men must die ; there is no need to grieve on our own account or that of the dead ; time will ease the sorrow, but let reason do it first.

The *Ad Marciam*, for all its show of Stoic hardness, has much that is noble and tender, and closes with a rapturous picture of the blissful existence of the sainted dead. The date of its composition is assigned by Waltz [e] to the period between A.D. 37 and 41.

The *Ad Polybium* and the *Ad Helviam* were written in exile and are interesting, but sad, commentaries on the quality of Seneca's Stoic fortitude. The first is seriously marred by much weakly complaint and base flattery of the emperor Claudius, while the other wins praise from its show of reasoned and cheerful acceptance of untoward fortune.

The mishaps [f] that might call forth a *consolatio* were as various as the misfortunes of men, but Seneca

---

[a] *Ad Fam.* v. 16.   [b] *Ad Fam.* iv. 5.
[c] *e.g.*, Epist. lxiii, xcix.
[d] *Cf.* Summers, Introd. to Letter lxiii. in *Select Letters* of Seneca.
[e] *Vie de Sénèque*, Introd. p 7, note 2.
[f] They are listed by Cicero in *Tusc. Disp.* iii. 81.

had no model for his task of penning comfort to Helvia; for here the mourned, "lifting his head from the bier," must himself give comfort to the chief mourner. Because of the novel situation the essay shows more eclecticism in argument, and is, consequently, the most original and human—and likewise the most orderly—of the three. The reasoning, developed from the two main propositions that neither the exile himself nor his mother is to be considered really unfortunate, smacks of the cleverness of Stoic paradox and is, on the whole, more ingenious than convincing.

The *De Vita Beata*, placed by Waltz in A.D. 58 or 59, is ostensibly a consideration of the questions of what true happiness is and how it is to be obtained. To live according to Nature or, in other words, to be able to rejoice in Stoic virtue is, clearly, the answer to the first; to pursue philosophy is, by implication, the answer to the second. In the actual showing, after a polemic against pleasure, reasoned discussion gives place, first, to a scathing arraignment of those who sneer at philosophy and, later, to a defence of the ownership of wealth, in which, believably, we may see Seneca's effort to answer his own critics.

The chronology of the *De Otio*—and of the *De Tranquillitate Animi* next in order—is wholly conjectural; the first is placed by Waltz after the return from exile in A.D. 49, the second in Seneca's declining years. The fragment of the *De Otio* opens with an attempt to reconcile the Stoic and the Epicurean attitude towards participation in public affairs, and closes with a plea for the life of philosophic leisure and contemplation.

In the *De Tranquillitate Animi* the author gives

much wise counsel to his young friend and disciple, Serenus, who is troubled by irresolution in coping with the appeal of luxury, public affairs, and literary fame. After an analysis of the causes of universal restlessness and boredom, guidance to inner peace and joy is given in a lengthy series of practical rules based broadly on reason and virtue.

The thesis of the *De Brevitate Vitae* is that the only true living consists in the pursuit of philosophy. To the philosopher life is never " short," for through books he may have access to all past ages, and learn from the sages both how to live and how to die. A discussion of how we waste time, and why consequently life seems too short prepares the way for the positive doctrine. In the spirited indictment [a] of scholarly research as a misuse of leisure it is tempting to see a covert satire upon the antiquarian interests of the eccentric Claudius. A clue to the date of composition is found in the author's apparent ignorance [b] of Claudius's extension of the *pomerium* in A.D. 50. The conclusion is that the treatise was written before that date, but after the return from exile.[c]

In the critical apparatus, A designates the *Codex Ambrosianus* at Milan, of the tenth or the eleventh century—the most important manuscript of the *Dialogues*. For the *Ad Marciam* and the *Ad Polybium* —of the latter A preserves but a scanty fragment— there is further a Florentine manuscript of the fifteenth century (designated F), and for the *Ad Polybium* alone a series of late manuscripts—one at Berlin (B), two at Milan (DE), one at Copenhagen (H),

---

[a] Ch. 13.   [b] Ch. 13. 8.
[c] Duff, *Literary History of Rome in the Silver Age*, p. 215.

one at Breslau (V), and one at Wolfenbüttel (G). The symbol O designates a consensus of BDEFH; C a consensus of any three or four of these.

The text is, with some necessary or desirable modifications, that of Hermes, Leipzig, 1905.

References to proper names, it will be found, are elucidated in the Index.

J. W. B.

PERUGIA, *July*, 1931.

BIBLIOGRAPHICAL NOTE (1979)

Edition:

L. *Annaei Senecae Dialogorum libri xii*, L. D. Reynolds, (OCT), 1977.

Studies:

Motto, A. L., *Seneca Sourcebook: Guide to the Thought of* ... (arranged by subject in alphabetical order), Amsterdam 1970. See also her bibliographical surveys in *Classical World* 54 (1960) and 64 (1971).

Griffin, Miriam T., *Seneca: A Philosopher in Politics*, Oxford, 1976.

SENECA
MORAL ESSAYS

L. ANNAEI SENECAE DIALOGORVM

LIBER VI

AD MARCIAM

DE CONSOLATIONE

1 1. Nisi te, Marcia, scirem tam longe ab infirmitate muliebris animi quam a ceteris vitiis recessisse et mores tuos velut aliquod antiquum exemplar aspici, non auderem obviam ire dolori tuo, cui viri quoque libenter haerent et incubant, nec spem concepissem tam iniquo tempore, tam inimico iudice, tam invidioso crimine posse me efficere, ut fortunam tuam absolveres. Fiduciam mihi dedit exploratum iam robur animi et magno experimento approbata virtus tua.

2 Non est ignotum, qualem te in persona patris tui gesseris, quem non minus quam liberos dilexisti, excepto eo quod non optabas superstitem. Nec scio an et optaveris; permittit enim sibi quaedam contra bonum morem magna pietas. Mortem A. Cremuti

---

a The particulars of Marcia's loss are known only from this dialogue. She was an intimate friend of the empress Livia (ch. 4), and the mother of four children, two sons and two daughters, of whom only the daughters survived (ch. 16). Her protracted mourning for a son Metilius (ch. 16) calls forth this effort of Seneca. In the opening

2

THE DIALOGUES OF
LUCIUS ANNAEUS SENECA

BOOK VI·

TO MARCIA

ON CONSOLATION

If I did not know, Marcia,[a] that you were as far removed from womanish weakness of mind as from all other vices, and that your character was looked upon as a model of ancient virtue, I should not dare to assail your grief—the grief that even men are prone to nurse and brood upon—nor should I have conceived the hope of being able to induce you to acquit Fortune of your complaint, at a time so unfavourable, with her judge so hostile, after a charge so hateful. But your strength of mind has been already so tested and your courage, after a severe trial, so approved that they have given me confidence.

How you bore yourself in relation to your father is common knowledge; for you loved him not less dearly than your children, save only that you did not wish him to outlive you. And yet I am not sure that you did not wish even that; for great affection sometimes ventures to break the natural law. The death of your

chapters elaborate reference is made to an earlier loss, when her father, the historian, A. Cremutius Cordus, accused of treason under Tiberius (A.D. 25), committed suicide.

3

Cordi parentis tui quantum poteras inhibuisti ;
postquam tibi apparuit inter Seianianos satellites
illam unam patere servitutis fugam, non favisti
consilio eius, sed dedisti manus victa fudistique
lacrimas palam et gemitus devorasti quidem, non
tamen hilari fronte texisti ; et haec illo saeculo, quo
3 magna pietas erat nihil impie facere. Ut vero
aliquam occasionem · mutatio temporum[1] dedit, ingenium patris tui, de quo sumptum erat supplicium,
in usum hominum reduxisti et a vera illum vindicasti
morte ac restituisti in publica monumenta libros,
quos vir ille fortissimus sanguine suo scripserat.
Optime meruisti de Romanis studiis : magna illorum
pars arserat ; optime de posteris, ad quos veniet
incorrupta rerum fides auctori suo magno imputata ;
optime de ipso, cuius viget vigebitque memoria, quam
diu in pretio fuerit Romana cognosci, quam diu quisquam erit, qui reverti velit ad acta maiorum, quam
diu quisquam qui velit scire, quid sit vir Romanus,
quid subactis iam cervicibus omnium et ad Seiania-
num iugum adactis indomitus, quid sit homo ingenio,
4 animo, manu liber. Magnum me hercules detrimentum res publica ceperat, si illum ob duas res
pulcherrimas in oblivionem coniectum, eloquentiam
et libertatem, non eruisses. Legitur, floret, in manus
hominum, in pectora receptus vetustatem nullam

---

[1] mutatio temporum *editors* : mutato tempore *AF*.

---

[a] The military terminology in the setting and the rhetoric
point to this interpretation of *fudisti*. It is commonly considered the equivalent of *effudisti*.

[b] *i.e.*, to commit no outrage on a parent.

[c] According to Tacitus, *Annals*, **iv.** 34. **1**, Cordus was
charged with treason for having lauded Brutus, and for
styling Cassius " the last of the Romans."

father, Aulus Cremutius Cordus, you delayed as long as you could ; after it became clear that, surrounded as he was by the minions of Sejanus, he had no other way of escape from servitude, favour his plan you did not, but you acknowledged defeat, and you routed *a* your tears in public and choked down your sobs, yet in spite of your cheerful face you did not conceal them—and these things in an age when the supremely filial was simply not to be unfilial ! *b* When, however, changed times gave you an opportunity, you recovered for the benefit of men that genius of your father which had brought him to his end, and thus saved him from the only real death, and the books which that bravest hero had written with his own blood you restored to their place among the memorials of the nation. You have done a very great service to Roman scholarship, for a large part of his writings had been burned ; a very great service to posterity, for history will come to them as an uncorrupted record whose honesty cost its author dear *c* ; and a very great service to the man himself, whose memory now lives and will ever live so long as it shall be worth while to learn the facts of Roman history—so long as there shall be anyone who will wish to hark back to the deeds of our ancestors, so long as there shall be anyone who will wish to know what it is to be a Roman hero, what it is to be unconquered when all necks are bowed and forced to bear the yoke of a Sejanus, what it is to be free in thought, in purpose, and in act. A great loss, in very truth, the state had suffered, had you not rescued this man who had been thrust into oblivion for the sake of two of the noblest things—eloquence and freedom. But he is now read, he lives, and ensconced in the hands and

5

timet; at illorum carnificum cito scelera quoque, quibus solis memoriam meruerunt, tacebuntur.[1]

5 Haec magnitudo animi tui vetuit me ad sexum tuum respicere, vetuit ad vultum, quem tot annorum continua tristitia, ut semel obduxit, tenet. Et vide, quam non subrepam tibi nec furtum facere affectibus tuis cogitem. Antiqua mala in memoriam reduxi et, ut scires[2] hanc quoque plagam esse sanandam, ostendi tibi aeque magni vulneris cicatricem. Alii itaque molliter agant et blandiantur ; ego confligere cum tuo maerore constitui et defessos exhaustosque oculos, si verum vis, magis iam ex consuetudine quam ex desiderio fluentis continebo, si fieri potuerit, favente te remediis tuis, si minus, vel invita, teneas licet et amplexeris dolorem tuum, quem tibi in filii locum superstitem fecisti. Quis enim erit finis ?

6 Omnia in supervacuum temptata sunt. Fatigatae adlocutiones amicorum, auctoritates magnorum et adfinium tibi virorum ; studia, hereditarium et paternum bonum, surdas aures irrito et vix ad brevem occupationem proficiente[3] solacio transeunt ; illud ipsum naturale remedium temporis, quod maximas quoque aerumnas componit, in te una vim suam

7 perdidit. Tertius iam praeterît annus, cum interim nihil ex primo illo impetu cecidit ; renovat se et corroborat cotidie luctus et iam sibi ius mora fecit

---

[1] tacebuntur *inferior* MSS. : tacebunt *A.*
[2] ut scires *Schultess* : uis scire *A.*
[3] proficiente *F* : proficientes *A* : proliciente *Waltz.*

hearts of men he fears no passing of the years ; but those cutthroats—even their crimes, by which alone they deserved to be remembered, will soon be heard of no more.

This evidence of the greatness of your mind forbade me to pay heed to your sex, forbade me to pay heed to your face, which, since sorrow once clouded it, unbroken sadness holds for all these years. And see! —I am not stealing upon you with stealth, nor am I planning to filch from you any of your sufferings. I have recalled to your memory old misfortunes, and, that you may know that even this deep-cut wound will surely heal, I have shown you the scar of an old wound that was not less severe. And so let others deal with you gently and ply soft words. I myself have determined to battle with your grief, and your eyes that are wearied and worn—weeping now, if I may speak the truth, more from habit than from sorrow —shall be checked by measures that, if so it may be, you welcome, if not, even against your will, even though you hug and embrace the sorrow that you have kept alive in place of your son. Else what end shall it have ? Every means has been tried in vain. The consolations of your friends, the influence of great men who were your relatives have been exhausted. Books, your love for which was a boon bequeathed by your father, now void of comfort and scarcely serving for brief distraction, make their appeal to unheeding ears. Even time, Nature's great healer, that allays even our most grievous sorrows, in your case only has lost its power. Three whole years have now passed, and yet the first violence of your sorrow has in no way abated. Your grief is renewed and grows stronger every day—by lingering

eoque adductus est, ut putet turpe desinere. Quemadmodum omnia vitia penitus insidunt, nisi, dum surgunt, oppressa sunt, ita haec quoque tristia et misera et in se saevientia ipsa novissime acerbitate pascuntur et fit infelicis animi prava voluptas dolor.

8 Cupissem itaque primis temporibus ad istam curationem accedere. Leniore medicina fuisset oriens adhuc restringenda vis; vehementius contra inveterata pugnandum est. Nam vulnerum quoque sanitas facilis est, dum a sanguine recentia sunt; tunc et uruntur et in altum revocantur et digitos scrutantium recipiunt, ubi corrupta in malum ulcus verterunt. Non possum nunc per obsequium nec molliter adsequi tam durum dolorem; frangendus est.

1 2. Scio a praeceptis incipere omnis, qui monere aliquem volunt, in exemplis desinere. Mutari hunc interim morem expedit; aliter enim cum alio agendum est. Quosdam ratio ducit, quibusdam nomina clara opponenda sunt et auctoritas, quae liberum non relin-

2 quat animum ad speciosa stupenti. Duo tibi ponam ante oculos maxima et sexus et saeculi tui exempla: alterius feminae, quae se tradidit ferendam dolori, alterius, quae pari adfecta casu, maiore damno, non tamen dedit longum in se malis suis dominium, sed

3 cito animum in sedem suam reposuit. Octavia et

it has established its right to stay, and has now reached the point that it is ashamed to make an end. Just as all vices become deep-rooted unless they are crushed when they spring up, so, too, such a state of sadness and wretchedness, with its self-afflicted torture, feeds at last upon its very bitterness, and the grief of an unhappy mind becomes a morbid pleasure. And so I should have liked to approach your cure in the first stages of your sorrow. While it was still young, a gentler remedy might have been used to check its violence; against inveterate evils the fight must be more vehement. This is likewise true of wounds—they are easy to heal while they are still fresh and bloody. When they have festered and turned into a wicked sore, then they must be cauterized and, opened up to the very bottom, must submit to probing fingers. As it is, I cannot possibly be a match for such hardened grief by being considerate and gentle ; it must be crushed.

I am aware that all those who wish to give anyone admonition commonly begin with precepts, and end with examples. But it is desirable at times to alter this practice ; for different people must be dealt with differently. Some are guided by reason, some must be confronted with famous names and an authority that does not leave a man's mind free, dazzled as he is by showy deeds. I shall place before your eyes but two examples—the greatest of your sex and century—one, of a woman who allowed herself to be swept away by grief, the other, of a woman who, though she suffered a like misfortune and even greater loss, yet did not permit her ills to have the mastery long, but quickly restored her mind to its accustomed state. Octavia and Livia, the one the

Livia, altera soror Augusti, altera uxor, amiserant filios iuvenes, utraque spe futuri principis certa.

Octavia Marcellum, cui et avunculus et socer incumbere coeperat, in quem onus imperii reclinare, adulescentem animo alacrem, ingenio potentem, sed frugalitatis continentiaeque in illis aut annis aut opibus non mediocriter admirandae, patientem laborum, voluptatibus alienum, quantumcumque imponere illi avunculus et, ut ita dicam, inaedificare voluisset, laturum ; bene legerat nulli cessura ponderi
4 fundamenta. Nullum finem per omne vitae suae tempus flendi gemendique fecit nec ullas admisit voces salutare aliquid adferentis ; ne avocari quidem se passa est, intenta in unam rem et toto animo adfixa. Talis per omnem vitam fuit, qualis in funere, non dico non ausa consurgere, sed adlevari recusans, secundam orbitatem iudicans lacrimas amittere. Nullam habere imaginem filii carissimi voluit, nullam sibi de illo fieri mentionem. Oderat omnes matres et in Liviam maxime furebat, quia videbatur ad illius filium transisse sibi promissa felicitas. Tenebris et solitudini familiarissima, ne ad fratrem quidem respiciens, carmina celebrandae Marcelli memoriae composita aliosque studiorum honores reiecit et aures suas adversus omne solacium clusit. A sollemnibus officiis seducta et ipsam magnitudinis fraternae

---

 a In 23 B.C. He had recently married Julia, daughter of Augustus.

 b Augustus had no son, and by his favours had apparently designated Marcellus as his successor. Later his choice fell upon Tiberius, the son of Livia.

 c Virgil has immortalized the memory of Marcellus in *Aeneid*, vi. 860 *sqq.*

10

sister of Augustus, the other his wife, had lost their
sons—both of them young men with the well-assured
hope of becoming emperor.

Octavia lost[a] Marcellus, upon whom Augustus, at
once his uncle and his father-in-law, had begun to
lean, upon whom he had begun to rest the burden of
empire—a young man of keen mind, of commanding
ability, yet withal marked by a frugality and self-
restraint that, for one of his years and wealth,
commanded the highest admiration, patient under
hardships, averse to pleasures, and ready to bear
whatever his uncle might wish to place or, so to speak,
to build upon him : well had he chosen a foundation
that would not sink beneath any weight. Through all
the rest of her life Octavia set no bounds to her tears
and moans, and closed her ears to all words that
offered wholesome advice ; with her whole mind fixed
and centred upon one single thing, she did not allow
herself even to relax. Such she remained during her
whole life as she was at the funeral—I do not say
lacking the courage to rise, but refusing to be uplifted, counting any loss of tears a second bereavement. Not a single portrait would she have of
her darling son, not one mention of his name in her
hearing. She hated all mothers, and was inflamed
most of all against Livia, because it seemed that
the happiness which had once been held out to
herself had passed to the other woman's son.[b]
Companioned ever by darkness and solitude, giving
no thought even to her brother, she spurned the
poems[c] that were written to glorify the memory of
Marcellus and all other literary honours, and closed
her ears to every form of consolation. Withdrawing from all her accustomed duties and hating

nimis circumlucentem fortunam exosa defodit se
et abdidit. Adsidentibus liberis, nepotibus lugubrem
vestem non deposuit, non sine contumelia omnium
suorum, quibus salvis orba sibi videbatur.

1   3. Livia amiserat filium Drusum, magnum futurum
principem, iam magnum ducem; intraverat penitus
Germaniam et ibi signa Romana fixerat,[1] ubi vix ullos
esse Romanos notum erat. In expeditione decesserat
ipsis illum hostibus aegrum cum veneratione et pace
mutua prosequentibus nec optare quod expediebat
audentibus. Accedebat ad hanc mortem, quam ille
pro re publica obierat, ingens civium provinciarumque
et totius Italiae desiderium, per quam effusis in
officium lugubre municipiis coloniisque usque in urbem
2 ductum erat funus triumpho simillimum. Non
licuerat matri ultima filii oscula gratumque extremi
sermonem oris haurire. Longo itinere reliquias
Drusi sui prosecuta tot per omnem Italiam ardentibus
rogis, quasi totiens illum amitteret, irritata, ut primum
tamen intulit tumulo, simul et illum et dolorem suum
posuit, nec plus doluit quam aut honestum erat
Caesare aut aequom Tiberio salvo.[2] Non desiit

[1] signa Romana fixerat *Muretus* : signum Romani
fixerunt *A* : signa Romani fixerunt *Bourgery, Favez.*

[2] aequom Tiberio salvo *Hermes after Gertz* (1889) : aequo
maluo *A* : aequom Nerone salvo *Schultess* : aequom alvo
Apelt after Ellis : aequum altero filio saluo *Waltz after
Gertz* (1886).

[a] Probably from Pavia to Rome in company with Augustus
(Tacitus, *Annals*, iii. 5. 1.

12

even the good fortune that her brother's greatness
shed all too brightly around her, she buried herself
in deep seclusion. Surrounded by children and
grandchildren, she would not lay aside her garb of
mourning, and, putting a slight on all her nearest,
accounted herself utterly bereft though they still
lived.

And Livia lost her son Drusus, who would have
made a great emperor, and had already shown himself
a great leader. For he had penetrated far into Germany, and had planted the Roman standards in a
region where it was scarcely known that any Romans
existed. He had died on the campaign, and his very
foes had reverently honoured his sick-bed by main-
taining peace along with us; nor did they dare to
desire what their interests demanded. And to
these circumstances of his death, which he had
met in the service of his country, there was added
the unbounded sorrow of his fellow-citizens, of the
provinces, and of all Italy, through the length of which
crowds poured forth from the towns and colonies,
and, escorting the funeral train all the way to the
city, made it seem more like a triumph. His mother
had not been permitted to receive her son's last
kisses and drink in the fond words of his dying lips.
On the long journey *a* through which she accompanied
the remains of her dear Drusus, her heart was harrowed by the countless pyres that flamed throughout
all Italy—for on each she seemed to be losing her son
afresh—, yet as soon as she had placed him in the tomb,
along with her son she laid away her sorrow, and
grieved no more than was respectful to Caesar or fair
to Tiberius, seeing that they were alive. And lastly,
she never ceased from proclaiming the name of her

13

denique Drusi sui celebrare nomen, ubique illum sibi
privatim publiceque repraesentare, libentissime de
illo loqui, de illo audire : cum memoria illius vixit ;
quam[1] nemo potest retinere et frequentare, qui illam
tristem sibi reddidit.

3   Elige itaque, utrum exemplum putes probabilius.
Si illud prius sequi vis, eximes te numero vivorum :
aversaberis et alienos liberos et tuos ipsumque quem[2]
desideras ; triste matribus omen occurres ; voluptates honestas, permissas, tamquam parum decoras
fortunae tuae reicies ; invisa haerebis in luce et aetati
tuae, quod non praecipitet te quam primum et finiat,
infestissima eris ; quod turpissimum alienissimumque
est animo tuo in meliorem noto partem, ostendes te
4 vivere nolle, mori non posse. Si ad hoc maximae
feminae te exemplum applicueris moderatius, mitius,
non eris in aerumnis nec te tormentis macerabis ;
quae enim, malum, amentia est poenas a se infelicitatis exigere et mala sua novo augere[3] ! Quam in
omni vita servasti morum probitatem et verecundiam,
in hac quoque re praestabis ; est enim quaedam et
dolendi modestia. Illum ipsum iuvenem, dignissi-
mum qui te laetam semper nominatus cogitatusque

---

[1] quam *added by Haase.*
[2] quem *added by Madvig.*
[3] novo augere *Madvig, Favez*   non augere *A* : augere
F : manu augere *Waltz.*

dear Drusus. She had him pictured everywhere, in private and in public places, and it was her greatest pleasure to talk about him and to listen to the talk of others—she lived with his memory. But no one can cherish and cling to a memory that he has rendered an affliction to himself.

Do you choose, therefore, which of these two examples you think the more laudable. If you prefer to follow the former, you will remove yourself from the number of the living; you will turn away your eyes both from other people's children and from your own, even from him whom you mourn; mothers will regard you as an unhappy omen; honourable and permissible pleasures you will renounce as ill-becoming to your plight; hating the light of day, you will linger in it, and your deepest offence will be your age, because the years do not hurry you on and make an end of you as soon as possible; you will show that you are unwilling to live and unable to die—a condition that is most disgraceful and foreign, too, to your character, which is conspicuous for its leaning toward the better course. If, on the other hand, you appropriate the example of the other most exalted lady, showing thus a more restrained and more gentle spirit, you will not dwell in sorrow, nor rack yourself with anguish. For what madness it is—how monstrous!—to punish one's self for misfortune and add new ill to present ills! That correctness of character and self-restraint which you have maintained all your life, you will exhibit in this matter also; for there is such a thing as moderation even in grieving. And as to the youth himself, who so richly deserved that the mention of his name and your thought of him should always bring you joy, you will set him in a more fitting place, if he

15

SENECA

faciat, meliore pones loco, si matri suae, qualis vivus
solebat, hilarisque et cum gaudio occurrit.

1   4. Nec te ad fortiora ducam praecepta, ut in-
humano ferre humana iubeam modo, ut ipso funebri
die oculos matris exsiccem. Ad arbitrum tecum
veniam ; hoc inter nos quaeretur, utrum magnus
dolor esse debeat an perpetuus. Non dubito quin
Iuliae Augustae, quam familiariter coluisti, magis
tibi placeat exemplum ; illa te ad suum consilium
2 vocat. Illa in primo fervore, cum maxime im-
patientes ferocesque sunt miseri, accessum Areo,
philosopho viri sui, praebuit et multum eam rem
profuisse sibi confessa est, plus quam populum
Romanum, quem nolebat tristem tristitia sua facere,
plus quam Augustum, qui subducto altero adminiculo
titubabat nec luctu suorum inclinandus erat, plus
quam Tiberium filium, cuius pietas efficiebat, ut in
illo acerbo et defleto gentibus funere nihil sibi nisi
3 numerum deesse sentiret. Hic, ut opinor, aditus
illi fuit, hoc principium apud feminam opinionis suae
custodem diligentissimam : "Usque in hunc diem,
Iulia, quantum quidem ego sciam—adsiduus viri tui
comes, cui non tantum quae in publicum emittuntur
nota, sed omnes sunt secretiores animorum vestrorum
motus—dedisti operam, ne quid esset quod in te
4 quisquam reprenderet ; nec id in maioribus modo

ᵃ Cf. Seneca, Cons. ad Polybium, xviii. 5: "et scio inveniri
quosdam (i.e. Stoics) durae magis quam fortis prudentiae
viros, qui negent doliturum esse sapientem."
    ᵇ i.e., Livia, who by the will of Augustus was adopted into
the Julian family (Tacitus, Annals, i. 8. 2).

comes before his mother as the same merry and joyous son that he used to be when he was alive.

Nor shall I direct your mind to precepts of the sterner sort,[a] so as to bid you bear a human fortune in inhuman fashion, so as to dry a mother's eyes on the very day of burial. But I shall come with you before an arbiter, and this will be the question at issue between us—whether grief ought to be deep or never-ending. I doubt not that the example of Julia Augusta,[b] whom you regarded as an intimate friend, will seem more to your taste than the other ; she summons you to follow her. She, during the first passion of grief, when its victims are most unsubmissive and most violent, made herself accessible to the philosopher Areus, the friend of her husband, and later confessed that she had gained much help from that source—more than from the Roman people, whom she was unwilling to sadden with this sadness of hers ; more than from Augustus, who was staggering under the loss of one of his main supports, and was in no condition to be further bowed down by the grief of his dear ones ; more than from her son Tiberius, whose devotion at that untimely funeral that made the nations weep kept her from feeling that she had suffered any loss except in the number of her sons. It was thus, I fancy, that Areus approached her, it was thus he commenced to address a woman who clung most tenaciously to her own opinion : " Up to this day, Julia, at least so far as I am aware—and, as the constant companion of your husband, I have known not only everything that was given forth to the public, but all the more secret thoughts of your minds —you have taken pains that no one should find anything at all in you to criticize ; and not only in the

17

observasti, sed in minimis, ne quid faceres, cui famam,
liberrimam principum iudicem, velles ignoscere.
Nec quicquam pulchrius existimo quam in summo
fastigio collocatos multarum rerum veniam dare,
nullius petere. Servandus itaque tibi in hac quoque
re tuus mos est, ne quid committas, quod minus
aliterve factum velis.

1   5. " Deinde oro atque obsecro, ne te difficilem
amicis et intractabilem praestes. Non est enim quod
ignores omnes hos nescire, quemadmodum se gerant,
loquantur aliquid coram te de Druso an nihil, ne aut
oblivio clarissimi iuvenis illi faciat iniuriam aut mentio
2 tibi. Cum secessimus et in unum convenimus, facta
eius dictaque quanto meruit suspectu celebramus ;
coram te altum nobis de illo silentium est. Cares
itaque maxima voluptate, filii tui laudibus, quas non
dubito quin vel impendio vitae, si potestas detur, in
3 aevum omne sis prorogatura. Quare patere, immo
accerse sermones, quibus ille narretur, et apertas
aures praebe ad nomen memoriamque filii tui ; nec
hoc grave duxeris ceterorum more, qui in eiusmodi
4 casu partem mali putant audire solacia. Nunc in-
cubuisti tota in alteram partem et oblita meliorum
fortunam tuam qua deterior est aspicis : non con-
vertis te ad convictus filii tui occursusque iucundos,

larger matters, but in the smallest trifles, you have
been on your guard not to do anything that you could
wish public opinion, that most frank judge of princes,
to excuse. And nothing, I think, is more admirable
than the rule that those who have been placed in high
position should bestow pardon for many things, should
seek pardon for none. And so in this matter also you
must still hold to your practice of doing nothing that
you could wish undone, or done otherwise.

" Furthermore, I beg and beseech of you, do not
make yourself unapproachable and difficult to your
friends. For surely you must be aware that none of
them know how to conduct themselves—whether they
should speak of Drusus in your presence or not—
wishing neither to wrong so distinguished a youth
by forgetting him, or to hurt you by mentioning
him. When we have withdrawn from your company
and are gathered together, we extol his deeds and
words with all the veneration he deserved ; in your
presence there is deep silence about him. And so
you are missing a very great pleasure in not hearing
the praises of your son, which I doubt not, you would
be glad, if you should be given the opportunity,
to prolong to all time even at the cost of your life.
Wherefore submit to conversation about your son, nay,
encourage it, and let your ears be open to his name
and memory ; and do not consider this burdensome,
after the fashion of some others, who in a calamity of
this sort count it an added misfortune to have to
listen to words of comfort. As it is, you have tended
wholly to the other extreme, and, forgetting the
better aspects of your fortune, you gaze only upon
its worse side. You do not turn your thought to the
pleasant intercourse and the meetings you had with

non ad pueriles dulcesque blanditias, non ad incrementa studiorum ; ultimam illam faciem rerum premis ; illi, tamquam si parum ipsa per se horrida
5 sit, quidquid potes congeris. Ne, obsecro te, concupieris perversissimam gloriam, infelicissima videri ! Simul cogita non esse magnum rebus prosperis fortem gerere, ubi secundo cursu vita procedit ; ne gubernatoris quidem artem tranquillum mare et obsequens ventus ostendit, adversi aliquid incurrat oportet,
6 quod animum probet. Proinde ne summiseris te, immo contra fige stabilem gradum et quicquid onerum supra cecidit sustine, primo dumtaxat strepitu conterrita. Nulla re maior invidia fortunae fit quam aequo animo." Post haec ostendit illi filium incolumem, ostendit ex amisso nepotes.

1   6. Tuum illic, Marcia, negotium actum, tibi Areus adsedit ; muta personam—te consolatus est. Sed puta, Marcia, ereptum tibi amplius quam ulla umquam mater amiserit—non permulceo te nec extenuo calamitatem tuam. Si fletibus fata vincuntur, con-
2 feramus ; eat omnis inter luctus dies, noctem sine somno tristitia consumat ; ingerantur lacerato pectori manus et in ipsam faciem impetus fiat atque omni se genere saevitiae profecturus maeror exerceat. Sed si nullis planctibus defuncta revocantur, si sors immota et in aeternum fixa nulla miseria mutatur et mors tenuit quicquid abstulit, desinat dolor qui perit.

your son, nor to his fond and boyish caresses, nor to the progress of his studies ; you dwell only on that last appearance of fortune, and just as if it were not horrible enough in itself, you add to it all the horror you can. Do not, I pray you, covet that most perverse distinction—that of being considered the most unhappy of women ! Reflect, too, that it is no great thing to show one's self brave in the midst of prosperity, when life glides on in a tranquil course ; a quiet sea and a favouring wind do not show the skill of a pilot either—some hardship must be encountered that will test his soul. Accordingly, do not be bowed down—nay, on the contrary, plant your feet firmly, and, terrified only at first by the din, support whatever burden may fall from above. Nothing casts so much contempt on Fortune as an unruffled spirit." After this he directed her to the son that was still alive, he directed her to the children of the son she had lost.

It was your trouble, Marcia, that was dealt with there, it was at your side that Areus sat ; change the rôle—it was you that he tried to comfort. But suppose, Marcia, more was snatched from you than any mother has ever lost—I am not trying to soothe you or to minimize your calamity. If tears can vanquish fate, let us marshal tears ; let every day be passed in grief, let every night be sleepless and consumed with sorrow ; let hands rain blows on a bleeding breast, nor spare even the face from their assault ; if sorrow will help, let us vent it in every kind of cruelty. But if no wailing can recall the dead, if no distress can alter a destiny that is immutable and fixed for all eternity, and if death holds fast whatever it has once carried off, then let grief, which is futile, cease. Wherefore let us steer our own ship,

3 Quare regamur nec nos ista vis transversos auferat!
Turpis est navigii rector, cui gubernacula fluctus
eripuit, qui fluvitantia vela deseruit, permisit tem-
pestati ratem; at ille vel in naufragio laudandus
quem obruit mare clavum tenentem et obnixum.

1 7. "At enim naturale desiderium suorum est."
Quis negat, quam diu modicum est? Nam discessu,
non solum amissione carissimorum necessarius morsus
est et firmissimorum quoque animorum contractio.
Sed plus est quod opinio adicit quam quod natura
2 imperavit. Aspice mutorum animalium quam
concitata sint desideria et tamen quam brevia:
vaccarum uno die alterove mugitus auditur, nec
diutius equarum vagus ille amensque discursus est;
ferae cum vestigia catulorum consectatae sunt et
silvas pervagatae, cum saepe ad cubilia expilata
redierint, rabiem intra exiguum tempus extinguunt;
aves cum stridore magno inanes nidos circum-
fremuerunt, intra momentum tamen quietae volatus
suos repetunt; nec ulli animali longum fetus sui
desiderium est nisi homini, qui adest dolori suo nec
tantum, quantum sentit, sed quantum constituit,
adficitur.

3 Ut scias autem non esse hoc naturale, luctibus
frangi, primum magis feminas quam viros, magis
barbaros quam placidae eruditaeque gentis homines,
magis indoctos quam doctos eadem orbitas vulnerat.
Atqui ea, quae a natura vim acceperunt, eandem in

and not allow this power to sweep us from the course ! He is a sorry steersman who lets the waves tear the helm from his hands, who has left the sails to the mercy of the winds, and abandoned the ship to the storm ; but he deserves praise, even amid shipwreck, whom the sea overwhelms still gripping the rudder and unyielding.

" But," you say, " Nature bids us grieve for our dear ones." Who denies it, so long as grief is tempered ? For not only the loss of those who are dearest to us, but a mere parting, brings an inevitable pang and wrings even the stoutest heart. But false opinion has added something more to our grief than Nature has prescribed. Observe how passionate and yet how brief is the sorrow of dumb animals. The lowing of cows is heard, for one or two days only, and that wild and frantic running about of mares lasts no longer ; wild beasts, after following the tracks of their stolen cubs, after wandering through the forests and returning over and over to their plundered lairs, within a short space of time quench their rage ; birds, making a great outcry, rage about their empty nests, yet in a trice become quiet and resume their ordinary flight ; nor does any creature sorrow long for its offspring except man— he nurses his grief, and the measure of his affliction is not what he feels, but what he wills to feel.

Moreover, in order that you may know that it is not by the will of Nature that we are crushed by sorrow, observe, in the first place, that, though they suffer the same bereavement, women are wounded more deeply than men, savage peoples more deeply than the peaceful and civilized, the uneducated, than the educated. But the passions that derive their

23

omnibus servant ; apparet non esse naturale quod
4 varium est. Ignis omnes aetates omniumque urbium
cives, tam viros quam feminas uret ; ferrum in omni
corpore exhibebit secandi potentiam. Quare ? quia
vires illi a natura datae sunt, quae nihil in personam
constituit. Paupertatem, luctum, ambitionem[1] alius
aliter sentit, prout illum consuetudo infecit, et imbecillum impatientemque reddit praesumpta opinio
de non timendis terribilis.

1   8. Deinde quod naturale est non decrescit mora ;
dolorem dies longa consumit. Licet contumacis-
simum, cotidie insurgentem et contra remedia ef-
fervescentem, tamen illum efficacissimum mitigandae
2 ferociae tempus enervat.   Manet quidem tibi, Marcia,
etiamnunc ingens tristitia et iam videtur duxisse
callum, non illa concitata, qualis initio fuit, sed
pertinax et obstinata ; tamen hanc quoque tibi aetas
minutatim eximet. Quotiens aliud egeris, animus
3 relaxabitur.   Nunc te ipsa custodis ; multum autem
interest, utrum tibi permittas maerere an imperes.
Quanto magis hoc morum tuorum elegantiae convenit, finem luctus potius facere quam expectare,
nec illum opperiri diem, quo te invita dolor desinat !
Ipsa illi renuntia !

1   9. " Unde ergo tanta nobis pertinacia in deplora-

---

[1] ambitionem *A* : damnationem *Madvig* : amissionem
Gertz : contemptionem *Waltz* : abitionem *Negro*.

---

[a] The word has little point here, and the Latin reading is
justly suspected.

power from Nature maintain the same hold upon all ;
therefore it is clear that a passion of variable power
is not ordered by Nature. Fire will burn alike people
of all ages and of all nationalities, men as well as
women ; steel will display its cutting force upon
every sort of flesh. And why ? Because each derives
its power from Nature, which makes no distinction of
persons. But poverty, grief, and ambition ^{a} are felt
differently by different people according as their
minds are coloured by habit, and a false presumption,
which arouses a fear of things that are not to be
feared, makes a man weak and unresisting.

In the second place, whatever proceeds from
Nature is not diminished by its continuance. But
grief is effaced by the long lapse of time. However
stubborn it may be, mounting higher every day and
bursting forth in spite of efforts to allay it, nevertheless the most powerful agent to calm its fierceness is
time—time will weaken it. There remains with you
even now, Marcia, an immense sorrow ; it seems
already to have grown calloused—no longer the
passionate sorrow it was at first, but still persistent
and stubborn ; yet this also little by little time will
remove. Whenever you engage in something else,
your mind will be relieved. As it is now, you keep
watch on yourself ; but there is a wide difference between permitting and commanding yourself to
mourn. How much better would it accord with the
distinction of your character to force, and not merely
to foresee, an end to your grief, and not to wait for
that distant day on which, even against your will,
your distress will cease ! Do yóu of your own will
renounce it !

" Why then," you ask, " do we all so persist in
25

tione nostri, si id non fit naturae iussu ? " Quod
nihil nobis mali, antequam eveniat, proponimus, sed
ut immunes ipsi et aliis pacatius ingressi iter alienis
2 non admonemur casibus illos esse communes. Tot
praeter domum nostram ducuntur exsequiae : de
morte non cogitamus ; tot acerba funera : nos togam
nostrorum infantium, nos militiam et paternae
hereditatis successionem agitamus animo ; tot
divitum subita paupertas in oculos incidit : et nobis
numquam in mentem venit nostras quoque opes
aeque in lubrico positas. Necesse est itaque magis
corruamus : quasi ex inopinato ferimur ; quae multo
3 ante provisa sunt, languidius incurrunt. Vis tu scire
te ad omnis expositum ictus stare et illa quae alios
tela fixerunt circa te vibrasse ! Velut murum
aliquem aut obsessum multo hoste locum et arduum
ascensu semermis adeas, expecta vulnus et illa superne
volantia cum sagittis pilisque saxa in tuum puta
librata corpus. Quotiens aliquis ad latus aut pone
tergum ceciderit, exclama : " Non decipies me,
fortuna, nec securum aut neglegentem opprimes.
Scio quid pares ; alium quidem percussisti, sed me
4 petisti." Quis umquam res suas quasi periturus
aspexit ? Quis umquam nostrum de exilio, de
egestate, de luctu cogitare ausus est ? Quis non,
si admoneatur ut cogitet, tamquam dirum omen

---

a Seneca probably has in mind the case of Theseus as
depicted in a play of Euripides (*Frag.* 964 Nauck)—a stock
example of one who foresaw and schooled himself to meet
all possible reversals of fortune. See Plutarch, *Consolatio ad
Apollonium,* *Mor.* 112 D ; Cicero, *Tusc. Disp.* iii. 14. 29.
26

lamenting what was ours, if it is not Nature's will that
we should ? " Because we never anticipate any evil
before it actually arrives, but, imagining that we ourselves are exempt and are travelling a less exposed
path, we refuse to be taught by the mishaps of others
that such are the lot of all. So many funerals pass our
doors, yet we never think of death ! So many deaths
are untimely, yet we make plans for our own infants—
how they will don the toga, serve in the army, and
succeed to their father's property ! So many rich
men are stricken before our eyes with sudden poverty,
yet it never occurs to us that our own wealth also
rests on just as slippery a footing ! Of necessity,
therefore, we are more prone to collapse ; we are
struck, as it were, off our guard ; blows that are long
foreseen fall less violently. And you wish to be told
that you stand exposed to blows of every sort, and
that the darts that have transfixed others have
quivered around you ! Just as if you were assaulting
some city wall, or were mounting, only half-armed,
against some lofty position manned by a host of the
enemy, expect to be wounded, and be sure that the
missiles that whirl above your head, the stones and
the arrows and the javelins, were all aimed at your
own person. Whenever anyone falls at your side or
behind you, cry out : " Fortune, you will not deceive
me, you will not fall upon me confident and heedless.
I know what you are planning ; it is true you struck
someone else, but you aimed at me." Who of us ever
looked upon his possessions with the thought that he
would die ?[a] Who of us ever ventured to think upon
exile, upon want, upon grief ? Who, if he were urged
to reflect upon these things, would not reject the idea
as an unlucky omen, and demand that those curses

27

respuat et in capita inimicorum aut ipsius in-
tempestivi monitoris abire illa iubeat? "Non
5 putavi futurum." Quicquam tu putas non futurum,
quod scis[1] posse fieri, quod multis vides evenisse?
Egregium versum et dignum qui non e pulpito exiret:

Cuivis potest accidere quod cuiquam potest!

Ille amisit liberos; et tu amittere potes. Ille dam-
natus est; et tua innocentia sub ictu est. Error
decipit hic, effeminat, dum patimur quae numquam
pati nos posse providimus. Aufert vim praesentibus
malis qui futura prospexit.

1   10. Quicquid est hoc, Marcia, quod circa nos ex
adventicio fulget, liberi, honores, opes, ampla atria et
exclusorum clientium turba referta vestibula, clarum
nomen,[2] nobilis aut formosa coniux ceteraque ex incerta et mobili sorte pendentia alieni commodatique
apparatus sunt; nihil horum dono datur. Conlaticiis et
ad dominos redituris instrumentis scaena adornatur;
alia ex his primo die, alia secundo referentur, pauca
2 usque ad finem perseverabunt. Itaque non est quod
nos suspiciamus tamquam inter nostra positi; mutua
accepimus. Usus fructusque noster est, cuius tempus
ille arbiter muneris sui temperat; nos oportet in
promptu habere quae in incertum diem data sunt et

---

[1] quod scis *Madvig*: quod multis scis *A.*
[2] nomen *supplied by Madvig.*

---

[a] Publilius Syrus, a writer of mimes under the late
Republic, famous for his adages.

pass over to the head of an enemy or even to that of his untimely adviser ? You say : " I did not think it would happen." Do you think there is anything that will not happen, when you know that it is possible to happen, when you see that it has already happened to many ? A striking verse this—too good to have come from the stage :

> Whatever can one man befall can happen just as well to all ! [a]

That man lost his children ; you also may lose yours. That man was condemned to death ; your innocence also is in imminent peril. Such is the delusion that deceives and weakens us while we suffer misfortunes which we never foresaw that we ourselves could possibly suffer. He robs present ills of their power who has perceived their coming beforehand.

All these fortuitous things, Marcia, that glitter about us—children, honours, wealth, spacious halls and vestibules packed with a throng of unadmitted clients, a famous name, a high-born or beautiful wife, and all else that depends upon uncertain and fickle chance—these are not our own but borrowed trappings ; not one of them is given to us outright. The properties that adorn life's stage have been lent, and must go back to their owners ; some of them will be returned on the first day, others on the second, only a few will endure until the end. We have, therefore, no reason to be puffed up as if we were surrounded with the things that belong to us ; we have received them merely as a loan. The use and the enjoyment are ours, but the dispenser of the gift determines the length of our tenure. On our part we ought always to keep in readiness the gifts that have been granted

appellatos sine querella reddere : pessimi debitoris est
3 creditori facere convicium. Omnes ergo nostros, et
quos superstites lege nascendi optamus et quos prae-
cedere iustissimum ipsorum votum est, sic amare debemus, tamquam nihil nobis de perpetuitate, immo
nihil de diuturnitate eorum promissum sit. Saepe
admonendus est animus, amet ut recessura, immo
tamquam recedentia. Quicquid a fortuna datum est,
4 tamquam exempto auctore[1] possideas. Rapite ex
liberis voluptates, fruendos vos in vicem liberis date
et sine dilatione omne gaudium haurite ; nihil de
hodierna nocte promittitur—nimis magnam advoca-
tionem dedi—, nihil de hac hora. Festinandum est,
instatur a tergo. Iam disicietur iste comitatus, iam
contubernia ista sublato clamore solventur. Rapina
rerum omnium est ; miseri nescitis in fuga vivere !
5   Si mortuum tibi filium doles, eius temporis quo
natus est crimen est ; mors enim illi denuntiata nascenti est; in hanc legem erat satus,[2] hoc illum fatum
6 ab utero statim prosequebatur. In regnum fortunae
et quidem durum atque invictum pervenimus, illius arbitrio digna atque indigna passuri. Corporibus nostris
impotenter, contumeliose, crudeliter abutetur. Alios
ignibus peruret vel in poenam admotis vel in remedium;
alios vinciet : id nunc hosti licebit, nunc civi ; alios

---

[1] exempto auctore *Madvig* : exemplum auctore *A* :
exemplum ab auctore *F* : exemptum auctore *Waltz* : exemp-
turo auctore *Favez after Pichon.*
[2] satus *Schultess (adding* erat): datus *A.*

---

[a] *i.e.*, the tenure of Fortune's gifts is insecure.
[b] *i.e.*, death threatens all; only the philosopher learns
not to fear it—he only knows how really to live.

for a time not fixed, and, when called upon, to restore them without complaint; it is a very mean debtor that reviles his creditor. And so we should love all of our dear ones, both those whom, by the condition of birth, we hope will survive us, and those whose own most just prayer is to pass on before us, but always with the thought that we have no promise that we may keep them forever—nay, no promise even that we may keep them for long. Often must the heart be reminded—it must remember that loved objects will surely leave, nay, are already leaving. Take whatever Fortune gives, remembering that it has no voucher.[a] Snatch the pleasures your children bring, let your children in turn find delight in you, and drain joy to the dregs without delay; no promise has been given you for this night—nay, I have offered too long a respite!—no promise has been given even for this hour. We must hurry, the enemy presses upon our rear. Soon these companions will all be scattered, soon the battle-cry will be raised, and these comrade ties sundered. Nothing escapes the pillage; poor wretches, amid the rout ye know not how to *live*![b]

If you grieve for the death of your son, the blame must go back to the time when he was born; for his death was proclaimed at his birth; into this condition was he begotten, this fate attended him straightway from the womb. We have come into the realm of Fortune, and harsh and invincible is her power; things deserved and undeserved must we suffer just as she wills. With violence, insult, and cruelty she will maltreat our bodies. Some she will burn with fire, applied, it may be, to punish, it may be, to heal; some she will bind with chains, committing the power now to an enemy, now to a fellow-countryman; some

31

per incerta nudos maria iactabit et luctatos cum
fluctibus ne in harenam quidem aut litus explodet,
sed in alicuius immensae ventrem beluae decondet;
alios morborum varis generibus emaceratos diu inter
vitam mortemque medios detinebit. Ut varia et libi-
dinosa mancipiorumque suorum neglegens domina et
poenis et muneribus errabit.

1 11. Quid opus est partes deflere? Tota flebilis
vita est; urgebunt nova incommoda, priusquam veteribus satis feceris. Moderandum est itaque vobis
maxime, quae immoderate fertis, et in multos dolores
humani pectoris vis[1] dispensanda. Quae deinde ista
suae publicaeque condicionis oblivio est? Mortalis
nata es, mortales peperisti. Putre ipsa fluidumque
corpus et causis morborum repetita[2] sperasti tam
2 imbecilla materia solida et aeterna gestasse? Decessit filius tuus; id est, decucurrit ad hunc finem, ad
quem quae feliciora partu tuo putas properant. Hoc
omnis ista quae in foro litigat, spectat[3] in theatris, in
templis precatur turba dispari gradu vadit; et quae
diligis, veneraris et quae despicis unus exaequabit
cinis. Hoc videlicet dicit[4] illa Pythicis oraculis ad-
3 scripta vox[5]: NOSCE TE. Quid est homo? Quolibet

----

[1] vis *added by Madvig.*

[2] causis morborum repetita *Gertz*: causis morbos repetitas
A: causis omnibus repetita *v.d. Vliet*: carnis morbo repetita
Madvig: carnis morbos sortita *Pfennig*: causis repleta
Waltz: causis morborum repleta *Apelt.*

[3] spectat *added by Gertz after* theatris.

[4] dicit *suggested addition of Hermes*: videlicet (illa) *A*:
videre iubet *Gertz*: indicat *Waltz*: videre licet *Favez.*

[5] vox *added by Erasmus*: voce *added by Favez.*

----

[a] Seneca translates the Greek saying, Γνῶθι σεαυτόν,
inscribed at Delphi and variously attributed to the Greek
sages or to Apollo himself. *Cf.* Coleridge (*Self-Knowledge*):

she will toss naked upon the fickle sea, and, when their struggle with the waves is over, she will not even cast them up on the sand or the shore, but will hide them away in the maw of some huge monster; others, when she has worn them down with divers diseases, she will long keep suspended between life and death. Like a mistress that is changeable and passionate and neglectful of her slaves, she will be capricious in both her rewards and her punishments.

What need is there to weep over parts of life? The whole of it calls for tears. New ills will press on before you have done with the old. Therefore you women especially must observe moderation, you who are immoderate in your grief, and against your many sorrows the power of the human breast must be arrayed. Again, why this forgetfulness of what is the individual and the general lot? Mortal have you been born, to mortals have you given birth. You, who are a crumbling and perishable body and oft assailed by the agents of disease,—can you have hoped that from such frail matter you gave birth to anything durable and imperishable? Your son is dead; that is, he has finished his course and reached that goal toward which all those whom you count more fortunate than your child are even now hastening. Toward this, at different paces, moves all this throng that now squabbles in the forum, that looks on at the theatres, that prays in the temples; both those whom you love and revere and those whom you despise one heap of ashes will make equal. This, clearly, is the meaning of that famous utterance ascribed to the Pythian oracle: KNOW THYSELF.[a] What

Γνῶθι σεαυτόν ! And is this the prime
And heaven-sprung adage of the olden time?

quassu vas et quolibet fragile iactatu. Non tempestate magna, ut dissiperis, opus est; ubicumque arietaveris, solveris. Quid est homo? Imbecillum corpus et fragile, nudum, suapte natura inerme, alienae opis indigens, ad omnis fortunae contumelias proiectum; cum bene lacertos exercuit, cuiuslibet ferae pabulum, cuiuslibet victima, ex infirmis fluidisque contextum et lineamentis exterioribus nitidum, frigoris, aestus, laboris impatiens, ipso rursus situ et otio iturum in tabem, alimenta metuens sua, quorum modo inopia deficit, modo copia[1] rumpitur; anxiae sollicitaeque tutelae, precarii spiritus et male haerentis, quem pavor repentinus aut auditus ex improviso[2] sonus auribus gravis excutit; sollicitudinis[3] semper 4 sibi nutrimentum, vitiosum et inutile. Miramur in hoc mortem, quae unius singultus opus est? Numquid enim, ut concidat, magni res molimenti est? Odor illi saporque et lassitudo et vigilia et umor et cibus et sine quibus vivere non potest mortifera sunt; quocumque se movit, statim infirmitatis suae conscium, non omne caelum ferens, aquarum novitatibus flatuque non familiaris aurae et tenuissimis causis atque offensionibus morbidum, putre, causarium, fletu vitam

[1] deficit modo copia *added by P. Thomas.*
[2] quem pavor repentinus aut auditus ex inproviso *Hermes conjectures*: qua parum repentinū audiet exinproviso *AF*: quem ex improviso sonus *Waltz.*
[3] sollicitudinis *Gertz*: solli *A*: periculi *Waltz*: inbecillitatis *Favez.*

is man? A vessel that the slightest shaking, the slightest toss will break. No mighty wind is needed to scatter you abroad; whatever you strike against, will be your undoing. What is man? A body weak and fragile, naked,[a] in its natural state defenceless, dependent upon another's help, and exposed to all the affronts of Fortune; when it has practised well its muscles, it then becomes the food of every wild beast, of everyone the prey ; a fabric of weak and unstable elements, attractive only in its outer features, unable to bear cold, heat, and toil, yet from mere rust and idleness doomed to decay ; fearful of the foods that feed it, it dies now from the lack of these, and now is burst open by their excess ; filled with anxiety and concern for its safety, it draws its very breath on sufferance, keeping but a feeble hold upon it—for sudden fear or a loud noise that falls unexpectedly upon the ears will drive it forth— and fosters ever its own unrest, a morbid and a useless thing. Do we wonder that in this thing is death, which needs but a single sigh ? Is it such a mighty undertaking to compass its destruction ? For it, smell and taste, weariness and loss of sleep, drink and food, and the things without which it cannot live are charged with death. Whithersoever it moves, it straightway becomes conscious of its frailty ; un- able to endure all climates, from strange waters, a blast of unfamiliar air, the most trifling causes and complaints, it sickens and rots with disease—having

[a] *Cf.* Lucretius, v. 222 *sqq.* :
> Tum porro puer, ut saevis proiectus ab undis
> navita, nudus humi iacet, infans, indigus omni
> vitali auxilio, cum primum in luminis oras
> nixibus ex alvo matris natura profudit.

auspicatum, cum interim quantos tumultus hoc tam
contemptum animal movet ! in quantas cogitationes
5 oblitum condicionis suae venit ! Immortalia, aeterna
volutat animo et in nepotes pronepotesque disponit,
cum interim longa conantem eum mors opprimit et
hoc, quod senectus vocatur, paucissimorum est[1] cir-
cuitus annorum.

1 12. Dolor tuus, si modo ulla illi ratio est, utrum
sua spectat incommoda an eius qui decessit ? Utrum
te in amisso filio movet, quod nullas ex illo voluptates
cepisti, an quod maiores, si diutius vixisset, percipere
potuisti ? Si nullas percepisse te dixeris, tolerabilius
efficies detrimentum tuum ; minus enim homines desiderant ea, ex quibus nihil gaudi laetitiaeque per-
ceperant. Si confessa fueris percepisse magnas
voluptates, oportet te non de eo quod detractum est
2 queri, sed de eo gratias agere quod contigit.   Pro-
venerunt enim satis magni fructus laborum tuorum ex
ipsa educatione, nisi forte ii, qui catulos avesque et
frivola animorum oblectamenta summa diligentia
nutriunt, fruuntur aliqua voluptate ex visu tactuque
et blanda adulatione mutorum, liberos nutrientibus
non fructus educationis ipsa educatio est. Licet itaque
nil tibi industria eius contulerit, nihil diligentia custo-
dierit, nihil prudentia suaserit, ipsum quod habuisti,
quod amasti, fructus est.

[1] paucissimorum est *Gertz*: paucissimo *A.*

started life with tears, what a mighty pother all the while does this despicable creature make! Forgetting his inevitable lot, to what mighty thoughts does man aspire! He ponders upon everlasting and eternal things, and makes plans for his grandchildren and great-grandchildren, while meantime, amid his far-reaching schemes, death overtakes him, and even this, which we call old age, is but the passing round of a pitifully few years.

But your sorrow—granting that there is any reason in it—tell me, does it have in view your own ills or the ills of him who is gone? In the loss of your son are you stirred by the thought that you have received no pleasures from him, or is it that you might have experienced greater pleasures if he had lived longer? If you answer that you have experienced none, you will render your loss more bearable; for the things from which men have experienced no joy and gladness are always less missed. If you confess that you have experienced great pleasures from him, then it is your duty not to complain about what has been withdrawn, but to give thanks for what you have had. Surely his rearing alone has yielded you ample reward for all your toil, unless perhaps it happens that those who spare no pains in raising pups and birds and other silly pets derive some slight pleasure from the sight and touch and fawning caresses of these dumb creatures, while those who raise children miss the rearer's reward that comes from the mere act of rearing them. And so although his industry may have gained you nothing, although his carefulness may have saved you nothing, although his wisdom may have taught you nothing, yet in having had him, in having loved him, lies your reward.

3 "At potuit longior esse, maior." Melius tamen
tecum actum est quam si omnino non contigisset,
quoniam, si ponatur electio, utrum satius sit non diu
felicem esse an numquam, melius est discessura nobis
bona quam nulla contingere. Utrumne malles de-
generem aliquem et numerum tantum nomenque filii
expleturum habuisse, an tantae indolis, quantae tuus
fuit, iuvenis cito prudens, cito pius, cito maritus, cito
pater, cito omnis officii curiosus, cito sacerdos, omnia
4 tamquam properans[1]? Nulli fere et magna bona et
diuturna contingunt; non durat nec ad ultimum exit
nisi lenta felicitas. Filium tibi dii immortales non diu
daturi statim talem dederunt, qualis diu effici potest.
Ne illud quidem dicere potes electam te a dis, cui frui
non liceret filio. Circumfer per omnem notorum,
ignotorum frequentiam oculos, occurrent tibi passi
ubique maiora. Senserunt ista magni duces, senserunt principes; ne deos quidem fabulae immunes
reliquerunt, puto, ut nostrorum funerum levamentum
esset etiam divina concidere. Circumspice, inquam,
omnis; nullam tam[2] miseram nominabis domum, quae
5 non inveniat in miseriore solacium. Non me hercules
tam male de moribus tuis sentio, ut putem posse te

---

[1] properans *Schultess et Pfennig*: propera *A*.
[2] tam *added by Muretus.*

---

[a] Obviously the demi-gods, such as Hercules and the
Dioscuri.

"But," you say, "it might have lasted longer, might have been greater." True, but you have been better dealt with than if you had never had a son; for if we should be given the choice—whether it is better to be happy for a short time only or never at all—it is better for us to have blessings that will flee than none at all. Would you rather have had a son who was a disgrace, someone who has possessed merely the place and the name of a son, or one with the fine qualities your son had, a youth who was early discerning, early dutiful, early a husband, early a father, who was early diligent in every public duty, early a priest, as though he were always hastening? Great and at the same time long-lasting blessings fall to scarcely any man's lot; it is only the good fortune which comes slowly that lasts and goes with us to the end. The immortal gods, not purposing to give him to you for a long time, gave to you from the first a son such as length of time is able to produce. And you cannot say even this—that the gods picked you out in order to deprive you of the enjoyment of your son. Cast your eyes upon the great company of people you know, or do not know—everywhere you will find those who have suffered greater losses than yours. Great generals have experienced such as yours, princes have experienced them; story has left not even the gods*a* exempt, in order, I fancy, that the knowledge that even divinities can perish may lighten our grief for the dead. Look about you, I say, at everyone; you will not mention a single home so wretched that it could not take comfort from knowing one more wretched. But I do not think so ill of your character—Heaven forbid!—as to believe that you would be able to bear your

levius pati casum tuum, si tibi ingentem lugentium numerum produxero. Malivolum solacii genus est turba miserorum ; quosdam tamen referam, non ut scias hoc solere hominibus accidere—ridiculum est enim mortalitatis exempla colligere—, sed ut scias fuisse multos, qui lenirent aspera placide ferendo. A felicissimo incipiam.

6 L. Sulla filium amisit, nec ea res aut malitiam eius et acerrimam virtutem in hostes civesque contudit aut effecit, ut cognomen illud usurpasse falso videretur, quod amisso filio adsumpsit nec odia hominum veritus, quorum malo illae nimis secundae res constabant, nec invidiam deorum, quorum illud crimen erat, Sulla tam felix. Sed istud inter res nondum iudicatas abeat, qualis Sulla fuerit—etiam inimici fatebuntur bene illum arma sumpsisse, bene posuisse. Hoc de quo agitur constabit, non esse maximum malum quod etiam ad felicissimos pervenit.

1 13. Ne nimis admiretur Graecia illum patrem, qui in ipso sacrificio nuntiata fili morte tibicinem tantum iussit tacere et coronam capiti detraxit, cetera rite perfecit, Pulvillus effecit pontifex, cui postem tenenti et Capitolium dedicanti mors filii nuntiata est. Quam

---

^a At the celebration of his triumph over Mithridates, Sulla, attributing his successes to the favour of the gods, claimed for himself the title of *Felix* (81 B.C.).

^b In his rivalry with Marius, Sulla was ostensibly the defender of the senate, and marched on Rome "to deliver her from her tyrants." Having finished his work, he resigned the dictatorship (79 B.C.), and retired to private life.

^c The story is told (Valerius Maximus, v. 10, *ext.* 2) of Xenophon, whose son Gryllus was killed in the cavalry fight at Mantinea (362 B.C.).

^d A detail of the ceremony of dedication, as Cicero shows, *De Domo*, 121 : "postem teneri in dedicatione oportere videor audisse templi."

own misfortune more lightly if I should bring before you a mighty number of mourners. The solace that comes from having company in misery smacks of ill-will. Nevertheless, I shall cite some others, not so much to show you that this calamity often befalls mankind—for it would be absurd to collect the examples of man's mortality—as to show you that there have been many who sweetened bitter fortune by enduring it calmly. I shall begin with a man who was most fortunate.

Lucius Sulla lost a son, but that circumstance neither blunted his malice and the great energy of his prowess against his enemies and his fellow-countrymen nor made it appear that he had wrongly used his famous title [a]; for he assumed it after the death of his son, fearing neither the hatred of men, by whose misfortune that excessive prosperity of his was purchased, nor the envy of the gods, whose reproach it was that Sulla was so truly " the Fortunate." The question, however, of Sulla's character may be left among the matters not yet decided—that he took up arms honourably [b] and honourably laid them aside even his enemies will admit. But the point at present involved will be clear—that an evil which reaches even the most fortunate men is not the greatest of evils.

Greece had a famous father,[c] who, having received news of the death of his son while he was in the very act of offering sacrifice, merely bade the flutist be silent, withdrew the chaplet from his head, and finished duly the rest of the ceremony ; but, thanks to Pulvillus, a Roman priest, Greece cannot give him too much glory. He was dedicating the temple on the Capitoline, and was still grasping the door-post [d] when he received news of the death of his son. But

ille exaudisse dissimulavit et sollemnia pontificii car-
minis verba concepit gemitu non interrumpente pre-
2 cationem et ad filii sui nomen Iove propitiato. Pu-
tasne eius luctus aliquem finem esse debere, cuius
primus dies et primus impetus ab altaribus publicis et
fausta nuncupatione non abduxit patrem ? Dignus
me hercules fuit memorabili dedicatione, dignus am-
plissimo sacerdotio, qui colere deos ne iratos quidem
destitit. Idem tamen ut redît domum, et implevit
oculos et aliquas voces flebiles misit et peractis, quae
mos erat praestare defunctis, ad Capitolinum illum
redît vultum.
3   Paulus circa illos nobilissimi triumphi dies, quo
vinctum ante currum egit Persen, incliti regis nomen,
duos filios in adoptionem dedit, duos[1] quos sibi serva-
verat extulit. Quales retentos putas, cum inter com-
modatos Scipio fuisset ? Non sine motu vacuum
Pauli currum populus Romanus aspexit. Contiona-
tus est tamen et egit dis gratias, quod compos voti
factus esset ; precatum enim se, ut, si quid ob ingentem victoriam invidiae dandum esset, id suo potius
4 quam publico damno solveretur. Vides quam magno
animo tulerit ? Orbitati suae gratulatus est. Et

---

[1] duos *added by Lipsius.*

---

[a] The last king of Macedonia, defeated by Paulus at
Pydna in 168 B.C.
[b] The younger, adopted into the family of the Scipios,
became the famous conqueror of Carthage, Scipio Africanus
Minor ; the other was adopted by Fabius Maximus.
[c] The general's children of tender age usually rode with
him in the triumphal car.

he pretended not to hear it, and repeated the words of the pontifical ritual in the appointed manner ; not a single moan interrupted the course of his prayer, and he entreated the favour of Jove with the name of his son ringing in his ears. Do you not think that such grief must have an end, when even the first day of it and its first fury failed to divert him, father though he was, from his duty at the public altar and from an auspicious delivery of his solemn proclamation ? Worthy, in truth, was he of the notable dedication, worthy was he to hold the most exalted priesthood—a man who did not desist from the worship of the gods even when they were angry ! Yet when he had returned to his home, this man's eyes were flooded with tears and he indulged in a few tearful laments, then, having completed the rites that custom prescribed for the dead, he resumed the expression he had worn at the Capitol.

Paulus, about the time of his most glorious triumph, in which he drove Perses,[a] that king of high renown, in chains before his car, gave over two of his sons[b] to be adopted by others, and the two whom he had kept for himself he buried. What manner of men, think you, were those whom he retained when Scipio was one of those whom he bestowed on others ! Not without emotion did the Roman people gaze upon the car of Paulus that now was empty.[c] Nevertheless he made a public address, and gave thanks to the gods for having granted his prayer ; for he had prayed that, if he should be required to make some payment to Envy on account of his mighty victory, the debt might be discharged by a loss to himself rather than to the state. Do you see with how noble a spirit he bore himself ? He con-

quem¹ magis poterat permovere tanta mutatio?
Solacia simul atque auxilia perdidit. Non contigit
tamen tristem Paulum Persi videre.

1   14. Quid nunc te per innumerabilia magnorum
virorum exempla ducam et quaeram miseros, quasi
non difficilius sit invenire felices? Quota enim quaeque domus usque ad exitum omnibus partibus suis
constitit? in qua non aliquid turbatum est²? Unum
quemlibet annum occupa et ex eo magistratus cita:
Lucium si vis Bibulum et C. Caesarem—videbis inter
collegas inimicissimos concordem fortunam.

2   L. Bibuli, melioris quam fortioris viri, duo simul filii
interfecti sunt, Aegyptio quidem militi ludibrio habiti,
ut non minus ipsa orbitate auctor eius digna res lacrimis esset. Bibulus tamen, qui toto honoris sui anno
ob invidiam collegae domi latuerat, postero die quam
geminum funus renuntiatum est, processit ad solita
imperii officia. Quis minus potest quam unum diem
duobus filiis dare? Tam cito liberorum luctum finivit,
qui consulatum anno luxerat.

3   C. Caesar cum Britanniam peragraret nec oceano
continere felicitatem suam posset, audît decessisse
filiam publica secum fata ducentem. In oculis erat

¹ et quem *A* : et quo eum *Hermes after Gertz.*
² turbatum est *Madvig* : turbatum sit *A* : in qua non
aliquid turbatum sit *Waltz omits.*

ᵃ Correctly, Marcus (Calpurnius) Bibulus, Caesar's
colleague in the consulship in 59 B.C.
ᵇ Bibulus's inactivity during his year of office was the
occasion of much waggery. *Cf.* Suetonius, *Iul.* 20. 2:
" unus (*i.e.* Caesar) ex eo tempore omnia in re publica et ad
arbitrium administravit, ut nonnulli urbanorum, cum quid
per iocum testandi gratia signarent, non Caesare et Bibulo,
sed Iulio et Caesare consulibus actum scriberent."
ᶜ He was at the time proconsul of Syria (51–50 B.C.).

gratulated himself on the loss of his children! And who would have had a better right to be deeply moved by so great a shift of fortune? He lost at the same time both his comfort and his stay. Yet Perses never had the pleasure of seeing Paulus sad!

But why should I now drag you through the countless examples of great men, and search for those who were unhappy just as though it were not more difficult to find those who were happy? For how few families have endured even to the end with all members intact? What one is there that has not known trouble? Take any one year you please and call for its magistrates. Take, if you like, Lucius[a] Bibulus and Gaius Caesar; you will see that, though these colleagues were the bitterest foes, their fortunes agreed.

Lucius Bibulus, a good, rather than a strong, man, had two sons murdered at the same time, and that, too, by Egyptian soldiery, who had subjected them to insult, so that not less than the bereavement itself the source of it was a matter that called for tears. Yet Bibulus, who, during the whole year of his consulship, on account of his jealousy of his colleague, had stayed at home in retirement,[b] on the day after he had heard of the twofold murder came forth and performed the routine duties of his office.[c] Who can devote less than one day to mourning for two sons? So quickly did he end his grief for his children—he who had grieved for the consulship a year.

Gaius Caesar, when he was traversing Britain, and could not endure that even the ocean should set bounds to his success, heard that his daughter[d] had departed; and with her went the fate of the republic.

[d] Julia, the wife of Pompey, whose sudden death in 54 B.C. precipitated the estrangement of Caesar and Pompey.

iam Cn. Pompeius non aequo laturus animo quemquam
alium esse in re publica magnum et modum impositurus incrementis, quae gravia illi videbantur, etiam
cum in commune crescerent. Tamen intra tertium
diem imperatoria obît munia et tam cito dolorem vicit
quam omnia solebat.

1   15. Quid aliorum tibi funera Caesarum referam?
Quos in hoc mihi videtur interim violare fortuna, ut
sic quoque generi humano prosint ostendentes ne eos
quidem, qui dis geniti deosque genituri dicantur, sic
suam fortunam in potestate habere quemadmodum
2 alienam. Divus Augustus amissis liberis, nepotibus,
exhausta Caesarum turba adoptione desertam domum
fulsit; tulit tamen tam fortiter quam cuius iam res
agebatur cuiusque maxime intererat de dis neminem
3 queri. Ti. Caesar et quem genuerat et quem adopta-
verat amisit; ipse tamen pro rostris laudavit filium
stetitque in conspectu posito corpore, interiecto tantummodo velamento, quod pontificis oculos a funere
arceret, et flente populo Romano non flexit vultum;
experiendum se dedit Seiano ad latus stanti, quam
patienter posset suos perdere.

4   Videsne quanta copia virorum maximorum sit, quos

ᵃ The Latin expression is reminiscent of Virgil, *Aeneid*,
ix. 641 *sq.*:

Macte nova virtute, puer; sic itur ad astra,
dis genite et geniture deos.

ᵇ An allusion to the later apotheosis of Augustus.

ᶜ Germanicus, his nephew.

ᵈ Drusus, who was poisoned by Sejanus, the imperial
favourite, in A.D. 23. (Tacitus, *Annals*, iv. 8.)

ᵉ *i.e.*, the emperor in his capacity of *Pontifex Maximus*.

ᶠ A veiled allusion to the spectacular overthrow of Sejanus
himself, eight years later.

46

It was already plain to his eyes that Gnaeus Pompeius would not endure with calmness that any other should become " great " in the commonwealth, and would place a check upon his own advancement, which seemed to cause him offence even when it was increasing to their common interest. Yet within three days he returned to his duties as a general, and conquered his grief as quickly as he was wont to conquer everything.

Why should I recall to you the bereavements of the other Caesars, whom Fortune seems to me at times deliberately to outrage in order that so also they may benefit the human race by showing that not even they who are said to be born from gods, and to be destined to give birth to gods,[a] can have the same power over their own fortune that they have over the fortune of others. The deified Augustus, when he had lost his children and his grandchildren, and the supply of Caesars had been exhausted, bolstered his depleted house by adoption ; nevertheless he bore his lot with the bravery of one who was already counting it a personal affair[b] and his deepest concern that no man should make complaint of the gods. Tiberius Caesar lost both the son he had begotten and the son he had adopted[c] ; nevertheless he himself delivered a panegyric upon his own son[d] from the Rostra, and he stood there beside the corpse, which lay in plain view, with but a veil intervening, so that the eyes of a high-priest[e] might not look upon a corpse, and, while the Roman people wept, he did not even change countenance. To Sejanus, standing by his side, he offered an example of how patiently he could endure the loss of his dear ones ![f]

You see how long is the list of men who were most

non excepit hic omnia prosternens casus, et in quos[1]
tot animi bona, tot ornamenta publice privatimque
congesta erant[2] ? Sed videlicet it in orbem ista tempestas et sine dilectu vastat omnia agitque ut sua.
Iube singulos conferre rationem ; nulli contigit im-
pune nasci.

1   16. Scio quid dicas : " Oblitus es feminam te con-
solari, virorum refers exempla." Quis autem dixit
naturam maligne cum mulierum ingeniis egisse et virtutes illarum in artum retraxisse ? Par illis, mihi
crede, vigor, par ad honesta, libeat, facultas est ;
dolorem laboremque ex aequo, si consuevere, patiun-
2 tur. In qua istud urbe, di boni, loquimur ? In qua
regem Romanis capitibus Lucretia et Brutus deiece-
runt : Bruto libertatem debemus, Lucretiae Brutum ;
in qua Cloeliam contempto et hoste et flumine ob in-
signem audaciam tantum non in viros transcripsimus :
equestri insidens statuae in sacra via, celeberrimo loco,
Cloelia exprobrat iuvenibus nostris pulvinum escen-
dentibus in ea illos urbe sic ingredi, in qua etiam
3 feminas equo donavimus. Quod si tibi vis exempla
referri feminarum, quae suos fortiter desideraverint,
non ostiatim quaeram ; ex una tibi familia duas Cor-

---

[1] et in quos *Koch* : et quos *A* : et quo *Madvig* : et, quos
Gertz (1889) : et quos *Hermes* : et quibus *Waltz*.
[2] congesta erant *A* : congesta sacrant *Gertz* : congesta
honestaverant *proposed by Hermes*.

---

[a] Brutus's resentment of the outrage upon Lucretia led
to the abolishment of the monarchy.
[b] An early Roman heroine, who escaped from the
Etruscans by swimming across the Tiber (Livy, ii. 13).

eminent and yet were not exempted from this misfortune that lays everything low—men, too, upon
whom so many gifts of mind had been heaped, so
many distinctions in public and private life ! But it
is very plain that this storm of disaster moves upon
its round, lays waste everything without distinction,
and drives everything before it as its prey. Order
all men one by one to compare their accounts ;
no man has escaped paying the penalty for being
born.

I know what you are saying : " You forget that
you are giving comfort to a woman ; the examples
you cite are of men." But who has asserted that
Nature has dealt grudgingly with women's natures
and has narrowly restricted their virtues ? Believe
me, they have just as much force, just as much
capacity, if they like, for virtuous action ; they are
just as able to endure suffering and toil when they
are accustomed to them. In what city, good
heavens, are we thus talking ? In the city where
Lucretia and Brutus[a] tore the yoke of a king from the
heads of the Romans—to Brutus we owe liberty, to
Lucretia we owe Brutus. In the city where Cloelia,[b]
who braved both the enemy and the river has been
almost transferred by us, on account of her signal
courage, to the list of heroes : the statue of Cloelia,
mounted upon a horse, stands on the Sacred Way in
the city's busiest quarter, and, as our young coxcombs
mount to their cushioned seats, she taunts them with
journeying in such a fashion in a city in which even
women have been presented with a horse ! But if you
wish me to cite examples of women who have bravely
suffered the loss of dear ones, I shall not go from door
to door to find them. From one family I shall present

49

nelias dabo : primam Scipionis filiam, Gracchorum
matrem. Duodecim illa partus totidem funeribus
recognovit. Et de ceteris facile est, quos nec editos
nec amissos civitas sensit ; Tiberium Gaiumque, quos
etiam qui bonos viros negaverit magnos fatebitur, et
occisos vidit et insepultos. Consolantibus tamen
miseramque dicentibus : " Numquam," inquit,
" non felicem me dicam, quae Gracchos peperi."

4 Cornelia Livi Drusi clarissimum iuvenem inlustris ingenii, vadentem per Gracchana vestigia imperfectis
tot rogationibus intra penates interemptum suos,
amiserat incerto caedis auctore. Tamen et acerbam
mortem filii et inultam tam magno animo tulit, quam
ipse leges tulerat.

5 Iam cum fortuna in gratiam, Marcia, reverteris, si
tela, quae in Scipiones Scipionumque matres ac filias
exegit, quibus Caesares petît, ne a te quidem continuit ? Plena et infesta variis casibus vita est, a quibus
nulli longa pax, vix indutiae sunt. Quattuor liberos
sustuleras, Marcia. Nullum aiunt frustra cadere
telum, quod in confertum agmen inmissum est :
mirum est tantam turbam non potuisse sine invidia

6 damnove praetervehi ? At hoc[1] iniquior fortuna fuit,
quod non tantum eripuit filios, sed elegit. Numquam

----

[1] at hoc *inferior* MSS. : adhoc *A Hermes.*

----

[a] M. Livius Drusus, while tribune in 91 B.C.

to you the two Cornelias—the first one, the daughter of Scipio and mother of the Gracchi. Twelve births did she recall by as many deaths. The rest whom the state never knew as either born or lost matter little; as for Tiberius and Gaius, who even the man who denies that they were good will admit were great men, she saw them not only murdered but left unburied. Yet to those who tried to comfort her and called her unfortunate she said: " Never shall I admit that I am not fortunate, I who have borne the Gracchi." Cornelia, the wife of Livius Drusus, had lost a son, a young man *a* of distinguished ability and very great renown, who, while following in the footsteps of the Gracchi, was killed at his own hearth by an unknown murderer, just when he had so many measures pending and was at the height of his fame. Yet she showed as much courage in supporting the death of her son, untimely and unavenged as it was, as he had shown in supporting his laws.

If Fortune, Marcia, has pierced the Scipios and the mothers and daughters of the Scipios with her darts, if with them she has assailed the Caesars, will you not now pardon her if she has not held them back even from you? Life is beset with full many and varied misfortunes; they grant to no one long-extended peace, scarcely even a truce. Four children, Marcia, you had borne. Not a single dart, they say, that is hurled into the thick of the line falls without a victim—is it surprising that such a company as yours has not been able to get by without incurring envy and harm? But Fortune was all the more unfair because she not only carried off your sons but chose them out! Yet you should never call it an in-

tamen iniuriam dixeris ex aequo cum potentiore dividere ; duas tibi reliquit filias et harum nepotes.   Et ipsum, quem maxime luges prioris oblita, non ex toto abstulit ; habes ex illo duas filias, si male fers, magna onera, si bene, magna solacia. In hoc te perduc, ut
7 illas cum videris, admonearis filii, non doloris ! Agricola eversis arboribus, quas aut ventus radicitus evulsit aut contortus repentino impetu turbo praefregit, subolem ex illis residuam fovet et in amissarum vicem[1] semina statim plantasque disponit ; et momento (nam ut ad damna, ita ad incrementa rapidum veloxque tempus est) adolescunt amissis laetiora.
8 Has nunc Metilii tui filias in eius vicem substitue et vacantem locum exple et unum dolorem geminato solacio leva ! Est quidem haec natura mortalium, ut nihil magis placeat quam quod amissum est ; iniquiores sumus adversus relicta ereptorum desiderio. Sed si aestimare volueris, quam valde tibi fortuna, etiam cum saeviret, pepercerit, scies te habere plus quam solacia ; respice tot nepotes, duas filias. Dic illud quoque, Marcia : " Moverer, si esset cuique fortuna pro moribus et numquam mala bonos sequerentur ; nunc video exempto discrimine eodem modo malos bonosque iactari."
1 17. "Grave est tamen, quem educaveris, iuvenem,

---

[1] in amissarum vicem *Favez* : in amissarum *inferior MSS.* : in missarum *A* : in vicem amissarum *Gertz* (1889) : in scissuram *Hermes after Schultess* : et amissarum *Waltz.*

justice to be forced to share equally with one more powerful; she has left you two daughters and the children of these. And even the son whom you, forgetful of an earlier loss, mourn so deeply has not been utterly taken from you; you still have the two daughters he left—great burdens if you are weak, great comforts if you are brave. Do bring yourself to this—whenever you see them, let them remind you of your son and not of your grief! When the farmer sees his fruit-trees all ruined—completely uprooted by the wind, or twisted and broken by the sudden fury of a cyclone—he nurses the young stock they have left, and immediately plants seeds and cuttings to replace the trees that were lost; and in a moment (for if time causes speedy and swift destruction, it likewise causes swift and speedy growth) more flourishing trees grow up than those he lost. Do you now put these daughters of your son Metilius in his stead, and fill the vacant place, and lighten your sorrow for one by drawing comfort from two! Yet such is the nature of mortals that they find nothing so pleasing as what they have lost; yearning for what is taken away makes us too unfair towards what is left. But if you are willing to count up how very merciful Fortune has been to you even when she was angry, you will find that she has left you much beside consolations; look at all your grandchildren, your two daughters. And, Marcia, say this also to yourself: " I might indeed be disturbed, if everyone's lot accorded with his conduct, and if evils never pursued the good; as it is, I see that there is no distinction and that the good and the bad are tossed to and fro after the same fashion.

" Nevertheless it is hard," you reply, " to lose a

iam matri iam patri praesidium ac decus, amittere."
Quis negat grave esse ? Sed humanum est. Ad hoc
genitus es, ut perderes, ut perires, ut sperares,
metueres, alios teque inquietares, mortem et timeres
et optares et, quod est pessimum, numquam scires,
cuius esses status.

2 Si quis Syracusas petenti diceret : " Omnia incommoda, omnes voluptates futurae peregrinationis tuae
ante cognosce, deinde ita naviga. Haec sunt, quae
mirari possis : videbis primum ipsam insulam ab Italia
angusto interscissam freto, quam continenti quondam
cohaesisse constat ; subitum illo mare irrupit et

Hesperium Siculo latus abscidit.

Deinde videbis (licebit enim tibi avidissimum maris
verticem perstringere) stratam illam fabulosam Cha-
rybdin, quam diu ab austro vacat, at, si quid inde vehementius spiravit, magno hiatu profundoque navigia
3 sorbentem. Videbis celebratissimum carminibus fon-
tem Arethusam, nitidissimi ac perlucidi ad imum
stagni, gelidissimas aquas profundentem, sive illas ibi
primum nascentis invenit, sive inlapsum terris flumen
integrum subter tot maria et ab confusione peioris
4 undae servatum reddidit. Videbis portum quietis-
simum omnium, quos aut natura posuit in tutelam
classium aut adiuvit manus, sic tutum, ut ne maxi-

---

^a Virgil, *Aen.* iii. 418.
^b In story Alpheus, a river-god in Arcadia, pursued the
nymph Arethusa to the distant island of Ortygia by passing
under the sea.
^c The Great Harbour of Syracuse.

son whom you have reared to young manhood just
when his mother, just when his father was finding him
their stay and pride." Who will deny that it is hard?
But it is the common lot. To this end were you born
—to lose, to perish, to hope, to fear, to disquiet yourself and others, both to fear death and to long for it,
and, worst of all, never to know the real terms of
your existence.

Suppose a man should be planning a visit to Syracuse and someone should say to him : " First inform
yourself of all the disagreeable and all the pleasurable
features of your future journey, and then set sail.
The things that may fill you with wonder are these.
First, you will see the island itself, cut off from Italy
by a narrow strait, but once evidently joined to the
mainland ; there the sea suddenly broke through, and

> Severed Sicily from Hesperia's side.[a]

Next, you will see Charybdis—for it will be possible
for you to skirt this greediest of whirlpools, so famous
in story—resting quietly so long as there is no wind
from the south, but whenever a gale blows from that
quarter, sucking down ships into its huge and deep
maw. You will see the fountain of Arethusa, oft
famed in song, with its bright gleaming pool, transparent to the very bottom, and pouring forth its icy
waters—whether it found them there where they
first had birth, or yielded up a river that had plunged
beneath the earth[b] and, gliding intact beneath so
many seas, had been kept from the contamination of
less pure water. You will see a harbour,[c] of all havens
the most peaceful—whether those that Nature has
set to give shelter to ships or that man's hand has
improved—and so safe that not even the fury of

marum quidem tempestatium furori locus sit. Videbis ubi Athenarum potentia fracta, ubi tot milia captivorum ille excisis in infinitam altitudinem saxis nativus carcer incluserat, ipsam ingentem civitatem et laxius territorium quam multarum urbium fines sunt, tepidissima hiberna et nullum diem sine interventu solis.
5 Sed cum omnia ista cognoveris, gravis et insalubris aestas hiberni caeli beneficia corrumpet. Erit Dionysius illic tyrannus, libertatis, iustitiae, legum exitium, dominationis cupidus etiam post Platonem, vitae etiam post exilium! Alios uret, alios verberabit, alios ob levem offensam detruncari iubebit, accerset ad libidinem mares feminasque et inter foedos regiae intemperantiae greges parum erit simul binis coire. Audisti quid te invitare possit, quid absterrere ; proinde aut naviga
6 aut resiste." Post hanc denuntiationem si quis dixisset intrare se Syracusas velle, satisne iustam querellam de ullo nisi de se habere posset, qui non incidisset in illa, sed prudens sciensque venisset ?

Dicit omnibus nobis natura : " Neminem decipio. Tu si filios sustuleris, poteris habere formosos, et deformes poteris ; fortasse muti nascentur. Esse aliquis ex illis tam servator patriae quam proditor poterit.
7 Non est quod desperes tantae dignationis futuros, ut nemo tibi propter illos male dicere audeat ; propone

---

ᵃ The ancient latomies, or quarries, near Syracuse, which were used as places of imprisonment. The so-called " Ear of Dionysius " is to-day a famous sight.
ᵇ Expelled from Syracuse by Timoleon, Dionysius is said to have lived a dissolute life in Corinth.

the most violent storms can have access there. You
will see where the might of Athens was broken,
where so many thousands of captives were confined
in that natural prison,[a] hewn out of solid rock to
an immeasurable depth—you will see the great city
itself, occupying a broader extent of territory than
many a metropolis can boast, where the winters are
the balmiest, and not a single day passes without the
appearance of the sun. But, having learned of all
these things, you will discover that the blessings of
its winter climate are ruined by oppressive and un-
wholesome summers. You will find there the tyrant
Dionysius, that destroyer of freedom, justice, and law,
greedy of power, even after knowing Plato, and of
life even after exile ![b] Some he will burn, some he
will flog, some for a slight offence he will order to be
beheaded, he will call for males and females to satisfy
his lust, and to enjoy two at one time of his shameful
victims will ill suffice for his royal excesses. You have
now heard what may attract, what repel you—now,
then, either set sail or stay at home !" If after such
a warning anyone should declare that he desired to
enter Syracuse, against whom but himself could he
find just cause for complaint, since he would not have
stumbled upon those conditions, but have come into
them purposely and with full knowledge ?

To all of us Nature says : " I deceive no one. If
you bear sons, it may be that they will be handsome,
it may be that they will be ugly ; perchance they will
be born dumb. Some one of them, it may be, will be
the saviour of his country, or as likely its betrayer. It
is not beyond hope that they will win so much esteem
that out of regard for them none will venture to speak
evil of you ; yet bear in mind, too, that they may sink

tamen et tantae futuros turpitudinis, ut ipsi maledicta
sint. Nihil vetat illos tibi suprema praestare et
laudari te a liberis tuis, sed sic te para tamquam in
ignem impositurus vel puerum vel iuvenem vel senem;
nihil enim ad rem pertinent anni, quoniam nullum
non acerbum funus est, quod parens sequitur." Post
has leges propositas, si liberos tollis, omni deos invidia
liberas, qui tibi nihil certi spoponderunt.

1   18. Hanc imaginem[1] agedum ad totius[2] vitae introitum refer. An Syracusas viseres deliberanti tibi
quicquid delectare poterat, quicquid offendere, ex-
posui ; puta nascenti me tibi venire in consilium :
" Intraturus es urbem dis, hominibus communem,
omnia complexam, certis legibus aeternisque devinc-
2 tam, indefatigata caelestium officia volventem. Videbis illic innumerabiles stellas micare, videbis uno sidere
omnia implere solem,[3] cotidiano cursu diei noctisque
spatia signantem, annuo aestates hiemesque aequa-
lius quidem dividentem. Videbis nocturnam lunae
successionem, a fraternis occursibus lene remissum-
que lumen mutuantem et modo occultam modo
toto ore terris imminentem, accessionibus damnisque
3 mutabilem, semper proximae dissimilem. Videbis
quinque sidera diversas agentia vias et in contrarium

---

[1] hanc imaginem A : ad hanc imaginem *Hermes and
commonly* :
[2] ad totius *inferior* $MS.$: totius A.
[3] inplere solem *Gertz* : inpleri solem AF ; *so P. Thomas,
transferring* videbis *before* uno *to position before* solem.

---

[a] Mercury, Venus, Mars, Jupiter, Saturn. *Cf.* Milton,
Paradise Lost, v. 177 ff.:

> And ye *five* other wandering fires, that move
> In mystic dance not without song, resound
> His praise.

to such great infamy that they themselves will become your curse.   There is nothing to forbid that they should perform the last sad rites for you, and that those who deliver your panegyric should be your children, but, too, hold yourself ready to place your son upon the pyre, be he lad or man or greybeard ; for years have nothing to do with the matter, since every funeral is untimely at which a parent follows the bier."   If, after these conditions have been set forth, you bring forth children, you must free the gods from all blame ; for they have made you no promises.

Come now, apply this picture to your entrance into life as a whole.   I have set forth what could there delight you, what offend you, if you were debating whether you should visit Syracuse ; consider that I am coming now to give you advice at your birth : " You are about to enter a city," I should say, " shared by gods and men—a city that embraces the universe, that is bound by fixed and eternal laws, that holds the celestial bodies as they whirl through their unwearied rounds.   You will see there the gleaming of countless stars, you will see one star flooding everything with his light—the sun that marks off the spaces of day and night in his daily course, and in his annual course distributes even more equably the periods of summer and winter.   You will see the moon taking his place by night, who as she meets her brother borrows from him a pale, reflected light, now quite hidden, now overhanging the earth with her whole face exposed, ever changing as she waxes and wanes, ever different from her last appearance.   You will see the five planets[a] pursuing their different courses and

praecipiti mundo nitentia : ex horum levissimis motibus fortunae populorum dependent et maxima ac
minima proinde formantur, prout aequum iniquumve
sidus incessit.   Miraberis conlecta nubila et cadentis
4 aquas et obliqua fulmina et caeli fragorem.   Cum
satiatus spectaculo supernorum in terram oculos
deieceris, excipiet te alia forma rerum aliterque mira-
bilis : hinc camporum in infinitum patentium fusa
planities, hinc montium magnis et nivalibus surgen-
tium iugis erecti in sublime vertices ; deiectus
fluminum et ex uno fonte in occidentem orientemque
diffusi amnes et summis cacuminibus nemora nutantia
et tantum silvarum cum suis animalibus aviumque con-
5 centu dissono ; varii urbium situs et seclusae nationes
locorum difficultate, quarum aliae se in erectos sub-
trahunt montes, aliae ripis lacubus vallibus pavidae[1]
circumfunduntur ; adiuta cultu seges et arbusta sine
cultore feritatis ; et rivorum lenis inter prata discursus et amoeni sinus et litora in portum recedentia ;
sparsae tot per vastum insulae, quae interventu suo
6 maria distinguunt.   Quid lapidum gemmarumque
fulgor et inter rapidorum torrentium aurum harenas
interfluens et in mediis terris medioque rursus mari
aëriae ignium faces et vinculum terrarum oceanus,

[1] ripis lacubus vallibus *Basore doubtfully* : ripis. lacu.
uallibus *AF* : pavidae *A* : palude *F* : ripis lacuum valli-
busque (paludibusque ?) pavidae *Madvig* : euripis, lacubus,
amnibus pavidae *Gertz* : ripis lacunalibus pavidae *Waltz* :
ripis lacuum, vallibus, paludibus *Favez*.

----

a The sphere of heaven was supposed to revolve about the
earth from east to west.

striving to stem the headlong whirl *a* of heaven; on even the slightest motions of these hang the fortunes of nations, and the greatest and smallest happenings are shaped to accord with the progress of a kindly or unkindly star. You will wonder at the piled-up clouds and the falling waters and the zigzag lightning and the roar of heaven. When your eyes are sated with the spectacle of things above and you lower them to earth, another aspect of things, and otherwise wonderful, will meet your gaze. On this side you will see level plains stretching out their boundless expanse, on the other, mountains rising in great, snow-clad ridges and lifting their peaks to heaven; descending streams and rivers that rise from one source flowing both to the east and to the west, and waving trees on the topmost summits and vast forests with the creatures that people them, and birds blending into harmony the discord of their songs. You will see cities in diverse places, and the nations fenced off by natural barriers, some of them withdrawn to mountain heights, and others in their fear hugging the river-banks, lakes, and valleys; corn-fields assisted by cultivation and orchards that need none to tend their wildness; and brooks flowing gently through the meadows, lovely bays, and shores curving inwards to form a harbour; the countless islands that are scattered over the deep and, breaking up its expanse, stud the seas. And what of the gleaming of precious stones and jewels, and the gold that rolls down amid the sands of rushing streams, and the flaming torches that soar from the midst of the land and at times even from the midst of the sea, and the ocean that encircles the lands, severing the continu-

continuationem gentium triplici sinu scindens et in-
7 genti licentia exaestuans ? Videbis hic inquietis et
sine vento fluctuantibus aquis innare excedenti ter-
restria magnitudine animalia, quaedam gravia et
alieno se magisterio moventia, quaedam velocia et
concitatis perniciora remigis, quaedam haurientia
undas et magno praenavigantium periculo efflantia.
Videbis hic navigia quas non novere terras quaerentia;
videbis nihil humanae audaciae intemptatum erisque
et spectator et ipse pars magna conantium ; disces
docebisque artes, alias quae vitam instruant, alias
8 quae ornent, alias quae regant. Sed istic erunt mille
corporum, animorum pestes, et bella et latrocinia et
venena et naufragia et intemperies caeli corporisque
et carissimorum acerba desideria et mors, incertum
facilis an per poenam cruciatumque. Delibera tecum
et perpende, quid velis : ut ad illa venias, per illa
exeundum est." Respondebis velle te vivere ?
Quidni ? immo, puto, ad id non accedes, ex quo
tibi aliquid decuti doles ! Vive ergo ut convenit.
" Nemo," inquis, " nos consuluit." Consulti sunt de
nobis parentes nostri, qui cum condicionem vitae
nossent, in hanc nos sustulerunt.
1   19. Sed ut ad solacia veniam, videamus primum
quid curandum sit, deinde quemadmodum. Movet

---

a Macrobius (*In Somn. Scip.* ii. 9. 7) specifies the Medi-
terranean Sea, Red Sea with the Persian Gulf, and the
Caspian. The earth was supposed to be an island surrounded
by the ocean.

b According to Pliny (*Nat. Hist.* ix. 186) a fish called the
musculus performed this office for whales.

ity of the nations by its three gulfs *a* and boiling up
in mighty rage ? Here you will see its waters
troubled and rising up in billows, stirred not by the
wind but by swimming monsters that surpass in
size all creatures of the land, some of them sluggish
and moving under the guidance *b* of another, others
nimble and more swift than rowers at full speed, and
still others that drink in the waters of the sea and
blow them out to the great peril of those who are sail-
ing by. You will see here ships searching for lands
that they do not know ; you will see man in his
audacity leaving nothing untried, and you will yourself be both a spectator and a partner of mighty enter-
prises ; you will learn and will teach the arts, of which
some serve to maintain life, some to adorn it, and
others to regulate it. But there, too, will be found a
thousand plagues, banes of the body as well as of the
mind, wars, robberies, poisons, shipwrecks, dis-
tempers of climate and of the body, untimely grief
for those most dear, and death—whether an easy one
or only after pain and torture no one can tell. Now
take counsel of yourself and weigh carefully the choice
you make ; if you would reach these wonders, you
must pass through these perils." Will your answer
be that you choose to live ? Of course it will—nay,
perhaps, on second thought, you will not enter upon a
state in which to suffer any loss causes you pain ! Live,
then, upon the terms you have accepted. " But,"
you say, "no one has consulted us." Yet our parents
have been consulted about us, and they, knowing the
terms of life, have reared us to accept them.

But, to come back now to the subject of consolation,
let us consider, first, what wound must be healed,
and, second, in what way. One source of grief is the

lugentem desiderium eius quem dilexit. Id per se tolerabile esse apparet ; absentis enim afuturosque, dum vivent, non flemus, quamvis omnis usus nobis illorum cum aspectu ereptus sit. Opinio est ergo, quae nos cruciat, et tanti quodque malum est, quanti illud taxavimus. In nostra potestate remedium habemus. Iudicemus illos abesse et nosmet ipsi fallamus, dimisimus illos, immo consecuturi praemisimus.

2 Movet et illud lugentem : "Non erit qui me defendat, qui a contemptu vindicet." Ut minime probabili sed vero solacio utar, in civitate nostra plus gratiae orbitas confert quam eripit, adeoque senectutem solitudo, quae solebat destruere, ad potentiam ducit, ut quidam odia filiorum simulent et liberos 3 eiurent, orbitatem manu faciant. Scio quid dicas : "Non movent me detrimenta mea ; etenim non est dignus solacio, qui filium sibi decessisse sicut mancipium moleste fert, cui quicquam in filio respicere praeter ipsum vacat." Quid igitur te, Marcia, movet ? utrum quod filius tuus decessit, an quod non diu vixit ? Si quod decessit, semper debuisti dolere ; semper enim scisti moriturum.

4 Cogita nullis defunctum malis adfici, illa, quae nobis inferos faciunt terribiles, fabulas esse, nullas imminere mortuis tenebras nec carcerem nec flumina

---

a An allusion to the widespread evil of legacy-hunting (*captatio*). Unmarried or childless persons were assiduously courted by those who hoped to benefit by their wills. Horace, *Sat.* ii. 5, gives the rules of the art.

longing we have for one that we have lost. But it is evident that this in itself is bearable ; for, so long as they are alive, we do not shed tears for those who are absent or will soon be absent, although along with the sight of them we are robbed of all enjoyment of them. What tortures us, therefore, is an opinion, and every evil is only as great as we have reckoned it to be. In our own hands we have the remedy. Let us consider that the dead are merely absent, and let us deceive ourselves ; we have sent them on their way— nay, we have sent them ahead and shall soon follow.

Another source of grief is the thought : " I shall have no one to protect me, no one to keep me from being despised." If I may employ a consolation by no means creditable but true, in this city of ours child-lessness bestows more influence than it takes away, and the loneliness that used to be a detriment to old age, now leads to so much power that some old men pretend to hate their sons and disown their children, and by their own act make themselves childless.[a] Yet I know what you will say : " My own losses do not stir me ; for no parent is worthy of consolation who sorrows over the loss of a son just as he would over the loss of a slave, who in the case of a son has room to consider anything except the son himself." What then, Marcia, is it that troubles you ?—the fact that your son has died, or that he did not live long ? If it is that he has died, then you had always reason to grieve ; for you always knew that he would have to die.

Reflect that there are no ills to be suffered after death, that the reports that make the Lower World terrible to us are mere tales, that no darkness is in store for the dead, no prison, no blazing streams of

igne flagrantia nec Oblivionem amnem nec tribunalia
et reos et in illa libertate tam laxa ullos iterum
tyrannos : luserunt ista poetae et vanis nos agitavere
5 terroribus. Mors dolorum omnium exsolutio est et
finis, ultra quem mala nostra non exeunt, quae nos in
illam tranquillitatem, in qua antequam nasceremur
iacuimus, reponit. Si mortuorum aliquis miseretur,
et non natorum misereatur. Mors nec bonum nec
malum est ; id enim potest aut bonum aut malum
esse, quod aliquid est ; quod vero ipsum nihil est et
omnia in nihilum redigit, nulli nos fortunae tradit ;
mala enim bonaque circa aliquam versantur materiam.
Non potest id fortuna tenere, quod natura dimisit, nec
6 potest miser esse qui nullus est. Excessit filius tuus
terminos, intra quos servitur, excepit illum magna et
aeterna pax. Non paupertatis metu, non divitiarum
cura, non libidinis per voluptatem animos carpentis
stimulis incessitur ; non invidia felicitatis alienae
tangitur, non suae premitur, ne conviciis quidem ullis
verecundae aures verberantur ; nulla publica clades
prospicitur, nulla privata ; non sollicitus futuri pendet
ex eventu semper incertiora rependenti. Tandem
ibi constitit, unde nil eum pellat, ubi nihil terreat.
1   20. O ignaros malorum suorum, quibus non mors ut
optimum inventum naturae laudatur expectaturque,
sive felicitatem includit, sive calamitatem repellit,

fire, no river of Lethe, that no judgement-seats are there, nor culprits, nor in that freedom so unfettered are there a second time any tyrants. All these things are the fancies of the poets, who have harrowed us with groundless terrors. Death is a release from all suffering, a boundary beyond which our ills cannot pass—it restores us to that peaceful state in which we lay before we were born. If anyone pities the dead, he must also pity those who have not been born. Death is neither a good nor an evil; for that only which is something is able to be a good or an evil. But that which is itself nothing and reduces all things to nothingness consigns us to neither sphere of fortune: for evils and goods must operate upon something material. Fortune cannot maintain a hold upon that which Nature has let go, nor can he be wretched who is non-existent. Your son has passed beyond those boundaries within which there is servitude; a great and everlasting peace has welcomed him. No fear of want assails him, no anxiety from riches, no stings of lust, that through the pleasure of the body rends the soul; envy of another's prosperity touches him not, envy of his own afflicts him not, no reproaches ever assail his unoffending ears; no disaster either to his country or to himself does he descry, nor does he, in suspense about the future, hang upon the distant outcome that ever repays with ever more uncertainty. At last he has an abiding-place from which nothing can drive him, where nothing can affright him.

O ignorant are they of their ills, who do not laud death and look forward to it as the most precious discovery of Nature! Whether it shuts off prosperity, or repels calamity, or terminates the satiety and

sive satietatem ac lassitudinem senis terminat, sive
iuvenile aevom dum meliora sperantur in flore deducit,
sive pueritiam ante duriores gradus revocat, omnibus
finis, multis remedium, quibusdam votum, de nullis
melius merita quam de is, ad quos venit antequam
2 invocaretur ! Haec servitutem invito domino remit-
tit ; haec captivorum catenas levat ; haec e carcere
educit quos exire imperium impotens vetuerat ; haec
exulibus in patriam semper animum oculosque ten-
dentibus ostendit nihil interesse, infra quos quis
iaceat ; haec, ubi res communis fortuna male divisit
et aequo iure genitos alium alii donavit, exaequat
omnia ; haec est, post quam nihil quisquam alieno
fecit arbitrio ; haec est, in qua nemo humilitatem
suam sensit ; haec est, quae nulli non patuit ; haec
est, Marcia, quam pater tuus concupît ; haec est,
inquam, quae efficit, ut nasci non sit supplicium,
quae efficit, ut non concidam adversus minas casuum,
ut servare animum salvum ac potentem sui possim :
3 habeo quod appellem. Video istic cruces non unius
quidem generis sed aliter ab aliis fabricatas : capite
quidam conversos in terram suspendere, alii per
obscena stipitem egerunt, alii brachia patibulo ex-
plicuerunt ; video fidiculas, video verbera, et membris
singulis articulis[1] singula nocuerunt[2] machinamenta.
At video et mortem. Sunt istic hostes cruenti, cives
superbi ; sed video istic et mortem. Non est molestum

[1] singulis articulis *A* : singulis et articulis *inferior* MSS. :
membris *deleted by Waltz.*
[2] nocuerunt *Madvig* : docuerunt *A* : admoverunt *Niemeyer* : texuerunt *Waltz* : dicaverunt *Favez.*

* *i.e.*, a powerful tyrant.

weariness of the old man, or leads off the youth in the bloom of life while he still hopes for happier things, or calls back the boy before the harsher stages of life are reached, it is to all the end, to many a relief, to some an answer to prayer, and to none does it show more favour than to those to whom it comes before it is asked for ! Death frees the slave though his master is unwilling ; it lightens the captive's chains ; from the dungeon it leads forth those whom unbridled power[a] had forbidden to leave it ; to exiles, whose eyes and minds are ever turning to their native land, death shows that it makes no difference beneath whose soil a man may lie. If Fortune has apportioned unjustly the common goods, and has given over one man to another though they were born with equal rights, death levels all things ; this it is, after whose coming no one any more does the will of another ; this it is, under whose sway no one is aware of his lowly estate ; this it is, that lies open to everyone ; this it is, Marcia, that your father eagerly desired ; this it is, I say, that keeps my birth from being a punishment, that keeps me from falling in the face of threatening misfortunes, that makes it possible to keep my soul unharmed and master of itself : I have a last appeal. Yonder I see instruments of torture, not indeed of a single kind, but differently contrived by different peoples ; some hang their victims with head toward the ground, some impale their private parts, others stretch out their arms on a fork-shaped gibbet ; I see cords, I see scourges, and for each separate limb and each joint there is a separate engine of torture ! But I see also Death. There, too, are bloodthirsty enemies and proud fellow-countrymen ; but yonder, too, I see Death. Slavery is no hardship when, if a

servire, ubi, si dominii pertaesum est, licet uno gradu
ad libertatem transire. Caram te, vita, beneficio
mortis habeo !

4 Cogita quantum boni opportuna mors habeat, quam
multis diutius vixisse nocuerit. Si Gnaeum Pompeium, decus istud firmamentumque imperii, Neapoli
valetudo abstulisset, indubitatus populi Romani princeps excesserat. At nunc exigui temporis adiectio
fastigio illum suo depulit. Vidit legiones in conspectu
suo caesas et ex illo proelio, in quo prima acies senatus
fuit,—quam infelices reliquiae sunt !—ipsum imperatorem superfuisse ; vidit Aegyptium carnificem et
sacrosanctum victoribus corpus satelliti praestitit,
etiam si incolumis fuisset, paenitentiam salutis ac-
turus : quid enim erat turpius quam Pompeium
vivere beneficio regis ?

5 M. Cicero si illo tempore, quo Catilinae sicas de-
vitavit, quibus pariter cum patria petitus est, conci-
disset, si[1] liberata re publica servator eius, si denique
filiae suae funus secutus esset, etiamtunc felix mori
potuit. Non vidisset strictos in civilia capita mucrones nec divisa percussoribus occisorum bona, ut
etiam de suo perirent, non hastam consularia spolia

---

[1] si added by Schultess.

[a] In 50 B.C. Juvenal (x. 283 sqq.) moralizes in the same vein :
  Provida Pompeio dederat Campania febres
  optandas, sed multae urbes et publica vota
  vicerunt, igitur Fortuna ipsius et urbis
  servatum victo caput abstulit.

[b] Seneca merely exaggerates a fact.
[c] i.e., Pompey himself survived the decisive battle of Pharsalus (48 B.C.), and lived to see Caesar master of the Roman
world.
[d] As Pompey was in the act of landing in Egypt, he was
stabbed by an agent of the Egyptian king.

man wearies of the yoke, by a single step he may pass to freedom. O Life, by the favour of Death I hold thee dear !

Think how great a boon a timely death offers, how many have been harmed by living too long ! If Gnaeus Pompeius, that glory and stay of the realm, had been carried off by his illness at Naples,[a] he would have departed the unchallenged head of the Roman people. But as it was, a very brief extension of time cast him down from his pinnacle. He saw his legions slaughtered before his eyes, and from that battle where the first line was the senate,[b] he saw—what a melancholy remnant [c] !—the commander himself left alive ! He saw an Egyptian his executioner, and yielded to a slave a body that was sacrosanct to the victors,[d] though even had he been unharmed, he would have repented of his escape ; for what were baser than that a Pompey should live by the bounty of a king !

If Marcus Cicero had fallen at the moment when he escaped the daggers of Catiline, which were aimed not less at him than at his country, if he had fallen as the saviour of the commonwealth which he had freed, if his death had followed close upon that of his daughter,[e] even then he might have died happy. He would not have seen swords drawn to take the lives of Roman citizens, nor assassins parcelling out the goods of their victims in order that these might even be murdered at their own cost, nor the spoils of a consul [f] put up at

---

[e] Tullia, who died in 45 B.C.
[f] *Cf.* Cicero, *Phil.* ii. 64 : " hasta posita pro aede Iovis Statoris bona Cn. Pompei (miserum me ! consumptis enim lacrimis tamen infixus haeret animo dolor), bona, inquam, Cn. Pompei Magni voci acerbissimae subiecta praeconis ! "

vendentem nec caedes locatas publice nec latrocinia,
bella, rapinas, tantum Catilinarum.

6 M. Catonem si a Cypro et hereditatis regiae dis-
pensatione redeuntem mare devorasset vel cum illa
ipsa pecunia, quam adferebat civili bello stipendium,
nonne illi bene actum foret ? Hoc certe secum tulis-
set, neminem ausurum coram Catone peccare. Nunc
annorum adiectio paucissimorum virum libertati non
suae tantum sed publicae natum coegit Caesarem
fugere, Pompeium sequi.

Nihil ergo illi mali immatura mors attulit ; omnium
etiam malorum remisit patientiam.

1 21. " Nimis tamen cito perît et immaturus." Primum puta illi superfuisse—comprende quantum plurimum procedere homini licet : quantum est ? Ad
brevissimum tempus editi, cito cessuri loco venienti
in pactum[1] hoc prospicimus hospitium. De nostris
aetatibus loquor, quas incredibili celeritate aevum
volvit ? Computa urbium saecula ; videbis quam
non diu steterint etiam quae vetustate glorientur.
Omnia humana brevia et caduca sunt et infiniti tem-
2 poris nullam partem occupantia. Terram hanc cum
urbibus populisque et fluminibus et ambitu maris
puncti loco ponimus ad universa referentes ; minorem
portionem aetas nostra quam puncti habet, si omni
tempori comparetur, cuius maior est mensura quam

---

[1] in pactum *A* : inpacatum *Madvig* : inpactum *Gertz* :
impacato *Waltz*.

---

[a] Left by King Ptolemy, who committed suicide soon after
Cato arrived to carry out the annexation of the island in 58 B.C.
Cato himself committed suicide after Caesar's victory at
Thapsus (46 B.C.).

public auction, nor murders contracted for officially, nor brigandage and war and pillage—so many new Catilines !

If the sea had swallowed up Marcus Cato as he was returning from Cyprus and his stewardship of the royal legacy,[a] and along with him even the money which he was bringing to defray the expense of the Civil War, would it not have been a blessing to him ? This much at least he might have taken with him then—the conviction that no one would have the effrontery to do wrong in the presence of Cato ! As it was, having gained the respite of a very few years, that hero, who was born no less for personal than for political freedom, was forced to flee from Caesar and to submit to Pompey.

To your son, therefore, though his death was premature, it brought no ill ; rather has it released him from suffering ills of every sort.

" Yet," you say, " he perished too soon and before his time." In the first place, suppose he had survived—grant him the very longest life a man can have —how many years are there after all ? Born as we are for the briefest space, and destined soon to yield place to another coming into his lease of time, we view our life as a sojourn at an inn. " Our " life do I say, when Time hurries it on with such incredible swiftness ? Count the centuries of cities ; you will see how even those that boast of their great age have not existed long. All things human are short-lived and perishable, and fill no part at all of infinite time. This earth with its cities and peoples, its rivers and the girdle of the sea, if measured by the universe, we may count a mere dot ; our life, if compared with all time, is relatively even less than a dot ; for the com-

mundi, utpote cum ille se intra huius spatium totiens
remetiatur. Quid ergo interest id extendere, cuius
quantumcumque fuerit incrementum non multum
aberit a nihilo ? Uno modo multum est quod vivimus,
3 si satis est. Licet mihi vivaces et in memoriam
traditae senectutis viros nomines, centenos denosque
percenseas annos : cum ad omne tempus dimiseris
animum, nulla erit illa brevissimi longissimique aevi
differentia, si inspecto quanto quis vixerit spatio com-
4 paraveris quanto non vixerit. Deinde sibi maturus
decessit ; vixit enim quantum debuit vivere, nihil illi
iam ultra supererat. Non una hominibus senectus
est, ut ne animalibus quidem. Intra quattuordecim
quaedam annos defetigavit, et haec illis longissima
aetas est quae homini prima ; dispar cuique vivendi
facultas data est. Nemo nimis cito moritur, quia vic-
5 turus diutius quam vixit non fuit. Fixus est cuique
terminus ; manebit semper, ubi positus est, nec illum
ulterius diligentia aut gratia promovebit. Sic habe,
te illum ex consilio perdidisse. Tulit suum

Metasque dati pervenit ad aevi.

6 Non est itaque quod sic te oneres : " Potuit diutius
vivere." Non est interrupta eius vita nec umquam se
annis casus intericit. Solvitur quod cuique promissum est ; eunt via sua fata nec adiciunt quicquam

---

ᵃ An allusion to the Stoic doctrine of cyclic conflagrations,
by which the existing universe was destroyed and the process
of creation renewed.
ᵇ Virgil, *Aeneid*, x. 472.

pass of eternity is greater than that of the world, since the world renews[a] itself over and over within the bounds of time. What, then, is to be gained by lengthening out that which, however much shall be added on to it, will still not be far from nothing? The time we live is much in only one way—if it is enough! You may name to me men who were long-lived and attained an age that has become proverbial, and you may count up a hundred and ten years for each, yet when you turn your thought upon eternal time, if you compare the space that you discover a man has lived with the space that he has not lived, not a whit of difference will you find between the shortest and the longest life. Again, your son himself was ripe for death; for he lived as long as he needed to live—nothing further was left for him to do. There is no uniform time for old age in the case of men, nor indeed of animals either. Some animals are exhausted within the space of fourteen years, and their longest life is no more than the first stage of a man's; to each has been given a different capacity for living. No man dies too soon, because he lives only as long as he was destined to live. For each the boundary-line is marked; where it has been once placed, it will always remain, and no endeavour or favour will move it farther on. Look at the matter thus—you lost your son in accordance with a fixed plan. He had his day

And reached the goal of his allotted years.[b]

And so you must not burden yourself with the thought: "He might have lived longer." His life has not been cut short, nor does Chance ever thrust itself into the years. What has been promised to each man, is paid; the Fates go their way, and neither add any-

nec ex promisso semel demunt. Frustra vota ac
studia sunt ; habebit quisque quantum illi dies primus
adscripsit. Ex illo quo primum lucem vidit, iter
mortis ingressus est accessitque fato propior et illi
ipsi qui adiciebantur adulescentiae anni vitae de-
trahebantur. In hoc omnes errore versamur, ut non
putemus ad mortem nisi senes inclinatosque iam ver-
gere, cum illo infantia statim et iuventa, omnis aetas
ferat. Agunt opus suum fata ; nobis sensum nostrae
necis auferunt, quoque facilius obrepat mors, sub ipso
vitae nomine latet ; infantiam in se pueritia convertit,
pueritiam pubertas, iuvenem senex abstulit. Incrementa ipsa, si bene computes, damna sunt.

1   22. Quereris, Marcia, non tam diu filium tuum
vixisse quam potuisset ? Unde enim scis an diutius
illi expedierit vivere ? an illi hac morte consultum
sit ? Quemquam invenire hodie potes, cuius res tam
bene positae sunt fundataeque, ut nihil illi procedenti
tempore timendum sit ? Labant humana ac fluunt
neque ulla pars vitae nostrae tam obnoxia aut tenera
est quam quae maxime placet, ideoque felicissimis
optanda mors est, quia in tanta inconstantia turbaque
2 rerum nihil nisi quod praeterît certum est. Quis tibi
recipit illud fili tui pulcherrimum corpus et summa
pudoris custodia inter luxuriosae urbis oculos con-

thing to what has once been promised, nor subtract from it. Prayers and struggles are all in vain ; each one will get just the amount that was placed to his credit on the first day of his existence. That day on which he first saw the light, he entered upon the path to death and drew ever nearer to his doom, and the very years that were added to his youth were subtracted from his life. We all fall into the error of thinking that only those who are old and already on the downward path are tending toward death, whereas earliest infancy, middle age, every period of life indeed leads in that direction. The Fates ply their work ; they keep us from being conscious that we are dying, and, to have it steal upon us the more easily, death lurks beneath the very name of life ; infancy changes into boyhood, boyhood into adolescence, and old age steals away the age of maturity. Our very gains, if you reckon them properly, are losses.

Do you complain, Marcia, that your son did not live as long as he might have lived ? For how do you know whether it was advisable for him to live longer ? whether his interest was served by such a death ? Can you this day find anyone whose fortunes are so happily placed and so firmly grounded that he has nothing to fear from the advance of time ? Human affairs are unstable and fleeting, and no part of our life is so frail and perishable as that which gives most pleasure, and therefore at the height of good fortune we ought to pray for death, since in all the inconstancy and turmoil of life we can feel sure of nothing except the past. And your son who was so handsome in body and under the eyes of a dissolute city had been kept pure by his strict regard for chastity—

servatum potuisse tot morbos ita evadere, ut ad senectutem inlaesum perferret formae decus? Cogita
animi mille labes; neque enim recta ingenia qualem
in adulescentia spem sui fecerant usque in senectutem
pertulerunt, sed interversa plerumque sunt; aut sera
eoque foedior luxuria invasit coepitque dehonestare
speciosa principia, aut in popinam ventremque pro-
cubuerunt toti summaque illis curarum fuit, quid
3 essent, quid biberent. Adice incendia, ruinas, naufragia lacerationesque medicorum ossa vivis legen-
tium et totas in viscera manus demittentium et non
simplici cum dolore pudenda curantium; post haec
exilium (non fuit innocentior filius tuus quam Rutilius),
carcerem (non fuit sapientior quam Socrates), volun-
tario vulnere transfixum pectus (non fuit sanctior quam
Cato). Cum ista perspexeris, scies optime cum is agi,
quos natura, quia illos hoc manebat vitae stipendium,
cito in tutum recepit. Nihil est tam fallax quam vita
humana, nihil tam insidiosum; non me hercules quisquam illam accepisset, nisi daretur inscientibus. Itaque si felicissimum est non nasci, proximum est, puto,
brevi aetate defunctos cito in integrum restitui.

4 Propone illud acerbissimum tibi tempus, quo Seianus patrem tuum clienti suo Satrio Secundo con-

---

^a His firmness and honesty in public life worked his ruin
(92 B.C.).
^b Cf. Sophocles, Oedipus Col. 1225 sq.:

Μὴ φῦναι τὸν ἅπαντα νικᾷ λόγοι· τὸ δ', ἐπεὶ φανῇ,
βῆναι κεῖθεν ὅθεν περ ἥκει, πολὺ δεύτερον, ὡς τάχιστα.

what assurance have you that he could have escaped
the many diseases there are, and so have preserved
the unimpaired beauty of his person down to old age ?
And think of the thousand taints of the soul ! For
even noble natures do not support continuously into
old age the expectations they had stirred in their
youth, but are often turned aside ; they either fall
into dissipation, which coming late is for that reason
the more disgraceful, and begins to tarnish the brilliance of their first years, or they sink wholly to the
level of the eating-house and the belly, and what they
shall eat and what they shall drink become their chief
concern. To this add fires and falling houses, and
shipwrecks and the agonies from surgeons as they
pluck bones from the living body, and thrust their
whole hands deep into the bowels, and treat the
private parts at the cost of infinite pain. And besides all these there is exile—surely your son was not
more blameless than Rutilius [a] !—and the prison—
surely he was not wiser than Socrates !—and the
suicide's dagger, piercing the heart—surely he was
not more holy than Cato ! If you will consider all
these possibilities, you will learn that those who are
treated most kindly by Nature are those whom she
removes early to a place of safety, because life had in
store some such penalty as this. Yes, nothing is so
deceptive as human life, nothing is so treacherous.
Heaven knows ! not one of us would have accepted it
as a gift, were it not given to us without our knowledge. If, therefore, the happiest lot is not to be
born, the next best, I think, is to have a brief life and
by death to be restored quickly to the original state. [b]

Recall that time, so bitter for you, when Sejanus
handed over your father to his client, Satrius

giarium dedit. Irascebatur illi ob unum aut alterum
liberius dictum, quod tacitus ferre non potuerat
Seianum in cervices nostras ne imponi quidem, sed
escendere. Decernebatur illi statua in Pompei
theatro ponenda, quod exustum Caesar reficiebat;
exclamavit Cordus tunc vere theatrum perire. Quid
5 ergo? Non rumperetur supra cineres Cn. Pompei
constitui Seianum et in monimentis maximi impera-
toris consecrari perfidum militem? Consecratur[1]
subscriptio, et acerrimi canes, quos ille ut sibi uni
mansuetos, omnibus feros haberet, sanguine humano
pascebat, circumlatrare hominem etiam illum iam
6 pedica captum[2] incipiunt. Quid faceret? Si vivere
vellet, Seianus rogandus erat, si mori, filia, uterque
inexorabilis. Constituit filiam fallere. Usus itaque
balineo, quo plus virium poneret, in cubiculum se
quasi gustaturus contulit et dimissis pueris quaedam
per fenestram, ut videretur edisse, proiecit; a cena
deinde, quasi iam satis in cubiculo edisset, abstinuit.
Altero quoque die et tertio idem fecit; quartus ipsa
infirmitate corporis faciebat indicium. Complexus
itaque te: " Carissima," inquit, " filia et hoc unum

---

[1] consecratur *AF*: *the reading of the MSS. rejected by
editors is retained by Basore for the sake of the irony;* con-
cinnatur *Madvig*: conflatur *Gertz*: consignatur *Waltz*.

[2] etiam illum iam pedica captum *Basore*: etiam illum
imperiatum *AF*: etiam in illo (illo in *Gertz*) imperio altum
Madvig: etiam tunc imperterritum *Niemeyer*: etiamtum
imperturbatum *Waltz*.

---

^a *i.e.*, the authority of Sejanus demanding the destruction
of Cordus was respected.

Secundus, as a largess. He was angry because your
father, not being able to endure in silence that a
Sejanus should be set upon our necks, much less climb
there, had spoken out once or twice rather boldly.
Sejanus was being voted the honour of a statue,
which was to be set up in the theatre of Pompey, just
then being restored by Tiberius after a fire. Whereupon Cordus exclaimed : " Now the theatre is ruined
indeed ! " What ! Was it not to burst with rage—
to think of a Sejanus planted upon the ashes of Gnaeus
Pompeius, a disloyal soldier hallowed by a statue in
a memorial to one of the greatest generals ? Hallowed, too, was the signature[a] of Sejanus ! and those
fiercest of dogs,[b] which, savage toward all others, he
kept friendly only to himself by feeding them on
human blood, began to bark around that great man,[c]
who was already caught in a trap. What was he to
do ? If he wished to live, he had to make his plea to
Sejanus ; if he wished to die, to his own daughter,
and both were inexorable. So he determined to
deceive his daughter. Therefore, having taken a
bath and seeking to reduce his strength still further,
he retired to his bedchamber, giving out that he
would have luncheon there ; then, having dismissed
the slaves, he threw part of the food out of the window
in order to have it appear that he had eaten it ; later
he refused dinner on the pretext that he had already
eaten enough in his room. He did the same thing
also on the second day and the third day ; on the
fourth, the very weakness of his body revealed the
truth. And so, taking you into his arms, he said :
" My dearest daughter, nothing in my whole life have

[b] The delators, or unscrupulous political accusers, who
were the tools of Sejanus.   [c] Cordus.

tota celata vita, iter mortis ingressus sum et iam
medium fere teneo; revocare me nec debes nec potes."
Atque ita iussit lumen omne praecludi et se in tene-
7 bras condidit. Cognito consilio eius publica voluptas
erat, quod e faucibus avidissimorum luporum edu-
ceretur praeda. Accusatores auctore Seiano adeunt
consulum tribunalia, queruntur mori Cordum, ut interpellarent[1] quod coegerant[2]; adeo illis Cordus videbatur effugere. Magna res erat in quaestione, an
mortis ius rei perderent; dum deliberatur, dum accusatores iterum adeunt, ille se absolverat. Videsne,
Marcia, quantae iniquorum temporum vices ex inopinato ingruant? Fles, quod alicui tuorum mori necesse
fuit? Paene non licuit!

1   23. Praeter hoc quod omne futurum incertum est
et ad deteriora certius, facillimum ad superos iter
est animis cito ab humana conversatione dimissis;
minimum enim faecis, ponderis traxerunt. Ante
quam obdurescerent et altius terrena conciperent
liberati leviores ad originem suam revolant et facilius
2 quicquid est illud obsoleti inlitique eluunt. Nec
umquam magnis ingenis cara in corpore mora est;
exire atque erumpere gestiunt, aegre has angustias

---

[1] interpellarent *inferior mss.* : interpella *A* : interpellaret
Waltz.
[2] quod coegerant *A* : quod coeperant *Waltz.*

---

[a] Again, the delators.

I ever concealed from you but this, but I have entered
upon the road to death, and am now almost half-way
there ; you cannot and you ought not to call me
back." And so, having ordered all light to be shut
out, he buried himself in deep darkness. When his
purpose was recognized, there was general rejoicing,
because the jaws of the ravening wolves *a* were
being cheated of their prey. At the instigation
of Sejanus, accusers of Cordus appeared before the
tribunal of the consuls, complained that their victim
was dying, and begged them to prevent the very
thing they had forced upon him ; so strongly did
they feel that Cordus was escaping them ! The
great question in dispute was whether an accused
man lost his right to die ; while the matter was being
debated, while his accusers were making their plea a
second time, he had already gained his freedom. Do
you not see, Marcia, what great vicissitudes of fortune assail us unexpectedly when the times are evil ?
Weep you because one of your dear ones was required
to die ? One was very nearly not allowed.

Besides the fact that all the future is uncertain,
and more certain to be worse than otherwise, it is
true that the souls that are quickly released from
intercourse with men find the journey to the gods
above most easy; for they carry less weight of earthly
dross. Set free before they become hardened, before
they are too deeply contaminated by the things of
earth, they fly back more lightly to the source of
their being, and more easily wash away all defilement
and stain. And souls that are great find no joy in
lingering in the body ; they yearn to go forth and
burst their bonds, and they chafe against these
narrow bounds, accustomed as they are to range far

ferunt, vagi per omne, sublimes et ex alto adsueti
humana despicere. Inde est quod Platon clamat :
sapientis animum totum in mortem prominere, hoc
velle, hoc meditari, hac semper cupidine ferri in
exteriora tendentem.

3   Quid ? tu, Marcia, cum videres senilem in iuvene
prudentiam, victorem omnium voluptatium animum,
emendatum, carentem vitio, divitias sine avaritia,
honores sine ambitione, voluptates sine luxuria ad-
petentem, diu tibi putabas illum sospitem posse contingere ? Quicquid ad summum pervenit, ab exitu
prope est. Eripit se aufertque ex oculis perfecta
virtus, nec ultimum tempus expectant quae in primo
4 maturuerunt. Ignis quo clarior fulsit, citius extinguitur ; vivacior est, qui cum lenta ac difficili materia
commissus fumoque demersus ex sordido lucet ;
eadem enim detinet causa, quae maligne alit. Sic
ingenia quo inlustriora, breviora sunt ; nam ubi in-
5 cremento locus non est, vicinus occasus est. Fabianus
ait, id quod nostri quoque parentes videre, puerum
Romae fuisse statura ingentis viri[1] ; sed hic cito
decessit, et moriturum brevi nemo prudens non ante
dixit[2] ; non poterat enim ad illam aetatem pervenire,
quam praeceperat. Ita est : indicium imminentis
exitii nimia maturitas est ; adpetit finis ubi incrementa consumpta sunt.

1   24. Incipe virtutibus illum, non annis aestimare ;
satis diu vixit. Pupillus relictus sub tutorum cura

---

[1] statura ingentis uiri ante *AF* (ante *commonly omitted*) :
staturae ingentis, virum antecellentis *Gertz* : staturae ingentis,
ui nitentem *Waltz*.

[2] prudens non ante dixit *Bourgery* : prudens dixit *A* :
Hermes and editors since Erasmus add non *before* prudens.

---

[a] *Cf. Phaedo.* 64 A.

aloft throughout the universe, and from on high to
look down in scorn upon the affairs of men. Hence
it is that Plato[a] cries out that the wise man reaches
out with all his mind toward death, longs for it, thinks
upon it, and because of this passion moves through
life striving ever for the things beyond.

Tell me, Marcia, when you saw in your son, youth
that he was, the wisdom of an old man, a mind victorious over all sensual pleasures, unblemished, fault-
less, seeking riches without greed, honours without
ostentation, pleasures without excess, did you think
that you could long have the good fortune to keep
him safe and unharmed? Whatever has reached
perfection, is near its end. Ideal Virtue hurries
away and is snatched from our eyes, and the fruits
that ripen in their first days do not wait long for
their last. The brighter a fire glows, the more
quickly it dies; the fire that is kindled with tough
and stubborn wood, and, shrouded in smoke, shines
with a murky light is longer lived; for the same condition keeps it alive that provides it grudging food.
So with men—the brighter their spirits, the briefer
their day; for when there is no room for increase,
destruction is near. Fabianus relates—our parents
also actually saw him—that there was at Rome a
boy who was as tall as a very tall man; but he
soon died, and every sensible person said beforehand
that he would promptly die, for he could not be expected to reach an age that he had already fore-
stalled. And so it is—ripe maturity is the sign of
impending destruction; when growth stops, the
end approaches.

Undertake to estimate him by his virtues, not by
his years, and you will see he lived long enough.
Left as a ward, he was under the care of guardians

usque ad quartum decimum annum fuit, sub matris
tutela semper. Cum haberet suos penates, relinquere tuos noluit et in materno contubernio, cum vix
paternum liberi ferant, perseveravit. Adulescens
statura, pulchritudine, certo corporis robore castris
2 natus militiam recusavit, ne a te discederet. Computa,
Marcia, quam raro liberos videant quae in diversis
domibus habitant; cogita tot illos perire annos
matribus et per sollicitudinem exigi, quibus filios
in exercitu habent : scies multum patuisse hoc tempus,
ex quo nil perdidisti. Numquam e conspectu tuo
recessit ; sub oculis tuis studia formavit excellentis
ingeni et aequaturi avum, nisi obstitisset verecundia,
3 quae multorum profectus silentio pressit. Adulescens
rarissimae formae in tam magna feminarum turba
viros corrumpentium nullius se spei praebuit, et cum
quarundam usque ad temptandum pervenisset im-
probitas, erubuit quasi peccasset, quod placuerat.
Hac sanctitate morum effecit, ut puer admodum
dignus sacerdotio videretur, materna sine dubio
suffragatione, sed ne mater quidem nisi pro bono
4 candidato valuisset. Harum contemplatione virtutum filium gere quasi sinu ! Nunc ille tibi magis
vacat, nunc nihil habet, quo avocetur ; numquam

---

^a Under the Empire the members of the various priest-
hoods at Rome were appointed by the emperor in his
capacity of *Pontifex Maximus*. The priesthoods at this
time were little more than useful ornaments, but supplied
a powerful source of patronage.

up to his fourteenth year, but his mother's guardian-ship lasted all his life. Although he had his own hearthstone, he did not wish to leave yours, and at an age when most children can scarcely endure the society of a father, he persisted in seeking that of his mother. As a young man, although by his stature, beauty, and sure bodily strength, born for the camp, he refused military service so as not to leave you. Consider, Marcia, how rarely it happens that mothers who live in separate houses see their chil-dren ; think of all the years that are lost to those mothers who have sons in the army, and they are spent in constant anxiety ; you will find that this period during which you suffered no loss has been very extended. Your son was never removed from your sight ; with an ability that was outstanding and would have made him the rival of his grandfather had he not been hampered by modesty, which in the case of many men checks their advancement by silence, he shaped all his studies beneath your eyes. Though he was a young man of the rarest beauty of person, and was surrounded by such a great horde of women, the corrupters of men, he lent himself to the hopes of none, and when some of them in their effron-tery went so far as to make advances to him, he blushed with shame as if he had sinned even by pleasing them. It was this purity of character that made him seem worthy of being appointed to the priesthood[a] while he was still a lad ; his mother's influence undoubtedly helped, but, unless the candi-date himself had been good, even a mother's influ-ence would have had no weight. In thinking of all these virtues hold again, as it were, your son in your arms ! He has now more leisure to devote to you, there is nothing now to call him away from you ;

tibi sollicitudini, numquam maerori erit. Quod
unum ex tam bono filio poteras dolere, doluisti;
cetera, exempta casibus, plena voluptatis sunt, si
modo uti filio scis, si modo quid in illo pretiosissimum
5 fuerit intellegis. Imago dumtaxat fili tui perît et
effigies non simillima; ipse quidem aeternus melioris-
que nunc status est, despoliatus oneribus alienis et
sibi relictus. Haec quae vides circumdata[1] nobis,
ossa nervos et obductam cutem vultumque et minis-
tras manus et cetera quibus involuti sumus, vincula
animorum tenebraeque sunt. Obruitur his, offocatur,
inficitur, arcetur a veris et suis in falsa coiectus.
Omne illi cum hac gravi carne certamen est, ne
abstrahatur et sidat; nititur illo, unde demissus est.
Ibi illum aeterna requies manet ex confusis crassisque
pura et liquida visentem.

1 25. Proinde non est quod ad sepulcrum fili tui
curras; pessima eius et ipsi molestissima istic iacent,
ossa cineresque, non magis illius partes quam vestes
aliaque tegimenta corporum. Integer ille nihilque
in terris relinquens sui fugit et totus excessit;
paulumque supra nos commoratus, dum expurgatur
et inhaerentia vitia situmque omnem mortalis aevi
excutit, deinde ad excelsa sublatus inter felices currit
animas. Excepit illum coetus sacer, Scipiones

---

[1] circumdata *Koch*: circum *A.*

never again will he cause you anxiety, never again any grief. The only sorrow you could possibly have from a son so good is the sorrow you have had ; all else is now exempt from the power of chance, and holds nought but pleasure if only you know how to enjoy your son, if only you come to understand what his truest value was. Only the image of your son— and a very imperfect likeness it was—has perished ; he himself is eternal and has reached now a far better state, stripped of all outward encumbrances and left simply himself. This vesture of the body which we see, bones and sinews and the skin that covers us, this face and the hands that serve us and the rest of our human wrapping—these are but chains and darkness to our souls. By these things the soul is crushed and strangled and stained and, imprisoned in error, is kept far from its true and natural sphere. It constantly struggles against this weight of the flesh in the effort to avoid being dragged back and sunk ; it ever strives to rise to that place from which it once descended. There eternal peace awaits it when it has passed from earth's dull motley to the vision of all that is pure and bright.

There is no need, therefore, for you to hurry to the tomb of your son ; what lies there is his basest part and a part that in life was the source of much trouble —bones and ashes are no more parts of him than were his clothes and the other protections of the body. He is complete—leaving nothing of himself behind, he has fled away and wholly departed from earth ; for a little while he tarried above us while he was being purified and was ridding himself of all the blemishes and stain that still clung to him from his mortal exist- ence, then soared aloft and sped away to join the souls of the blessed. A saintly band gave him wel-

Catonesque, interque contemptores vitae et veneficio[1]
2 liberos parens tuus, Marcia. Ille nepotem suum—
quamquam illic omnibus omne cognatum est—
applicat sibi nova luce gaudentem et vicinorum
siderum meatus docet, nec ex coniectura sed omnium
ex vero peritus in arcana naturae libens ducit ; utque
ignotarum urbium monstrator hospiti gratus est, ita
sciscitanti caelestium causas domesticus interpres.
Et in profunda terrarum permittere aciem iubet ;
3 iuvat enim ex alto relicta respicere. Sic itaque te,
Marcia, gere, tamquam sub oculis patris filique posita,
non illorum, quos noveras, sed tanto excelsiorum et
in summo locatorum. Erubesce quicquam humile
aut volgare cogitare[2] et mutatos in melius tuos flere !
Aeternarum rerum per libera et vasta spatia dimissi
sunt[3] ; non illos interfusa maria discludunt nec alti-
tudo montium aut inviae valles aut incertarum vada
Syrtium : omnia ibi plana[4] et ex facili mobiles et
expediti et in vicem pervii sunt intermixtique
sideribus.

1 26. Puta itaque ex illa arce caelesti patrem tuum
Marcia, cui tantum apud te auctoritatis erat quantum
tibi apud filium tuum, non illo ingenio, quo civilia
bella deflevit, quo proscribentis in aeternum ipse
proscripsit, sed tanto elatiore, quanto est ipse sub-

---

[1] veneficio *Apelt* : beneficio *A* : mortis beneficio *editors
commonly* : *Gertz adds* suo *after* (*Favez before*) beneficio.
[2] cogitare *added by Hermes*.
[3] dimissi sunt *Gertz* : dimissi A[1] : dimissos *F*.
[4] omnia ibi plana *Gertz* : omnium plana *A* : omnia
plana *F* : omnia in plano habent *Waltz*.

---

[a] In Stoic physics the soul was a fiery substance identical
with the divine fire ; the stars were likewise fiery and
divine. The exuberant language seems to represent that
the purified soul becomes one with the stars.

come—the Scipios and the Catos and, joined with those who scorned life and through a draught of poison found freedom, your father, Marcia. Although there all are akin with all, he keeps his grandson near him, and, while your son rejoices in the new-found light, he instructs him in the movement of the neighbouring stars, and gladly initiates him into Nature's secrets, not by guesswork, but by experience having true knowledge of them all ; and just as a stranger is grateful for a guide through an unknown city, so your son, as he searches into the causes of celestial things, is grateful for a kinsman as his instructor. He bids him also turn his gaze upon the things of earth far below ; for it is a pleasure to look back upon all that has been left behind. Do you therefore, Marcia, always act as if you knew that the eyes of your father and your son were set upon you—not such as you once knew them, but far loftier beings, dwelling in the highest heaven. Blush to have a low or common thought, and to weep for those dear ones who have changed for the better ! Throughout the free and boundless spaces of eternity they wander ; no intervening seas block their course, no lofty mountains or pathless valleys or shallows of the shifting Syrtes ; there every way is level, and, being swift and unencumbered, they easily are pervious to the matter of the stars and, in turn, are mingled with it.[a]

Consider, therefore, Marcia, that your father, whose influence upon you was not less great than was yours upon your son, using no longer that tone in which he bewailed the civil wars, in which he himself proscribed for all time the sponsors of proscription, but the loftier tone that befits his more exalted state,

2 limior, dicere ; " Cur te, filia, tam longa tenet aegri-
tudo ? Cur in tanta veri ignoratione versaris, ut
inique actum cum filio tuo iudices, quod integro
domus statu integer ipse se[1] ad maiores recepit suos ?
Nescis quantis fortuna procellis disturbet omnia ?
Quam nullis benignam facilemque se praestiterit, nisi
qui minimum cum illa contraxerant ? Regesne tibi
nominem felicissimos futuros, si maturius illos mors
instantibus subtraxisset malis ? an Romanos duces,
quorum nihil magnitudini deerit, si aliquid aetati
detraxeris ? an nobilissimos viros clarissimosque
ad ictum militaris gladi composita cervice curvatos ?
3 Respice patrem atque avum tuum : ille in alieni
percussoris venit arbitrium ; ego nihil in me cuiquam
permisi et cibo prohibitus ostendi tam magno me
quam uidebar animo scripsisse.[2] Cur in domo nostra
diutissime lugetur qui felicissime moritur ? Coimus
omnes in unum videmusque non alta nocte cir-
cumdati nil apud vos, ut putatis, optabile, nil excel-
sum, nil splendidum, sed humilia cuncta et gravia et
anxia et quotam partem luminis nostri cernentia !
4 Quid dicam nulla hic arma mutuis furere concursibus
nec classes classibus frangi nec parricidia aut fingi
aut cogitari nec fora litibus strepere dies perpetuos,

---

[1] se *added by Haase.*
[2] tam magno me quam videbar animo scripsisse *Haase*:
quam magno me quam uibar animo scribsisse (magno me
quam *in the margin*) A^1 : tam magno me quam vivebam
animo scripsisse *Waltz.*

speaks to you from the citadel of high heaven and says : " Why, my daughter, are you held by such lengthy sorrow ? Why do you live in such ignorance of the truth as to believe that your son was unfairly treated because, leaving his family fortunes whole, he himself returned to his forefathers, safe and whole ? Do you not know how mighty are the storms of Fortune that demolish everything ? How if she shows herself kindly and indulgent, it is only to those who have the fewest possible dealings with her ? Need I name to you the kings who would have been the happiest of mortals if death had removed them sooner from the evils that were threatening ? or even the Roman leaders who would lose not a tithe of greatness if you should subtract some years from their life ? or those heroes of the highest birth and fame who calmly bowed their necks to receive the stroke of a soldier's sword ? Look back upon your father and your grandfather. Your grandfather fell into the power of a foreign assassin ; I myself suffered no man to have any power over me, and, having cut myself off from food, I proved that I was as courageous as I seemed to have been in my writings. Why should that member who has had the happiest death be longest mourned in our family ? We are all together in one place, and, released from the deep night that envelops you, we discover among you nothing that is, as you think, desirable, nothing that is lofty, nothing glorious, but all is lowly, heavy laden, and troubled, and beholds how small a fraction of the light in which we dwell ! Why need I say that here are no rival armies clashing in their rage, no fleets to shatter one another, no parricides are here either conceived or planned, no forums ring with strife the

nihil in obscuro, detectas mentes et aperta praecordia
et in publico medioque vitam et omnis aevi prospec-
tum venientiumque ?

5 " Iuvabat unius me saeculi facta componere in parte
ultima mundi et inter paucissimos gesta. Tot saecula,
tot aetatium contextum, seriem, quicquid annorum
est, licet visere ; licet surrectura, licet ruitura regna
prospicere et magnarum urbium lapsus et maris

6 novos cursus. Nam si tibi potest solacio esse desideri
tui commune fatum, nihil quo stat loco stabit, omnia
sternet abducetque secum vetustas. Nec hominibus
solum (quota enim ista fortuitae potentiae portio
est ?), sed locis, sed regionibus, sed mundi partibus
ludet. Totos supprimet montes et alibi rupes in
altum novas exprimet ; maria sorbebit, flumina
avertet et commercio gentium rupto societatem
generis humani coetumque dissolvet ; alibi hiatibus
vastis subducet urbes, tremoribus quatiet et ex infimo
pestilentiae halitus mittet et inundationibus quicquid
habitatur obducet necabitque omne animal orbe
submerso et ignibus vastis torrebit incendetque
mortalia. Et cum tempus advenerit, quo se mundus
renovaturus extinguat, viribus ista se suis caedent
et sidera sideribus incurrent et omni flagrante materia

---

* Cordus was *laudator* of the era of the Republic.
ᵇ *i.e.*, the earth, remote from the speaker's position in
heaven.

livelong day, that no secrecy is here, but minds are uncovered and hearts revealed and our lives are open and manifest to all, while every age and things to come are ranged before our sight ?

" It was once my delight to compile the history of what took place in a single epoch[a] in the most distant region[b] of the universe and among the merest handful of people. Now I may have the view of countless centuries, the succession and train of countless ages, the whole array of years : I may behold the rise and fall of future kingdoms, the downfall of great cities, and new invasions of the sea. For, if the common fate can be a solace for your yearning, know that nothing will abide where it is now placed, that time will lay all things low and take all things with it. And not simply men will be its sport—for how small a part are they of Fortune's domain !—but places, countries, and the great parts of the universe. It will level whole mountains, and in another place will pile new rocks on high ; it will drink up seas, turn rivers from their courses, and, sundering the communication of nations, break up the association and intercourse of the human race ; in other places it will swallow up cities in yawning chasms, will shatter them with earthquakes, and from deep below send forth a pestilential vapour ; it will cover with floods the face of the inhabited world, and, deluging the earth, will kill every living creature, and in huge conflagration it will scorch and burn all mortal things. And when the time shall come for the world to be blotted out in order that it may begin its life anew, these things will destroy themselves by their own power, and stars will clash with stars, and all the fiery matter of the world that now shines in orderly array will blaze

uno igni quicquid nunc ex disposito lucet ardebit.
7 Nos quoque felices animae et aeterna sortitae, cum
deo visum erit iterum ista moliri, labentibus cunctis
et ipsae parva ruinae ingentis accessio in antiqua
elementa vertemur."

Felicem filium tuum, Marcia, qui ista iam novit !

up in a common conflagration. Then also the souls of the blest, who have partaken of immortality, when it shall seem best to God to create the universe anew—we, too, amid the falling universe, shall be added as a tiny fraction to this mighty destruction, and shall be changed again into our former elements."

Happy, Marcia, is your son, who already knows these mysteries !

LIBER VII

AD GALLIONEM

DE VITA BEATA

1 1. Vivere, Gallio frater, omnes beate volunt, sed
ad pervidendum, quid sit quod beatam vitam efficiat,
caligant ; adeoque non est facile consequi beatam
vitam, ut eo quisque ab ea longius recedat, quo ad
illam concitatius fertur, si via lapsus est ; quae ubi
in contrarium ducit, ipsa velocitas maioris intervalli
causa fit.

Proponendum est itaque primum, quid sit quod ad-
petamus ; tunc circumspiciendum, qua contendere
illo celerrime possimus, intellecturi in ipso itinere, si
modo rectum erit, quantum cotidie profligetur quanto-
que propius ab eo simus, ad quod nos cupiditas
2 naturalis impellit. Quam diu quidem passim vaga-
mur non ducem secuti sed fremitum et clamorem
dissonum in diversa vocantium, conteretur vita inter
errores brevis, etiam si dies noctesque bonae menti
laboremus. Decernatur itaque, et quo tendamus et

---

a Annaeus Novatus, known after his adoption as L. Iunius
Gallio, was the elder brother of Seneca. He had a
senatorial career, was governor of the province of Achaia
(A.D. 52), and has the fame of being the Roman official
before whom the Jews accused the apostle Paul (Acts, xviii.

BOOK VII

TO GALLIO

ON THE HAPPY LIFE

To live happily, my brother Gallio,[a] is the desire of all men, but their minds are blinded to a clear vision of just what it is that makes life happy ; and so far from its being easy to attain the happy life, the more eagerly a man strives to reach it, the farther he recedes from it if he has made a mistake in the road ; for when it leads in the opposite direction, his very speed will increase the distance that separates him.

First, therefore, we must seek what it is that we are aiming at ; then we must look about for the road by which we can reach it most quickly, and on the journey itself, if only we are on the right path, we shall discover how much of the distance we overcome each day, and how much nearer we are to the goal toward which we are urged by a natural desire. But so long as we wander aimlessly, having no guide, and following only the noise and discordant cries of those who call us in different directions, life will be consumed in making mistakes—life that is brief even if we should strive day and night for sound wisdom. Let us, therefore, decide both upon the goal and upon the

12-17). He died by his own hand in A.D. 66. To him, apparently before his adoption, are addressed the three books of the *De Ira. Cf.* Vol. I, Introd. pp. vii, xiii.

qua, non sine perito aliquo, cui explorata sint ea, in quae procedimus, quoniam quidem non eadem hic quae in ceteris peregrinationibus condicio est. In illis comprensus aliquis limes et interrogati incolae non patiuntur errare, at hic tritissima quaeque via 3 et celeberrima maxime decipit. Nihil ergo magis praestandum est, quam ne pecorum ritu sequamur antecedentium gregem, pergentes non quo eundum est, sed quo itur. Atqui nulla res nos maioribus malis implicat, quam quod ad rumorem componimur, optima rati ea, quae magno adsensu recepta sunt, quodque exempla nobis multa sunt, nec ad rationem sed ad similitudinem vivimus. Inde ista tanta coacer- 4 vatio aliorum super alios ruentium. Quod in strage hominum magna evenit, cum ipse se populus premit —nemo ita cadit, ut non et alium in se adtrahat, primique exitio sequentibus sunt—, hoc in omni vita accidere videas licet. Nemo sibi tantummodo errat, sed alieni erroris et causa et auctor est; nocet enim applicari antecedentibus et, dum unusquisque mavult credere quam iudicare, numquam de vita iudicatur, semper creditur versatque nos et praecipitat traditus per manus error. Alienis perimus exemplis; sanabi-

way, and not fail to find some experienced guide who has explored the region towards which we are advancing ; for the conditions of this journey are different from those of most travel. On most journeys some well-recognized road and inquiries made of the inhabitants of the region prevent you from going astray ; but on this one all the best beaten and the most frequented paths are the most deceptive. Nothing, therefore, needs to be more emphasized than the warning that we should not, like sheep, follow the lead of the throng in front of us, travelling, thus, the way that all go and not the way that we ought to go. Yet nothing involves us in greater trouble than the fact that we adapt ourselves to common report in the belief that the best things are those that have met with great approval,—the fact that, having so many to follow, we live after the rule, not of reason, but of imitation. The result of this is that people are piled high, one above another, as they rush to destruction. And just as it happens that in a great crush of humanity, when the people push against each other, no one can fall down without drawing along another, and those that are in front cause destruction to those behind—this same thing you may see happening everywhere in life. No man can go wrong to his own hurt only, but he will be both the cause and the sponsor of another's wrongdoing. For it is dangerous to attach one's self to the crowd in front, and so long as each one of us is more willing to trust another than to judge for himself, we never show any judgement in the matter of living, but always a blind trust, and a mistake that has been passed on from hand to hand finally involves us and works our destruction. It is the example of other people that is our undoing ; let

5 mur, separemur modo a coetu. Nunc vero stat contra
rationem defensor mali sui populus. Itaque id evenit
quod in comitiis, in quibus eos factos esse praetores
idem qui fecere mirantur, cum se mobilis favor circum-
egit. Eadem probamus, eadem reprehendimus ; hic
exitus est omnis iudicii, in quo secundum plures
datur.

1   2. Cum de beata vita agetur, non est quod mihi illud
discessionum more respondeas : " Haec pars maior
esse videtur." Ideo enim peior est. Non tam bene
cum rebus humanis agitur, ut meliora pluribus
2 placeant ; argumentum pessimi turba est. Quaeramus ergo, quid optimum factu sit, non quid usitatis-
simum, et quid nos in possessione felicitatis aeternae
constituat, non quid vulgo, veritatis pessimo inter-
preti, probatum sit. Vulgum autem tam chlamydatos quam coronatos voco ; non enim colorem
vestium, quibus praetexta sunt corpora, aspicio.
Oculis de homine non credo ; habeo melius et certius
lumen, quo a falsis vera diiudicem. Animi bonum
animus inveniat. Hic, si umquam respirare illi et
recedere in se vacaverit, o quam sibi ipse verum tortus
3 a se fatebitur ac dicet : " Quicquid feci adhuc infec-

ᵃ Literally, " those who wear cloaks than those who wear
crowns." The antithesis between *chlamydatos* and *coronatos*,
which the rhetoric requires, is admittedly obscure, yet the
ms. reading is clearly attested. The Greek chlamys, or
mantle, among the Romans was characteristically a garb
of elegance and distinction. It here evidently designates a
superior social class. The significance of *coronatos*, *i.e.*, the
slave class, I have derived from the custom of crowning
captives put up for sale as slaves (Gellius, vi. (vii.) 4), seen
in the common phrase *sub corona vendere* (*venire*). *Cf.*

us merely separate ourselves from the crowd, and we shall be made whole. But as it is, the populace, defending its own iniquity, pits itself against reason. And so we see the same thing happening that happens at the elections, where, when the fickle breeze of popular favour has shifted, the very same persons who chose the praetors wonder that those praetors were chosen. The same thing has one moment our favour, the next our disfavour ; this is the outcome of every decision that follows the choice of the majority.

When the happy life is under debate, there will be no use for you to reply to me, as if it were a matter of votes : "This side seems to be in a majority." For that is just the reason it is the worse side. Human affairs are not so happily ordered that the majority prefer the better things ; a proof of the worst choice is the crowd. Therefore let us find out what is best to do, not what is most commonly done— what will establish our claim to lasting happiness, not what finds favour with the rabble, who are the worst possible exponents of the truth. But by the rabble I mean no less the servants of the court than the servants of the kitchen *a* ; for I do not regard the colour of the garments that clothe the body. In rating a man I do not rely upon eyesight ; I have a better and surer light, by which I may distinguish the false from the true. Let the soul discover the good of the soul. If the soul ever has leisure to draw breath and to retire within itself—ah ! to what self-torture will it come, and how, if it confesses the truth to itself, it will say : " All that I have done hitherto,

Tacitus, *Annals*, xiii. 39. 7 : " et imbelle vulgus sub corona venundatum, reliqua praeda victoribus cessit."

tum esse mallem, quicquid dixi cum recogito, mutis
invideo,[1] quicquid optavi inimicorum exsecrationem
puto, quicquid timui, di boni, quanto levius fuit quam
quod concupii ! Cum multis inimicitias gessi et in
gratiam ex odio, si modo ulla inter malos gratia est,
redii ; mihi ipsi nondum amicus sum. Omnem
operam dedi, ut me multitudini educerem et aliqua
dote notabilem facerem. Quid aliud quam telis me
opposui et malevolentiae quod morderet ostendi ?
4 Vides istos, qui eloquentiam laudant, qui opes sequuntur, qui gratiae adulantur, qui potentiam extollunt ?
Omnes aut sunt hostes aut, quod in aequo est, esse
possunt. Quam magnus mirantium tam magnus
invidentium populus est. Quin potius quaero aliquod
usu bonum, quod sentiam, non quod ostendam ?
Ista, quae spectantur, ad quae consistitur, quae alter
alteri stupens monstrat, foris nitent, introrsus misera
sunt."

1 3. Quaeramus aliquod non in speciem bonum, sed
solidum et aequale et a secretiore parte formosius ;
hoc eruamus. Nec longe positum est ; invenietur,
scire tantum opus est quo manum porrigas. Nunc
velut in tenebris vicina transimus offensantes ea ipsa
quae desideramus.

2 Sed ne te per circumitus traham, aliorum quidem

<hr />

[1] mutis invideo *Gruter*: in multis uideo *A.*

I would were undone ; when I think of all that I have
said, I envy the dumb ; of all that I have prayed for,
I rate my prayers as the curses of my enemies ; of all
that I have feared—ye gods ! how much lighter it
would have been than the load of what I have
coveted ! With many I have been at enmity, and,
laying aside hatred, have been restored to friendship
with them—if only there can be any friendship between
the wicked ; with myself I have not yet entered into
friendship. I have made every effort to remove myself from the multitude and to make myself note-
worthy by reason of some endowment. What have
I accomplished save to expose myself to the darts of
malice and show it where it can sting me ? See you
those who praise your eloquence, who trail upon your
wealth, who court your favour, who exalt your power ?
All these are either now your enemies, or—it amounts
to the same thing—can become such. To know how
many are jealous of you, count your admirers. Why
do I not rather seek some real good—one which I could
feel, not one which I could display ? These things
that draw the eyes of men, before which they halt,
which they show to one another in wonder, outwardly glitter, but are worthless within."

Let us seek something that is a good in more than
appearance—something that is solid, constant, and
more beautiful in its more hidden part ; for this
let us delve. And it is placed not far off ; you will
find it—you need only to know where to stretch out
your hand. As it is, just as if we groped in darkness,
we pass by things near at hand, stumbling over the
very objects we desire.

Not to bore you, however, with tortuous details, I
shall pass over in silence the opinions of other philo-

opiniones praeteribo—nam et enumerare illas longum
est et coarguere. Nostram accipe. Nostram autem
cum dico, non alligo me ad unum aliquem ex Stoicis
proceribus; est et mihi censendi ius. Itaque aliquem
sequar, aliquem iubebo sententiam dividere, fortasse
et post omnes citatus nihil improbabo ex iis, quae
priores decreverint, et dicam : " Hoc amplius censeo."
3 Interim, quod inter omnis Stoicos convenit, rerum
naturae adsentior ; ab illa non deerrare et ad illius
legem exemplumque formari sapientia est.

Beata est ergo vita conveniens naturae suae, quae
non aliter contingere potest, quam si primum sana
mens est et in perpetua possessione sanitatis suae ;
deinde fortis ac vehemens, tunc pulcherrime patiens,
apta temporibus, corporis sui pertinentiumque ad id
curiosa non anxie, tum aliarum rerum quae vitam
instruunt diligens sine admiratione cuiusquam, usura
4 fortunae muneribus, non servitura. Intellegis, etiam
si non adiciam, sequi perpetuam tranquillitatem,
libertatem depulsis iis, quae aut irritant nos aut terri-
tant ; nam voluptatibus et timoribus proiectis[1] pro
illis, quae parva ac fragilia sunt et ipsis flagitiis noxia,
ingens gaudium subit, inconcussum et aequale, tum
pax et concordia animi et magnitudo cum mansuetudine ; omnis enim ex infirmitate feritas est.

---

[1] timoribus proiectis *supplied by Basore*: voluptatibus et
pro illis *A* : doloribus spretis *supplied by Reitzenstein* :
voluptatibus et illiciis *Bourgery.*

---

[a] *Cf.* Seneca, *Epistles*, xxi. 9: " quod fieri in senatu solet,
faciendum ego in philosophia quoque existimo: cum censuit
aliquis, quod ex parte mihi placeat, iubeo illum dividere
sententiam et sequor quod probo."

[b] The Stoic doctrine of ἀθαυμαστία, Horace's *nil admirari.*

sophers, for it would be tedious to enumerate and refute them all. Do you listen to ours. But when I say "ours," I do not bind myself to some particular one of the Stoic masters; I, too, have the right to form an opinion. Accordingly, I shall follow so-and-so, I shall request so-and-so to divide the question;[a] perhaps, too, when called upon after all the rest, I shall impugn none of my predecessors' opinions, and shall say: "I simply have this much to add." Meantime, I follow the guidance of Nature—a doctrine upon which all Stoics are agreed. Not to stray from Nature and to mould ourselves according to her law and pattern—this is true wisdom.

The happy life, therefore, is a life that is in harmony with its own nature, and it can be attained in only one way. First of all, we must have a sound mind and one that is in constant possession of its sanity; second, it must be courageous and energetic, and, too, capable of the noblest fortitude, ready for every emergency, careful of the body and of all that concerns it, but without anxiety; lastly, it must be attentive to all the advantages that adorn life, but with over-much love for none[b]—the user, but not the slave, of the gifts of Fortune. You understand, even if I do not say more, that, when once we have driven away all that excites or affrights us, there ensues unbroken tranquillity and enduring freedom; for when pleasures and fears have been banished, then, in place of all that is trivial and fragile and harmful just because of the evil it works, there comes upon us first a boundless joy that is firm and unalterable, then peace and harmony of the soul and true greatness coupled with kindliness; for all ferocity is born from weakness.

1 **4.** Potest aliter quoque definiri bonum nostrum, id est eadem sententia non isdem comprendi verbis. Quemadmodum idem exercitus modo latius panditur modo in angustum coartatur et aut in cornua sinuata media parte curvatur aut recta fronte explicatur, vis illi, utcumque ordinatus est, eadem est et voluntas pro eisdem partibus standi : ita finitio summi boni alias diffundi potest et exporrigi, alias colligi et in
2 se cogi. Idem itaque erit, si dixero : " Summum bonum est animus fortuita despiciens, virtute laetus " aut " Invicta vis animi, perita rerum, placida in actu cum humanitate multa et conversantium cura." Licet et ita finire, ut beatum dicamus hominem eum, cui nullum bonum malumque sit nisi bonus malusque animus, honesti cultorem, virtute contentum, quem nec extollant fortuita nec frangant, qui nullum maius bonum eo quod sibi ipse dare potest noverit, cui vera
3 voluptas erit voluptatum contemptio. Licet, si evagari velis, idem in aliam atque aliam faciem salva et integra potestate transferre ; quid enim prohibet nos beatam vitam dicere liberum animum et erectum et interritum ac stabilem, extra metum, extra cupiditatem positum, cui unum bonum sit honestas, unum malum turpitudo, cetera vilis turba rerum nec de-

It is possible also to define this good of ours in other terms—that is, the same idea may be expressed in different language. Just as an army remains the same, though at one time it deploys with a longer line, now is massed into a narrow space and either stands with hollowed centre and wings curved forward, or extends a straightened front, and, no matter what its formation may be, will keep the selfsame spirit and the same resolve to stand in defence of the selfsame cause,—so the definition of the highest good may at one time be given in prolix and lengthy form, and at another be restrained and concise. So it will come to the same thing if I say : " The highest good is a mind that scorns the happenings of chance, and rejoices only in virtue," or say : " It is the power of the mind to be unconquerable, wise from experience, calm in action, showing the while much courtesy and consideration in intercourse with others." It may also be defined in the statement that the happy man is he who recognizes no good and evil other than a good and an evil mind—one who cherishes honour, is content with virtue, who is neither puffed up, nor crushed, by the happenings of chance, who knows of no greater good than that which he alone is able to bestow upon himself, for whom true pleasure will be the scorn of pleasures. It is possible, too, if one chooses to be discursive, to transfer the same idea to various other forms of expression without injuring or weakening its meaning. For what prevents us from saying that the happy life is to have a mind that is free, lofty, fearless and steadfast—a mind that is placed beyond the reach of fear, beyond the reach of desire, that counts virtue the only good, baseness the only evil, and all else but a worthless mass of things, which come

trahens quicquam beatae vitae nec adiciens, sine auctu ac detrimento summi boni veniens ac recedens ?

4 Hunc ita fundatum necesse est, velit nolit, sequatur hilaritas continua et laetitia alta atque ex alto veniens, ut qui suis gaudeat nec maiora domesticis cupiat. Quidni ista bene penset cum minutis et frivolis et non perseverantibus corpusculi motibus ? Quo die infra voluptatem fuerit, et infra dolorem erit ; vides autem, quam malam et noxiosam servitutem serviturus sit quem voluptates doloresque, incertissima dominia

5 impotentissimaque, alternis possidebunt. Ergo exeundum ad libertatem est. Hanc non alia res tribuit quam fortunae neglegentia. Tum illud orietur inaestimabile bonum, quies mentis in tuto conlocatae et sublimitas expulsisque erroribus ex cognitione veri gaudium grande et immotum comitasque et diffusio animi, quibus delectabitur non ut bonis sed ut ex bono suo ortis.

1 5. Quoniam liberaliter agere coepi, potest beatus dici qui nec cupit nec timet beneficio rationis, quoniam et saxa timore et tristitia carent nec minus pecudes ; non ideo tamen quisquam felicia dixerit, quibus non

2 est felicitatis intellectus. Eodem loco pone homines, quos in numerum pecorum et inanimalium[1] redegit

---

[1] inanimalium *Hermes after Reitzenstein*: animalium *A*.

and go without increasing or diminishing the highest
good, and neither subtract any part from the happy
life nor add any part to it ?

A man thus grounded must, whether he wills or
not, necessarily be attended by constant cheerfulness
and a joy that is deep and issues from deep within,
since he finds delight in his own resources, and desires
no joys greater than his inner joys.   Should not such
joys as these be rightly matched against the paltry
and trivial and fleeting sensations of the wretched
body ?   The day a man becomes superior to pleasure,
he will also be superior to pain ; but you see in what
wretched and baneful bondage he must linger whom
pleasures and pains, those most capricious and tyran-
nical of masters, shall in turn enslave.   Therefore
we must make our escape to freedom.   But the
only means of procuring this is through indifference
to Fortune.   Then will be born the one inestimable
blessing, the peace and exaltation of a mind now
safely anchored, and, when all error is banished, the
great and stable joy that comes from the discovery
of truth, along with kindliness and cheerfulness of
mind ; and the source of a man's pleasure in all of
these will not be that they are good, but that they
spring from a good that is his own.

Seeing that I am employing some freedom in treat-
ing my subject, I may say that the happy man is one
who is freed from both fear and desire because of the
gift of reason; since even rocks are free from fear and
sorrow, and no less are the beasts of the field, yet for all
that no one could say that these things are " blissful,"
when they have no comprehension of bliss.   Put in
the same class those people whose dullness of nature
and ignorance of themselves have reduced them to

hebes natura et ignoratio sui. Nihil interest inter hos et illa, quoniam illis nulla ratio est, his prava et malo suo atque in perversum sollers ; beatus enim
3 dici nemo potest extra veritatem proiectus. Beata ergo vita est in recto certoque iudicio stabilita et immutabilis. Tunc enim pura mens est et soluta omnibus malis, quae non tantum lacerationes sed etiam vellicationes effugerit, statura semper ubi constitit ac sedem suam etiam irata et infestante fortuna
4 vindicatura. Nam quod ad voluptatem pertinet, licet circumfundatur undique et per omnis vias influat animumque blandimentis suis leniat aliaque ex aliis admoveat, quibus totos partesque nostri sollicitet, quis mortalium, cui ullum superest hominis vestigium, per diem noctemque titillari velit et deserto animo corpori operam dare ?

1 6. " Sed animus quoque," inquit, " voluptates habebit suas." Habeat sane sedeatque luxuriae et voluptatium arbiter ; impleat se eis omnibus, quae oblectare sensus solent, deinde praeterita respiciat et exoletarum voluptatium memor exsultet prioribus futurisque iam immineat ac spes suas ordinet et, dum corpus in praesenti sagina iacet, cogitationes ad futuram praemittat : hoc mihi videbitur miserior, quoniam mala pro bonis legere dementia est. Nec

---

ᵃ Literally, " pluckings."

the level of beasts of the field and of inanimate things. There is no difference between the one and the other, since in one case they are things without reason, and in the other their reason is warped, and works their own hurt, being active in the wrong direction ; for no man can be said to be happy if he has been thrust outside the pale of truth. Therefore the life that is happy has been founded on correct and trustworthy judgement, and is unalterable. Then, truly, is the mind unclouded and freed from every ill, since it knows how to escape not only deep wounds, but even scratches,[a] and, resolved to hold to the end whatever stand it has taken, it will defend its position even against the assaults of an angry Fortune. For so far as sensual pleasure is concerned, though it flows about us on every side, steals in through every opening, softens the mind with its blandishments, and employs one resource after another in order to seduce us in whole or in part, yet who of mortals, if he has left in him one trace of a human being, would choose to have his senses tickled night and day, and, forsaking the mind, devote his attention wholly to the body ?

" But the mind also," it will be said, " has its own pleasures." Let it have them, in sooth, and let it pose as a judge of luxury and pleasures ; let it gorge itself with all the things that are wont to delight the senses, then let it look back upon the past, and, re-calling faded pleasures, let it intoxicate itself with former experiences and be eager now for those to come, and let it lay its plans, and, while the body lies helpless from present cramming, let it direct its thoughts to that to come—yet from all this, it seems to me, the mind will be more wretched than ever, since it is madness to choose evils instead of goods. But

sine sanitate quisquam beatus est nec sanus, cui
2 obfutura pro optimis adpetuntur. Beatus ergo est
iudicii rectus ; beatus est praesentibus, qualiacumque
sunt, contentus amicusque rebus suis ; beatus est is,
cui omnem habitum rerum suarum ratio commendat.
1 7. Vident et in iliis qui summum bonum dixerunt,
quam turpi illud loco posuerint. Itaque negant posse
voluptatem a virtute diduci et aiunt nec honeste
quemquam vivere, ut non iucunde vivat, nec iucunde,
ut non honeste quoque. Non video quomodo ista
tam diversa in eandem copulam coiciantur. Quid
est, oro vos, cur separari voluptas a virtute non possit ?
Videlicet, quia omne bonis ex virtute principium est,
ex huius radicibus etiam ea, quae vos et amatis et
expetitis, oriuntur ? Sed si ista indiscreta essent,
non videremus quaedam iucunda sed non honesta-
quaedam vero honestissima sed aspera, per dolores
2 exigenda. Adice nunc, quod voluptas etiam ad vitam
turpissimam venit, at virtus malam vitam non admittit, et infelices quidam non sine voluptate, immo
ob ipsam voluptatem sunt, quod non eveniret, si
virtuti se voluptas immiscuisset, qua virtus saepe
3 caret, numquam indiget. Quid dissimilia, immo
diversa componitis ? Altum quiddam est virtus, ex-
celsum et regale, invictum, infatigabile ; voluptas

---

[a] Epicurus, Κύριαι Δόξαι, 140, v. (Bailey): οὐκ ἔστιν ἡδέως
ζῆν ἄνευ τοῦ φρονίμως καὶ καλῶς καὶ δικαίως ⟨οὐδὲ φρονίμως καὶ
καλῶς καὶ δικαίως⟩ ἄνευ τοῦ ἡδέως.

no man can be happy unless he is sane, and no man can be sane who searches for what will injure him in place of what is best. The happy man, therefore, is one who has right judgement; the happy man is content with his present lot, no matter what it is, and is reconciled to his circumstances; the happy man is he who allows reason to fix the value of every condition of existence.

Even those who declare that the highest good is in the belly see in what a dishonourable position they have placed it. And so they say that it is not possible to separate pleasure from virtue, and they aver that no one can live virtuously without also living pleasantly, nor pleasantly without also living virtuously.[a] But I do not see how things so different can be cast in the same mould. What reason is there, I beg of you, why pleasure cannot be separated from virtue? Do you mean, since all goods have their origin in virtue, even the things that you love and desire must spring from its roots? But if the two were inseparable, we should not see certain things pleasant, but not honourable, and certain things truly most honourable, but painful and capable of being accomplished only through suffering. Then, too, we see that pleasure enters into even the basest life, but, on the other hand, virtue does not permit life to be evil, and there are people who are unhappy not without pleasure—nay, are so on account of pleasure itself—and this could not happen if pleasure were indissolubly joined to virtue; virtue often lacks pleasure, and never needs it. Why do you couple things that are unlike, nay, even opposites? Virtue is something lofty, exalted and regal, unconquerable, and unwearied; pleasure is something lowly, servile,

humile, servile, imbecillum, caducum, cuius statio ac domicilium fornices et popinae sunt. Virtutem in templo convenies, in foro, in curia, pro muris stantem, pulverulentam, coloratam, callosas habentem manus ; voluptatem latitantem saepius ac tenebras captantem circa balinea ac sudatoria ac loca aedilem metuentia, mollem, enervem, mero atque unguento madentem, pallidam aut fucatam et medicamentis
4 pollinctam. Summum bonum immortale est, nescit exire nec satietatem habet nec paenitentiam ; numquam enim recta mens vertitur nec sibi odio est nec quicquam mutavit a vita[1] optima. At voluptas tunc, cum maxime delectat, extinguitur ; non multum loci habet, itaque cito implet et taedio est et post primum impetum marcet. Nec id umquam certum est, cuius in motu natura est. Ita ne potest quidem ulla eius esse substantia, quod venit transitque celerrime in ipso usu sui periturum ; eo enim pertendit, ubi desinat, et, dum incipit, spectat ad finem.
1 8. Quid, quod tam bonis quam malis voluptas inest nec minus turpes dedecus suum quam honestos egregia delectant ? Ideoque praeceperunt veteres optimam sequi vitam, non iucundissimam, ut rectae ac bonae voluntatis non dux sed comes sit voluptas. Natura enim duce utendum est ; hanc ratio observat,
2 hanc consulit. Idem est ergo beate vivere et secun-

---

[1] a vita *supplied by Hermes after Rossbach.*

---

[a] First follow Nature, and your judgement frame
By her just standard, which is still the same.
　　　　　　　　　　Pope, *Essay on Criticism,* 68 f.

weak, and perishable, whose haunt and abode are the brothel and the tavern.   Virtue you will find in the temple, in the forum, in the senate-house—you will find her standing in front of the city walls, dusty and stained, and with calloused hands ; pleasure you will more often find lurking out of sight, and in search of darkness, around the public baths and the sweating-rooms and the places that fear the police—soft, enervated, reeking with wine and perfume, and pallid, or else painted and made up with cosmetics like a corpse.   The highest good is immortal, it knows no ending, it permits neither surfeit nor regret ; for the right-thinking mind never alters, it neither is filled with self-loathing nor suffers any change in its life, that is ever the best.   But pleasure is extinguished just when it is most enjoyed ; it has but small space, and thus quickly fills it—it grows weary and is soon spent after its first assault.   Nor is anything certain whose nature consists in movement. So it is not even possible that there should be any substance in that which comes and goes most swiftly and will perish in the very exercise of its power ; for it struggles to reach a point at which it may cease, and it looks to the end while it is beginning.

What, further, is to be said of the fact that pleasure belongs alike to the good and the evil, and that the base delight no less in their disgrace than do the honourable in fair repute ? And therefore the ancients have enjoined us to follow, not the most pleasant, but the best life, in order that pleasure should be, not the leader, but the companion of a right and proper desire.   For we must use Nature as our guide ; she it is that Reason heeds, it is of her that it takes counsel.[a] Therefore to live happily is the same thing as to live

dum naturam. Hoc quid sit, iam aperiam. Si corporis dotes et apta naturae conservarimus diligenter et impavide tamquam in diem data et fugacia, si non subierimus eorum servitutem nec nos aliena possederint, si corpori grata et adventicia eo nobis loco fuerint, quo sunt in castris auxilia et armaturae leves— serviant ista, non imperent—, ita demum utilia sunt 3 menti. Incorruptus vir sit externis et insuperabilis miratorque tantum sui, fidens animo atque in utrumque paratus, artifex vitae ; fiducia eius non sine scientia sit, scientia non sine constantia ; maneant illi semel placita nec ulla in decretis eius litura sit. Intellegitur, etiam si non adiecero, compositum ordinatumque fore talem virum et in iis quae aget 4 cum comitate magnificum. Externa ratio quaerat sensibus irritata et capiens inde principia—nec enim habet aliud, unde conetur aut unde ad verum impetum capiat—, at[1] in se revertatur. Nam mundus quoque cuncta complectens rectorque universi deus in exteriora quidem tendit, sed tamen introrsum undique in se redit. Idem nostra mens faciat ; cum secuta sensus suos per illos se ad externa porrexerit, 5 et illorum et sui potens sit. Hoc modo una efficietur

---

[1] at *supplied by Gertz.*

---

[a] In Stoic teaching the universe (*mundus*) was identified with deity—the active element of the universe, described by various names, which pervaded the vast mass of passive matter. According to the monistic theory of the older Stoics this was creative Fire. Acting upon itself, by a process of mutation it produced the other forms of matter, which in turn by the reverse process were resolved into primal Fire. The reference here is to some such integrity of the ruling principle.

according to Nature. What this is, I shall proceed
to make clear. If we shall guard the endowments
of the body and the needs of Nature with care and
fearlessness, in the thought that they have been given
but for a day and are fleeting, if we shall not be their
slaves, nor allow these alien things to become our
masters, if we shall count that the gratifications of
the body, unessential as they are, have a place like
to that of the auxiliaries and light-armed troops in
camp—if we let them serve, not command—thus and
thus only will these things be profitable to the mind.
Let a man not be corrupted by external things, let
him be unconquerable and admire only himself,
courageous in spirit and ready for any fate, let him
be the moulder of his own life ; let not his confidence
be without knowledge, nor his knowledge without
firmness ; let his decisions once made abide, and
let not his decrees be altered by any erasure. It
will be understood, even without my adding it,
that such a man will be poised and well ordered,
and will show majesty mingled with courtesy in
all his actions. Let reason search into external
things at the instigation of the senses, and, while
it derives from them its first knowledge—for it
has no other base from which it may operate, or
begin its assault upon truth—yet let it fall back
upon itself. For God also, the all-embracing
world and the ruler of the universe, reaches forth
into outward things, yet, withdrawing from all
sides, returns into himself.[a] And our mind should
do the same ; when, having followed the senses
that serve it, it has through them reached to things
without, let it be the master both of them and of itself. In this way will be born an energy that is united,

vis ac potestas concors sibi et ratio illa certa nascetur
non dissidens nec haesitans in opinionibus compren-
sionibusque nec in persuasione, quae cum se disposuit
et partibus suis consensit et, ut ita dicam, concinuit,
summum bonum tetigit. Nihil enim pravi, nihil
lubrici superest, nihil in quo arietet aut labet.
6 Omnia faciet ex imperio suo nihilque inopinatum accidet, sed quicquid agetur in bonum exibit facile et
parate et sine tergiversatione agentis ; nam pigritia
et haesitatio pugnam et inconstantiam ostendit.
Quare audaciter licet profitearis summum bonum
esse animi concordiam ; virtutes enim ibi esse de-
bebunt, ubi consensus atque unitas erit. Dissident
vitia.

1   9. " Sed tu quoque," inquit, " virtutem non ob
aliud colis, quam quia aliquam ex illa speras voluptatem." Primum non, si voluptatem praestatura
virtus est, ideo propter hanc petitur ; non enim hanc
praestat, sed et hanc, nec huic laborat, sed labor eius,
2 quamvis aliud petat, hoc quoque adsequetur. Sicut
in arvo, quod segeti proscissum est, aliqui flores inter-
nascuntur, non tamen huic herbulae, quamvis delectet
oculos, tantum operis insumptum est—aliud fuit
serenti propositum, hoc supervenit—, sic voluptas non
est merces nec causa virtutis sed accessio, nec quia

a power that is at harmony with itself, and that dependable reason which is not divided against itself, nor uncertain either in its opinions, or its perceptions, or in its convictions ; and this reason, when it has regulated itself, and established harmony between all its parts, and, so to speak, is in tune, has attained the highest good. For no crookedness, no slipperiness is left to it, nothing that will cause it to stumble or fall. It will do everything under its own authority and nothing unexpected will befall it, but whatever it does will turn out a good, and that, too, easily and readily and without subterfuge on the part of the doer ; for reluctance and hesitation are an indication of conflict and instability. Wherefore you may boldly declare that the highest good is harmony of the soul ; for where concord and unity are, there must the virtues be. Discord accompanies the vices.

" But even you," it is retorted, " cultivate virtue for no other reason than because you hope for some pleasure from it." But, in the first place, even though virtue is sure to bestow pleasure, it is not for this reason that virtue is sought ; for it is not this, but something more than this that she bestows, nor does she labour for this, but her labour, while directed toward something else, achieves this also. As in a ploughed field, which has been broken up for corn, some flowers will spring up here and there, yet it was not for these poor little plants, although they may please the eye, that so much toil was expended—the sower had a different purpose, these were superadded—just so pleasure is neither the cause nor the reward of virtue, but its by-product, and we do not accept virtue because she delights us, but

121

3 delectat placet, sed, si placet, et delectat. Summum
bonum in ipso iudicio est et habitu optimae mentis,
quae cum cursum[1] suum implevit et finibus se suis
cinxit, consummatum est summum bonum nec quicquam amplius desiderat ; nihil enim extra totum est,
4 non magis quam ultra finem. Itaque erras, cum interrogas, quid sit illud, propter quod virtutem petam ;
quaeris enim aliquid supra summum. Interrogas,
quid petam ex virtute ? Ipsam. Nihil enim habet
melius, ipsa pretium sui. An hoc parum magnum
est ? Cum tibi dicam : " Summum bonum est in-
fragilis animi rigor et providentia et sublimitas
et sanitas et libertas et concordia et decor," aliquid
etiamnunc exigis maius, ad quod ista referantur ?
Quid mihi voluptatem nominas ? Hominis bonum
quaero, non ventris, qui pecudibus ac beluis laxior
est !

1   10. " Dissimulas," inquit, " quid a me dicatur ;
ego enim nego quemquam posse iucunde vivere, nisi
simul et honeste vivit, quod non potest mutis contingere animalibus nec bonum suum cibo metientibus.
Clare, inquam, ac palam testor hanc vitam, quam ego
iucundam voco, non nisi adiecta virtute contingere."
2 Atqui quis ignorat plenissimos esse voluptatibus
vestris stultissimos quosque et nequitiam abundare
iucundis animumque ipsum genera voluptatis prava

---

[1] cursum *supplied by Hermes after Schultess.*

if we accept her, she also delights us. The highest good lies in the very choice of it, and the very attitude of a mind made perfect, and when the mind has completed its course and fortified itself within its own bounds, the highest good has now been perfected, and nothing further is desired; for there can no more be anything outside of the whole than there can be some point beyond the end. Therefore you blunder when you ask what it is that makes me seek virtue; you are looking for something beyond the supreme. Do you ask what it is that I seek in virtue? Only herself. For she offers nothing better—she herself is her own reward. Or does this seem to you too small a thing? When I say to you, " The highest good is the inflexibility of an unyielding mind, its foresight, its sublimity, its soundness, its freedom, its harmony, its beauty," do you require of me something still greater to which these blessings may be ascribed? Why do you mention to me pleasure? It is the good of man that I am searching for, not that of his belly—the belly of cattle and wild beasts is more roomy!

"You are misrepresenting what I say," you retort; " for I admit that no man can live pleasantly without at the same time living virtuously as well, and this is patently impossible for dumb beasts and for those who measure their good by mere food. Distinctly, I say, and openly I testify that the life that I denominate pleasant is impossible without the addition of virtue." Yet who does not know that those who are most apt to be filled with your sort of pleasure are all the greatest fools, and that wickedness abounds in enjoyments, and that the mind itself supplies many kinds of pleasure that are

sibi[1] multa suggerere ?—in primis insolentiam et nimiam aestimationem sui tumoremque elatum super ceteros et amorem rerum suarum caecum et improvidum, delicias fluentis et ex minimis ac puerilibus causis exsultationem, iam dicacitatem ac superbiam contumeliis gaudentem, desidiam dissolutionemque 3 segnis animi, indormientis sibi. Haec omnia virtus discutit et aurem pervellit et voluptates aestimat, antequam admittat, nec quas probavit, magni pendit aut utique etiam admittit, nec usu earum sed temperantia laeta est. Temperantia autem cum voluptates[2] minuat, summi boni iniuria est. Tu voluptatem complecteris, ego compesco ; tu voluptate frueris, ego utor ; tu illam summum bonum putas, ego nec bonum ; tu omnia voluptatis causa facis, ego nihil.

1 11. Cum dico me nihil voluptatis causa, de illo loquor sapiente, cui soli concedis[3] voluptatem. Non voco autem sapientem, supra quem quicquam est, nedum voluptas. Atqui ab hac occupatus quomodo resistet labori et periculo, egestati et tot humanam vitam circumstrepentibus minis ? Quomodo conspectum mortis, quomodo dolores feret, quomodo mundi fragores et tantum acerrimorum hostium, a tam molli[4] adversario victus ? "Quicquid voluptas suaserit faciet." Age, non vides quam multa suasura 2 sit ? "Nihil," inquit, "poterit turpiter suadere,

---

[1] sibi *Haase*: sed *A*.
[2] voluptates *omitted by Hermes after Reitzenstein.*
[3] concedis *A* : concedimus *Hermes after Joh. Müller.*
[4] a tam molli *Muretus*: an molli *A*.

---

[a] The gesture was an appeal to memory, since, as Pliny (*Nat. Hist.* xi. 251) explains, "est in aure ima memoriae locus." So Virgil (*Copa*, 38):

Mors aurem vellens "vivite," ait, "venio."

vicious ? Foremost are haughtiness, a too high opinion of one's self and a puffed-up superiority to others, a blind and unthinking devotion to one's own interests, dissolute luxury, extravagant joy springing from very small and childish causes, and, besides a biting tongue and the arrogance that takes pleasure in insults, sloth, and the degeneracy of a sluggish mind that falls asleep over itself. All these things Virtue tosses aside, and she plucks the ear,[a] and appraises pleasures before she permits them, and those that she approves she sets no great store by, or even just permits them, and it is not her use of them, but her temperance that gives her joy. Since, however, temperance reduces our pleasures, injury results to your highest good. You embrace pleasure, I enchain her ; you enjoy pleasure, I use it ; you think it the highest good, I do not think it even a good ; you do everything for the sake of pleasure, I, nothing.

When I say that " I " do nothing for the sake of pleasure, I am speaking of the ideal wise man, to whom alone you are willing to concede pleasure. But I do not call him a wise man who is dominated by anything, still less by pleasure. And yet if he is engrossed by this, how will he withstand toil and danger and want and all the threatening ills that clamour about the life of man ? How will he endure the sight of death, how grief, how the crashes of the universe and all the fierce foes that face him, if he has been subdued by so soft an adversary ? You say : " He will do whatever pleasure advises." But come, do you not see how many things it will be able to advise ? " It will not be able to advise anything

quia adiuncta virtuti est." Non vides iterum, quale
sit summum bonum, cui custode opus est, ut bonum
sit ? Virtus autem quomodo voluptatem reget,
quam sequitur, cum sequi parentis sit, regere im-
perantis ? A tergo ponis quod imperat ? Egregium
autem habet virtus apud vos officium voluptates
3 praegustare ! Sed videbimus, an apud quos tam
contumeliose tractata virtus est, adhuc virtus sit,
quae habere nomen suum non potest, si loco cessit.
Interim, de quo agitur, multos ostendam voluptatibus obsessos, in quos fortuna omnia munera sua
4 effudit, quos fatearis necesse est malos. Aspice
Nomentanum et Apicium, terrarum ac maris, ut isti
vocant, bona concoquentis et super mensam recog-
noscentis omnium gentium animalia ; vide hos eosdem
in suggestu rosae despectantis popinam suam, aures
vocum sono, spectaculis oculos, saporibus palatum
suum delectantes ; mollibus lenibusque fomentis
totum lacessitur eorum corpus et, ne nares interim
cessent, odoribus variis inficitur locus ipse, in quo
luxuriae parentatur. Hos esse in voluptatibus dices ;
nec tamen illis bene erit, quia non bono gaudent.
1   12. " Male," inquit, " illis erit, quia multa inter-
veniunt, quae perturbent animum, et opiniones inter

[a] A reference to the office of a slave (*praegustator*) who
tasted his master's food before serving it. So Virtue serves
the voluptuary in providing him safe pleasure. In the same
vein, Cicero (*De Fin.* ii. 21. 69) pictures pleasure as a queen
served by the virtues as handmaids : " nos quidem virtutes
sic natae sumus ut tibi serviremus ; aliud negoti nihil habemus."

[b] A notorious epicure in the time of Tiberius, best known
from Seneca, *Dial.* xii. 10. 8-11. Nomentanus, often the
type of spendthrift in the *Satires* of Horace (*e.g.*, i. 1. 102 ;
ii. 1. 22), appears here as a *homo gulosus*.

base," you say, " because it is linked with virtue."
But once more, do you not see what sort of thing
that highest good must be if it needs a guardian in
order to become a good ? And how shall Virtue
guide Pleasure if she follows her, since it is the part
of one who obeys to follow, of one who commands
to guide ? Do you station in the rear the one that
commands ? Truly a fine office that you assign to
Virtue—to be the foretaster [a] of your pleasures !
We shall see later whether to those who have treated
virtue so contemptuously she still remains virtue ;
for she cannot keep her name if she yields her place.
Meanwhile—for this is the point here—I shall show
that there are many who are besieged by pleasures,
upon whom Fortune has showered all her gifts, and
yet, as you must needs admit, are wicked men.
Look at Nomentanus and Apicius,[b] digesting, as they
say, the blessings of land and sea, and reviewing the
creations of every nation arrayed upon their board !
See them, too, upon a heap of roses, gloating over their
rich cookery, while their ears are delighted by the
sound of music, their eyes by spectacles, their palates
by savours ; soft and soothing stuffs caress with
their warmth the length of their bodies, and, that
the nostrils may not meanwhile be idle, the room
itself, where sacrifice is being made to Luxury, reeks
with varied perfumes. You will recognize that these
are living in the midst of pleasures, and yet it will
not be well with them, because what they delight
in is not a good.

" It will be ill with them," you say, " because
many things will intrude that perturb [c] the soul,

[c] *i.e.*, they will not be true Epicureans, since they lack
ἀταραξία.

se contrariae mentem inquietabunt." Quod ita esse concedo ; sed nihilo minus illi ipsi stulti et inaequales et sub ictu paenitentiae positi magnas percipient voluptates, ut fatendum sit tam longe tum illos ab omni molestia abesse quam a bona mente et, quod plerisque contingit, hilarem insaniam insanire ac per
2 risum furere. At contra sapientium remissae voluptates et modestae ac paene languidae sunt compressaeque et vix notabiles, ut quae neque accersitae veniant nec, quamvis per se accesserint, in honore sint neque ullo gaudio percipientium exceptae ; miscent enim illas et interponunt vitae ut ludum iocumque inter seria.

3 Desinant ergo inconvenientia iungere et virtuti voluptatem implicare, per quod vitium pessimis quibusque adulantur. Ille effusus in voluptates, ructabundus semper atque ebrius, quia scit se cum voluptate vivere, credit et cum virtute ; audit enim voluptatem separari a virtute non posse, deinde vitiis suis sapientiam inscribit et abscondenda profitetur.
4 Itaque non ab Epicuro impulsi luxuriantur, sed vitiis dediti luxuriam suam in philosophiae sinu abscondunt et eo concurrunt, ubi audiant laudari voluptatem. Nec aestimant, voluptas illa Epicuri—ita enim me

---

[a] " Epicurus himself says in his letters that he was content with nothing but water and a bit of bread. ' Send me,' he says, ' some preserved cheese, that when I like I may have a feast ' " (Bailey, *Vita Epicuri*, 11).

and opinions, conflicting with one another, will disquiet the mind." That this is so I grant; but none the less these very men, foolish as they are and inconsistent and subject to the pangs of remorse, will have experience of very great pleasures, so that you must admit that, while in that state they lack all pain, they no less lack a sound mind, and, as is the case with very many others, that they make merry in madness and laugh while they rave. But, on the other hand, the pleasures of the wise man are calm, moderate, almost listless and subdued, and scarcely noticeable inasmuch as they come unsummoned, and, although they approach of their own accord, are not held in high esteem and are received without joy on the part of those who experience them; for they only let them mingle now and then with life as we do amusements and jests with serious affairs.

Let them cease, therefore, to join irreconcilable things and to link pleasure with virtue—a vicious procedure which flatters the worst class of men. The man who has plunged into pleasures, in the midst of his constant belching and drunkenness, because he knows that he is living with pleasure, believes that he is living with virtue as well; for he hears first that pleasure cannot be separated from virtue, then dubs his vices wisdom, and parades what ought to be concealed. And so it is not Epicurus who has driven them to debauchery, but they, having surrendered themselves to vice, hide their debauchery in the lap of philosophy and flock to the place where they may hear the praise of pleasure, and they do not consider how sober and abstemious[a] the " pleasure " of Epicurus really is—for so, in

hercules sentio—quam sobria ac sicca sit, sed ad
nomen ipsum advolant quaerentes libidinibus suis
5 patrocinium aliquod ac velamentum. Itaque quod
unum habebant in malis bonum perdunt, peccandi
verecundiam. Laudant enim ea, quibus erubesce-
bant, et vitio gloriantur ; ideoque ne resurgere
quidem adulescentiae[1] licet, cum honestus turpi
desidiae titulus accessit. Hoc est cur ista voluptatis
laudatio perniciosa sit, quia honesta praecepta intra
latent, quod corrumpit apparet.

1   13. In ea quidem ipse sententia sum—invitis hoc
nostris popularibus dicam—sancta Epicurum et recta
praecipere et, si propius accesseris, tristia ; voluptas
enim illa ad parvum et exile revocatur et, quam nos
virtuti legem dicimus, eam ille dicit voluptati : iubet
illam parere naturae. Parum est autem luxuriae
2 quod naturae satis est. Quid ergo est ? Ille, quisquis desidiosum otium et gulae ac libidinis vices
felicitatem vocat, bonum malae rei quaerit auctorem
et, cum illo venit blando nomine inductus, sequitur
voluptatem non quam audit, sed quam attulit, et vitia
sua cum coepit putare similia praeceptis, indulget
illis non timide, nec obscure luxuriatur sed iam inde
aperto capite. Itaque non dicam, quod plerique
nostrorum, sectam Epicuri flagitiorum magistram
esse, sed illud dico : male audit, infamis est, et im-

---

[1] adulescentiae *A* : erubescentiae *Madvig* : displicentiae
Gertz.

---

[a] *i.e.*, their youthful point of view.
[b] *i.e.*, has become an Epicurean.
[e] Literally, " with uncovered head."

all truth, I think it—but they fly to a mere name
seeking some justification and screen for their lusts.
And thus they lose the sole good that remained to
them in their wickedness—shame for wrongdoing.
For they now praise the things that used to make
them blush, and they glory in vice; and therefore
they cannot even recover their youth,[a] when once an
honourable name has given warrant to their shameful laxity. The reason why your praise of pleasure
is pernicious is that what is honourable in your teaching lies hid within, what corrupts is plainly visible.

Personally I hold the opinion—I shall express it
though the members of our school may protest—
that the teachings of Epicurus are upright and holy
and, if you consider them closely, austere; for his
famous doctrine of pleasure is reduced to small and
narrow proportions, and the rule that we Stoics
lay down for virtue, this same rule he lays down for
pleasure—he bids that it obey Nature. But it takes
a very little luxury to satisfy Nature! What then is
the case? Whoever applies the term " happiness "
to slothful idleness and the alternate indulgence in
gluttony and lust, looks for a good sponsor for his
evil course, and when, led on by an attractive name,
he has found this one,[b] the pleasure he pursues is
not the form that he is taught, but the form that
he has brought, and when he begins to think that
his vices accord with the teacher's maxims, he
indulges in them no longer timidly, and riots in
them, not now covertly, but from this time on in broad
daylight.[c] And so I shall not say, as do most of our
sect, that the school of Epicurus is an academy of
vice, but this is what I say—it has a bad name,
is of ill repute, and yet undeservedly. How can

3 merito. Hoc scire qui potest nisi interius admissus ? Frons eius ipsa dat locum fabulae et ad malam spem irritat. Hoc tale est, quale vir fortis stolam indutus ; constat tibi pudicitia, virilitas salva est, nulli corpus tuum turpi patientiae vacat, sed in manu tympanum est ! Titulus itaque honestus eligatur et inscriptio ipsa excitans animum ; quae stat, ad eam[1] venerunt vitia.

4 Quisquis ad virtutem accessit, dedit generosae indolis specimen ; qui voluptatem sequitur, videtur enervis, fractus, degenerans viro, perventurus in turpia, nisi aliquis distinxerit illi voluptates, ut sciat, quae ex eis intra naturale desiderium desistant, quae praeceps ferantur infinitaeque sint et, quo magis 5 implentur, eo magis inexplebiles. Agedum, virtus antecedat, tutum erit omne vestigium. Et voluptas nocet nimia ; in virtute non est verendum, ne quid nimium sit, quia in ipsa est modus. Non est bonum, quod magnitudine laborat sua. Rationalem porro sortitis naturam quae melius res quam ratio proponitur ? Et si placet ista iunctura, si hoc placet ad beatam vitam ire comitatu, virtus antecedat, comitetur voluptas et circa corpus ut umbra versetur. Virtutem quidem, excelsissimam dominam, voluptati tradere ancillam nihil magnum animo capientis est.

[1] stat ad eam *Bourgery*: statim *A* : *Hermes after Reitzenstein supplies* quae stat, corpori adulatur invitavitque, *before* quae statim.

---

[a] Here the symbol of something enervated and effeminate. The tambourine was associated with the orgiastic worship of Cybele. Her priests were emasculated.
[b] *i.e.*, a life combining virtue and pleasure.

anyone know this who has not been admitted to the inner shrine? Its mere outside gives ground for scandal and incites to evil hopes. The case is like that of a strong man dressed up in a woman's garb; you maintain your chastity, your virility is unimpaired, your body is free from base submission—but in your hand is a tambourine *a*! Therefore you should choose some honourable superscription and a motto that in itself appeals to the mind; the one that stands has attracted only the vices.

Whosoever has gone over to the side of virtue, has given proof of a noble nature; he who follows pleasure is seen to be weakly, broken, losing his manhood, and on the sure path to baseness unless someone shall establish for him some distinction between pleasures, so that he may know which of them lie within the bounds of natural desire, which sweep headlong onward and are unbounded and are the more insatiable the more they are satisfied. Come then! let virtue lead the way, and every step will be safe. Then, too, it is the excess of pleasure that harms; but in the case of virtue there need be no fear of any excess, for in virtue itself resides moderation. That cannot be a good that suffers from its own magnitude. Besides, to creatures endowed with a rational nature what better guide can be offered than reason? Even if that combination *b* pleases you, if you are pleased to proceed toward the happy life in such company, let virtue lead the way, let pleasure attend her — let it hover about the body like its shadow. To hand over virtue, the loftiest of mistresses, to be the handmaid of pleasure is the part of a man who has nothing great in his soul.

1   14. Prima virtus eat, haec ferat signa. Habebimus
nihilo minus voluptatem, sed domini eius et tempera-
tores erimus ;   aliquid nos exorabit, nihil coget.
At ei, qui voluptati tradidere principia, utroque
caruere ;   virtutem enim amittunt, ceterum non
ipsi voluptatem, sed ipsos voluptas habet, cuius aut
inopia torquentur aut copia strangulantur, miseri,
si deseruntur ab illa, miseriores, si obruuntur ; sicut
deprensi mari Syrtico modo in sicco relinquuntur,
2 modo torrente unda fluctuantur. Evenit autem
hoc nimia intemperantia et amore caeco rei ; nam
mala pro bonis petenti periculosum est adsequi.   Ut
feras cum labore periculoque venamur et captarum
quoque illarum sollicita possessio est—saepe enim
laniant dominos—, ita habent se magnae voluptates ;
in magnum malum evasere captaeque cepere.   Quae
quo plures maioresque sunt, eo ille minor ac plurium
3 servus est, quem felicem vulgus appellat.   Permanere libet in hac etiamnunc huius rei imagine.
Quemadmodum qui bestiarum cubilia indagat et

Laqueo captare feras

magno aestimat et

Latos canibus circumdare saltus,

ut illarum vestigia premat, potiora deserit multisque

    ᵃ Sandbanks off the northern coast of Africa, proverbially
perilous to the sailor.   *Cf.* Horace, *Odes*, ii. 6. 3 *sq.* :
                Barbaras Syrtes, ubi Maura semper
                aestuat unda.
So on St. Paul's stormy voyage to Italy, " fearing lest they
should be cast upon the Syrtis, they lowered the gear, and
so were driven " (Acts, xxvii. 17).
    ᵇ Virgil, *Georg.* i. 139 *sq.*, though Seneca has cited *laqueo*
for *laqueis* and *latos* for *magnos*.

Let virtue go first, let her bear the standard. We shall none the less have pleasure, but we shall be the master and control her; at times we shall yield to her entreaty, never to her constraint. But those who surrender the leadership to pleasure, lack both; for they lose virtue, and yet do not possess pleasure, but are possessed by it, and they are either tortured by the lack of it or strangled by its excess—wretched if it deserts them, more wretched if it overwhelms them—they are like sailors who have been caught in the waters around the Syrtes,[a] and now are left on the dry shore, and again are tossed by the seething waves. But this results from a complete lack of self-control and blind love for an object; for, if one seeks evils instead of goods, success becomes dangerous. As the hunt for wild beasts is fraught with hardship and danger, and even those that are captured are an anxious possession—for many a time they rend their masters—so it is as regards great pleasures; for they turn out to be a great misfortune, and captured pleasures become now the captors. And the more and the greater the pleasures are, the more inferior will that man be whom the crowd calls happy, and the more masters will he have to serve. I wish to dwell still further upon this comparison. Just as the man who tracks wild animals to their lairs, and counts it a great delight

> With noose the savage beasts to snare,[b]

and

> Around the spreading woods to fling a line of hounds,

in order that he may follow upon their tracks, leaves things that are more worth while and forsakes

135

officiis renuntiat, ita qui sectatur voluptatem omnia postponit et primam libertatem neglegit ac pro ventre dependit, nec voluptates sibi emit, sed se voluptatibus vendit.

1 15. " Quid tamen," inquit, " prohibet in unum virtutem voluptatemque confundi et ita effici summum bonum, ut idem et honestum et iucundum sit ? " Quia pars honesti non potest esse nisi honestum, nec summum bonum habebit sinceritatem suam, si aliquid 2 in se viderit dissimile meliori. Ne gaudium quidem quod ex virtute oritur, quamvis bonum sit, absoluti tamen boni pars est, non magis quam laetitia et tranquillitas, quamvis ex pulcherrimis causis nascantur ; sunt enim ista bona, sed consequentia 3 summum bonum, non consummantia. Qui vero virtutis voluptatisque societatem facit et ne ex aequo quidem, fragilitate alterius boni quicquid in altero vigoris est hebetat libertatemque illam, ita demum, si nihil se pretiosius novit, invictam, sub iugum mittit. Nam, quae maxima servitus est, incipit illi opus esse fortuna ; sequitur vita anxia, suspiciosa, trepida, 4 casum pavens, temporum suspensa momentis. Non das virtuti fundamentum grave, immobile, sed iubes illam in loco volubili stare ; quid autem tam volubile est, quam fortuitorum expectatio et corporis rerumque corpus adficientium varietas ? Quomodo hic potest deo parere et quicquid evenit bono animo excipere

---

ᵃ *i.e.,* which belongs to virtue : virtue frees, pleasure enslaves.

many duties, so he who pursues pleasures makes everything else secondary, and first of all gives up liberty, and he pays this price at the command of his belly; nor does he buy pleasures for himself, but he sells himself to pleasures.

"Nevertheless," someone asks, "what is there to prevent the blending of virtue and pleasure into one, and constituting the highest good in such a way that the honourable and the agreeable may be the same thing?" The answer is that the honourable can have no part that is not honourable, nor will the highest good preserve its integrity if it sees in itself something that is different from its better part. Even the joy that springs from virtue, although it is a good, is not nevertheless a part of the absolute good, any more than are cheerfulness and tranquillity, although they spring from the noblest origins; for goods they are, yet they only attend on the highest good but do not consummate it. But whoever forms an alliance between virtue and pleasure—and that too, not an equal one—by the frailty of one good dulls whatever power the other may have, and sends beneath the yoke that liberty *a* which remains unconquered only so long as it finds nothing more precious than itself. For it begins to need the help of Fortune, and this is the depth of servitude; there follows a life of anxiety, suspicion, and alarm, a dread of mishap and worry over the changes time brings. You do not give to virtue a foundation solid and immovable, but bid her stand on unstable ground; yet what is so unstable as trust in the hazards of chance and the vicissitudes of the body and the things that affect the body? How is such a man able to obey God and to receive in cheerful spirit whatever happens, and, interpreting

137

nec de fato queri casuum suorum benignus interpres,
si ad voluptatum dolorumque punctiunculas con-
cutitur ? Sed ne patriae quidem bonus tutor aut vin-
dex est nec amicorum propugnator, si ad voluptates
5 vergit. Illo ergo summum bonum escendat, unde
nulla vi detrahitur, quo neque dolori neque spei nec
timori sit aditus[1] nec ulli rei, quae deterius summi
boni ius faciat ; escendere autem illo sola virtus
potest. Illius gradu clivus iste frangendus est ; illa
fortiter stabit et quicquid evenerit feret non patiens
tantum sed etiam volens, omnemque temporum
difficultatem sciet legem esse naturae et ut bonus
miles feret volnera, numerabit cicatrices, et transver-
beratus telis moriens amabit eum, pro quo cadet,
imperatorem ; habebit illud in animo vetus praecep-
6 tum : deum sequere ! Quisquis autem queritur et
plorat et gemit, imperata facere vi cogitur et invitus
rapitur ad iussa nihilo minus. Quae autem dementia
est potius trahi quam sequi ! Tam me hercules quam
stultitia et ignoratio condicionis est suae dolere, quod
dest[2] aliquid tibi aut incidit durius, aeque mirari aut
indigne ferre ea, quae tam bonis accidunt quam
malis,—morbos dico, funera, debilitates et cetera
ex transverso in vitam humanam incurrentia. Quicquid ex universi constitutione patiendum est, magno

---

[1] timori sit aditus A^5 : timoris ita ditus A^1 : timori est
Gertz : timorist *Hermes* : timori sit *Bourgery*.

[2] quod dest (deest) *Hermes after Madvig* : quod est A.

---

[a] *Cf.* the picture of the sage in Horace (*Odes*, iv. 9. 51 *sq*.):

> Non ille pro caris amicis
> aut patria timidus perire.

In Cicero (*De Fin*. i. 20) the Epicurean eloquently defends
the school against the criticism that the doctrine of pleasure
was incompatible with the maintenance of true friendship.

[b] *Cf.* Cicero, *De Finibus*, iii. 22: " quaeque sunt vetera

his mishaps indulgently, never to complain of Fate, if he is agitated by the petty prickings of pleasure and pain ? But he is not even a good guardian or avenger of his country, nor a defender of his friends[a] if he has a leaning toward pleasures. Therefore let the highest good mount to a place from which no force can drag it down, where neither pain nor hope nor fear finds access, nor does any other thing that can lower the authority of the highest good ; but Virtue alone is able to mount to that height. We must follow her footsteps to find that ascent easy ; bravely will she stand, and she will endure whatever happens, not only patiently, but even gladly ; she will know that every hardship that time brings comes by a law of Nature, and like a good soldier she will submit to wounds, she will count her scars, and, pierced by darts, as she dies she will love him for whose sake she falls—her commander ; she will keep in mind that old injunction, "Follow God[b]!" But whoever complains and weeps and moans, is compelled by force to obey commands, and, even though he is unwilling, is rushed none the less to the bidden tasks. But what madness to prefer to be dragged rather than to follow ! As much so, in all faith, as it is great folly and ignorance of one's lot to grieve because of some lack or some rather bitter happening, and in like manner to be surprised or indignant at those ills that befall the good no less than the bad—I mean sickness and death and infirmities and all the other unexpected ills that invade human life. All that the very constitution of the universe obliges us to suffer,

praecepta sapientium, qui iubent 'tempori parere' et 'sequi deum' et 'se noscere' et 'nihil nimis,' haec sine physicis quam vim habeant (et habent maximam) videre nemo potest."

7 suscipiatur animo. Ad hoc sacramentum adacti sumus, ferre mortalia nec perturbari iis, quae vitare non est nostrae potestatis. In regno nati sumus; deo parere libertas est.[a]

1 16. Ergo in virtute posita est vera felicitas. Quid haec tibi virtus suadebit? Ne quid aut bonum aut malum existimes, quod nec virtute nec malitia continget; deinde, ut sis immobilis et contra malum 2 et[1] ex bono, ut, qua fas est, deum effingas. Quid tibi pro hac expeditione promittit? Ingentia et aequa divinis. Nihil cogeris, nullo indigebis, liber eris, tutus, indemnis; nihil frustra temptabis, nihil prohibeberis; omnia tibi ex sententia cedent, nihil adversum accidet, nihil contra opinionem ac volunta- 3 tem. "Quid ergo? Virtus ad beate vivendum sufficit?" Perfecta illa et divina quidni sufficiat, immo superfluat? Quid enim deesse potest extra desiderium omnium posito? Quid extrinsecus opus est ei, qui omnia sua in se collegit? Sed ei, qui ad virtutem tendit, etiam si multum processit, opus est aliqua fortunae indulgentia adhuc inter humana luctanti, dum nodum illum exsolvit et omne vinculum mortale. Quid ergo interest? Quod arte alligati sunt alii, adstricti alii, districti[b] quoque. Hic, qui ad superiora progressus est et se altius extulit,

---

[1] et *supplied by Madvig.*

---

[a] *Cf.* "Whose service is perfect freedom," in a *Collect for Peace* of the English Liturgy.

[b] The Latin word-play shows a different metaphor. *Districti* is "outstretched," "spread-eagled," as if upon a cross.

must be borne with high courage. This is the sacred obligation by which we are bound—to submit to the human lot, and not to be disquieted by those things which we have no power to avoid. We have been born under a monarchy; to obey God is freedom.[a]

Therefore true happiness is founded upon virtue. And what is the counsel this virtue will give to you? That you should not consider anything either a good or an evil that will not be the result of either virtue or vice; then, that you should stand unmoved both in the face of evil and by the enjoyment of good, to the end that—as far as is allowed—you may body forth God. And what does virtue promise you for this enterprise? Mighty privileges and equal to the divine. You shall be bound by no constraint, nothing shall you lack, you shall be free, safe, unhurt; nothing shall you essay in vain, from nothing be debarred; all things shall happen according to your desire, nothing adverse shall befall you, nothing contrary to your expectations and wish. "What! does virtue alone suffice for living happily?" Perfect and divine as it is, why should it not suffice—nay, suffice to overflowing? For if a man has been placed beyond the reach of any desire, what can he possibly lack? If a man has gathered into himself all that is his, what need does he have of any outside thing? But the man who is still on the road to virtue, who, even though he has proceeded far, is still struggling in the toils of human affairs, does have need of some indulgence from Fortune until he has loosed that knot and every mortal bond. Where then lies the difference? In that some are closely bound, others fettered—even hand and foot.[b] He who has advanced toward the higher realm and has

laxam catenam trahit nondum liber, iam tamen pro libero.

1 17. Si quis itaque ex istis, qui philosophiam conlatrant, quod solent dixerit : " Quare ergo tu fortius loqueris quam vivis ? Quare et superiori verba summittis et pecuniam necessarium tibi instrumentum existimas et damno moveris et lacrimas audita coniugis aut amici morte demittis et respicis famam 2 et malignis sermonibus tangeris ? Quare cultius rus tibi est quam naturalis usus desiderat ? Cur non ad praescriptum tuum cenas ? Cur tibi nitidior supellex est ? Cur apud te vinum aetate tua vetustius bibitur ? Cur aviarium[1] disponitur ? Cur arbores nihil praeter umbram daturae conseruntur ? Quare uxor tua locupletis domus censum auribus gerit ? Quare paedagogium pretiosa veste succingitur ? Quare ars est apud te ministrare nec temere et ut libet conlocatur argentum sed perite servitur[2] et est aliquis scindendi obsonii magister ? " Adice, si vis : " Cur trans mare possides ? Cur plura quam nosti ? Turpiter[3] aut tam neglegens es, ut non noveris pauculos servos, aut tam luxuriosus, ut plures habeas quam quorum notitiae memoria sufficiat ! " 3 Adiuvabo postmodo convicia et plura mihi quam putas obiciam, nunc hoc respondeo tibi : " Non sum sapiens et, ut malivolentiam tuam pascam, nec ero. Exige itaque a me, non ut optimis par sim,

---

[1] aviarium *Bourgery after Wesenberg* : auruum *A*.
[2] ser uitur *A* : struitur *Hermes after Lipsius*.
[3] *Hermes adds* cur *before* turpiter.

---

a *i.e.,* the ideal wise man of the Stoics.

lifted himself to higher levels drags a loosened chain;
he is not yet free, but still is as good as free.

If, therefore, any of those who bark against philosophy, should ask the usual thing : " Why then do
you talk so much more bravely than you live ? Why
do you speak humbly in the presence of a superior
and deem money a necessary equipment, and why
are you moved by a loss, and why do you shed tears
on hearing of the death of your wife or a friend, and
why do you have regard for your reputation and let
slander affect you ? Why do you till broader acres
than your natural need requires ? Why do your
dinners not conform to your own teaching ? Why
do you have such elegant furniture ? Why is the
wine that is drunk at your table older than you
are yourself ? Why this show of an aviary ? Why
do you plant trees that will supply nothing but shade ?
Why does your wife wear in her ears the revenue of
a rich house ? Why are your young slaves dressed
in costly stuffs ? Why is it an art to attend at your
table and instead of the plate being set out carelessly
and as you please why is there expertness of service,
and why to carve your meat is there a professional ? "
Add, too, if you like : " Why do you have domains
across the sea ? Why more than you have seen ? And
shame to you !—you are either so careless that you
do not know your handful of slaves by sight, or so
pampered that you have more than your memory
can recall to your knowledge ! " Later I shall outdo
your reproaches and bestow on myself more blame
than you think of ; for the moment I shall make this
reply : " I am not a ' wise man,' [a] nor—to feed your
malevolence !—shall I ever be. And so require not
from me that I should be equal to the best, but that I

143

sed ut malis melior. Hoc mihi satis est, cotidie
aliquid ex vitiis meis demere et errores meos ob-
4 iurgare. Non perveni ad sanitatem, ne perveniam
quidem ; delenimenta magis quam remedia podagrae
meae compono, contentus, si rarius accedit et si
minus verminatur ; vestris quidem pedibus com-
paratus, debilis[1] cursor sum." Haec non pro me
loquor—ego enim in alto vitiorum omnium sum—,
sed pro illo, cui aliquid acti est.
1 18. " Aliter," inquis, " loqueris, aliter vivis."
Hoc, malignissima capita et optimo cuique inimicissima, Platoni obiectum est, obiectum Epicuro,
obiectum Zenoni ; omnes enim isti dicebant non
quemadmodum ipsi viverent, sed quemadmodum
esset ipsis vivendum. De virtute, non de me loquor,
et cum vitiis convicium facio, in primis meis facio.
2 Cum potuero, vivam quomodo oportet. Nec mali-
gnitas me ista multo veneno tincta deterrebit ab
optimis ; ne virus quidem istud, quo alios spargitis,
quo vos necatis, me impediet, quo minus perseverem
laudare vitam, non quam ago, sed quam agendam
scio, quo minus virtutem adorem et ex intervallo
3 ingenti reptabundus sequar. Expectabo scilicet,
ut quicquam malivolentiae inviolatum sit, cui sacer
nec Rutilius fuit nec Cato ? Curet aliquis, an istis
nimis dives videatur, quibus Demetrius Cynicus
parum pauper est ? Virum acerrimum et contra
omnia naturae desideria pugnantem, hoc pauperiorem
quam ceteros Cynicos quod, cum sibi interdixerint

---

[1] debilis *A* : debiles (*voc. plu.*) *Gronovius and Bentley,*
Hermes.

---

[a] Seneca's stock types of virtue. *Cf.* Index.
[b] *Cf.* Index.

should be better than the wicked. It is enough for me
if every day I reduce the number of my vices, and
blame my mistakes. I have not attained to perfect
health, nor indeed shall I attain it ; my gout I con-
trive to alleviate rather than to cure, content if it
comes more rarely and gives less pain ; but when I
compare your feet, crippled though I am, I am a
racer ! " What I say is not spoken on my own
behalf—for I am sunk deep in vice of every kind—
but on behalf of the man who has actually achieved
something.

" You talk one way, you live another," you say.
The same reproach, O ye creatures most spiteful,
most hostile to all the best of men, has been made
against Plato, against Epicurus, against Zeno ; for
all these told, not how they themselves were living,
but how they ought to live. It is of virtue, not of
myself, that I am speaking, and my quarrel is against
all vices, more especially against my own. When I
shall be able, I shall live as I ought. And your spitefulness, deep-dyed with venom, shall not deter me
from what is best, nor shall even this poison with
which you besprinkle others, with which, too, you are
killing yourselves, hinder me from continuing to vaunt
the life, not that I lead, but that I know ought to be
led—from worshipping virtue and from following her,
albeit a long way behind and with very halting pace.
Am I, in sooth, to expect that spite will spare anything when it held neither Rutilius nor Cato [a] sacred ?
Should anyone be concerned whether he seems too
rich in the eyes of those to whom Demetrius the Cynic [b]
seems not poor enough ? This boldest of heroes, fighting against all the desires of nature, and poorer than
the rest of the Cynics in that, while they banned

habere, interdixit et poscere, negant satis egere!
Vides enim : non virtutis scientiam sed egestatis
professus est.

1   19. Diodorum, Epicureum philosophum, qui intra
paucos dies finem vitae suae manu sua imposuit,
negant ex decreto Epicuri fecisse, quod sibi gulam
praesecuit. Alii dementiam videri volunt factum
hoc eius, alii temeritatem ; ille interim beatus ac
plenus bona conscientia reddidit sibi testimonium
vita excedens laudavitque aetatis in portu et ad
ancoram actae quietem et dixit, quod vos inviti
audistis, quasi vobis quoque faciendum sit :

Vixi et quem dederat cursum fortuna peregi.

2 De alterius vita, de alterius morte disputatis et ad
nomen magnorum ob aliquam eximiam laudem
virorum, sicut ad occursum ignotorum hominum
minuti canes, latratis ; expedit enim vobis neminem
videri bonum, quasi aliena virtus exprobratio/ de-
lictorum vestrum[1] omnium sit. Invidi splendida
cum sordibus vestris confertis nec intellegitis, quanto
id vestro detrimento audeatis. Nam si illi, qui
virtutem sequuntur, avari libidinosi ambitiosique
sunt, quid vos estis, quibus ipsum nomen virtutis odio
3 est? Negatis quemquam praestare, quae loquitur,
nec ad exemplar orationis suae vivere. Quid
mirum, cum loquantur fortia, ingentia, omnis humanas

---

[1] vestrum *supplied by Bourgery.*

---

[a] Elsewhere unknown.
[b] Virgil, *Aeneid*, iv. 653.
[c] Diodorus set over against Demetrius

possessions, he banned even the desire of them—this
man they say has not enough poverty ! But you see
—he has not professed a knowledge of virtue but of
poverty.

And they say that Diodorus,[a] the Epicurean philosopher, who within the last few days put an end to
his life with his own hand, was not following the
teaching of Epicurus when he slashed his own throat.
Some would see in his suicide an act of madness,
others of recklessness ; he, meanwhile, happy and
filled with a good conscience bore testimony to himself as he was departing from life ; he praised the
tranquillity of the years he had passed safe at anchor
in a haven, and uttered the words which you never
have liked to hear, as though you also must do the
same thing :

> I've lived; my destined course I now have run.[b]

You argue about the life of the one, about the death
of the other,[c] and when you hear the name of men
who have become great on account of some distinguished merit, you bark, just as small dogs do
when they meet with strangers ; for you find it to
your interest that no man should appear to be good,
as though virtue in another cast reproach upon the
shortcomings of all of you. You jealously compare
their glorious appearance with your squalor, and fail
to understand with what great disadvantage to yourself you dare to do so. For if those who pursue virtue
are avaricious, lustful, and ambitious, what are you
yourselves, to whom the very name of virtue is hateful ? You say that no one of them practises what
he preaches, or models his life upon his own words.
But what wonder, since their words are heroic,

tempestates evadentia ? Cum refigere se crucibus conentur, in quas unusquisque vestrum clavos suos ipse adigit, ad supplicium tamen acti stipitibus singulis pendent ; hi, qui in se ipsi animum advertunt, quot cupiditatibus tot crucibus distrahuntur. At maledici et in[1] alienam contumeliam venusti sunt. Crederem illis hoc vacare, nisi quidam ex patibulo suo spectatores conspuerent !

1   20. " Non· praestant philosophi quae loquuntur." Multum tamen praestant quod loquuntur, quod honesta mente concipiunt ; namque idem si et paria dictis agerent, quid esset illis beatius ? Interim non est quod contemnas bona verba et bonis cogitationibus plena praecordia. Studiorum salutarium etiam 2 citra effectum laudanda tractatio est. Quid mirum, si non escendunt in altum ardua adgressi ? Sed si vir es, suspice, etiam si decidunt, magna conantis. Generosa res est respicientem non ad suas sed ad naturae suae vires conari, alta temptare et mente maiora concipere, quam quae etiam ingenti animo 3 adornatis effici possunt. Qui sibi hoc proposuit : " Ego mortem eodem voltu comoediamque videbo. Ego laboribus, quanticumque illi erunt, parebo animo

---

[1] maledici et in *Hermes after Koch*: male dici ||| in *A*: ii maledici et in *Bourgery*.

[a] *i.e.*, their sins.
[b] *i.e.*, the worldling *desires* to sin.
[c] The *stipes* was the upright part of the cross or gibbet, the *patibulum* the transverse beam.
[d] *i.e.*, while suffering for their own sins.

mighty, and survive all the storms of human life? Though they strive to release themselves from their crosses—those crosses [a] to which each one of *you* nails himself with his own hand [b]—yet they, when brought to punishment, hang each upon a single gibbet [c]; but these others who bring upon themselves their own punishment are stretched upon as many crosses as they had desires. Yet they are slanderous and witty in heaping insult on others. I might believe that they were free to do so, did not some of them spit upon spectators from their own cross [d]!

" Philosophers do not practise what they preach," you say. Yet they do practise much that they preach, much that their virtuous minds conceive. For indeed if their actions always matched their words, who would be more happy than they? Meanwhile you have no reason to despise noble words and hearts that are filled with noble thoughts. The pursuit of salutary studies is praiseworthy, even if they have no practical result. What wonder that those who essay the steep path do not mount to the summit? But if you are a man, look up to those who are attempting great things, even though they fall. The man that measures his effort, not by his own strength, but by the strength of his nature, that aims at high things, and conceives in his heart greater undertakings than could possibly be accomplished even by those endowed with gigantic courage, shows the mark of nobility. The man who has set before himself such ideals as these : " As for me, I shall look upon death or a comedy with the same expression of countenance. As for me, I shall submit to all hardships, no matter how great they be, staying my body

fulciens corpus. Ego divitias et praesentis et absentis aeque contemnam, nec si aliubi iacebunt, tristior, nec si circa me fulgebunt, animosior. Ego fortunam nec venientem sentiam nec recedentem. Ego terras omnis tamquam meas videbo, meas tamquam omnium. Ego sic vivam quasi sciam aliis esse me natum et naturae rerum hoc nomine gratias agam ; quo enim melius genere negotium meum 4 agere potuit ? Unum me donavit omnibus, uni mihi omnis. Quicquid habebo, nec sordide custodiam nec prodige spargam. Nihil magis possidere me credam quam bene donata. Non numero nec pondere beneficia nec ulla nisi accipientis aestimatione perpendam ; numquam id mihi multum erit, quod dignus accipiet. Nihil opinionis causa, omnia conscientiae faciam. Populo spectante fieri credam 5 quicquid me conscio faciam. Edendi mihi erit bibendique finis desideria naturae restinguere, non implere alvum et exinanire. Ero amicis iucundus, inimicis mitis et facilis. Exorabor, antequam roger, et honestis precibus occurram. Patriam meam esse mundum sciam et praesides deos, hos supra me circaque me stare factorum dictorumque censores. Quandoque aut natura spiritum repetet aut ratio dimittet, testatus exibo bonam me conscientiam

---

[a] Suicide was recognized by the Stoics as a desirable and heroic release from unbearable misfortune.

by the spirit. As for me, I shall despise riches alike when I have them and when I have them not, being neither cast down if they shall lie elsewhere, nor puffed up if they shall glitter around me. As for me, I shall pay no heed to Fortune, either when she comes or when she goes. As for me, I shall view all lands as my own, my own as belonging to all others. As for me, I shall always live as if I were aware that I had been born for service to others, and on this account I shall render my thanks to Nature; for how could she better have served my interest? She has given me, the individual, to all men and all men to me, the individual. Whatever I may possess, I shall neither hoard as a miser, nor as a spendthrift squander. Nothing shall seem to me so truly my possessions as the gifts I have wisely bestowed. I shall not estimate my benefactions by their number, nor by their size, nor by anything except my estimation of the recipient; never shall what a worthy man receives seem great in my eyes. Nothing shall I ever do for the sake of opinion, everything for the sake of my conscience. Whatever I shall do when I alone am witness I shall count as done beneath the gaze of the Roman people. In eating and drinking my aim shall be to quench the desires of Nature, not to fill and empty my belly. I shall be agreeable to my friends, to my enemies mild and indulgent. I shall give pardon before it is asked, and hasten to grant all honourable requests. I shall know that the whole world is my country, that its rulers are the gods, and that they abide above me and around me, the censors of my words and deeds. And whenever Nature demands back my breath, or my reason releases *a* it, I shall depart, bearing witness that I have loved a good

amasse, bona studia, nullius per me libertatem de-
minutam, minime meam "—qui haec facere proponet,
volet, temptabit, ad deos iter faciet, ne ille, etiam
si non tenuerit,

> Magnis tamen excidit ausis.

6 Vos quidem, quod virtutem cultoremque eius odistis,
nihil novi facitis. Nam et solem lumina aegra
formidant et aversantur diem splendidum nocturna
animalia, quae ad primum eius ortum stupent et
latibula sua passim petunt, abduntur in aliquas rimas
timida lucis. Gemite et infelicem linguam bonorum
exercete convicio, hiate, commordete ; citius multo
frangetis dentes quam imprimetis.

1 21. " Quare ille philosophiae studiosus est et tam
dives vitam agit ? Quare opes contemnendas dicit
et habet ? Vitam contemnendam putat et tamen
vivit ? Valetudinem contemnendam et tamen illam
diligentissime tuetur atque optimam mavult ? Et
exilium vanum nomen putat et ait : ' Quid enim
est mali mutare regiones ? ' et tamen, si licet, senescit
in patria ? Et inter longius tempus et brevius nihil
interesse iudicat, tamen, si nihil prohibet, extendit
aetatem et in multa senectute placidus viret ? "
2 Ait ista debere contemni, non, ne habeat, sed ne
sollicitus habeat ; non abigit illa a se, sed abeuntia

---

conscience and all good endeavour, that I have been guilty of nothing that impaired the liberty of any man, least of all my own "—the man who shall resolve, shall wish, and shall essay to do these things will be following the path toward the gods—ah! such a man, even if he shall not reach them,

> Yet fails in a high emprise.[a]

But as for you, your hatred of virtue and of those who practise it is in no way strange. For sickly lights quail before the sun, and creatures of the night abhor the shining day—they stand aghast at the first signs of dawn, and seek everywhere their lairs, and, finding some hole, hide themselves away from fear of the light. Croak, and ply your wretched tongues in abuse of the good, show your fangs, bite hard; you will break your teeth long before they leave a mark!

"Why," you ask, "does that man espouse philosophy and yet live in such opulence? Why does he say that riches ought to be despised and yet have them? Why does he think that life ought to be despised and yet live? That health ought to be despised and yet guard it most carefully, and prefer it to be excellent? And why does he think that exile is an empty name and say : ' What evil is there in a change of country,' and yet, if he is allowed, grow old in his native land? Why does he decide that there is no difference between a long and short existence, yet, if nothing prevents him, prolong his life and peacefully flourish in a green old age?" He says these things ought to be despised, not to keep him from having them, but to keep him from being worried about having them; he does not drive them away, but if they leave him, he escorts them to the door without

securus prosequitur. Divitias quidem ubi tutius
fortuna deponet quam ibi, unde sine querella red-
dentis receptura est ?

3   M. Cato cum laudaret Curium et Coruncanium et
illud saeculum, in quo censorium crimen erat paucae
argenti lamellae, possidebat ipse quadragies sestertium, minus sine dubio quam Crassus, plus quam
Censorius Cato. Maiore spatio, si comparentur,
proavum vicerat, quam a Crasso vinceretur, et, si
4 maiores illi obvenissent opes, non sprevisset. Nec
enim se sapiens indignum ullis muneribus fortuitis
putat. Non amat divitias, sed mavult ; non in
animum illas, sed in domum recipit, nec respuit
possessas, sed continet et maiorem virtuti suae
materiam subministrari vult.

22. Quid autem dubii est, quin haec maior materia
sapienti viro sit animum explicandi suum in divitiis
quam in paupertate, quom[1] in hac unum genus virtutis sit non inclinari nec deprimi, in divitiis et temperantia et liberalitas et diligentia et dispositio
et magnificentia campum habeat patentem ? Non
contemnet se sapiens, etiam si fuerit minimae
staturae, esse tamen se procerum volet. Et exilis
corpore aut amisso[2] oculo valebit, malet tamen sibi
esse corporis robur, et hoc ita, ut sciat esse aliud in

---

[1] quom *Gertz*: quam *A*.
[2] aut amisso *Bourgery after Goelzer* : acamisso *A*.

---

[a] *i.e.*, the Younger, supporter of the senate against Caesar.
His great-grandfather, Cato the Censor (234-149 B.C.), was
noted for his austerity. *Cf.* Index.

[b] Seneca himself was the possessor of lordly wealth (Tac.
Ann. xv. 64. 6; Juv. x. 16; Cassius Dio, lxi. 10. 2), and
here gives spirited answer to his own critics.

[c] The author contrasts physical and mental well-being;

the least concern. Where, indeed, will Fortune deposit riches more securely than with one who will return them without protest when she recalls them ?

Marcus Cato,[a] when he was vaunting Curius and Coruncanius and that age in which it was a censorial offence to have a few small silver coins, himself possessed four million sesterces, fewer without doubt than Crassus, but more than Cato the Censor. If comparison be made, the distance by which he had outstripped his great-grandfather was greater than that by which Crassus outstripped him, and, if greater wealth had fallen to his lot, he would not have scorned it. For indeed the wise man does not deem himself undeserving of any of the gifts of Fortune. He does not love riches, but he would rather have them ; he does not admit them to his heart, but to his house, and he does not reject the riches he has, but he keeps them and wishes them to supply ampler material for exercising his virtue.

Who, however, can doubt that the wise man[b] finds in riches, rather than in poverty, this ampler material for displaying his powers, since in poverty there is room for only one kind of virtue—not to be bowed down and crushed by it—while in riches moderation and liberality and diligence and orderliness and grandeur all have a wide field ? The wise man will not despise himself even if he has the stature of a dwarf, but nevertheless he will wish to be tall. And if he is feeble in body, or deprived of one eye, he will still be strong,[c] but nevertheless he will prefer to have strength of body, and this too, though he knows that there is something else in him that is stronger

the latter may exist without the former, but it is desirable to have both.

se valentius. Malam valetudinem tolerabit, bonam
3 optabit. Quaedam enim, etiam si in summam rei
parva sunt et subduci sine ruina principalis boni
possunt, adiciunt tamen aliquid ad perpetuam
laetitiam ex virtute nascentem. Sic illum adficiunt
divitiae et exhilarant, ut navigantem secundus et
ferens ventus, ut dies bonus et in bruma ac frigore
4 apricus locus. Quis porro sapientium—nostrorum
dico, quibus unum est bonum virtus—negat etiam
haec, quae indifferentia vocamus, habere aliquid
in se pretii et alia esse potiora? Quibusdam ex iis
tribuitur aliquid honoris, quibusdam multum. Ne
5 erres itaque, inter potiora divitiae sunt. "Quid
ergo," inquis, "me derides, cum eundem apud te
locum habeant, quem apud me?" Vis scire, quam
non eundem habeant locum? Mihi divitiae si
effluxerint, nihil auferent nisi semet ipsas, tu stupebis
et videberis tibi sine te relictus, si illae a te recesserint;
apud me divitiae aliquem locum habent, apud te
summum; ad postremum divitiae meae sunt, tu
divitiarum es.

1 23. Desine ergo philosophis pecunia interdicere;
nemo sapientiam paupertate damnavit. Habebit
philosophus amplas opes, sed nulli detractas nec
alieno sanguine cruentas, sine cuiusquam iniuria
partas, sine sordidis quaestibus, quarum tam honestus

---

a Indifferentia, representing the Stoic ἀδιάφορα, is a
technical term characterizing the things that lie outside of
the categories of *virtus* and *dedecus*, the sole good and the
sole evil.

than body. If his health is bad he will endure it, but he will wish for good health. For certain things, even if they are trifles in comparison with the whole, and can be withdrawn without destroying the essential good, nevertheless contribute something to the perpetual joy that springs from virtue. As a favourable wind, sweeping him on, gladdens the sailor, as a bright day and a sunny spot in the midst of winter and cold give cheer, just so riches have their influence upon the wise man and bring him joy. And besides, who among wise men—I mean those of our school, who count virtue the sole good—denies that even those things which we call " indifferent " [a] do have some inherent value, and that some are more desirable than others? To some of them we accord little honour, to others much. Do not, therefore, make a mistake—riches are among the more desirable things. " Why then," you say, " do you make game of me, since they occupy the same place in your eyes that they do in mine?" Do you want to know what a different place they occupy? In my case, if riches slip away, they will take from me nothing but themselves, while if they leave you, you will be dumbfounded, and you will feel that you have been robbed of your real self; in my eyes riches have a certain place, in yours they have the highest; in fine, I own my riches, yours own you.

Cease, therefore, forbidding to philosophers the possession of money; no one has condemned wisdom to poverty. The philosopher shall own ample wealth, but it will have been wrested from no man, nor will it be stained with another's blood—wealth acquired without harm to any man, without base dealing, and the outlay of it will be not less honourable than was

sit exitus quam introitus, quibus nemo ingemescat
nisi malignus. In quantum vis exaggera illas;
honestae sunt, in quibus cum multa sint, quae sua
quisque dici velit, nihil est, quod quisquam suum
2 possit dicere. Ille vero fortunae benignitatem a
se non summovebit et patrimonio per honesta quaesito
nec gloriabitur nec erubescet. Habebit tamen
etiam quo glorietur, si aperta domo et admissa in
res suas civitate poterit dicere : "Quod quisque
agnoverit, tollat." O magnum virum, O[1] optime
divitem, si post hanc vocem tantundem habuerit!
Ita dico : si tuto et securus scrutationem populo
praebuerit, si nihil quisquam apud illum invenerit,
quoi manus iniciat, audaciter et propalam erit dives.
3 Sapiens nullum denarium intra limen suum admittet
male intrantem ; idem magnas opes, munus fortunae
fructumque virtutis, non repudiabit nec excludet.
Quid enim est quare illis bono loco invideat ? Veniant, hospitentur. Nec iactabit illas nec abscondet
—alterum infruniti animi est, alterum timidi et pusilli,
velut magnum bonum intra sinum continentis—nec,
4 ut dixi, eiciet illas e domo. Quid enim dicet ?
Utrumne "Inutiles estis" an "Ego uti divitiis
nescio"? Quemadmodum etiam pedibus suis
poterit iter conficere, escendere tamen vehiculum
malet, sic pauper etsi[2] poterit esse, dives volet.

---

[1] O *supplied by Lipsius.*
[2] pauper etsi *Hermes after Schultess* : paup' si *A.*
158

its acquisition; it will make no man groan except the spiteful. Pile up that wealth of his as high as you like; it will be honourable, if, while it includes much that each man would like to call his own, it includes nothing that any man is able to call his own. But he, surely, will not thrust aside the generosity of Fortune, and an inheritance that has been honourably acquired will give him no cause either to blush or to boast. Yet he will even have reason to boast if, throwing open his mansion and admitting the whole city to view his possessions, he shall be able to say: "If any one recognizes anything as his own, let him take it." O! a great man, O! a man excellently rich, if after these words he shall possess just as much! I mean this: if without risk and concern he has allowed the people to make search, if no man shall have found in his possession a single thing to lay his hands upon, then he will be rich boldly and in all openness. Not one penny will a wise man admit within his threshold that makes a dishonest entry; yet he will not repulse or exclude great wealth that is the gift of Fortune and the fruit of virtue. For what reason has he to grudge it good quarters? Let it come, let it be welcomed. But he will not flaunt it, neither will he hide it—the one is the part of a silly mind, the other of a timid and petty mind, that makes him keep a great blessing as it were, in his pocket—nor, as I said before, will he expel it from the house. For what shall he say to it? Will it be—"You are of no use," or "I do not know how to use riches"? In the same way that, even if he is able to accomplish a journey on foot, he will prefer to mount into a carriage, so, even if he is able to be poor, he will prefer to

Habebit itaque opes, sed tamquam leves et avola-
turas, nec ulli alii eas nec sibi graves esse patietur.
5 Donabit—quid erexisti aures? quid expediti
sinum?—donabit aut bonis aut eis, quos facere
poterit bonos, donabit cum summo consilio dignis-
simos eligens, ut qui meminerit tam expensorum
quam acceptorum rationem esse reddendam, donabit
ex recta et probabili causa, nam inter turpes iacturas
malum munus est; habebit sinum facilem, non
perforatum, ex quo multa exeant, et nihil excidat.

1 24. Errat, si quis existimat facilem rem esse
donare; plurimum ista res habet difficultatis, si modo
consilio tribuitur, non casu et impetu spargitur.
Hunc promereor, illi reddo; huic succurro, huius
misereor; illum instruo dignum quem non deducat
paupertas nec occupatum teneat; quibusdam non
dabo, quamvis desit, quia, etiam si dedero, erit de-
futurum; quibusdam offeram, quibusdam etiam
inculcabo. Non possum in hac re esse neglegens;
numquam magis nomina facio quam cum dono.

2 " Quid? tu," inquis, " recepturus donas ? " Immo
non perditurus; eo loco sit donatio, unde repeti non
debeat, reddi possit. Beneficium conlocetur, quem-
160

be rich. And so he will possess wealth, but with the knowledge that it is fickle and likely to fly away, and he will not allow it to be a burden either to himself or to anyone else. He will give of it—why do you prick up your ears ? why do you get ready your pocket ?—he will give of it either to good men or to those whom he will be able to make good men ; choosing the most worthy after the utmost deliberation, he will give of his wealth, as one who rightly remembers that he must render account no less of his expenditures than of his receipts ; he will give of it only for a reason that is just and defensible, for wrong giving is no other than a shameful waste ; he will have his pocket accessible, but it will have no hole in it—a pocket from which much can appear and nothing can drop.

Whoever believes that giving is an easy matter, makes a mistake ; it is a matter of very great difficulty, provided that gifts are made with wisdom, and are not scattered at haphazard and by caprice. To this man I do a service, to that one make return ; this one I succour, this one I pity ; I supply this other one because he does not deserve to be dragged down by poverty and have it engross him ; to some I shall not give although they are in need, because, even if I should give, they would still be in need ; to some I shall proffer my help, upon certain ones even thrust it. In this matter I cannot afford to be careless ; never am I more careful to register names than when I am giving.

" What ! " you say, " do you give with the intention of taking back ? " No, with the intention of not wasting ; the status of giving should be that no return ought to be asked, yet that a return is possible.

admodum thensaurus alte obrutus, quem non eruas,
nisi fuerit necesse. Quid ? Domus ipsa divitis viri
3 quantam habet bene faciendi materiam ! Quis enim
liberalitatem tantum ad togatos vocat ? Hominibus
prodesse natura me iubet. Servi liberine sint hi,
ingenui an libertini, iustae libertatis an inter amicos
datae, quid refert ? Ubicumque homo est, ibi bene-
fici locus est. Potest itaque pecunia etiam intra
limen suum diffundi et liberalitatem exercere, quae
non quia liberis debetur, sed quia a libero animo
proficiscitur, ita nominata est. Haec apud sapientem
nec umquam in turpes indignosque impingitur nec
umquam ita defetigata errat, ut non, quotiens dignum
invenerit, quasi ex pleno fluat.

4   Non est ergo, quod perperam exaudiatis, quae
honeste, fortiter, animose a studiosis sapientiae dicuntur. Et hoc primum adtendite : aliud est studiosus sapientiae, aliud iam adeptus sapientiam. Ille
tibi dicet : " Optime loquor, sed adhuc inter mala
volutor plurima. Non est, quod me ad formulam
meam exigas. Cum maxime facio me et formo et
ad exemplar ingens attollo ; si processero quantumcumque proposui, exige ut dictis facta respondeant."
Adsecutus vero humani boni summam aliter tecum

---

[a] The badge of Roman citizenship. *Cf.* Virgil's proud
line (*Aeneid*, i. 282) :

Romanos rerum dominos gentemque togatam.

[b] Seneca's own generosity, to which Tacitus alludes
(*Annals*, xv. 62. 1) in the account of his death, seems from
Juvenal (v. 108 *sq.*) to have become proverbial :

Nemo petit, *modicis* quae mittebantur amicis
a Seneca.

A benefit should be stored away like a deep buried treasure, which you would not dig up except from necessity. Why, the very house of a rich man— what an opportunity it offers for conferring benefit! Whose voice invokes liberality only for the man that wears a toga *a*? Nature bids me do good to all mankind—whether slaves or freemen, freeborn or freed-men, whether the laws gave them freedom or a grant in the presence of friends—what difference does it make? Wherever there is a human being there is the opportunity for a kindness. And so it is possible to be lavish with money even inside the threshold and to find there a field for one's liberality, which is so called, not because it is owed to a free man, but because it is born from a free mind. This, in the case of a wise man, is never hurled at base and unworthy men, and never makes the mistake of being so exhausted that it cannot flow from a full hand, as it were, as often as it finds a worthy object.*b*

You have no excuse, therefore, for hearing wrongly the honourable, brave, and heroic utterances of those who pursue wisdom. And pay heed first to this—it is one thing to pursue wisdom, and another to have already attained wisdom. A man of the first type will say to you : " My words are most excellent, but I still wallow in evils, very many of them. You have no right to require me to live up to my own standard. Just now I am still fashioning and mould- ing myself and trying to lift myself to the height of a lofty ideal ; when I shall have accomplished all that I have set before me, then require me to make my actions accord with my words." But he who has already attained the height of human good will plead with you otherwise, and will say :

aget et dicet : " Primum non est, quod tibi permittas
de melioribus ferre sententiam ; mihi iam, quod
5 argumentum est recti, contigit malis displicere. Sed,
ut tibi rationem reddam, qua nulli mortalium invideo,
audi quid promittam et quanti quaeque aestimem.
Divitias nego bonum esse ; nam si essent, bonos
facerent. Nunc, quoniam quod apud malos depren-
ditur dici bonum non potest, hoc illis nomen nego.
Ceterum et habendas esse et utiles et magna com-
moda vitae adferentis fateor.

1   25. " Quid ergo sit, quare illas non in bonis numerem,
et quid praestem in illis aliud quam vos, quoniam
inter utrosque convenit habendas, audite. Pone in
opulentissima me domo, pone aurum argentumque
ubi¹ in promiscuo usu sit ; non suspiciam me ob ista,
quae etiam si apud me, extra me tamen sunt. In
sublicium pontem me transfer et inter egentes abice ;
non ideo tamen me despiciam, quod in illorum numero
consedero, qui manum ad stipem porrigunt. Quid
enim ad rem, an frustum panis desit, cui non deest
mori posse ? Quid ergo est ? Domum illam splen-
2 didam malo quam pontem. Pone in² instrumentis
splendentibus et delicato apparatu ; nihilo me
feliciorem credam, quod mihi molle erit amiculum,
quod purpura convivis meis substernetur. Muta

---

¹ ubi *supplied by Hermes.*   ² in *commonly supplied.*

ᵃ An ancient wooden bridge across the Tiber, swept away
by a flood a few years after Seneca's death (Tacitus, *Hist.*
i. 86). The Roman bridges were so favoured a haunt of
beggars that Juvenal (xiv. 134) uses the phrase *aliquis de
ponte* to designate a beggar.

" In the first place, you have no right to permit your-self to pass judgement on your betters. As for me, I have already had the good fortune to win the displeasure of the wicked, which is proof enough of my uprightness. But, that I may give you the explanation that I grudge to no mortal man, hear what I maintain and what value I set on each thing. I deny that riches are a good ; for if they were, they would make men good. As it is, since that which is found in the hands of the wicked cannot be called a good, I refuse to apply the term to riches. Nevertheless I admit that they are desirable, that they are useful, and that they add great comforts to living.

" Hear, then, since we both agree that they are desirable, what reason I have for not including them in the number of goods, and in what respect my attitude toward them differs from yours. Place me in a house that is most sumptuous, place me where I may have gold and silver plate for common use ; I shall not look up to myself on account of these things, which, even though they belong to me, are nevertheless no part of me. Take me to the Sublician Bridge [a] and cast me among the beggars ; nevertheless I shall not find reason to look down upon myself because I sit in the company of those who stretch out their hands for alms. For what difference does it make whether a man lacks a piece of bread when he does not lack the possibility of dying ? And what is the conclusion ? I prefer that gorgeous house to the Bridge ! Place me in the midst of sumptuous furnishings and the trappings of luxury ; I shall not think myself one whit happier because I have a soft mantle, because my guests recline on purple. Change my mattress ; I shall

165

stragula mea ; nihilo miserius ero, si lassa cervix mea
in maniculo faeni adquiescet, si super Circense tomentum per sarturas veteris lintei effluens incubabo.
Quid ergo est ?   Malo, quid mihi animi sit, ostendere
praetextatus et calceatus[1] quam nudis scapulis aut
3 sectis plantis.[2]   Omnes mihi ex voto dies cedant,
novae gratulationes prioribus subtexantur ; non ob
hoc mihi placebo.   Muta in contrarium hanc indulgentiam temporis, hinc illinc percutiatur animus
damno, luctu, incursionibus varis, nulla hora sine aliqua querella sit ; non ideo me dicam inter miserrima
miserum, non ideo aliquem execrabor diem ; provisum est enim a me, ne quis mihi ater dies esset.
Quid ergo est ?   Malo gaudia temperare, quam
dolores compescere."

4   Hoc tibi ille Socrates dicet : " Fac me victorem
universarum gentium, delicatus ille Liberi currus
triumphantem usque ad Thebas a solis ortu vehat,
iura reges nationum petant a me[3] ; hominem esse
maxime cogitabo, cum deus undique consalutabor.
Huic tam sublimi fastigio coniunge protinus praecipi-
tem mutationem ; in alienum imponar fericulum exor-

---

[1] calceatus *Schultess* : causatus *A*.
[2] sectis plantis (*cf. Virg.* Ecl. x. 49) *Schultess* : sententis *A*.
[3] nationum petant a me *Gertz* : penatium petant me *A*.

---

[a] The exact nature of the article designated by *Circense
tomentum* is not clear.   That, however, it was despised and
stuffed with reeds—the poor man's substitute for Leuconic
wool—is shown by Martial, xiv. 160 :

> Tomentum concisa palus Circense vocatur :
>   haec pro Leuconico stramina pauper emit.

[b] *i.e.*, the supreme philosopher.
[c] Bacchus, who travelled throughout the world introducing
the culture of the vine and the early arts of civilization, is

be not a whit more wretched if my wearied neck must rest on a handful of hay, if I shall sleep on a cushion [a] of the Circus with the stuffing spilling out through its patches of old cloth. And what is the conclusion ? I prefer to display the state of my soul clad rather in the toga and shoes than showing naked shoulders and with cuts on my feet. Let all my days pass according to my desire, let new felicitations be added to the old ; I shall not on this account be puffed up. Change this kindness of time to just the opposite ; from this quarter and that let my soul be smitten by loss, by grief, by various adversities, let no hour lack some cause for complaint ; I shall not for that reason call myself the most wretched of the wretched ; I shall not for that reason curse any one day ; for I have seen to it that for me no day shall be black. And what is the conclusion ? I prefer to temper my joys, rather than to stifle my sorrows."

This is what a Socrates [b] will say to you : " Make me victor over the nations of the world, let the voluptuous car of Bacchus convey me in triumph from the rising [c] of the sun all the way to Thebes, let the kings of the nations seek laws from me ; when from every side I shall be greeted as a god, I shall then most of all remember that I am a man. Then with such a lofty height connect straightway a headlong fall to altered fortune ; let me be placed upon a foreign barrow [d] to grace the procession of a proud and

here pictured as returning from his triumphal journey to India.

[d] The *fericulum* was a structure on which the spoils and sometimes noble captives were displayed in the triumphal procession.

naturus victoris superbi ac feri pompam ; non humilior
sub alieno curru agar quam in meo steteram." Quid
5 ergo est ? Vincere tamen quam capi malo. Totum
fortunae regnum despiciam, sed ex illo, si dabitur
electio, meliora sumam. Quicquid ad me venerit,
bonum fiet, sed malo faciliora ac iucundiora veniant
et minus vexatura tractantem. Non est enim, quod
existimes ullam esse sine labore virtutem, sed quae-
6 dam virtutes stimulis, quaedam frenis egent. Quemadmodum corpus in proclivi retineri debet, adversus
ardua impelli, ita quaedam virtutes in proclivi sunt,
quaedam clivum subeunt. An dubium sit, quin
escendat, nitatur, obluctetur patientia, fortitudo, per-
severantia et quaecumque alia duris opposita virtus
7 est et fortunam subigit ? Quid ergo ? Non aeque
manifestum est per devexum ire liberalitatem, tem-
perantiam, mansuetudinem ? In his continemus
animum, ne prolabatur, in illis exhortamur in-
citamusque acerrime. Ergo paupertati adhibebimus
illas, quae pugnare sciunt, fortiores, divitiis illas dili-
gentiores, quae suspensum gradum ponunt et pondus
8 suum sustinent. Cum hoc ita divisum sit, malo has
in usu mihi esse, quae exercendae tranquillius sunt,
quam eas, quarum experimentum sanguis et sudor
est. " Ergo non ego aliter," inquit sapiens, " vivo
168

brutal victor; no whit more humble shall I be when I am driven in front of the chariot of another than when I stood erect upon my own." And what is the conclusion? After all, I prefer to conquer rather than to be captured. The whole domain of Fortune I shall despise, but, if the choice be offered, I shall choose the better part of it. Whatever befalls me will turn into a good, but I prefer that what befalls me should be the more pleasant and agreeable things and those that will be less troublesome to manage. For while you are not to suppose that any virtue is acquired without effort, yet certain virtues need the spur, certain ones the bridle. Just as the body must be held back upon a downward path, and be urged up a steep ascent, so certain virtues follow the downward path, and certain others struggle up the hill. Would anyone doubt that patience, fortitude, and perseverance, and every virtue that pits itself against hardships and subdues Fortune must mount and strive and struggle? And tell me, is it not just as evident that liberality, moderation, and kindness take the downward path? In the case of these we must put a check upon the soul for fear that it may slip, in the case of the others, with all our power we urge and spur it on. Therefore for poverty we shall make use of those more hardy virtues that know how to fight, for riches those more cautious virtues that advance on tiptoe and yet keep their balance. Since there exists this distinction between them, I prefer to appropriate for myself the virtues that can be practised with comparative tranquillity, rather than those whose exercise draws blood and sweat. "Consequently," says the wise man, "I do not live one way and talk another, but I talk one

169

quam loquor, sed vos aliter auditis ; sonus tantummodo verborum ad aures vestras pervenit : quid significent non quaeritis."

1 26. " Quid ergo inter me stultum et te sapientem interest, si uterque habere volumus ? " Plurimum ; divitiae enim apud sapientem virum in servitute sunt, apud stultum in imperio ; sapiens divitiis nihil permittit, vobis divitiae omnia ; vos, tamquam aliquis vobis aeternam possessionem earum promiserit, adsuescitis illis et cohaeretis, sapiens tunc maxime paupertatem meditatur, cum in mediis divitiis constitit. 2 Numquam imperator ita paci credit, ut non se praeparet bello, quod etiam si non geritur, indictum est. Vos domus formosa, tamquam nec ardere nec ruere possit, insolentes, vos opes, tamquam periculum omne transcenderint maioresque sint vobis quam quibus consumendis satis virium habeat fortuna, 3 obstupefaciunt. Otiosi divitiis luditis nec providetis illarum periculum, sicut barbari plerumque inclusi, ut ignari machinarum, segnes laborem obsidentium spectant nec quo illa pertineant, quae ex longinquo struuntur, intellegunt. Idem vobis evenit ; marcetis in vestris rebus nec cogitatis, quot casus undique immineant iam iamque pretiosa spolia laturi. 4 Sapientis quisquis abstulerit divitias, omnia illi sua relinquet ; vivit enim praesentibus laetus, futuri securus.

---

[a] *Cf.* Horace (*Epist.* i. 10. 47) :
    Imperat aut servit collecta pecunia cuique.
[b] Compare the retort of the philosopher Stilbo cited by Seneca in *De Constantia Sap.* 5. 6.

way and you hear another—only the sound of my words reaches your ears, what they mean you do not inquire."

"What then," you say, " is the difference between you, the wise man, and me, the fool, if we both wish to have riches?" The very greatest; for in the eyes of a wise man riches are a slave, in the eyes of fools a master[a]; the wise man grants no importance to riches, to you riches are everything. You accustom yourself to them and cling to them just as if some-one had assured you that they would be a lasting possession; the wise man never reflects so much upon poverty as when he abides in the midst of riches. No general ever trusts so wholly to peace as to fail to make ready for a war that has been declared, even if it is not yet being waged. As for you, a beautiful house makes you arrogant, just as if it could never be burned or tumble down; you are stupefied by your wealth, just as if it had escaped every risk and had become so great that Fortune had lost all power to destroy it. Idly you play with your riches, and do not descry the danger they are in—you are like the barbarians who, usually, when they are blockaded, having no knowledge of the engines of war, watch with indifference the effort of the besiegers, and do not surmise the purpose of the constructions that are being erected afar. So it is with you; you loll in the midst of your possessions, and give no heed to the many disasters that threaten from every side and all too soon will carry off the costly spoils. But the wise man—whoever steals away his riches will still leave to him all that is his own[b]; for he ever lives happy in the present and unconcerned about the future.

171

" Nihil magis," inquit ille Socrates, aut aliquis alius, ius[1] cui idem adversus humana atque eadem potestas est, " persuasi mihi, quam ne ad opiniones vestras actum vitae meae flecterem. Solita conferte undique verba ; non conviciari vos putabo sed vagire
5 velut infantes miserrimos." Haec dicet ille, cui sapientia contigit, quem animus vitiorum immunis increpare alios, non quia odit, sed in remedium iubet. Adiciet his illa : " Existimatio me vestra non meo nomine sed vestro movet, quia clamitantis odisse et lacessere virtutem bonae spei eiuratio est. Nullam mihi iniuriam facitis, sed ne dis quidem hi qui aras evertunt. Sed malum propositum apparet malumque
6 consilium etiam ibi, ubi nocere non potuit. Sic vestras halucinationes fero quemadmodum Iuppiter optimus maximus ineptias poetarum, quorum alius illi alas imposuit, alius cornua, alius adulterum illum induxit et abnoctantem, alius saevum in deos, alius iniquum in homines, alius raptorem ingenuorum et cognatorum quidem, alius parricidam et regni alieni paternique expugnatorem. Quibus nihil aliud actum est, quam ut pudor hominibus peccandi demeretur,
7 si tales deos credidissent. Sed quamquam ista me nihil laedant, vestra tamen vos moneo causa. Suspicite virtutem, credite iis, qui illam diu secuti magnum quiddam ipsos et quod in dies maius appareat

---

[1] ius *supplied by Joh. Müller.*

---

[a] The allusions are to the familiar amours of Jupiter with Leda in the form of a swan, with Europa in the form of a bull, and with Alcmena, who became the mother of Hercules.
    [b] *e.g.,* Vulcan.   [c] *e g.,* Ganymedes.

" Upon nothing," says a Socrates, or any other who has like authority and like ability to cope with human affairs, " am I more strongly resolved than not to change my course of life to suit your opinion. Heap upon me from every side the usual taunts ; I shall not consider that you are railing at me, but that you are wailing like poor little babies." These will be the words of him who has found wisdom, whose soul, free from all vices, bids him chide others, not because he hates them, but in order to cure them. And, too, he will add others : " Your opinion of me moves me, not on my own account, but on yours ; for to hate and to assail virtue with your outcry, is to disavow the hope of being good. You do me no harm, but neither do men harm the gods when they overturn their altars. But evil intention and an evil purpose are apparent even where there has been no power to harm. I put up with your babblings even as Jupiter Greatest and Best puts up with the silly fancies of the poets, one of whom gives to him wings, another horns, another pictures him as the great adulterer staying out all night,[a] another as cruel toward the gods,[b] another as unjust toward men, another as the ravisher of freeborn youths[c] and even of his kinsmen, another as a parricide and usurper of another's throne—his own father's too. All that they have accomplished is that men are relieved of shame at doing wrong if they believe that the gods are such. But although your words do me no harm, nevertheless for your own sake I proffer advice. Have respect for virtue, give credence to those who, having long pursued her, proclaim that they themselves are pursuing something that is great and that every day seems

sequi clamant, et ipsam ut deos ac professores eius ut antistites colite et, quotiens mentio sacrarum litterarum intervenerit, favete linguis."[a] Hoc verbum non, ut plerique existimant, a favore trahitur, sed imperat silentium, ut rite peragi possit sacrum nulla voce mala obstrepente. Quod multo magis necessarium est imperari vobis, ut, quotiens aliquid ex illo proferetur oraculo, intenti et compressa voce audiatis.

8 Cum sistrum aliquis concutiens ex imperio mentitur, cum aliquis secandi lacertos suos artifex brachia atque umeros suspensa manu cruentat, cum aliqua genibus per viam repens ululat laurumque linteatus senex et medio lucernam die praeferens conclamat iratum aliquem deorum, concurritis et auditis ac divinum esse eum, invicem mutum alentes stuporem, adfirmatis.[b]

1 27. Ecce Socrates ex illo carcere, quem intrando purgavit omnique honestiorem curia reddidit, proclamat : "Qui iste furor, quae ista inimica dis hominibusque natura est infamare virtutes et malignis sermonibus sancta violare ? Si potestis, bonos laudate, si minus, transite ; quod si vobis exercere taetram istam licentiam placet, alter in

---

[a] " Favete linguis "=εὐφημεῖτε. During religious ceremonies it was important that no words of ill omen should be heard, and as the safest way to avoid them was to keep silent, the phrase, which originally was a call to utter good words (*bona verba*), acquired the meaning " keep silent."
[b] Used in the mystical worship of Isis. The woman and the old man mentioned below were, apparently, also the votaries of Isis, while the other type represents the Cory-

greater, and do you reverence her as you do the gods, and her exponents as the priests of the gods, and whenever any mention is made of sacred writings, 'be favourable with your tongues.'[a]" This expression is not derived, as very many imagine, from " favour " in the sense of " applause," but enjoins silence in order that sacrifice may be performed according to ritual without the interruption of an ill-omened word. But it is far more necessary that you lay this command upon yourself, in order that, whenever utterance is delivered from that oracle, you may listen with attentive ear and hushed voice. Whenever someone, shaking the rattle,[b] pretends to speak with authority, whenever someone dexterous in slashing his muscles makes bloody his arms and his shoulders with light hand, whenever some woman howls as she creeps along the street on her knees, and an old man, clad in linen and carrying a lamp in broad daylight and a branch of laurel, cries out that some one of the gods is angry, you gather in a crowd and give ear and, fostering each other's dumb amazement, affirm that he is divine !

Lo ! from that prison, which he purified by entering it and made more honourable than any senate-house, Socrates cries out : " What madness is this, what instinct is this at war with gods and men that leads you to calumniate the virtues and by your wicked talk to profane holy things ? If you are able, praise the good, if not, ignore them ; but if you take pleasure in indulging in your foul abuse, assail you one

bantes, the frenzied worshippers of Cybele ; *cf.* Lucretius, ii. 630 *sq.* :

> Inter se forte quod armis
> ludunt in numerumque exultant sanguinolenti.

alterum incursitate. Nam cum in caelum insanitis, non dico sacrilegium facitis sed operam perditis.

2 Praebui ego aliquando Aristophani materiam iocorum, tota illa comicorum poetarum manus in me venenatos sales suos effudit. Inlustrata est virtus mea per ea ipsa, per quae petebatur ; produci enim illi et temptari expedit, nec ulli magis intellegunt, quanta sit, quam qui vires eius lacessendo senserunt. Duritia

3 silicis nullis magis quam ferientibus nota est. Praebeo me non aliter quam rupes aliqua mari destituta, quam fluctus non desinunt, undecumque moti sunt, verberare, nec ideo aut loco eam movent aut per tot aetates crebro incursu suo consumunt. Adsilite, facite impetum ; ferendo vos vincam. In ea, quae firma et inexsuperabilia sunt, quicquid incurrit malo suo vim suam exercet. Proinde quaerite aliquam mollem cedentemque materiam, in qua tela vestra figantur."

4 Vobis autem vacat aliena scrutari mala et sententias ferre de quoquam ? " Quare hic philosophus laxius habitat ? Quare hic lautius cenat ?" Papulas observatis alienas, obsiti plurimis ulceribus. Hoc tale est, quale si quis pulcherrimorum corporum naevos aut verrucas derideat, quem foeda scabies

5 depascitur. Obicite Platoni, quod petierit pecuniam,

ᵃ Notably in the *Clouds.*

ᵇ *Cf.* Horace, *Sat.* i. 6. 65 *sqq.*:

  Atqui si vitiis mediocribus ac mea paucis
  mendosa est natura, alioqui recta, velut si
  egregio insparsos reprehendas corpore naevos, *etc.*

ᶜ Diogenes Laertius reports that Plato received more than eighty talents from Dionysius of Syracuse (iii. 9), that Aristotle tutored Alexander at the court of Philip (v. 4), that Epicurus spent no less than a mina a day on food (x. 7);

another. For when you rage against heaven I do not
say, ' You are committing sacrilege,' but ' You are
wasting your time.' I once afforded Aristophanes [a]
subject matter for his jokes, the whole company of
comic poets has poured upon me their envenomed wit.
Yet their very efforts to assail my virtue added to its
lustre ; for it profits from being exposed and tested,
and none understand better how great it is than
those who have perceived its strength by attacking
it. None know better the hardness of flint than
those who strike it. I show myself like some lonely
rock in the sea, which the waves never cease to beat
upon from whatever quarter they have come, yet
for all that they cannot move it from its base nor
wear it away by their ceaseless attack through countless ages. Leap upon me, make your assault ; I
shall conquer you by enduring. Whatever strikes
against that which is firm and unconquerable ex-
pends its power to its own hurt. Accordingly, seek
some soft and yielding object in which to stick your
darts."

But as for you, have you the leisure to search
out others' evils and to pass judgement upon
anybody ? " Why does this philosopher have such a
spacious house ? " " Why does this one dine so
sumptuously ? " you say. You look at the pimples of
others when you yourselves are covered with a mass of
sores. This is just as if someone who was devoured
by a foul itch should mock at the moles [b] and the
warts on bodies that are most beautiful. Taunt Plato [c]
because he sought for money, Aristotle because he

on Democritus Cicero (*De Fin.* v. 29. 87) comments :
" patrimonium neglexit, agros deseruit incultos, quid
quaerens aliud nisi vitam beatam."

Aristoteli, quod acceperit, Democrito, quod ne-
glexerit, Epicuro, quod consumpserit; mihi ipsi Alci-
biadem et Phaedrum obiectate, evasuri maxime
felices, cum primum vobis imitari vitia nostra con-
6 tigerit! Quin potius mala vestra circumspicitis,
quae vos ab omni parte confodiunt, alia grassantia
extrinsecus, alia in visceribus ipsis ardentia? Non
eo loco res humanae sunt, etiam si statum vestrum
parum nostis, ut vobis tantum otii supersit, ut in
probra meliorum agitare linguam vacet.

1 28. Hoc vos non intellegitis et alienum fortunae
vestrae vultum geritis, sicut plurimi, quibus in circo
aut theatro desidentibus iam funesta domus est nec
adnuntiatum malum. At ego ex alto prospiciens
video, quae tempestates aut immineant vobis paulo
tardius rupturae nimbum suum, aut iam vicinae vos
ac vestra rapturae propius accesserint. Quid porro?
Nonne nunc quoque, etiam si parum sentitis, turbo
quidam animos vestros rotat et involvit, fugientes
petentesque eadem et nunc in sublime adlevatos
nunc in infima adlisos? . . . .

---

^a Notorious for his amours and debaucheries. The
scandalous charges made by Cassius Dio (lxi. 10) against
Seneca give point to the allusion.
^b The rest of the essay is lost.

accepted it, Democritus because he disregarded it, Epicurus because he spent it; fling Alcibiades[a] and Phaedrus in my own teeth—though it will prove your happiest time when you are so fortunate as to copy my vices! Why do you not rather look about you at your own sins that rend you on every side, some assailing you from without, others raging in your very vitals. Human affairs—even if you have insufficient knowledge of your own position—have not yet reached the situation in which you may have such superfluity of spare time as to find leisure to wag your tongue in abusing your betters.

This you do not understand, and you wear an air that ill accords with your condition—you are like the many who lounge in the Circus or in a theatre while their home is already wrapped in mourning and they have not yet heard the evil news. But I, looking from the heights, see the storms that threaten and a little later will burst upon you in a flood, or, already near, have drawn still closer to sweep away both you and yours. Why say more? Are not your minds even now—though you little know-it—whirled and spun about as if some hurricane had seized them, while they flee and pursue the selfsame things, and now are lifted to the skies, and now are dashed to the lowest depths? . . .[b]

LIBER VIII

AD SERENVM

DE OTIO

1 1. [28.] . . . . . . cit, nobis magno consensu vitia
commendant. Licet nihil aliud, quod sit salutare,
temptemus, proderit tamen per se ipsum secedere;
meliores erimus singuli. Quid, quod secedere ad
optimos viros et aliquod exemplum eligere, ad
quod vitam derigamus, licet? Quod nisi[1] in otio
non fit. Tunc potest obtineri quod semel placuit,
ubi nemo intervenit, qui iudicium adhuc imbecillum
populo adiutore detorqueat; tunc potest vita
aequali et uno tenore procedere, quam propositis
2 diversissimis scindimus. Nam inter cetera mala
illud pessimum est, quod vitia ipsa mutamus. Sic
ne hoc quidem nobis contingit permanere in malo
iam familiari. Aliud ex alio placet vexatque nos hoc
quoque, quod iudicia nostra non tantum prava, sed
etiam levia sunt. Fluctuamur aliudque ex alio com-

---

[1] nisi *added by Gronovius.*

---

[a] This fragment appears in the MSS. as a continuation
of the *De Vita Beata.* Both essays have suffered loss. In
its extant form the *De Otio* begins abruptly in the
midst of a plea for the life of retirement. The theme,
apparently, was part of the introduction of the essay, since
180

BOOK VIII

TO SERENUS

ON LEISURE

. . . *a* with great accord commend to us the vices.
Although we attempt nothing else that would be
beneficial, nevertheless retirement in itself will do us
good ; we shall be better by ourselves. And what
of the opportunity to retire to the society of the best
men,*b* and to select some model by which we may direct
our own lives ? But we can do this only in leisure.
Only then is it possible for us to maintain what we
have once resolved upon, when there is no one who
can interfere and with the help of the crowd turn
aside our decision while it is still weak ; only then
is it possible for life, in which we are now distracted
by the most diverse aims, to progress along an even
and single course. For among all the rest of our
ills this is the worst—the habit of changing our very
vices. So we do not have even the good fortune to
persist in an evil that we already know. We find
pleasure first in one and then in another, and the
trouble is that our choices are not only wrong, but
also fickle. We are tossed about and clutch at one

the formal division of the subject is preserved at the end of
Chapter 2.
 b *i.e.*, the company of the best books.

3 prendimus, petita relinquimus, relicta repetimus,
alternae inter cupiditatem nostram et paenitentiam
vices sunt; pendemus enim toti ex alienis iudiciis
et id optimum nobis videtur, quod petitores lauda-
toresque multos habet, non id quod laudandum
petendumque est, nec viam bonam ac malam per
se aestimamus, sed turba vestigiorum, in quibus
nulla sunt redeuntium.

4   Dices mihi : " Quid agis, Seneca ? Deseris partes ?
Certe Stoici vestri dicunt: 'Usque ad ultimum vitae
finem in actu erimus, non desinemus communi bono
operam dare, adiuvare singulos, opem ferre etiam
inimicis senili manu. Nos sumus, qui nullis annis
vacationem damus et, quod ait ille vir disertissimus,

Canitiem galea premimus.

Nos sumus, apud quos usque eo nihil ante mortem
otiosum est, ut, si res patitur, non sit ipsa mors
otiosa.' Quid nobis Epicuri praecepta in ipsis
Zenonis principiis loqueris ? Quin tu bene gnaviter,
si partium piget, transfugis potius quam prodis ? "

5 Hoc tibi in praesentia respondebo : " Numquid vis
amplius, quam ut me similem ducibus meis praestem ? Quid ergo est ? Non quo miserint me illi,
sed quo duxerint, ibo."

1   2. [29.] Nunc probabo tibi non descicere me a
praeceptis Stoicorum ; nam ne ipsi quidem a suis

---

a *i.e.*, they have passed to destruction. In the fable of
The Fox and the Sick Lion (Aesop, 197), when the wary fox
was urged by the lion to enter his cave, he replied: "ἀλλ'
ἔγωγε εἰσῆλθον ἄν, εἰ μὴ ἑώρων πολλῶν εἰσιόντων ἴχνη, ἐξιόντο
δὲ οὐδενός."
b Virgil, *Aeneid*, ix. 612.
c *i.e.*, he inclines to follow their example, not their precept.

thing after another; what we have sought we abandon, and what we have abandoned we seek again, and oscillate ever between desire and repentance. For we depend wholly on the judgements of others, and that which the many seek and praise seems to us the best—not that which deserves to be sought and praised—and we do not consider whether the way in itself is good or bad, but the number of footprints it has; and none of these are of men who are coming back![a]

You will say to me: "What are you doing, Seneca? Are you deserting your party? Surely you Stoics say: 'We shall engage in affairs to the very end of life, we shall never cease to work for the common good, to help each and all, to give aid even to our enemies when our hand is feeble with age. We are those who grant no exemption from service by reason of years, and, as that most gifted poet puts it,

Upon our hoary heads we thrust the helm.[b]

We are those who hold so strongly that there should be no leisure before death that, if circumstance permits, we take no leisure for death itself.' Why in the very headquarters of Zeno do you preach the doctrines of Epicurus? Why, if you are tired of your party, do you not with all speed desert it rather than betray it?" For the present I shall have only this reply to make to you: "What more do you expect of me than that I should imitate my leaders? And what then? I shall not go whither they despatch me, but whither they lead me."[c]

Right now I shall prove to you that I am not in revolt against the teachings of the Stoics; for they themselves have not revolted against their own teach-

desciverunt; et tamen excusatissimus essem, etiam
si non praecepta illorum sequerer, sed exempla.
Hoc quod dico in duas dividam partes : primum,
ut possit aliquis vel a prima aetate contemplationi
veritatis totum se tradere, rationem vivendi quaerere
2 atque exercere secreto; deinde, ut possit hoc
aliquis emeritis iam stipendiis, profligatae aetatis,
iure optimo facere et ad alios actus animum[1] referre
virginum Vestalium more, quae annis inter officia
divisis discunt facere sacra et cum didicerunt docent.
1 3. [30.] Hoc Stoicis quoque placere ostendam, non
quia mihi legem dixerim nihil contra dictum Zenonis
Chrysippive committere, sed quia res ipsa patitur
me ire in illorum sententiam, quoniam si quis semper
unius sequitur, non in curia sed in factione est.
Utinam quidem iam tenerentur omnia et in aperto
confessa veritas esset nihilque ex decretis mutare-
mus ! Nunc veritatem cum eis ipsis qui docent
quaerimus.
2 Duae maxime et in hac re dissident sectae,
Epicureorum et Stoicorum, sed utraque ad otium
diversa via mittit. Epicurus ait : "Non accedet
ad rem publicam sapiens, nisi si quid intervenerit";
Zenon ait : "Accedet ad rem publicam, nisi si
3 quid impedierit." Alter otium ex proposito petit,

---

[1] animum *Ruhkopf*: animos *A*.

[a] For as Seneca himself shows at the end of chapter 5 :
"ne contemplatio quidem sine actione est."
[b] Cf. *Frag. Epicurea*, ᴅ 87 (Bailey).
[c] Cf. *Frag. of Zeno*, 170 (Pearson).

ings either. And yet I might plead a very good excuse even if I did follow their examples and not their teachings. What I have to say I shall develop under two heads, showing, first, that it is possible for a man to surrender himself wholly to the contemplation of truth, to search out the art of living, and to practise it in retirement, even from his earliest years; secondly, that, when a man has now earned release from public service and his life is almost over, it is possible that he may with perfect justice do the same thing and turn his mind to quite different activities,[a] after the manner of the Vestal virgins, whose years are allotted to varied duties while they are learning to perform the sacred rites, and, when they have learned, they begin to teach.

I shall show, too, that the Stoics also accept this doctrine, not because I have made it my rule to set up nothing contrary to the teaching of Zeno or Chrysippus, but because the matter itself suffers me to adopt their opinion; for if a man always follows the opinion of one person, his place is not in the senate, but in a faction. Would that all things were now understood, that truth were uncovered and revealed, and that we never altered our mandates! As it is, we are in search of truth in company with the very men that teach it.

The two sects, the Epicureans and the Stoics, are at variance, as in most things, in this matter also; they both direct us to leisure, but by different roads. Epicurus[b] says: "The wise man will not engage in public affairs except in an emergency." Zeno[c] says: "He will engage in public affairs unless something prevents him." The one seeks leisure by fixed pur-

185

alter ex causa ; causa autem illa late patet. Si res
publica corruptior est quam ut[1] adiuvari possit, si
occupata est malis, non nitetur sapiens in supervacuum
nec se nihil profuturus impendet. Si parum habebit
auctoritatis aut virium nec illum erit admissura
4 res publica, si valetudo illum impediet, quomodo
navem quassam non deduceret in mare, quomodo
nomen in militiam non daret debilis, sic ad iter, quod
inhabile sciet, non accedet. Potest ergo et ille, cui
omnia adhuc in integro sunt, antequam ullas ex-
periatur tempestates, in tuto subsistere et protinus
commendare se bonis artibus et inlibatum otium
exigere, virtutium cultor, quae exerceri etiam
5 quietissimis possunt. Hoc nempe ab homine ex-
igitur, ut prosit hominibus, si fieri potest, multis,
si minus, paucis, si minus, proximis, si minus, sibi.
Nam cum se utilem ceteris efficit, commune agit
negotium. Quomodo qui se deteriorem facit non
sibi tantummodo nocet, sed etiam omnibus eis,
quibus melior factus prodesse potuisset, sic quisquis bene de se meretur hoc ipso aliis prodest, quod
illis profuturum parat.

1 4. [31.] Duas res publicas animo complectamur,
alteram magnam et vere publicam, qua dii atque
homines continentur, in qua non ad hunc angulum re-
spicimus aut ad illum, sed terminos civitatis nostrae
cum sole metimur ; alteram, cui nos adscripsit condicio

___
1 ut *commonly supplied.*

pose, the other for a special cause ; but the term " cause " has here broad application. If the state is too corrupt to be helped, if it is wholly dominated by evils, the wise man will not struggle to no purpose, nor spend himself when nothing is to be gained. If he is lacking in influence or power and the state is unwilling to accept his services, if he is hampered by ill health, he will not enter upon a course for which he knows he is unfitted, just as he would not launch upon the sea a battered ship, just as he would not enlist for service in the army if he were disabled. Consequently, it is also possible that a man whose fortunes are still unharmed may establish himself in a safe retreat before he experiences any of the storms of life, and thenceforth devote himself to the liberal studies and demand uninterrupted leisure to cultivate the virtues, which even those who are most retired are able to practise. It is of course required of a man that he should benefit his fellow-men— many if he can, if not, a few ; if not a few, those who are nearest ; if not these, himself. For when he renders himself useful to others, he engages in public affairs. Just as the man that chooses to become worse injures not only himself but all those whom, if he had become better, he might have benefited, so whoever wins the approval of himself benefits others by the very fact that he prepares what will prove beneficial to them.

Let us grasp the idea that there are two commonwealths—the one, a vast and truly common state, which embraces alike gods and men, in which we look neither to this corner of earth nor to that, but measure the bounds of our citizenship by the path of the sun ; the other, the one to which we have

nascendi. Haec aut Atheniensium erit aut Carthaginiensium, aut alterius alicuius urbis, quae non ad omnis
pertineat homines sed ad certos. Quidam eodem
tempore utrique rei publicae dant operam, maiori
minorique, quidam tantum minori, quidam tantum
2 maiori. Huic maiori rei publicae et in otio de-
servire possumus, immo vero nescio an in otio melius,
ut quaeramus quid sit virtus, una pluresne sint ;
natura an ars bonos viros faciat ; unum sit hoc,
quod maria terrasque et mari ac terris inserta
complectitur, an multa eiusmodi corpora deus
sparserit ; continua sit omnis et plena materia,
ex qua cuncta gignuntur, an diducta et solidis inane
permixtum ; qui sit deus ; deses opus suum spectet
an tractet ; utrumne extrinsecus illi circumfusus
sit an toti inditus ; immortalis sit mundus an inter
caduca et ad tempus nata numerandus. Haec
qui contemplatur, quid deo praestat ? Ne tanta
eius opera sine teste sit.

1   5. Solemus dicere summum bonum esse secundum
naturam vivere. Natura nos ad utrumque genuit, et
contemplationi rerum et actioni. [32] Nunc id pro-
bemus, quod prius diximus. Quid porro ? Hoc non
erit probatum, si se unusquisque consuluerit, quantam cupidinem habeat ignota noscendi, quam ad
2 omnis fabulas excitetur ? Navigant quidam et

---

[a] The Stoic view.

[b] The Epicureans taught that there were countless
worlds throughout infinite space.

[c] The Stoics denied the existence of void, while the
Epicureans in turn made it a basic doctrine.

been assigned by the accident of birth. This will be the commonwealth of the Athenians or of the Carthaginians, or of any other city that belongs, not to all, but to some particular race of men. Some yield service to both commonwealths at the same time— to the greater and to the lesser—some only to the lesser, some only to the greater. This greater commonwealth we are able to serve even in leisure—nay, I am inclined to think, even better in leisure—so that we may inquire what virtue is, and whether it is one or many; whether it is nature or art that makes men good ; whether this world, which embraces seas and lands and the things that are contained in the sea and land, is a solitary creation *a* or whether God has strewn about many systems *b* of the same sort; whether all the matter from which everything is formed is continuous and compact, *c* or whether it is disjunctive and a void is intermingled with the solid ; what God is —whether he idly gazes upon his handiwork, or directs it ; whether he encompasses it without, or pervades the whole of it ; whether the world is eternal, or is to be counted among the things that perish and are born only for a time. And what service does he who ponders these things render unto God ? He keeps the mighty works of God from being without a witness !

We are fond of saying that the highest good is to live according to Nature. Nature has begotten us for both purposes—for contemplation and for action. Let me now prove the first statement. But why anything more ? Will not this be proved if each one of us shall take counsel simply of himself, and ponder how great is his desire to gain knowledge of the unknown, and how this desire is stirred by tales of every sort ? Some sail the sea and endure the hardships of

labores peregrinationis longissimae **una** mercede
perpetiuntur cognoscendi aliquid abditum remotum-
que. Haec res ad spectacula populos contrahit,
haec cogit praeclusa rimari, secretiora exquirere,
antiquitates evolvere, mores barbararum audire
3 gentium. Curiosum nobis natura ingenium dedit
et artis sibi ac pulchritudinis suae conscia spectatores
nos tantis rerum spectaculis genuit, perditura fructum sui, si tam magna, tam clara, tam subtiliter
ducta, tam nitida et non uno genere formosa soli-
4 tudini ostenderet. Ut scias illam spectari voluisse,
non tantum aspici, vide quem nobis locum dederit.
In media nos sui parte constituit et circumspectum
omnium nobis dedit; nec erexit tantummodo
hominem, sed etiam habilem contemplationi factura,
ut ab ortu sidera in occasum labentia prosequi
posset et vultum suum circumferre cum toto, sublime
fecit illi caput et collo flexili imposuit; deinde sena
per diem, sena per noctem signa perducens nullam
non partem sui explicuit, ut per haec, quae optulerat
oculis eius, cupiditatem faceret etiam ceterorum.
5 Nec enim omnia nec tanta visimus quanta sunt,
sed acies nostra aperit sibi investigandi viam et
fundamenta vero iacit, ut inquisitio transeat ex
apertis in obscura et aliquid ipso mundo inveniat
antiquius : unde ista sidera exierint; quis fuerit
190

journeying to distant lands for the sole reward of discovering something hidden and remote. It is this that collects people everywhere to see sights, it is this that forces them to pry into things that are closed, to search out the more hidden things, to unroll the past, and to listen to the tales of the customs of barbarous tribes. Nature has bestowed upon us an inquisitive disposition, and being well aware of her own skill and beauty, has begotten us to be spectators of her mighty array, since she would lose the fruit of her labour if her works, so vast, so glorious, so artfully contrived, so bright and so beautiful in more ways than one, were displayed to a lonely solitude. That you may understand how she wished us, not merely to behold her, but to gaze upon her, see the position in which she has placed us. She has set us in the centre of her creation, and has granted us a view that sweeps the universe ; and she has not only created man erect, but in order to fit him for contemplation of herself, she has given him a head to top the body, and set it upon a pliant neck, in order that he might follow the stars as they glide from their rising to their setting and turn his face about with the whole revolving heaven. And besides, guiding on their course six constellations by day, and six by night, she left no part of herself unrevealed, hoping that by these wonders which she had presented to man's eyes she might also arouse his curiosity in the rest. For we have not beheld them all, nor the full compass of them, but our vision opens up a path for its investigation, and lays the foundations of truth so that our research may pass from revealed to hidden things and discover something more ancient than the world itself—whence yon stars came forth, what

universi status, antequam singula in partes dis-
cederent; quae ratio mersa et confusa diduxerit;
quis loca rebus adsignaverit, suapte natura gravia
descenderint, evolaverint levia, an praeter nisum
pondusque corporum altior aliqua vis legem singulis
dixerit; an illud verum sit, quo maxime probatur
homines divini esse spiritus, partem ac veluti scintillas
quasdam astrorum in terram desiluisse atque alieno
6 loco haesisse. Cogitatio nostra caeli munimenta
perrumpit nec contenta est id, quod ostenditur,
scire. "Illud," inquit, "scrutor, quod ultra mundum
iacet, utrumne profunda vastitas sit an et hoc
ipsum terminis suis cludatur; qualis sit habitus
exclusis, informia et confusa sint, in omnem partem
tantundem loci obtinentia, an et illa in aliquem
cultum discripta sint; huic cohaereant mundo,
an longe ab hoc secesserint et hic vacuo volutentur;
individua sint, per quae struitur omne quod natum
futurumque est, an continua eorum materia sit
et per totum mutabilis; utrum contraria inter se
elementa sint, an non pugnent sed per diversa con-

---

a The Epicureans, who were pure materialists, taught
that the great parts of the world—earth, sea, air, and ether
—were formed from the chance combination of atoms of
varying size and weight, and that on the principle of gravity
the heavier substances sank and the lighter soared aloft.
Cf. Lucretius, v. 449-494.
   b The Stoics were practically pantheists and, positing an
intelligent Creator of the world, saw "God in the stone."
They identified primary fire with Divinity, and each of the
four elements in turn contained some proportion of Divine
heat.
   c Lucretius's vivid lines (i. 72 *sq.*) are warrant for the
metaphor:

> Ergo vivida vis animi pervicit, et extra
> processit longe flammantia moenia mundi.

was the state of the universe before the several
elements separated to form its parts, what principle
separated the engulfed and confused elements, who
appointed their places to things, whether the heavy
elements sank and the light ones flew aloft by reason
of their own nature,[a] or apart from the energy and
gravity of matter some higher power[b] has appointed
laws for each of them, or whether that theory is true
which strives especially to prove that man is part of
the divine spirit, that some part, sparks, as it were,
of the stars fell down to earth and lingered here in a
place that is not their own. Our thought bursts
through the ramparts[c] of the sky, and is not content
to know that which is revealed. " I search out
that," it says, " which lies beyond the world—
whether the vastness of space is unending, or whether
this also is enclosed within its own boundaries ;
what is the appearance of whatever exists outside,
whether it is formless and disordered, occupying the
same amount of room in every direction, or whether
that also has been arranged into some show of
elegance ; whether it clings close to this world, or
has withdrawn far from it and revolves there in the
void ; whether it is atoms[d] by means of which everything that has been born and will be born is built
up or whether the matter of things is continuous
and throughout is capable of change[e] ; whether
the elements are hostile to each other, or whether
they are not at war, but while they differ are in

---

[d] The Epicurean view.
[e] An allusion to the Stoic doctrine of the transmutation
of the four elements in fixed order. See note, Vol. I. p. 204.

7 spirent." Ad haec quaerenda natus, aestima, quam
non multum acceperit temporis, etiam si illud
totum sibi vindicat. Cui licet nihil facilitate eripi,
nihil neglegentia patiatur excidere, licet horas
suas avarissime servet et usque in ultimum aetatis
humanae terminum procedat nec quicquam illi
ex eo, quod natura constituit, fortuna concutiat,
tamen homo ad immortalium cognitionem nimis
8 mortalis est. Ergo secundum naturam vivo, si
totum me illi dedi, si illius admirator cultorque sum.
Natura autem utrumque facere me voluit, et agere
et contemplationi vacare. Utrumque facio, quoniam
ne contemplatio quidem sine actione est.

1 6. " Sed refert," inquis, " an ad illam voluptatis
causa accesseris nihil aliud ex illa petens quam adsi-
duam contemplationem sine exitu ; est enim dulcis
et habet inlecebras suas." Adversus hoc tibi
respondeo : aeque refert, quo animo civilem agas
vitam, an semper inquietus sis nec tibi umquam
sumas ullum tempus, quo ab humanis ad divina
2 respicias. Quomodo res adpetere sine ullo virtutum
amore et sine cultu ingeni ac nudas edere operas
minime probabile est — misceri enim ista inter se
et conseri debent—, sic imperfectum ac languidum
bonum est in otium sine actu proiecta virtus, num-
3 quam id, quod didicit, ostendens. Quis negat
illam debere profectus suos in opere temptare,

---

harmony." Since man was born for inquiring into
such matters as these, consider how little time has
been allotted to him even if he claims the whole of
it for himself. Though he allows none of it to be
snatched from him by ease, none of it to be lost
through carelessness, though he guards his hours
with most miserly care, and attains to the utmost
limit of human life, though Fortune wrecks no part
of that which Nature has appointed for him, yet
man is too mortal to comprehend things immortal.
Consequently I live according to Nature if I surrender myself entirely to her, if I become her admirer
and worshipper. But Nature intended me to do both
—to be active and to have leisure for contemplation. And really I do both, since even the contempla-
tive life is not devoid of action.[a]

"But it makes a difference," you say, "whether
you have resorted to that merely for the sake of
pleasure, demanding nothing from it except unbroken contemplation without practical result; for
that life is pleasant and has its own charms." In
answer to this I say that it makes just as much
difference in what spirit you engage in public life—
whether you are always distraught, and never take
any time to turn your eyes from human affairs to the
things of heaven. Just as to seek wealth without
any love of the virtues and without the cultivation
of character, and to display an interest in bare work
only is by no means to be commended—for all these
must be combined and go hand in hand—so when
virtue is banished to leisure without action it is an imperfect and spiritless good, that never brings what it
has learned into the open. Who will deny that Virtue
ought to test her progress by open deed, and should

nec tantum quid faciendum sit cogitare, sed etiam aliquando manum exercere et ea, quae meditata sunt, ad verum perducere? Quodsi per ipsum sapientem non est mora, si non actor deest, sed agenda desunt, ecquid illi secum esse permittes?

4 Quo animo ad otium sapiens secedit? Ut sciat se tum quoque ea acturum, per quae posteris prosit. Nos certe sumus qui dicimus et Zenonem et Chrysippum maiora egisse, quam si duxissent exercitus, gessissent honores, leges tulissent. Quas non uni civitati, sed toti humano generi tulerunt. Quid est ergo, quare tale otium non conveniat viro bono, per quod futura saecula ordinet nec apud paucos contionetur, sed apud omnis omnium gentium

5 homines, quique sunt quique erunt? Ad summam quaero, an ex praeceptis suis vixerint Cleanthes et Chrysippus et Zenon. Non[1] dubie respondebis sic illos vixisse, quemadmodum dixerant esse vivendum. Atqui nemo illorum rem publicam administravit. "Non fuit," inquis, "illis aut ea fortuna aut ea dignitas, quae admitti ad publicarum rerum tractationem solet." Sed idem nihilo minus non segnem egere vitam; invenerunt, quemadmodum plus quies ipsorum hominibus prodesset quam aliorum discursus et sudor. Ergo nihilo minus hi multum egisse visi sunt, quamvis nihil publice agerent.

1 7. Praeterea tria genera sunt vitae, inter quae quod sit optimum quaeri solet. Unum voluptati

---

[1] non *commonly added.*

not only consider what ought to be done, but also at times apply her hand and bring into reality what she has conceived ? But if the hindrance is not in the wise man himself—if what is lacking is not the doer, but the things to be done, will you then permit him to court his own soul ? And with what thought does the wise man retire into leisure ? In the knowledge that there also he will be doing something that will benefit posterity. Our school at any rate is ready to say that both Zeno and Chrysippus accomplished greater things than if they had led armies, held public office, and framed laws. The laws they framed were not for one state only, but for the whole human race. Why, therefore, should such leisure as this not be fitting for the good man, who by means of it may govern the ages to come, and speak, not to the ears of the few, but to the ears of all men of all nations, both those who now are and those who shall be ? In brief, I ask you whether Cleanthes and Chrysippus and Zeno lived in accordance with their teachings. Undoubtedly you will reply that they lived just as they taught that men ought to live. And yet no one of them governed a state. You reply : " They had neither the fortune nor the rank which ordinarily admit one to the management of public affairs." But, nevertheless, they did not lead a life of sloth ; they found a way to make their own repose a greater help to mankind than all the pother and sweat of others. Therefore, though they played no public part, they none the less have been thought to have played a great part.

Moreover, there are three kinds of life, and it is a common question as to which of them is best. One

vacat, alterum contemplationi, tertium actioni.
Primum deposita contentione depositoque odio
quod implacabile diversa sequentibus indiximus,
videamus, ut haec omnia ad idem sub alio atque
alio titulo perveniant. Nec ille, qui voluptatem probat, sine contemplatione est, nec ille, qui contemplationi inservit, sine voluptate est, nec ille, cuius
vita actionibus destinata est, sine contemplatione
2 est. " Plurimum," inquis, " discriminis est, utrum
aliqua res propositum sit an propositi alterius accessio." Sit sane grande discrimen, tamen alterum
sine altero non est. Nec ille sine actione contemplatur, nec hic sine contemplatione agit, nec
ille tertius, de quo male existimare consensimus,
voluptatem inertem probat, sed eam, quam ratione
3 efficit firmam sibi ; ita et haec ipsa voluptaria secta
in actu est. Quidni in actu sit ? cum ipse dicat
Epicurus aliquando se recessurum a voluptate,
dolorem etiam adpetiturum, si aut voluptati im-
minebit paenitentia aut dolor minor pro graviore
4 sumetur ? Quo pertinet haec dicere ? Ut appareat
contemplationem placere omnibus ; alii petunt
illam, nobis haec statio, non portus est.
1   8. Adice nunc,[1] quod e lege Chrysippi vivere
otioso licet ; non dico, ut otium patiatur, sed ut
eligat. Negant nostri sapientem ad quamlibet rem

---

[1] nunc *Haase*: nunc huc *A*.

---

[a] Evidently an Epicurean. The fragmentary sentence
at the beginning of the essay is possibly a remnant of some
discussion of the type.

[b] *Cf. Frag. Epicurea*, D. 62 (Bailey).

is devoted to pleasure, a second to contemplation, a third to action. Having first put away our strife and having put away the hatred which we have relentlessly declared against those who pursue ends different from ours, let us see how all these, under different names, come to the same thing. For he who sanctions pleasure is not without contemplation, nor he who surrenders to contemplation without pleasure, nor is he whose life is devoted to action without contemplation. But you say: " Whether something is a chief aim or is merely attached to some other chief aim makes a very great difference." Yes, grant that there is a huge difference, nevertheless the one does not exist without the other. That man is not given to contemplation without action, nor this one to action without contemplation, nor does that third one *a*—concerning whom we have agreed to form a bad opinion—give sanction to idle pleasure, but to the pleasure that he renders stable for himself by his reason; thus even this pleasure-loving sect is itself committed to action. Clearly is it committed to action! since Epicurus himself declares that he will at times withdraw from pleasure, will even seek pain if he foresees that he will either repent of pleasure, or will be able to substitute a lesser pain for one that is greater.*b* And what is my purpose in stating these things? To make it clear that contemplation is favoured by all. Some men make it their aim; for us it is a roadstead, but not the harbour.

Add, further, that on the authority of Chrysippus a man has a right to live a life of leisure; I do not mean, that he may tolerate leisure, but that he may choose it. Our school refuses to allow the wise man

199

publicam accessurum ; quid autem interest, quomodo sapiens ad otium veniat, utrum quia res
publica illi deest, an quia ipse rei publicae, si non
ubivis futura res publica est? Semper autem
deerit fastidiose quaerentibus. Interrogo, ad quam
rem publicam sapiens sit accessurus. Ad Atheniensium, in qua Socrates damnatur, Aristoteles, ne
damnetur, fugit ? in qua opprimit invidia virtutes ?
Negabis mihi accessurum ad hanc rem publicam
2 sapientem. Ad Carthaginiensium ergo rem publicam sapiens accedet, in qua adsidua seditio et
optimo cuique infesta libertas est, summa aequi
ac boni vilitas, adversus hostes inhumana crudelitas, etiam adversus suos hostilis ? Et hanc
3 fugiet. Si percensere singulas voluero, nullam
inveniam, quae sapientem aut quam sapiens pati
possit. Quodsi non invenitur illa res publica,
quam nobis fingimus, incipit omnibus esse otium
necessarium, quia quod unum praeferri poterat otio,
4 nusquam est. Si quis dicit optimum esse navigare,
deinde negat navigandum in eo mari, in quo naufragia fieri soleant et frequenter subitae tempestates
sint, quae rectorem in contrarium rapiant, puto hic
me vetat navem solvere, quamquam[1] laudet navi-
gationem.

---

[1] quamquam *Hermes*: quam *A.*

---

[a] The essay is apparently incomplete.

to attach himself to any sort of state. But what difference does it make in what manner the wise man arrives at leisure—whether because no state is available to him or because he is not available to the state—if he is nowhere to find a state? Besides, no state will ever be available to the fastidious searcher. I ask you to what state should the wise man attach himself? To that of the Athenians, in which Socrates was sentenced to death, from which Aristotle fled to avoid being sentenced? in which all the virtues are crushed by envy? Surely you will say that no wise man will wish to attach himself to this state. Shall the wise man, then, attach himself to the state of the Carthaginians, in which faction is always rife and all the best men find " freedom " their foe, in which justice and goodness have supreme contempt, and enemies are treated with inhuman cruelty and fellow-citizens like enemies? From this state also will he flee. If I should attempt to enumerate them one by one, I should not find a single one which could tolerate the wise man or which the wise man could tolerate. But if that state which we dream of can nowhere be found, leisure begins to be a necessity for all of us, because the one thing that might have been preferred to leisure nowhere exists. If anyone says that the best life of all is to sail the sea, and then adds that I must not sail upon a sea where shipwrecks are a common occurrence and there are often sudden storms that sweep the helmsman in an adverse direction, I conclude that this man, although he lauds navigation, really forbids me to launch my ship.[a]

LIBER IX

DE TRANQUILLITATE ANIMI

1 1. SERENUS[1] : Inquirenti mihi in me quaedam
vitia apparebant, Seneca,[2] retecta, in aperto posita,
quae manu prenderem, quaedam obscuriora et in
recessu, quaedam non continua sed ex intervallis
redeuntia, quae vel molestissima dixerim, ut hostis
vagos et ex occasionibus adsilientis, per quos neutrum
licet, nec tamquam in bello paratum esse nec tamquam in pace securum.

2 Illum tamen habitum in me maxime deprendo
(quare enim non verum ut medico fatear ?) nec bona
fide liberatum me iis, quae timebam et oderam,
nec rursus obnoxium ; in statu ut non pessimo, ita
maxime querulo et moroso positus sum : nec aegroto
3 nec valeo. Non est, quod dicas omnium virtutium
tenera esse principia, tempore illis duramentum et
robur accedere. Non ignoro etiam quae in speciem

---

[1] Serenus *added by Haase.*
[2] Seneca *added by Gertz.*

---

[a] Annaeus Serenus, to whom this and the preceding dialogue and the *De Constantia Sapientis* are addressed, was a
young prefect of Nero's nightwatch, for whom Seneca had

BOOK IX

ON TRANQUILLITY OF MIND

SERENUS [a]: When I made examination of myself, it became evident, Seneca, that some of my vices are uncovered and displayed so openly that I can put my hand upon them, some are more hidden and lurk in a corner, some are not always present but recur at intervals; and I should say that the last are by far the most troublesome, being like roving enemies that spring upon one when the opportunity offers, and allow one neither to be ready as in war, nor to be off guard as in peace.

Nevertheless the state in which I find myself most of all—for why should I not admit the truth to you as to a physician?—is that I have neither been honestly set free from the things that I hated and feared, nor, on the other hand, am I in bondage to them; while the condition in which I am placed is not the worst, yet I am complaining and fretful—I am neither sick nor well. There is no need for you to say that all the virtues are weakly at the beginning, that firmness and strength are added by time. I am well aware also

the deepest affection. His premature death in A.D. 63 is the subject of a touching tribute in *Epistles*, lxiii. 14-16. *Cf.* Vol. I. Introd. p. xii.

laborant, dignitatem dico et eloquentiae famam et quicquid ad alienum suffragium venit, mora convalescere—et quae veras vires parant et quae ad placendum fuco quodam subornant,[1] expectant annos, donec paulatim colorem diuturnitas ducat—, sed ego vereor, ne consuetudo, quae rebus adfert constantiam, hoc vitium mihi altius figat. Tam malorum quam bonorum longa conversatio amorem induit.

4 Haec animi inter utrumque dubii nec ad recta fortiter nec ad prava vergentis infirmitas qualis sit, non tam semel tibi possum quam per partes ostendere ; dicam quae accidant mihi : tu morbo 5 nomen invenies. Tenet me summus amor parsimoniae, fateor ; placet non in ambitionem cubile compositum, non ex arcula prolata vestis, non ponderibus ac mille tormentis splendere cogentibus expressa, sed domestica et vilis, nec servata nec 6 sumenda sollicite ; placet cibus, quem nec parent familiae nec spectent, non ante multos imperatus dies nec multorum manibus ministratus, sed parabilis facilisque, nihil habens arcessiti pretiosive, ubilibet non defuturus, nec patrimonio nec corpori gravis, non 7 rediturus qua intraverit ; placet minister incultus et rudis vernula, argentum grave rustici patris sine ullo nomine artificis, et mensa non varietate macu-

---

[1] subornant *Gertz* : subornantur *A*.

that the virtues that struggle for outward show, I
mean for position and the fame of eloquence and all
that comes under the verdict of others, do grow
stronger as time passes—both those that provide real
strength and those that trick us out with a sort of
dye with a view to pleasing, must wait long years
until gradually length of time develops colour—but
I greatly fear that habit, which brings stability to
most things, may cause this fault of mine to become
more deeply implanted. Of things evil as well as
good long intercourse induces love.

The nature of this weakness of mind that halts
between two things and inclines strongly neither to
the right nor to the wrong, I cannot show you so
well all at once as a part at a time; I shall tell you
what befalls me—you will find a name for my malady.
I am possessed by the very greatest love of frugality,
I must confess; I do not like a couch made up
for display, nor clothing brought forth from a chest
or pressed by weights and a thousand mangles to
make it glossy, but homely and cheap, that is
neither preserved nor to be put on with anxious
care; the food that I like is neither prepared nor
watched by a household of slaves, it does not need to
be ordered many days before nor to be served by
many hands, but is easy to get and abundant; there
is nothing far-fetched or costly about it, nowhere will
there be any lack of it, it is burdensome neither to
the purse nor to the body, nor will it return by the
way it entered; the servant that I like is a young
home-born slave without training or skill; the silver
is my country-bred father's heavy plate bearing no
stamp of the maker's name, and the table is not
notable for the variety of its markings or known to

larum conspicua nec per multas dominorum ele-
gantium successiones civitati nota, sed in usum posita,
quae nullius convivae oculos nec voluptate moretur
8 nec accendat invidia. Cum bene ista placuerunt,
praestringit animum apparatus alicuius paedagogii,
diligentius quam in tralatu vestita et auro culta
mancipia et agmen servorum nitentium ; iam domus
etiam qua calcatur pretiosa et divitiis per omnes
angulos dissipatis tecta ipsa fulgentia et adsectator
comesque patrimoniorum pereuntium populus. Quid
perlucentis ad imum aquas et circumfluentes ipsa
convivia, quid epulas loquar scaena sua dignas ?
9 Circumfudit me ex longo frugalitatis situ venientem
multo splendore luxuria et undique circumsonuit.
Paulum titubat acies, facilius adversus illam animum
quam oculos attollo. Recedo itaque non peior, sed
tristior, nec inter illa frivola mea tam altus incedo
tacitusque morsus subit et dubitatio, numquid illa
meliora sint. Nihil horum me mutat, nihil tamen
non concutit.

10 Placet imperia praeceptorum[1] sequi et in mediam
ire rem publicam ; placet honores fascisque non
scilicet purpura aut virgis abductum capessere, sed
ut amicis propinquisque et omnibus civibus, omnibus
deinde mortalibus paratior utiliorque sim. Promptus,

---

[1] imperia praeceptorum *Gertz* : inpreceptorum *A.*

the town from the many fashionable owners through whose hands it has passed, but one that stands for use, and will neither cause the eyes of any guest to linger upon it with pleasure nor fire them with envy. Then, after all these things have had my full approval, my mind is dazzled by the magnificence of some training-school for pages, by the sight of slaves bedecked with gold and more carefully arrayed than the leaders of a public procession, and a whole regiment of glittering attendants ; by the sight of a house where one even treads on precious stones and riches are scattered about in every corner, where the very roofs glitter, and the whole town pays court and escorts an inheritance on the road to ruin. And what shall I say of the waters, transparent to the bottom, that flow around the guests even as they banquet, what of the feasts that are worthy of their setting ? Coming from a long abandonment to thrift, luxury has poured around me the wealth of its splendour, and echoed around me on every side. My sight falters a little, for I can lift up my heart towards it more easily than my eyes. And so I come back, not worse, but sadder, and I do not walk among my paltry possessions with head erect as before, and there enters a secret sting and the doubt whether the other life is not better. None of these things changes me, yet none of them fails to disturb me.

I resolve to obey the commands of my teachers and plunge into the midst of public life ; I resolve to try to gain office and the consulship, attracted of course, not by the purple or by the lictor's rods, but by the desire to be more serviceable and useful to my friends and relatives and all my countrymen and then to all mankind. Ready and determined, I follow

compositus sequor Zenona, Cleanthen, Chrysippum, quorum tamen nemo ad rem publicam accessit, et
11 nemo non misit. Ubi aliquid animum insolitum arietari percussit, ubi aliquid occurrit aut indignum, ut in omni vita humana multa sunt, aut parum ex facili fluens, aut multum temporis res non magno aestimandae poposcerunt, ad otium convertor et, quemadmodum pecoribus fatigatis quoque, velocior domum gradus est. Placet intra parietes suos vitam coercere : " Nemo ullum auferat diem nihil dignum tanto impendio redditurus ; sibi ipse animus haereat, se colat, nihil alieni agat, nihil quod ad iudicem spectet ; ametur expers publicae privataeque curae
12 tranquillitas." Sed ubi lectio fortior erexit animum et aculeos subdiderunt exempla nobilia, prosilire libet in forum, commodare alteri vocem, alteri operam, etiam si nihil profuturam, tamen conaturam prodesse, alicuius coercere in foro superbiam male secundis rebus elati.
13 In studiis puto me hercules melius esse res ipsas intueri et harum causa loqui, ceterum verba rebus permittere, ut qua duxerint, hac inelaborata sequatur oratio : " Quid opus est saeculis duratura componere? Vis tu non id agere, ne te posteri taceant ? Morti natus es, minus molestiarum habet funus tacitum !

---

^a Cf. De Otio, 3. 2.
^b i.e., that needs the approval of another.

Zeno,[a] Cleanthes, and Chrysippus, of whom none the less not one entered upon public life, and not one failed to urge others to do so. And then, whenever something upsets my mind, which is unused to meeting shocks, whenever something happens that is either unworthy of me, and many such occur in the lives of all human beings, or that does not proceed very easily, or when things that are not to be accounted of great value demand much of my time, I turn back to my leisure, and just as wearied flocks too do, I quicken my pace towards home. I resolve to confine my life within its own walls : " Let no one," I say, " who will make me no worthy return for such a loss rob me of a single day ; let my mind be fixed upon itself, let it cultivate itself, let it busy itself with nothing outside, nothing that looks towards an umpire [b] ; let it love the tranquillity that is remote from public and private concern." But when my mind has been aroused by reading of great bravery, and noble examples have applied the spur, I want to rush into the forum, to lend my voice to one man ; to offer such assistance to another as, even if it will not help, will be an effort to help ; or to check the pride of someone in the forum who has been unfortunately puffed up by his successes.

And in my literary studies I think that it is surely better to fix my eyes on the theme itself, and, keeping this uppermost when I speak, to trust meanwhile to the theme to supply the words so that unstudied language may follow it wherever it leads. I say : " What need is there to compose something that will last for centuries ? Will you not give up striving to keep posterity from being silent about you ? You were born for death ; a silent funeral is less troublesome !

Itaque occupandi temporis causa, in usum tuum, non
in praeconium aliquid simplici stilo scribe ; minore
14 labore opus est studentibus in diem." Rursus ubi
se animus cogitationum magnitudine levavit, am-
bitiosus in verba est altiusque ut spirare ita eloqui
gestit et ad dignitatem rerum exit oratio ; oblitus
tum legis pressiorisque iudicii sublimius feror et ore
iam non meo.

15 Ne singula diutius persequar, in omnibus rebus
haec me sequitur bonae mentis infirmitas. Quin ne[1]
paulatim defluam vereor, aut quod est sollicitius,
ne semper casuro similis pendeam et plus[2] fortasse
sit quam quod ipse pervideo ; familiariter enim
domestica aspicimus et semper iudicio favor officit.
16 Puto multos potuisse ad sapientiam pervenire, nisi
putassent se pervenisse, nisi quaedam in se dis-
simulassent, quaedam opertis oculis transiluissent.
Non est enim, quod magis aliena iudices adulatione
nos perire quam nostra. Quis sibi verum dicere
ausus est ? Quis non inter laudantium blandien-
tiumque positus greges plurimum tamen sibi ipse
17 adsentatus est ? Rogo itaque, si quod habes remedium, quo hanc fluctuationem meam sistas,
dignum me putes qui tibi tranquillitatem debeam.
Non esse periculosos hos[3] motus animi nec quicquam
tumultuosi adferentis scio ; ut vera tibi similitudine

---

[1] quin ne *Lipsius* : cuine *A* : sic ne *Gertz.*
[2] plus *A* : peius *Gertz.*
[3] hos *added by Koch.*

And so to pass the time, write something in simple style, for your own use, not for publication ; they that study for the day have less need to labour." Then again, when my mind has been uplifted by the greatness of its thoughts, it becomes ambitious of words, and with higher aspirations it desires higher expression, and language issues forth to match the dignity of the theme ; forgetful then of my rule and of my more restrained judgement, I am swept to loftier heights by an utterance that is no longer my own.

Not to indulge longer in details, I am in all things attended by this weakness of good intention. In fact I fear that I am gradually losing ground, or, what causes me even more worry, that I am hanging like one who is always on the verge of falling, and that perhaps I am in a more serious condition than I myself perceive ; for we take a favourable view of our private matters, and partiality always hampers our judgement. I fancy that many men would have arrived at wisdom if they had not fancied that they had already arrived, if they had not dissembled about certain traits in their character and passed by others with their eyes shut. For there is no reason for you to suppose that the adulation of other people is more ruinous to us than our own. Who dares to tell himself the truth ? Who, though he is surrounded by a horde of applauding sycophants, is not for all that his own greatest flatterer ? I beg you, therefore, if you have any remedy by which you could stop this fluctuation of mine, to deem me worthy of being indebted to you for tranquillity. I know that these mental disturbances of mine are not dangerous and give no promise of a storm ; to express what I complain of in apt

id, de quo queror, exprimam, non tempestate vexor
sed nausea. Detrahe ergo quicquid hoc est mali et
succurre in conspectu terrarum laboranti.

1 2. SENECA[1] : Quaero me hercules iam dudum,
Serene, ipse tacitus, cui talem adfectum animi
similem putem, nec ulli propius admoverim exemplo
quam eorum, qui ex longa et gravi valetudine expliciti
motiunculis levibusque interim offensis perstringun-
tur et, cum reliquias effugerunt, suspicionibus tamen
inquietantur medicisque iam sani manum porrigunt
et omnem calorem corporis sui calumniantur. Horum,
Serene, non parum sanum est corpus, sed sanitati
parum adsuevit; sicut est quidam tremor etiam
tranquilli maris, utique cum ex tempestate requievit.
2 Opus est itaque non illis durioribus, quae iam trans-
cucurrimus, ut alicubi obstes tibi, alicubi irascaris,
alicubi instes gravis, sed illo, quod ultimum venit,
ut fidem tibi habeas et recta ire te via credas, nihil
avocatus transversis multorum vestigiis passim
discurrentium, quorundam circa ipsam errantium
3 viam. Quod desideras autem magnum et summum
est deoque vicinum, non concuti.

Hanc stabilem animi sedem Graeci euthymian
vocant, de qua Democriti volumen egregium est;
ego tranquillitatem voco. Nec enim imitari et

---

[1] Seneca *added by Haase.*

metaphor, I am distressed,' not by a tempest, but by sea-sickness. Do you, then, take from me this trouble, whatever it be, and rush to the rescue of one who is struggling in full sight of land.

SENECA : In truth, Serenus, I have for a long time been silently asking myself to what I should liken such a condition of mind, and I can find nothing that so closely approaches it as the state of those who, after being released from a long and serious illness, are sometimes touched with fits of fever and slight disorders, and, freed from the last traces of them, are nevertheless disquieted with mistrust, and, though now quite well, stretch out their wrist to a physician and complain unjustly of any trace of heat in their body. It is not, Serenus, that these are not quite well in body, but that they are not quite used to being well ; just as even a tranquil sea will show some ripple, particularly when it has just subsided after a storm. What you need, therefore, is not any of those harsher measures which we have already left behind, the necessity of opposing yourself at this point, of being angry with yourself at that, of sternly urging yourself on at another, but that which comes last— confidence in yourself and the belief that you are on the right path, and have not been led astray by the many cross-tracks of those who are roaming in every direction, some of whom are wandering very near the path itself. But what you desire is something great and supreme and very near to being a god—to be unshaken.

This abiding stability of mind the Greeks call *euthymia*, " well-being of the soul," on which there is an excellent treatise by Democritus ; I call it tranquillity. For there is no need to imitate and repro-

transferre verba ad illorum formam necesse est ;
res ipsa, de qua agitur, aliquo signanda nomine est,
quod appellationis Graecae vim debet habere, non
4 faciem. Ergo quaerimus, quomodo animus semper
aequali secundoque cursu eat propitiusque sibi sit
et sua laetus aspiciat et hoc gaudium non inter-
rumpat, sed placido statu maneat nec adtollens se
umquam nec deprimens. Id tranquillitas erit. Quomodo ad hanc perveniri possit, in universum quaeramus ; sumes tu ex publico remedio quantum voles.
5 Totum interim vitium in medium protrahendum est,
ex quo agnoscet quisque partem suam ; simul tu
intelleges, quanto minus negotii habeas cum fastidio
tui quam ii, quos ad professionem speciosam alligatos
et sub ingenti titulo laborantis in sua simulatione
pudor magis quam voluntas tenet.
6   Omnes in eadem causa sunt, et hi qui levitate
vexantur ac taedio adsiduaque mutatione propositi,
quibus semper magis placet quod reliquerunt, et illi,
qui marcent et oscitantur. Adice eos, qui non aliter
quam quibus difficilis somnus est versant se et hoc
atque illo modo componunt, donec quietem lassitudine inveniant. Statum vitae suae reformando[1]
subinde in eo novissime manent, in quo illos non
mutandi odium sed senectus ad novandum pigra
deprendit. Adice et illos, qui non constantiae vitio
parum leves sunt sed inertiae, et vivunt non quo-
7 modo volunt, sed quomodo coeperunt. Innumerabiles

[1] reformando *Koch* : formando *A.*

duce words in their Greek shape ; the thing itself, which is under discussion, must be designated by some name which ought to have, not the form, but the force, of the Greek term. What we are seeking, therefore, is how the mind may always pursue a steady and favourable course, may be well-disposed towards itself, and may view its condition with joy, and suffer no interruption of this joy, but may abide in a peaceful state, being never uplifted nor ever cast down. This will be " tranquillity." Let us seek in a general way how it may be obtained ; then from the universal remedy *you* will appropriate as much as you like. Meanwhile we must drag forth into the light the whole of the infirmity, and each one will then recognize his own share of it ; at the same time you will understand how much less trouble *you* have with your self-depreciation than those who, fettered to some showy declaration and struggling beneath the burden of some grand title, are held more by shame than by desire to the pretence they are making.

All are in the same case, both those, on the one hand, who are plagued with fickleness and boredom and a continual shifting of purpose, and those, on the other, who loll and yawn. Add also those who, just like the wretches who find it hard to sleep, change their position and settle first in one way and then in another, until finally they find rest through weariness. By repeatedly altering the condition of their life they are at last left in that in which, not the dislike of making a change, but old age, that shrinks from novelty, has caught them. And add also those who by fault, not of firmness of character, but of inertia, are not fickle enough, and live, not as they wish, but as they have begun. The characteristics of the malady

deinceps proprietates sunt sed unus effectus vitii,
sibi displicere. Hoc oritur ab intemperie animi et
cupiditatibus timidis aut parum prosperis, ubi aut
non audent, quantum concupiscunt, aut non con-
sequuntur et in spem toti prominent; semper in-
stabiles mobilesque sunt, quod necesse est accidere
pendentibus. Ad vota sua omni via tendunt et inhonesta se ac difficilia docent coguntque, et ubi sine
praemio labor est, torquet illos irritum dedecus, nec
8 dolent prava se sed[1] frustra voluisse. Tunc illos et
paenitentia coepti tenet et incipiendi timor subrepit-
que illa animi iactatio non invenientis exitum, quia
nec imperare cupiditatibus suis nec obsequi possunt,
et cunctatio vitae parum se explicantis et inter
9 destituta vota torpentis animi situs. Quae omnia
graviora sunt, ubi odio infelicitatis operosae ad otium
perfugerunt, ad secreta studia, quae pati non potest
animus ad civilia erectus agendique cupidus et natura
inquies, parum scilicet in se solaciorum habens; ideo
detractis oblectationibus, quas ipsae occupationes dis-
currentibus praebent, domum, solitudinem, parietes
non fert, invitus aspicit se sibi relictum.

10 Hinc illud est taedium et displicentia sui et nusquam residentis animi volutatio et otii sui tristis

---

[1] sed *added by Haase.*

are countless in number, but it has only one effect—
to be dissatisfied with oneself. This springs from
a lack of mental poise and from timid or unfulfilled
desires, when men either do not dare, or do not
attain, as much as they desire, and become entirely
dependent upon hope; such men are always unstable
and changeable, as must necessarily be the fate of
those who live in suspense. They strive to attain their
prayers by every means, they teach and force themselves to do dishonourable and difficult things, and,
when their effort is without reward, they are tortured
by the fruitless disgrace and grieve, not because they
wished for what was wrong, but because they wished
in vain. Then regret for what they have begun lays
hold upon them, and the fear of beginning again,
and then creeps in the agitation of a mind which can
find no issue, because they can neither rule nor obey
their desires, and the hesitancy of a life which fails
to find its way clear, and then the dullness of a soul
that lies torpid amid abandoned hopes. And all these
tendencies are aggravated when from hatred of
their laborious ill-success men have taken refuge in
leisure and in solitary studies, which are unendurable
to a mind that is intent upon public affairs, desirous
of action, and naturally restless, because assuredly it
has too few resources within itself; when, therefore,
the pleasures have been withdrawn which business
itself affords to those who are busily engaged, the
mind cannot endure home, solitude, and the walls
of a room, and sees with dislike that it has been left
to itself.

From this comes that boredom and dissatisfaction
and the vacillation of a mind that nowhere finds rest,
and the sad and languid endurance of one's leisure;

atque aegra patientia ; utique ubi causas fateri pudet et tormenta introsus egit verecundia, in angusto inclusae cupiditates sine exitu se ipsae strangulant. Inde maeror marcorque et mille fluctus mentis incertae, quam spes inchoatae suspensam habent, deploratae tristem ; inde ille adfectus otium suum detestantium querentiumque nihil ipsos habere, quod agant et alienis incrementis inimicissima invidia. Alit enim livorem infelix inertia et omnes destrui 11 cupiunt, quia se non potuere provehere ; ex hac deinde aversatione alienorum processuum et suorum desperatione obirascens fortunae animus et de saeculo querens et in angulos se retrahens et poenae incubans suae, dum illum taedet sui pigetque. Natura enim humanus animus agilis est et pronus ad motus. Grata omnis illi excitandi se abstrahendique materia est, gratior pessimis quibusque ingeniis, quae occupationibus libenter deteruntur. Ut ulcera quaedam nocituras manus adpetunt et tactu gaudent, et foedam 12 corporum scabiem delectat quicquid exasperat, non aliter dixerim his mentibus, in quas[1] cupiditates velut mala ulcera eruperunt, voluptati esse laborem vexationemque. Sunt enim quaedam, quae corpus quoque nostrum cum quodam dolore delectent, ut versare se et mutare nondum fessum latus, et alio atque alio positu ventilari. Qualis ille Homericus Achilles est, modo pronus, modo supinus, in varios habitus se ipse

---

[1] in quas *A* : in quis *Lipsius.*

especially when one is ashamed to confess the real causes of this condition and bashfulness drives its tortures inward; the desires pent up within narrow bounds, from which there is no escape, strangle one another. Thence comes mourning and melancholy and the thousand waverings of an unsettled mind, which its aspirations hold in suspense and then disappointment renders melancholy. Thence comes that feeling which makes men loathe their own leisure and complain that they themselves have nothing to be busy with; thence too the bitterest jealousy of the advancements of others. For their unhappy sloth fosters envy, and, because they could not succeed themselves, they wish every one else to be ruined; then from this aversion to the progress of others and despair of their own their mind becomes incensed against Fortune, and complains of the times, and retreats into corners and broods over its trouble until it becomes weary and sick of itself. For it is the nature of the human mind to be active and prone to movement. Welcome to it is every opportunity for excitement and distraction, and still more welcome to all those worst natures which willingly wear themselves out in being employed. Just as there are some sores which crave the hands that will hurt them and rejoice to be touched, and as a foul itch of the body delights in whatever scratches, exactly so, I would say, do these minds upon which, so to speak, desires have broken out like wicked sores find pleasure in toil and vexation. For there are certain things that delight our body also while causing it a sort of pain, as turning over and changing a side that is not yet tired and taking one position after another to get cool. Homer's hero Achilles is like that—lying now on his face, now

componens, quod proprium aegri est, nihil diu pati
et mutationibus ut remediis uti.

13 Inde peregrinationes suscipiuntur vagae et invia
litora[1] pererrantur et modo mari se modo terra ex-
peritur semper praesentibus infesta levitas. " Nunc
Campaniam petamus." Iam delicata fastidio sunt :
" Inculta videantur, Bruttios et Lucaniae saltus
persequamur." Aliquid tamen inter deserta amoeni
requiritur, in quo luxuriosi oculi longo locorum
horrentium squalore releventur : " Tarentum petatur
laudatusque portus et hiberna caeli mitioris et regio
vel antiquae satis opulenta turbae." Nimis diu a
plausu et fragore aures vacaverunt, iuvat iam et
humano sanguine frui : " Iam flectamus cursum
14 ad urbem."[2] Aliud ex alio iter suscipitur et spectacula spectaculis mutantur. Ut ait Lucretius :

> Hoc se quisque modo semper fugit.

Sed quid prodest, si non effugit ? Sequitur se ipse
15 et urget gravissimus comes. Itaque scire debemus
non locorum vitium esse quo laboramus, sed nostrum ;
infirmi sumus ad omne tolerandum, nec laboris
patientes nec voluptatis nec nostri nec ullius rei
diutius. Hoc quosdam egit ad mortem, quod pro-
posita saepe mutando in eadem revolvebantur et non

---

[1] invia litora *Castiglioni* : et inlitora *A* : et aliena litora
Joh. Müller.
[2] iam flectamus cursum ad urbem *transferred by Hermes*
(*after Gertz*) *from a position after* turbae.

---

[a] A reference to Homer's picture of the restlessness of
Achilles grieving for his friend Patroclus (*Iliad*, xxiv. 9 *sqq.*):

> Τῶν μιμνησκόμενος θαλερὸν κατὰ δάκρυον εἶβεν,
> ἄλλοτ' ἐπὶ πλευρὰς κατακείμενος, ἄλλοτε δ' αὖτε
> ὕπτιος, ἄλλοτε δὲ πρηνής.

[b] *De Rerum Natura*, iii. 1068.

on his back,[a] placing himself in various attitudes, and, just as sick men do, enduring nothing very long and using changes as remedies.

Hence men undertake wide-ranging travel, and wander over remote shores, and their fickleness, always discontented with the present, gives proof of itself now on land and now on sea. " Now let us head for Campania," they say. And now when soft living palls, " Let us see the wild parts," they say, " let us hunt out the passes of Bruttium and Lucania." And yet amid that wilderness something is missing— something pleasant wherein their pampered eyes may find relief from the lasting squalor of those rugged regions : " Let us head for Tarentum with its famous harbour and its mild winter climate, and a territory rich enough to have a horde of people even in antiquity." Too long have their ears missed the shouts and the din ; it delights them by now even to enjoy human blood : " Let us now turn our course toward the city." They undertake one journey after another and change spectacle for spectacle. As Lucretius says [b] :

Thus ever from himself doth each man flee.

But what does he gain if he does not escape from himself ? He ever follows himself and weighs upon himself as his own most burdensome companion. And so we ought to understand that what we struggle with is the fault, not of the places, but of ourselves ; when there is need of endurance, we are weak, and we cannot bear toil or pleasure or ourselves or anything very long. It is this that has driven some men to death, because by often altering their purpose they were always brought back to the same things

reliquerant novitati locum. Fastidio esse illis coepit
vita et ipse mundus, et subît illud tabidarum de-
liciarum : " Quousque eadem ? "

1   3. Adversus hoc taedium quo auxilio putem
utendum quaeris. Optimum erat, ut ait Athenodorus, actione rerum et rei publicae tractatione et
officiis civilibus se detinere. Nam ut quidam sole
atque exercitatione et cura corporis diem educunt
athletisque longe utilissimum est lacertos suos
roburque, cui se uni dicaverunt, maiore temporis
parte nutrire, ita vobis animum ad rerum civilium
certamen parantibus in opere esse uno[1] longe pulcherrimum est. Nam cum utilem se efficere civibus
mortalibusque propositum habeat, simul et exercetur
et proficit, qui in mediis se officiis posuit communia
2 privataque pro facultate administrans. " Sed quia
in hac," inquit, " tam insana hominum ambitione
tot calumniatoribus in deterius recta torquentibus
parum tuta simplicitas est et plus futurum semper
est quod obstet quam quod succedat, a foro quidem
et publico recedendum est, sed habet ubi se etiam in
privato laxe explicet magnus animus ; nec ut leonum
animaliumque impetus caveis coercetur, sic hominum,
3 quorum maximae in seducto actiones sunt. Ita
tamen delituerit, ut ubicumque otium suum abs-

----

[1] uno *Stangl* : non *A* : nostro *Gertz*.

----

[a] Not to be certainly identified, but probably the Stoic
philosopher of Tarsus who visited Rome as the friend of the
younger Cato.

and had left themselves no room for anything new. They began to be sick of life and the world itself, and from the self-indulgences that wasted them was born the thought : " How long shall I endure the same things ? "

You ask what help, in my opinion, should be employed to overcome this tedium. The best course would be, as Athenodorus [a] says, to occupy oneself with practical matters, the management of public affairs, and the duties of a citizen. For as some men pass the day in seeking the sun and in exercise and care of the body, and as athletes find it is most profitable by far to devote the greater part of the day to the development of their muscles and the strength to which alone they have dedicated themselves ; so for you, who are training your mind for the struggle of political life, by far the most desirable thing is to be busy at one task. For, whenever a man has the set purpose to make himself useful to his countrymen and all mortals, he both gets practice and does service at the same time when he has placed himself in the very midst of active duties, serving to the best of his ability the interests both of the public and of the individual. " But because," he continues, " in this mad world of ambition where chicanery so frequently twists right into wrong, simplicity is hardly safe, and is always sure to meet with more that hinders than helps it, we ought indeed to withdraw from the forum and public life, but a great mind has an opportunity to display itself freely even in private life ; nor, just as the activity of lions and animals is restrained by their dens, is it so of man's, whose greatest achievements are wrought in retirement. Let a man, however, hide himself away bearing in mind that,

223

conderit, prodesse velit singulis universisque ingenio, voce, consilio. Nec enim is solus rei publicae prodest, qui candidatos extrahit et tuetur reos et de pace belloque censet, sed qui iuventutem exhortatur, qui in tanta bonorum praeceptorum inopia virtutem instillat[1] animis, qui ad pecuniam luxuriamque cursu ruentis prensat ac retrahit et, si nihil aliud, certe
4 moratur, in privato publicum negotium agit. An ille plus praestat, qui inter peregrinos et cives aut urbanus praetor adeuntibus adsessoris verba pronuntiat, quam qui quid sit iustitia, quid pietas, quid patientia, quid fortitudo, quid mortis contemptus, quid deorum intellectus, quam tutum gratuitumque bonum[2] sit
5 bona conscientia? Ergo si tempus in studia conferas, quod subduxeris officiis, non deserueris nec munus detrectaveris. Neque enim ille solus militat, qui in acie stat et cornu dextrum laevumque defendit, sed et[3] qui portas tuetur et statione minus periculosa, non otiosa tamen fungitur vigiliasque servat et armamentario praeest; quae ministeria, quamvis incruenta sint, in numerum stipendiorum veniunt.
6 Si te ad studia revocaveris, omne vitae fastidium effugeris nec noctem fieri optabis taedio lucis, nec tibi gravis eris nec aliis supervacuus; multos in amicitiam adtrahes adfluetque ad te optumus quisque.

---

[1] instillat *Haase* : instituat *A* : insinuat *Petschenig.*
[2] quam tutum gratuitumque bonum *Joh. Müller* : quantum gratuitorum hominum *A.*
[3] et *commonly added.*

---

[a] The *praetor peregrinus* presided over civil suits in which one party or both were foreigners; the *praetor urbanus*, over those in which citizens only were concerned. In the condensed form of the Latin allusion is made to both offices.

wherever he secretes his leisure, he should be willing
to benefit the individual man and mankind by his
intellect, his voice, and his counsel. For the man that
does good service to the state is not merely he who
brings forward candidates and defends the accused
and votes for peace and war, but he also who ad-
monishes young men, who instils virtue into their
minds, supplying the great lack of good teachers,
who lays hold upon those that are rushing wildly in
pursuit of money and luxury, and draws them back,
and, if he accomplishes nothing else, at least retards
them—such a man performs a public service even in
private life. Or does he accomplish more who in the
office of praetor,ᵃ whether in cases between citizens
and foreigners or in cases between citizens, delivers
to suitors the verdict his assistant has formulated,
than he who teaches the meaning of justice, of piety,
of endurance, of bravery, of contempt of death, of
knowledge of the gods, and how secure and free is
the blessing of a good conscience? If, then, the time
that you have stolen from public duties is bestowed
upon studies, you will neither have deserted, nor
refused, your office. For a soldier is not merely one
who stands in line and defends the right or the left
wing, but he also who guards the gates and fills,
not an idle, but a less dangerous, post, who keeps
watch at night and has charge of the armoury;
these offices, though they are bloodless, yet count as
military service. If you devote yourself to studies,
you will have escaped all your disgust at life, you will
not long for night to come because you are weary
of the light, nor will you be either burdensome
to yourself or useless to others; you will attract
many to friendship and those that gather about you

Numquam enim quamvis obscura virtus latet, sed mittit sui signa; quisquis dignus fuerit, vestigiis 7 illam colliget. Nam si omnem conversationem tollimus et generi humano renuntiamus vivimusque in nos tantum conversi, sequetur hanc solitudinem omni studio carentem inopia rerum agendarum. Incipiemus aedificia alia ponere, alia subvertere et mare summovere et aquas contra difficultatem locorum educere et male dispensare tempus, quod nobis natura 8 consumendum dedit. Alii parce illo utimur, alii prodige; alii sic impendimus, ut possimus rationem reddere, alii, ut nullas habeamus reliquias, qua re nihil turpius est. Saepe grandis natu senex nullum aliud habet argumentum, quo se probet diu vixisse, praeter aetatem."

1   4. Mihi, carissime Serene, nimis videtur summisisse temporibus se Athenodorus, nimis cito refugisse. Nec ego negaverim aliquando cedendum, sed sensim relato gradu et salvis signis, salva militari dignitate; sanctiores tutioresque sunt hostibus suis, qui in fidem cum armis veniunt. Hoc puto virtuti 2 faciendum studiosoque virtutis. Si praevalebit fortuna et praecidet agendi facultatem, non statim aversus inermisque fugiat latebras quaerens, quasi ullus locus sit, quo non possit fortuna persequi, sed parcius se inferat officiis et cum dilectu inveniat

will be the most excellent. For virtue, though obscured, is never concealed, but always gives signs of its presence ; whoever is worthy will trace her out by her footsteps. But if we give up society altogether and, turning our backs upon the human race, live with our thoughts fixed only upon ourselves, this solitude deprived of every interest will be followed by a want of something to be accomplished. We shall begin to put up some buildings, to pull down others, to thrust back the sea, to cause waters to flow despite the obstacles of nature, and shall make ill disposition of the time which Nature has given us to be used. Some use it sparingly, others wastefully ; some of us spend it in such a way that we are able to give an account of it, others in such a way—and nothing can be more shameful—that we have no balance left. Often a man who is very old in years has no evidence to prove that he has lived a long time other than his age."

To me, my dearest Serenus, Athenodorus seems to have surrendered too quickly to the times, to have retreated too quickly. I myself would not deny that sometimes one must retire, but it should be a gradual retreat without surrendering the standards, without surrendering the honour of a soldier ; those are more respected by their enemies and safer who come to terms with their arms in their hands. This is what I think Virtue and Virtue's devotee should do. If Fortune shall get the upper hand and shall cut off the opportunity for action, let a man not straightway turn his back and flee, throwing away his arms and seeking some hiding-place, as if there were anywhere a place where Fortune could not reach him, but let him devote himself to his duties more sparingly, and, after

3 aliquid, in quo utilis civitati sit. Militare non licet?
Honores petat. Privato vivendum est? Sit orator.
Silentium indictum est? Tacita advocatione cives
iuvet. Periculosum etiam ingressu forum est? In
domibus, in spectaculis, in conviviis bonum con-
tubernalem, fidelem amicum, temperantem convivam
4 agat. Officia civis amisit? Hominis exerceat.
Ideo magno animo nos non unius urbis moenibus
clusimus, sed in totius orbis commercium emisimus
patriamque nobis mundum professi sumus, ut liceret
latiorem virtuti campum dare. Praeclusum tibi
tribunal est et rostris prohiberis aut comitiis?
Respice post te quantum latissimarum regionum
pateat, quantum populorum; numquam ita tibi
magna pars obstruetur, ut non maior relinquatur.
5 Sed vide, ne totum istud tuum vitium sit; non vis
enim nisi consul aut prytanis aut ceryx aut sufes
administrare rem publicam. Quid si militare nolis
nisi imperator aut tribunus? Etiam si alii primam
frontem tenebunt, te sors inter triarios posuerit, inde
voce, adhortatione, exemplo, animo milita; prae-
cisis quoque manibus ille in proelio invenit, quod
partibus conferat, qui stat tamen et clamore iuvat.
6 Tale quiddam facias. Si a prima te rei publicae parte
fortuna summoverit, stes tamen et clamore iuves et,

---

* The highest official in various Greek free states.
  b A Carthaginian high magistrate.

making choice, let him find something in which he may be useful to the state. Is he not permitted to be a soldier? Let him seek public office. Must he live in a private station? Let him be a pleader. Is he condemned to silence? Let him help his countrymen by his silent support. Is it dangerous even to enter the forum? In private houses, at the public spectacles, at feasts let him show himself a good comrade, a faithful friend, a temperate feaster. Has he lost the duties of a citizen? Let him exercise those of a man. The very reason for our magnanimity in not shutting ourselves up within the walls of one city, in going forth into intercourse with the whole earth, and in claiming the world as our country, was that we might have a wider field for our virtue. Is the tribunal closed to you, and are you barred from the rostrum and the hustings? Look how many broad stretching countries lie open behind you, how many peoples; never can you be blocked from any part so large that a still larger will not be left to you. But take care that this is not wholly your own fault; you are not willing to serve the state except as a consul or prytanis [a] or herald or sufete.[b] What if you should be unwilling to serve in the army except as a general or a tribune? Even if others shall hold the front line and your lot has placed you among those of the third line, from there where you are do service with your voice, encouragement, example, and spirit; even though a man's hands are cut off, he finds that he can do something for his side in battle if he stands his ground and helps with the shouting. Some such thing is what you should do. If Fortune has removed you from the foremost position in the state, you should, nevertheless, stand your ground

si quis fauces oppresserit, stes tamen et silentio iuves. Numquam inutilis est opera civis boni ; auditus visusque, voltu, nutu, obstinatione tacita 7 incessuque ipso prodest. Ut salutaria quaedam,[1] quae citra gustum tactumque odore proficiunt, ita virtus utilitatem etiam ex longinquo et latens fundit. Sive spatiatur et se utitur suo iure, sive precarios habet excessus cogiturque vela contrahere, sive otiosa mutaque est et in[2] angusto circumsaepta, sive adaperta, in quocumque habitu est, proficit. Quid tu parum utile putas exemplum bene quiescentis ? 8 Longe itaque optimum est miscere otium rebus, quotiens actuosa vita impedimentis fortuitis aut civitatis condicione prohibebitur ; numquam enim usque eo interclusa sunt omnia, ut nulli actioni locus honestae sit.

1 5. Numquid potes invenire urbem miseriorem quam Atheniensium fuit, cum illam triginta tyranni divellerent ? Mille trecentos cives, optimum quemque occiderant nec finem ideo faciebant, sed irritabat se ipsa saevitia. In qua civitate erat Areos pagos, religiosissimum iudicium, in qua senatus populusque senatu similis, coibat cotidie carnificum triste collegium et infelix curia tyrannis angustabatur[3] ! Poteratne illa civitas conquiescere, in qua tot tyranni

---

[1] quaedam *added by P. Thomas.*   [2] in *added by P. Thomas.*
[3] angustabatur *Gertz* : angusta *A.*

---

[a] *i.e.,* by the crowd of men, since every " hanger-on " was a tyrant.

and help with the shouting, and if someone stops your throat, you should, nevertheless, stand your ground and help in silence. The service of a good citizen is never useless ; by being heard and seen, by his expression, by his gesture, by his silent stubbornness, and by his very walk he helps. As there are certain salutary things that without our tasting and touching them benefit us by their mere odour, so virtue sheds her advantage even from a distance, and in hiding. Whether she walks abroad and of her own right makes herself active, or has her appearances on sufferance and is forced to draw in her sails, or is inactive and mute and pent within narrow bounds, or is openly displayed, no matter what her condition is, she always does good. Why, then, do *you* think that the example of one who lives in honourable retirement is of little value ? Accordingly, the best course by far is to combine leisure with business, whenever chance obstacles or the condition of the state shall prevent one's living a really active life ; for a man is never so completely shut off from all pursuits that no opportunity is left for any honourable activity.

Can you find any city more wretched than was that of the Athenians when it was being torn to pieces by the Thirty Tyrants ? They had slain thirteen hundred citizens, all the best men, and were not for that reason ready to stop, but their very cruelty fed its own flame. In the city in which there was the Areopagus, a most god-fearing court, in which there was a senate and a popular assembly that was like a senate, there gathered together every day a sorry college of hangmen, and the unhappy senate-house was made too narrow by tyrants [a] ! Could that city ever find peace in which there were as many tyrants

231

erant quot satellites[1] essent ? Ne spes quidem
ulla recipiendae libertatis animis poterat offerri, nec
ulli remedio locus apparebat contra tantam vim
malorum. Unde enim miserae civitati tot Harmo-

2 dios ? Socrates tamen in medio erat et lugentis
patres consolabatur et desperantis de re publica
exhortabatur et divitibus opes suas metuentibus ex-
probrabat seram periculosae avaritiae paenitentiam
et imitari volentibus magnum circumferebat exemplar, cum inter triginta dominos liber incederet.

3 Hunc tamen Athenae ipsae in carcere occiderunt, et
qui tuto insultaverat agmini tyrannorum, eius libertatem libertas non tulit. Licet scias et in adflicta re
publica esse occasionem sapienti viro ad se proferendum et in florenti ac beata petulantiam,[2] invidiam,

4 mille alia inertia vitia regnare. Utcumque ergo
se res publica dabit, utcumque fortuna permittet,
ita aut explicabimus nos aut contrahemus, utique
movebimus nec alligati metu torpebimus. Immo ille
vir fuerit, qui periculis undique imminentibus, armis
circa et catenis frementibus non alliserit virtutem
nec absconderit ; non est enim servare se obruere.

5 Vere,[3] ut opinor, Curius Dentatus aiebat, malle se
esse mortuum quam vivere ; ultimum malorum est
e vivorum numero exire, antequam moriaris. Sed
faciendum erit, si in rei publicae tempus minus

---

[1] *Hermes after Madvig adds* satis *before* satellites.
[2] petulantiam *Lipsius* : pecuniam *A*.
[3] vere *added by Haupt*.

---

[a] Harmodius, along with Aristogiton, was instrumental in
the overthrow of the Pisistratidae at Athens.

[b] Some such rendering seems necessary, and various conjectures have been made, such as *vivere mortuum viv*[*um,
torp*]*ere.*

as there might be satellites? No hope even of recovering liberty could offer itself, nor did there seem to be room for any sort of help against such mighty strength of wicked men. For where could the wretched state find enough Harmodiuses[a]? Yet Socrates was in their midst and comforted the mourning city fathers, he encouraged those that were despairing of the state, reproached the rich men that were now dreading their wealth with a too late repentance of their perilous greed, while to those willing to imitate him he carried round with him a great example, as he moved a free man amid thirty masters. Yet this was the man that Athens herself murdered in prison, and Freedom herself could not endure the freedom of one who had mocked in security at a whole band of tyrants. And so you may learn both that the wise man has opportunity to display his power when the state is torn by trouble, and that effrontery, envy, and a thousand other cowardly vices hold sway when it is prosperous and happy. Therefore we shall either expand or contract our effort according as the state shall lend herself to us, according as Fortune shall permit us, but in any case we shall keep moving, and shall not be tied down and numbed by fear. Nay, he will be truly a man who, when perils are threatening from every side, when arms and chains are rattling around him, will neither endanger, nor conceal, his virtue; for saving oneself does not mean burying oneself. Curius Dentatus said, truly as I think, that he would rather be a dead man than a live one dead[b]; for the worst of ills is to leave the number of the living before you die. But if you should happen upon a time when it is not at all easy to serve the state,

tractabile incideris, ut plus otio ac litteris vindices, nec aliter quam in periculosa navigatione subinde portum petas nec expectes, donec res te dimittant, sed ab illis te ipse diiungas.

1 6. Inspicere autem debebimus primum nosmet ipsos, deinde ea quae adgrediemur negotia, deinde eos, quorum causa aut cum quibus.

2 Ante omnia necesse est se ipsum aestimare, quia fere plus nobis videmur posse quam possumus. Alius eloquentiae fiducia prolabitur, alius patrimonio suo plus imperavit quam ferre posset, alius infirmum corpus laborioso pressit officio. Quorundam parum idonea est verecundia rebus civilibus, quae firmam frontem desiderant ; quorundam contumacia non facit ad aulam ; quidam non habent iram in potestate et illos ad temeraria verba quaelibet indignatio effert ; quidam urbanitatem nesciunt continere nec periculosis abstinent salibus. Omnibus his utilior negotio quies est ; ferox impatiensque natura irritamenta nociturae libertatis evitet.

3 Aestimanda sunt deinde ipsa, quae adgredimur, et vires nostrae cum rebus, quas temptaturi sumus, comparandae ; debet enim semper plus esse virium in actore quam in opere ; necesse est opprimant

4 onera, quae ferente maiora sunt. Quaedam praeterea non tam magna sunt negotia quam fecunda

your necessary course will be to claim more time for leisure and for letters, and, just as if you were making a perilous voyage, to put into harbour from time to time, and, without waiting for public affairs to release you, to separate yourself from them of your own accord.

Our duty, however, will be, first, to examine our own selves, then, the matters that we shall undertake, and lastly, those for whose sake or in whose company we are undertaking them.

Above all it is necessary for a man to estimate himself truly, because we commonly think that we can do more than we are able. One man blunders by relying upon his eloquence, another makes more demand upon his fortune than it can stand, another burdens a weakly body with laborious tasks. Some men by reason of their modesty are quite unsuited to civil affairs, which need a strong front; some by reason of their stubborn pride are not fitted for court; some do not have their anger under control, and any sort of provocation hurries them to rash words; some do not know how to restrain their pleasantry and cannot abstain from dangerous wit. For all these retirement is more serviceable than employment; a headstrong and impatient nature should avoid all incitements to a freedom of speech that will prove harmful.

Next, we must estimate the matters themselves that we are undertaking, and must compare our strength with the things that we are about to attempt; for the doer must always be stronger than his task; burdens that are too heavy for their bearer must necessarily crush him. There are certain undertakings, moreover, that are not so much great as they are prolific, and thus lead to many fresh under-

multumque negotiorum ferunt. Et haec refugienda
sunt, ex quibus nova occupatio multiplexque nascetur,
nec accedendum eo, unde liber regressus non sit;
iis admovenda manus est, quorum finem aut facere
aut certe sperare possis, relinquenda, quae latius actu
procedunt nec ubi proposueris desinunt.

1 7. Hominum utique dilectus habendus est : an
digni sint quibus partem vitae nostrae impendamus,
an ad illos temporis nostri iactura perveniat ; quidam
2 enim ultro officia nobis nostra imputant.ᵃ Athenodorus ait ne ad cenam quidem se iturum ad eum, qui
sibi nil pro hoc debiturus sit. Puto intellegis multo
minus ad eos iturum, qui cum amicorum officiis paria
mensa faciunt, qui fericula pro congiaris numerant,
quasi in alienum honorem intemperantes sint. Deme
illis testes spectatoresque, non delectabit popina
secreta.

Considerandum est, utrum natura tua agendis
rebus an otioso studio contemplationique aptior sit,
et eo inclinandum, quo te vis ingenii feret. Isocrates
Ephorum iniecta manu a foro subduxit utiliorem
componendis monumentis historiarum ratus ; male
enim respondent coacta ingenia, reluctante natura
irritus labor est.¹

3 Nihil tamen aeque oblectaverit animum, quam
amicitia fidelis et dulcis. Quantum bonum est, ubi
praeparata sunt pectora, in quae tuto secretum omne
descendat, quorum conscientiam minus quam tuam

---

¹ *The paragraph, evidently out of place, is assigned by
Haase to a position before* necesse est 6. 2 : *alii alia.*

ᵃ *i.e.,* they make us out their debtor because they sacrifice
their time in accepting our favours.
ᵇ The celebrated historian of the fourth century B.C.
ᶜ See critical note.

takings. Not only ought you to avoid those that give birth to new and multifarious employment, but you ought not to approach a task from which you are not free to retreat; you must put your hand to those that you can either finish, or at least hope to finish, leaving those untouched that grow bigger as you progress and do not cease at the point you intended.

And we must be particularly careful in our choice of men, and consider whether they are worthy of having us devote some part of our life to them, or whether the sacrifice of our time extends to theirs also; for certain people actually charge against us [a] the services we do them. Athenodorus says that he would not go to dine with a man who would not feel indebted to him for doing so. You understand, I suppose, that much less would he go to dinner with those who recompense the services of friends by their table, who set down the courses of a meal as largesses, as if they were being intemperate to do honour to others. Take away the spectators and witnesses, and solitary gluttony will give them no pleasure.

You must consider whether your nature is better adapted to active affairs or to leisurely study and contemplation, and you must turn towards that course to which the bent of your genius shall direct you. Isocrates laid hands upon Ephorus [b] and led him away from the forum, thinking that he would be more useful in compiling the records of history; for inborn tendencies answer ill to compulsion, and where Nature opposes labour is in vain.[c]

Nothing, however, gives the mind so much pleasure as fond and faithful friendship. What a blessing it is to have those to whose waiting hearts every secret may be committed with safety, whose knowledge of you

timeas, quorum sermo sollicitudinem leniat, sententia
consilium expediat, hilaritas tristitiam dissipet, conspectus ipse delectet! Quos scilicet vacuos, quantum fieri poterit, a cupiditatibus eligemus; serpunt
enim vitia et in proximum quemque transiliunt et
4 contactu nocent. Itaque quemadmodum[1] in pestilentia curandum est, ne correptis iam corporibus et
morbo flagrantibus adsideamus, quia pericula tra-
hemus adflatuque ipso laborabimus, ita in amicorum
legendis ingeniis dabimus operam, ut quam minime
inquinatos adsumamus; initium morbi est aegris
sana miscere. Nec hoc praeceperim tibi, ut neminem
nisi sapientem sequaris aut adtrahas. Ubi enim
istum invenies, quem tot saeculis quaerimus? Pro
5 optimo sit minime malus! Vix tibi esset facultas
dilectus felicioris, si inter Platonas et Xenophontas
et illum Socratici fetus proventum bonos quaereres,
aut si tibi potestas Catonianae fieret aetatis, quae
plerosque dignos tulit, qui Catonis saeculo nasceren-
tur, sicut multos peiores quam umquam alias maxi-
morumque molitores scelerum; utraque enim turba
opus erat, ut Cato posset intellegi: habere debuit
et bonos, quibus se adprobaret, et malos, in quibus vim
6 suam experiretur. Nunc vero in tanta bonorum
egestate minus fastidiosa fiat electio. Praecipue

[1] quemadmodum *Hermes*: ut quod *A*: ut quondam
Gertz: ut id *Petschenig*.

you fear less than your knowledge of yourself, whose conversation soothes your anxiety, whose opinion assists your decision, whose cheerfulness scatters your sorrow, the very sight of whom gives you joy ! We shall of course choose those who are free, as far as may be, from selfish desires ; for vices spread un-noticed, and quickly pass to those nearest and do harm by their contact. And so, just as in times of pestilence we must take care not to sit near those whose bodies are already infected and inflamed with disease, because we shall incur risks and be in danger from their very breath, so, in choosing our friends, we shall have regard for their character, so that we may appropriate those who are marked with fewest stains ; to combine the sick with the sound is to spread disease. Yet I would not lay down the rule that you are to follow, or attach to yourself, none but a wise man. For where will you find him whom we have been seeking for so many centuries ? In place of the best man take the one least bad ! Opportunity for a happier choice scarcely could you have, were you searching for a good man among the Platos and the Xenophons and the rest of that glorious com-pany of the Socratic breed, or, too, if you had at your command the age of Cato, which bore many men who were worthy to be born in Cato's time, just as it also bore many that were worse than had ever been known, and contrivers of the most monstrous crimes ; for both classes were necessary in order that Cato might be understood—he needed to have good men that he might win their approval, and bad men that he might prove his strength. But now, when there is such a great dearth of good men, you must be less squeamish in making your choice. Yet those are

tamen vitentur tristes et omnia deplorantes, quibus nulla non causa in querellas placet. Constet illi licet fides et benivolentia, tranquillitati tamen inimicus est comes perturbatus et omnia gemens.

1 8. Transeamus ad patrimonia, maximam humanarum aerumnarum materiam; nam si omnia alia quibus angimur compares, mortes, aegrotationes, metus, desideria, dolorum laborumque patientiam, cum iis quae nobis mala pecunia nostra exhibet, haec 2 pars multum praegravabit. Itaque cogitandum est, quanto levior dolor sit non habere quam perdere; et intellegemus paupertati eo minorem tormentorum quo minorem damnorum esse materiam. Erras enim, si putas animosius detrimenta divites ferre; maximis minimisque corporibus par est dolor vulneris.

3 Bion eleganter ait non minus molestum esse calvis quam comatis pilos velli. Idem scias licet de pauperibus locupletibusque, par illis esse tormentum; utrique enim pecunia sua obhaesit nec sine sensu revelli potest. Tolerabilius autem est, ut dixi, faciliusque non adquirere quam amittere, ideoque laetiores videbis, quos numquam fortuna respexit, quam quos 4 deseruit. Vidit hoc Diogenes, vir ingentis animi, et effecit, ne quid sibi eripi posset. Tu istud paupertatem, inopiam, egestatem voca, quod voles ignominiosum securitati nomen impone. Putabo hunc non esse felicem, si quem mihi alium inveneris, cui nihil pereat. Aut ego fallor, aut regnum est inter

especially to be avoided who are melancholy and bewail everything, who find pleasure in every opportunity for complaint. Though a man's loyalty and
friendliness be assured, yet the companion who is
always upset and bemoans everything is a foe to
tranquillity.

Let us pass now to the matter of fortunes, which
are the greatest source of human sorrow ; for if you
compare all the other ills from which we suffer—
deaths, sicknesses, fears, longings, the endurance of
pains and labours—with the evils which our money
brings, this portion will far outweigh the other. And
so we must reflect how much lighter is the sorrow of
not having money than of losing it ; and we shall
understand that, the less poverty has to lose, the
less chance it has to torment us. For you are wrong
if you think that the rich suffer losses more cheer-
fully ; the pain of a wound is the same in the largest
and smallest bodies. Bion says neatly that it hurts
the bald-head just as much as the thatched-head to
have his hairs plucked. You may be sure that the
same thing holds for the poor and the rich, that their
suffering is just the same ; for their money has a fast
grip on both, and cannot be torn away without their
feeling it. But, as I have said, it is more endurable
and easier not to acquire it than to lose it, and therefore you will see that those whom Fortune has never
regarded are more cheerful than those whom she has
forsaken. Diogenes, that high-souled man, saw this,
and made it impossible for anything to be snatched
from him. Do *you* call such a state poverty, want, need,
give this security any disgraceful name you please.
I shall not count the man happy, if you can find
anyone else who has nothing to lose ! Either I am

241

avaros, circumscriptores, latrones, plagiarios unum
5 esse, cui noceri non possit. Si quis de felicitate
Diogenis dubitat, potest idem dubitare et de deorum
immortalium statu, an parum beate degant, quod
illis nec praedia nec horti sint nec alieno colono rura
pretiosa nec grande in foro faenus. Non te pudet,
quisquis divitiis adstupes? Respice agedum mundum; nudos videbis deos, omnia dantis, nihil habentis.
Hunc tu pauperem putas an dis immortalibus similem,
6 qui se fortuitis omnibus exuit? Feliciorem tu
Demetrium Pompeianum vocas, quem non puduit
locupletiorem esse Pompeio? Numerus illi cotidie
servorum velut imperatori exercitus referebatur, cui
iam dudum divitiae esse debuerant duo vicarii et
7 cella laxior. At Diogeni servus unicus fugit nec
eum reducere, cum monstraretur, tanti putavit.
"Turpe est," inquit, "Manen sine Diogene posse
vivere, Diogenen sine Mane non posse." Videtur
mihi dixisse: "Age tuum negotium, fortuna; nihil
apud Diogenen iam tui est. Fugit mihi servus, immo
8 liber abii!" Familia petit vestiarium victumque;
tot ventres avidissimorum animalium tuendi sunt,
emenda vestis et custodiendae rapacissimae manus
et flentium detestantiumque ministeriis utendum.

---

^a An allusion to the practice of acquiring lands overseas.
Cf. Epistles, lxxxix. 20: "hoc quoque parum est, nisi lati-
fundiis vestris maria cinxistis, nisi trans Hadriam et Ionium
Aegaeumque vester vilicus regnat."

deceived, or it is a regal thing to be the only one amid all the misers, the sharpers, the robbers, and plunderers who cannot be harmed. If anyone has any doubt about the happiness of Diogenes, he may likewise have doubt about the condition of the immortal gods as well—whether they are living quite unhappily because they have neither manors nor gardens nor costly estates farmed by a foreign tenant,[a] nor a huge yield of interest in the forum. All ye who bow down to riches, where is your shame ? Come, turn your eyes upon heaven ; you will see the gods quite needy, giving all and having nothing. Do you think that he who stripped himself of all the gifts of Fortune is a poor man or simply like the immortal gods ? Would you say that Demetrius, the freedman of Pompey, who was not ashamed to be richer than Pompey, was a happier man ? He, to whom two underlings and a roomier cell would once have been wealth, used to have the number of his slaves reported to him every day as if he were the general of an army ! But the only slave Diogenes had ran away from him once, and, when he was pointed out to him, he did not think it worth while to fetch him back. " It would be a shame," he said, " if Diogenes is not able to live without Manes when Manes is able to live without Diogenes." But he seems to me to have cried : " Fortune, mind your own business ; Diogenes has now nothing of yours. My slave has run away—nay, it is I that have got away free ! " A household of slaves requires clothes and food ; so many bellies of creatures that are always hungry have to be filled, we have to buy clothing for them, and watch their most thievish hands, and use the services of people weeping and cursing. How much

Quanto ille felicior, qui nihil ulli debet, nisi cui
9 facillime negat, sibi ! Sed quoniam non est nobis
tantum roboris, angustanda certe sunt patrimonia,
ut minus ad iniurias fortunae simus exposti.
Habiliora sunt corpora in bello illa, quae in arma
sua contrahi possunt, quam quae superfunduntur et
undique magnitudo sua vulneribus obicit. Optimus
pecuniae modus est, qui nec in paupertatem cadit,
nec procul a paupertate discedit.

1 9. Placebit autem haec nobis mensura, si prius
parsimonia placuerit, sine qua nec ullae opes sufficiunt, nec ullae non[1] satis patent, praesertim cum in
vicino remedium sit et possit ipsa paupertas in divitias
2 se advocata frugalitate convertere. Adsuescamus a
nobis removere pompam, et usus rerum, non ornamenta, metiri. Cibus famem domet, potio sitim,
libido qua necesse est fluat ; discamus membris
nostris inniti, cultum victumque non ad nova exempla
componere, sed ut maiorum mores suadent ; discamus continentiam augere, luxuriam coercere,
gloriam temperare, iracundiam lenire, paupertatem
aequis oculis aspicere, frugalitatem colere, etiam si
multos pudebit, eo plus[2] desideriis naturalibus parvo
parata remedia adhibere, spes effrenatas et animum
in futura imminentem velut sub vinculis habere, id
agere, ut divitias a nobis potius quam a fortuna peta-
3 mus. Non potest umquam tanta varietas et iniquitas casuum ita depelli, ut non multum procellarum

---

[1] nec ulle non *A* : nec cum illa ullae non *Haase* : nec cum
illa non *Gertz* : nec ullae domus *Schultess* : nec ullae sortes
Birt.

[2] pudebit, eo plus *Basore* : pudebit ej plus *A* : pudebit
templi eius *Madvig* : pudebit eius cultus *Koch* : pudebit eius
Rossbach : pudebit eius ; placeat *Schultess* : *alii alia.*

happier is he whose only obligation is to one whom he can most easily refuse—himself! Since, however, we do not have such strength of character, we ought at least to reduce our possessions, so as to be less exposed to the injuries of Fortune. In war those men are better fitted for service whose bodies can be squeezed into their armour than those whose bodies spill over, and whose very bulk everywhere exposes them to wounds. In the case of money, an amount that does not descend to poverty, and yet is not far removed from poverty, is the most desirable.

Moreover, we shall be content with this measure if we were previously content with thrift, without which no amount of wealth is sufficient, and no amount is not sufficiently ample, especially since the remedy is always near at hand, and poverty of itself is able to turn itself into riches by summoning economy. Let us form the habit of putting away from us mere pomp and of measuring the uses of things, not their decorative qualities. Let food subdue hunger, drink quench thirst; let lust follow the course of nature; let us learn to rely upon our limbs and to conform our dress and mode of life, not to the new fashions, but to the customs our ancestors approved; let us learn to increase our self-control, to restrain luxury, to moderate ambition, to soften anger, to view poverty with unprejudiced eyes, to cultivate frugality, even if many shall be ashamed, all the more to apply to the wants of nature the remedies that cost little, to keep unruly hopes and a mind that is intent upon the future, as it were, in chains, and to determine to seek our riches from ourselves rather than from Fortune. It is never possible that all the diversity and injustice of mischance can be so repulsed, that many storms

irruat magna armamenta pandentibus. Cogendae in
artum res sunt, ut tela in vanum cadant, ideoque
exilia interim calamitatesque in remedium cessere et
levioribus incommodis graviora sanata sunt. Ubi
parum audit praecepta animus nec curari mollius
potest, quidni consulatur ei, si paupertas ei, ignominia, rerum eversio adhibetur, malo malum opponi-
tur ? Adsuescamus ergo cenare posse sine populo et
servis paucioribus servire et vestes parare in quod
inventae sunt et habitare contractius. Non in cursu
tantum circique certamine, sed in his spatiis vitae
interius flectendum est.

4   Studiorum quoque quae liberalissima impensa est
tam diu rationem habet, quam diu modum. Quo innumerabiles libros et bybliothecas, quarum dominus
vix tota vita indices perlegit ? Onerat discentem
turba, non instruit, multoque satius est paucis te
5 auctoribus tradere, quam errare per multos. Qua-
draginta milia librorum Alexandriae arserunt ; pulcherrimum regiae opulentiae monimentum alius
laudaverit, sicut T. Livius, qui elegantiae regum
curaeque egregium id opus ait fuisse. Non fuit
elegantia illud aut cura, sed studiosa luxuria, immo
ne studiosa quidem, quoniam non in studium sed in

---

a Literally, "in these circuits of life." In the ancient
chariot-races the chariots usually made seven circuits (*spatia*)
of the arena, and were kept as nearly as possible to the inner
course in rounding the turning posts (*metae*). By a common
metaphor *spatium* was identified with life or, as here, with a
portion of life.

b When Julius Caesar stormed the city in 47 B.C. (Cassius
Dio, xlii. 38). The extent of the loss is variously given, but
in no other authority is the estimate placed so low. See J. W.
White, *Scholia on the Aves of Aristophanes*, Introd. p. xxxiv.

will not sweep down upon those who are spreading great sail. We must draw in our activities to a narrow compass in order that the darts of Fortune may fall into nothingness, and for this reason exiles and disasters have turned out to be benefits, and more serious ills have been healed by those that are lighter. When the mind is disobedient to precepts and cannot be restored by gentler means, why should it not be for its own good to have poverty, disgrace, and a violent overthrow of fortune applied to it—to match evil with evil? Let us then get accustomed to being able to dine without the multitude, to being the slave of fewer slaves, to getting clothes for the purpose for which they were devised, and to living in narrower quarters. Not only in the race and the contests of the Circus, but also in the arena of life[a] we must keep to the inner circle.

Even for studies, where expenditure is most honourable, it is justifiable only so long as it is kept within bounds. What is the use of having countless books and libraries, whose titles their owners can scarcely read through in a whole lifetime? The learner is, not instructed, but burdened by the mass of them, and it is much better to surrender yourself to a few authors than to wander through many. Forty thousand books were burned[b] at Alexandria; let someone else praise this library as the most noble monument to the wealth of kings, as did Titus Livius, who says[c] that it was the most distinguished achievement of the good taste and solicitude of kings. There was no "good taste" or "solicitude" about it, but only learned luxury—nay, not even "learned," since they had collected the books, not for the sake of learning,

---

[c] Livy's narrative of the event (Bk. cxii.) has been lost.

spectaculum comparaverant, sicut plerisque ignaris
etiam puerilium litterarum libri non studiorum
instrumenta sed cenationum ornamenta sunt. Pare-
tur itaque librorum quantum satis sit, nihil in appara-
6 tum. "Honestius," inquis, "hoc se impensae quam
in Corinthia pictasque tabulas effuderint." Vitiosum
est ubique, quod nimium est. Quid habes, cur
ignoscas homini armaria e¹ citro atque ebore cap-
tanti, corpora conquirenti aut ignotorum auctorum
aut improbatorum et inter tot milia librorum oscitanti,
cui voluminum suorum frontes maxime placent
7 titulique? Apud desidiosissimos ergo videbis quicquid orationum historiarumque est, tecto tenus
exstructa loculamenta; iam enim inter balnearia et
thermas bybliotheca quoque ut necessarium domus
ornamentum expolitur. Ignoscerem plane, si studiorum nimia cupidine erraretur. Nunc ista conquisita,
cum imaginibus suis discripta sacrorum opera ingeniorum in speciem et cultum parietum comparantur.
1   10. At in aliquod genus vitae difficile incidisti et
tibi ignoranti vel publica fortuna vel privata laqueum
impegit, quem nec solvere possis nec rumpere.
Cogita compeditos primo aegre ferre onera et impedimenta crurum; deinde ubi non indignari illa
sed pati proposuerunt, necessitas fortiter ferre docet,
consuetudo facile. Invenies in quolibet genere
vitae oblectamenta et remissiones et voluptates, si

¹ e *added by Gertz.*

but to make a show, just as many who lack even a child's knowledge of letters use books, not as the tools of learning, but as decorations for the dining-room. Therefore, let just as many books be acquired as are enough, but none for mere show. " It is more respectable," you say, " to squander money on these than on Corinthian bronzes and on pictures." But excess in anything becomes a fault. What excuse have you to offer for a man who seeks to have book-cases of citrus-wood and ivory, who collects the works of unknown or discredited authors and sits yawning in the midst of so many thousand books, who gets most of his pleasure from the outsides of volumes and their titles ? Consequently it is in the houses of the laziest men that you will see a full collection of ora-tions and history with the boxes piled right up to the ceiling ; for by now among cold baths and hot baths a library also is equipped as a necessary orna-ment of a great house. I would readily pardon these men if they were led astray by their excessive zeal for learning. But as it is, these collections of the works of sacred genius with all the portraits that adorn them are bought for show and a decoration of their walls.

But it may be that you have fallen upon some phase of life which is difficult, and that, before you are aware, your public or your private fortune has you fastened in a noose which you can neither burst nor untie. But reflect that it is only at first that prisoners are worried by the burdens and shackles upon their legs ; later, when they have determined not to chafe against them, but to endure them, necessity teaches them to bear them bravely, habit to bear them easily. In any sort of life you will find that there are amuse-ments and relaxations and pleasures if you are

volueris mala putare levia potius quam invidiosa
2 facere. Nullo melius nomine de nobis natura meruit,
quae cum sciret quibus aerumnis nasceremur, calami-
tatum mollimentum consuetudinem invenit, cito in
familiaritatem gravissima adducens. Nemo duraret,
si rerum adversarum eandem vim adsiduitas haberet
3 quam primus ictus. Omnes cum fortuna copulati
sumus. Aliorum aurea catena est et laxa, aliorum
arta et sordida ; sed quid refert ? Eadem custodia
universos circumdedit alligatique sunt etiam qui
alligaverunt, nisi forte tu leviorem in sinistra catenam
putas. Alium honores, alium opes vinciunt ; quosdam
nobilitas, quosdam humilitas premit ; quibusdam
aliena supra caput imperia sunt, quibusdam sua ;
quosdam exilia uno loco tenent, quosdam sacerdotia.
4 Omnis vita servitium est. Adsuescendum est itaque
condicioni suae et quam minimum de illa querendum
et quicquid habet circa se commodi adprendendum ;
nihil tam acerbum est, in quo non aequus animus
solacium inveniat. Exiguae saepe areae in multos
usus discribentis arte patuerunt et quamvis angustum
pedem¹ dispositio fecit habitabilem. Adhibe rationem difficultatibus ; possunt et dura molliri et angusta laxari et gravia scite ferentis minus premere.
5 Non sunt praeterea cupiditates in longinquum
mittendae, sed in vicinum illis egredi permittamus,

¹ angustum pedem *A* : angustam sedem *Cornelissen.*

---

i.e., of the custodian who is chained to his prisoner, as
Seneca shows in *Epistles,* v. 7: "quemadmodum eadem
catena et custodiam et militem copulat, sic ista quae tam
dissimilia sunt, pariter incedunt."
ᵇ The flamens were subject to many ceremonial restric-
tions. Except by special dispensation, a flamen of Jupiter

willing to consider your evils lightly rather than to make them hateful. On no score has Nature more deserved our thanks, who, since she knew to what sorrows we were born, invented habit as an alleviation for disasters, and thus quickly accustoms us to the most serious ills. No one could endure adversity if, while it continued, it kept the same violence that its first blows had. All of us are chained to Fortune. Some are bound by a loose and golden chain, others by a tight chain of baser metal; but what difference does it make? The same captivity holds all men in its toils, those who have bound others have also been bound—unless perhaps you think that a chain on the left hand[a] is a lighter one. Some are chained by public office, others by wealth; some carry the burden of high birth, some of low birth; some bow beneath another's empire, some beneath their own; some are kept in one place by exile, others by priest-hoods.[b] All life is a servitude. And so a man must become reconciled to his lot, must complain of it as little as possible, and must lay hold of whatever good it may have; no state is so bitter that a calm mind cannot find in it some consolation. Even small spaces by skilful planning often reveal many uses; and arrangement will make habitable a place of ever so small dimensions. Apply reason to difficulties; it is possible to soften what is hard, to widen what is narrow, and burdens will press less heavily upon those who bear them skilfully.

Moreover, we must not send our desires upon a distant quest, but we should permit them to have access to what is near, since they do not endure to

could not leave the city for a single night (Livy, v. 52. 13).

quoniam includi ex toto non patiuntur. Relictis iis, quae aut non possunt fieri aut difficulter possunt, prope posita speique nostrae adludentia sequamur, sed sciamus omnia aeque levia esse, extrinsecus diversas facies habentia, introrsus pariter vana. Nec invideamus altius stantibus ; quae excelsa videbantur, praerupta sunt.

6   Illi rursus, quos sors iniqua in ancipiti posuit, tutiores erunt superbiam detrahendo rebus per se superbis et fortunam suam quam maxime poterunt in planum deferendo. Multi quidem sunt, quibus necessario haerendum sit in fastigio suo, ex quo non possunt nisi cadendo descendere, sed hoc ipsum testentur maximum onus suum esse, quod aliis graves esse cogantur, nec sublevatos se sed suffixos. Iustitia, mansuetudine, humanitate, larga et benigna manu praeparent multa ad secundos casus praesidia, quorum spe securius pendeant. Nihil tamen aeque nos ab his animi fluctibus vindicaverit, quam semper aliquem incrementis terminum figere, nec fortunae arbitrium desinendi dare, sed ipsos multo quidem citra exempla hortentur consistere. Sic et aliquae cupiditates animum acuent et finitae non in immensum incertumque producent.

1   11. Ad imperfectos et mediocres et male sanos hic meus sermo pertinet, non ad sapientem. Huic non timide nec pedetemptim ambulandum est ; tanta enim fiducia sui est, ut obviam fortunae ire

be shut up altogether. Leaving those things that either cannot be done, or can be done only with difficulty, let us pursue what lies near at hand and allures our hope, but let us be aware that they all are equally trivial, diverse outwardly in appearance, within alike vain. And let us not envy those who stand in higher places ; where there appeared heights, there are precipices.

Those, on the other hand, whom an unkind lot has placed in a critical position, will be safer by reducing their pride in the things that are in themselves proud and lowering their fortune, so far as they shall be able, to the common level. While there are many who must necessarily cling to their pinnacle, from which they cannot descend without falling, yet they may bear witness that their greatest burden is the very fact that they are forced to be burdensome to others, being not lifted, but nailed on high. By justice, by kindness, by courtesy, and by lavish and kindly giving let them prepare many safeguards against later mishaps, in hope whereof they may be more easy in their suspense. Yet nothing can free us from these mental waverings so effectively as always to establish some limit to advancement and not leave to Fortune the decision of when it shall end, but halt of our own accord far short of the limit that the examples of others urge. In this way there will be some desires to prick on the mind, and yet, because bounds have been set to them, they will not lead it to that which is unlimited and uncertain.

These remarks of mine apply, not to the wise man, but to those who are not yet perfect, to the mediocre, and to the unsound. The wise man does not need to walk timidly and cautiously ; for so great is his confidence in himself that he does not hesitate to

non dubitet nec umquam loco illi cessurus sit. Nec habet, ubi illam timeat, quia non mancipia tantum possessionesque et dignitatem, sed corpus quoque suum et oculos et manum et quicquid cariorem vitam facit viro seque ipsum inter precaria numerat vivitque ut commodatus sibi et reposcentibus sine tristitia 2 redditurus. Nec ideo vilis est sibi, quia scit se suum non esse, sed omnia tam diligenter faciet, tam circumspecte, quam religiosus homo sanctusque solet tueri fidei commissa. Quandoque autem reddere iubebitur, non queretur cum fortuna, sed dicet: 3 " Gratias ago pro eo, quod possedi habuique. Magna quidem res tuas mercede colui, sed quia ita imperas, do, cedo gratus libensque. Si quid habere me tui volueris etiamnunc, servabo; si aliud placet, ego vero factum signatumque argentum, domum familiamque meam reddo, restituo." Appellaverit natura quae prior nobis credidit, et huic dicemus : " Recipe animum meliorem quam dedisti. Non tergiversor nec refugio; paratum habes a volente quod non 4 sentienti dedisti: aufer." Reverti unde veneris quid grave est ? Male vivet quisquis nesciet bene mori. Huic itaque primum rei pretium detrahendum est et spiritus inter vilia numerandus. Gladiatores, ut ait Cicero, invisos habemus, si omni modo vitam impetrare cupiunt ; favemus, si contemptum eius

---

^a *Pro Milone*, 92.

go against Fortune, and will never retreat before her.
Nor has he any reason to fear her, for he counts not
merely his chattels and his possessions and his position, but even his body and his eyes and his hand and
all else that makes life very dear to a man, nay, even
himself, among the things that are given on sufferance, and he lives as one who has been lent to himself
and will return everything without sorrow when it is
reclaimed. Nor is he therefore cheap in his own eyes,
because he knows that he does not belong to himself,
but he will perform all his duties as diligently and as
circumspectly as a devout and holy man is wont to
guard the property entrusted to his protection. When,
however, he is bidden to give them up, he will not
quarrel with Fortune, but will say : " I give thanks
for what I have possessed and held. I have managed
your property to great advantage, but, since you order
me, I give it up, I surrender it gratefully and gladly.
If you still wish me to have anything of yours, I shall
guard it ; if your pleasure is otherwise, I give back
and restore to you my silver, both wrought and
coined, my house, and my household." Should
Nature recall what she previously entrusted us with,
we shall say to her also : " Take back the spirit that is
better than when you gave it. I do not quibble or
hang back ; of my own free will I am ready for you to
take what you gave me before I was conscious—away
with it ! " What hardship is there in returning to
the place from which you came ? That man will live
ill who will not know how to die well. Therefore we
must take from the value we set upon this thing, and
the breath of life must be counted as a cheap matter.
As Cicero says,[a] we feel hostility to gladiators if they
are eager to save their life no matter how ; if they

prae se ferunt. Idem evenire nobis scias; saepe
5 enim causa moriendi est timide mori. Fortuna illa,
quae ludos sibi facit: " Quo," inquit, " te reservem,
malum et trepidum animal? Eo magis convulnera-
beris et confodieris, quia nescis praebere iugulum
At tu et vives diutius et morieris expeditius, qui
ferrum non subducta cervice nec manibus oppositis
6 sed animose recipis." Qui mortem timebit, nihil
umquam pro homine vivo faciet. At qui sciet hoc
sibi cum conciperetur statim condictum, vivet ad
formulam et simul illud quoque eodem animi robore
praestabit, ne quid ex iis, quae eveniunt, subitum
sit. Quicquid enim fieri potest, quasi futurum sit,
prospiciendo malorum omnium impetus molliet, qui
ad praeparatos expectantesque nihil adferunt novi;
securis et beata tantum spectantibus graves veniunt.
Morbus est, captivitas, ruina, ignis; nihil horum
7 repentinum est: sciebam, in quam tumultuosum me
contubernium natura clusisset. Totiens in vicinia
mea conclamatum est; totiens praeter limen im-
maturas exequias fax cereusque praecessit; saepe a
latere ruentis aedificii fragor sonuit; multos ex iis, quos
forum, curia, sermo mecum contraxerat, nox abstulit
et iunctas sodalium manus capulus[1] interscidit.

---

[1] capulus *Basore*: copulas *codex Ambros. C* 293: copu-
latas (l *added by first hand*) *A*: copiates *Madvig*: speculator
Gertz: *others change or omit* iunctas.

display contempt for it, we favour them. The same thing, you may know, applies to us ; for often the cause of death is the fear of dying. Mistress Fortune, who uses us for her sport, says : " Why should I save you, you base and cowardly creature ? You will be hacked and pierced with all the more wounds, because you do not know how to offer your throat. But you, who receive the steel courageously and do not with-draw your neck or put out your hands to stop it, shall both live longer and die more easily." He who fears death will never do anything worthy of a man who is alive. But he who knows that these were the terms drawn up for him at the moment of his conception will live according to the bond, and at the same time will also with like strength of mind guarantee that none of the things that happen shall be un-expected. For by looking forward to whatever can happen as though it would happen, he will soften the attacks of all ills, which bring nothing strange to those who have been prepared beforehand and are expecting them ; it is the unconcerned and those that expect nothing but good fortune upon whom they fall heavily. Sickness comes, captivity, disaster, conflagration, but none of them is unex-pected—I always knew in what disorderly company Nature had confined me. Many times has wailing for the dead been heard in my neighbourhood ; many times have the torch and the taper led untimely funerals past my threshold ; often has the crash of a falling building resounded at my side ; many of those whom the forum, the senate-house and conversation had bound to me a night has carried off, and the hands that were joined in friendship have been sundered by the grave. Should I be surprised if the

257

Mirer ad me aliquando pericula accessisse, quae circa me semper erraverint? Magna pars hominum est, quae navigatura de tempestate non cogitat. 8 Numquam me in voce[1] bona mali pudebit auctoris. Publilius, tragicis comicisque vehementior ingeniis, quotiens mimicas ineptias et verba ad summam caveam spectantia reliquit, inter multa alia coturno, non tantum sipario, fortiora et hoc ait:

> Cuivis potest accidere quod cuiquam potest.

Hoc si quis in medullas demiserit et omnia aliena mala, quorum ingens cotidie copia est, sic aspexerit, tamquam liberum illis et ad se iter sit, multo ante se 9 armabit quam petatur; sero animus ad periculorum patientiam post pericula instruitur. "Non putavi hoc futurum" et "Umquam tu hoc eventurum credidisses?" Quare autem non? Quae sunt divitiae, quas non egestas et fames et mendicitas a tergo sequatur? Quae dignitas, cuius non prae-textam et augurale et lora patricia sordes comitentur et exprobratio notae et mille maculae et extrema contemptio? Quod regnum est, cui non parata sit ruina et proculcatio et dominus et carnifex? Nec magnis ista intervallis divisa, sed horae momentum 10 interest inter solium et aliena genua. Scito ergo omnem condicionem versabilem esse et quicquid in ullum incurrit posse in te quoque incurrere. Locuples

---

[1] voce *added by Gertz.*

[a] *Cf. Ad Marciam,* 9. 5, and note.
[b] *Lorum* is "leather strap," and since the uses of such were manifold, the allusion in *lora patricia* is not wholly clear. In the interpretation adopted *lora* is a metonymy for *mulleus,* the red-coloured boot worn by curule magistrates on great public occasions.

dangers that always have wandered about me should at some time reach me ? The number of men that will plan a voyage without thinking of storms is very great. I shall never be ashamed to quote a bad author if what he says is good. Publilius, who, whenever he abandoned the absurdities of farce and language directed to the gallery, had more vigour than the writers of comedy and tragedy, among many other utterances more striking than any that came from the buskined—to say nothing of the comic curtain's —stage, has also this :

> Whatever can one man befall can happen just as well to all.[a]

If a man lets this sink deep into his heart, and, when he looks upon the evils of others, of which there is a huge supply every day, remembers that they are free to come to him also, he will arm himself against them long before they attack him. It is too late to equip the soul to endure dangers after the dangers have arisen. You say : " I did not think this would happen," and " Would you have believed that this would happen ? " But why not ? Where are the riches that do not have poverty and hunger and beggary following close behind ? What rank is there whose bordered robe and augur's wand and patrician boot-laces[b] do not carry in their train rags and branded disgrace—a thousand stigmas and utter disrepute? What kingdom is there for which ruin and a trampling under foot and the tyrant and the hangman are not in store ? Nor are such things cut off by long intervals, but between the throne and bending at another's knees there is but an hour's space. Know, then, that every lot in life is changeable, and that whatever befalls any man can befall you also. You are rich : but are you any

SENECA

es : numquid divitior Pompeio ? Cui cum Gaius,
vetus cognatus, hospes novus, aperuisset Caesaris
domum, ut suam cluderet, defuit panis, aqua ! Cum
tot flumina possideret in suo orientia, in suo cadentia,
mendicavit stilicidia. Fame ac siti periit in palatio
cognati, dum illi heres publicum funus esurienti
11 locat ! Honoribus summis functus es ; numquid aut
tam magnis aut tam insperatis aut tam universis
quam Seianus ? Quo die illum senatus deduxerat,
populus in frusta divisit ; in quem quicquid congeri
poterat di hominesque contulerant, ex eo nihil super-
12 fuit, quod carnifex traheret ! Rex es : non ad Croesum
te mittam, qui rogum suum et accendi vivus et
extingui vidit, factus non regno tantum, sed[1] etiam
morti suae superstes, non ad Iugurtham, quem
populus Romanus intra annum, quam timuerat,
spectavit. Ptolemaeum Africae regem, Armeniae
Mithridaten inter Gaianas custodias vidimus ; alter
in exilium missus est, alter ut meliore fide mitteretur,
optabat ! In tanta rerum susum ac deorsum euntium

[1] sed *commonly added.*

a Identified by Dessau (*Prosopogr. Imp. Rom.* iii. 450)
with Sextus Pompeius, consul in A.D. 14.
b If this Pompey could be considered a descendant of
Sextus Pompey, son of Pompey the Great, his relationship
with Gaius might be established through the line of Sextus's
wife, who was the niece of Scribonia, wife of Augustus and
great-grandmother of Gaius. But no male descendant of
Sextus is elsewhere known.
c From attendance upon a meeting of the senate Sejanus
was hurried to prison under official escort, and on the same
day was there executed. His dramatic overthrow, a commonplace of later literature, forms the subject of Ben Jonson's
Sejanus his Fall.
d An allusion to the story of Herodotus (i. 86 *sq.*) that
260

richer than Pompey *a* ? Yet he lacked even bread
and water when Gaius, an old kinsman *b* but a new
sort of host, had opened to him the house of Caesar
in order that he might have a chance to close his
own ! Though he owned so many rivers that had their
source within his own lands and their mouth within
his own lands, he had to beg for drops of water. In
the palace of his kinsman he perished from hunger
and thirst, and, while he was starving, his heir was
arranging to give him a state funeral ! You have
held the highest offices ; but have you held any as
great, as unlooked for, as comprehensive as those of
Sejanus ? Yet on the day on which the senate played
the escort,*c* the people tore him to pieces ! Of the
man who had had heaped upon him all that gods and
men were able to bestow nothing was left for the
executioner to drag to the river ! You are a king : it
will not be Croesus to whom I shall direct you, who
lived to see his own pyre both lighted and extinguished,*d* who was forced to survive, not his kingdom
only, but even his own death, nor Jugurtha, whom
the Roman people gazed upon as a captive in less
than a year after he had made them afraid. We
ourselves have seen Ptolemy, king of Africa, and
Mithridates, king of Armenia, under the charge of
Gaius's guards ; the one was sent into exile—the
other was anxious to be sent there in better faith ! *e*
In view of this great mutability of fortune, that

after Croesus had been placed upon the pyre, on which he
was to be burned alive, and the flames had been lighted,
Cyrus, his conqueror, relented and ordered his release.

e Ptolemy, king of Mauretania, was " exiled " to Rome
and there killed (Suetonius, *Calig.* 35) ; Mithridates was
later restored to his throne.

versatione si non quicquid fieri potest pro futuro
habes, das in te vires rebus adversis, quas infregit
quisquis prior vidit.

1 12. Proximum ab his erit, ne aut in supervacuis
aut ex supervacuo laboremus, id est, ne quae aut non
possumus consequi concupiscamus, aut adepti vanitatem cupiditatium nostrarum sero post multum
pudorem intellegamus. Id est, ne aut labor irritus
sit sine effectu aut effectus labore indignus ; fere
enim ex his tristitia sequitur, si aut non successit aut
2 successus pudet. Circumcidenda concursatio, qualis
est magnae parti hominum domos et theatra et fora
pererrantium ; alienis se negotiis offerunt, semper
aliquid agentibus similes. Horum si aliquem exeuntem e domo interrogaveris : " Quo tu ? Quid
cogitas ? " respondebit tibi : " Non me hercules scio ;
3 sed aliquos videbo, aliquid agam." Sine proposito
vagantur quaerentes negotia nec quae destinaverunt
agunt, sed in quae incucurrerunt. Inconsultus illis
vanusque cursus est, qualis formicis per arbusta re-
pentibus, quae in summum cacumen et inde in imum
inanes aguntur ; his plerique similem vitam agunt,
quorum non immerito quis inquietam inertiam dixerit.
4 Quorundam quasi ad incendium currentium misere-
beris ; usque eo impellunt obvios et se aliosque
praecipitant, cum interim cucurrerunt aut salutaturi
aliquem non resalutaturum aut funus ignoti hominis

moves now upward, now downward, unless you consider that whatever can happen is likely to happen to you, you surrender yourself into the power of adversity, which any man can crush if he sees her first.

Our next concern will be not to labour either for useless ends or uselessly, that is, not to desire either what we are not able to accomplish, or what, if attained, will cause us to understand too late and after much shame the emptiness of our desires. In other words, neither should our labour be in vain and without result, nor the result unworthy of our labour ; for as a rule sadness attends upon it, if there has been either lack of success or shame for success. We must curtail the restlessness that a great many men show in wandering through houses and theatres and forums ; they thrust themselves into the affairs of others, and always appear to be busily engaged. If you ask one of these as he comes out of the house : " Where are you going ? What have you in mind ? " he will reply to you : " Upon my word, I really do not know ; but I shall see some people, I shall do something." They wander without any plan looking for employment, and they do, not what they have determined to do, but whatever they have stumbled upon. Their course is as aimless and idle as that of ants crawling among bushes, which idly bustle to the top of a twig and then to the bottom ; many men are like these in their way of life, which one may not unjustly call " busy idleness." When you see some of them running as if they were going to a fire, you will be sorry for them ; so often do they collide with those they meet and send themselves and others sprawling, though all the while they have been rushing to pay a call to someone who will not return it, or to attend

prosecuturi aut ad iudicium saepe litigantis aut ad sponsalia saepe nubentis et lecticam adsectati quibusdam locis etiam tulerunt. Dein domum cum supervacua redeuntes lassitudine iurant nescire se ipsos, quare exierint, ubi fuerint, postero die erraturi 5 per eadem illa vestigia. Omnis itaque labor aliquo referatur, aliquo respiciat ! Non industria inquietos, sed insanos falsae rerum imagines agitant. Nam ne illi quidem sine aliqua spe moventur ; proritat illos alicuius rei species, cuius vanitatem capta mens non 6 coarguit. Eodem modo unumquemque ex his, qui ad augendam turbam exeunt, inanes et leves causae per urbem circumducunt ; nihilque habentem, in quod laboret, lux orta expellit, et cum multorum frustra liminibus inlisus nomenculatores persalutavit, a multis exclusus neminem ex omnibus difficilius domi 7 quam se convenit. Ex hoc malo dependet illud taeterrimum vitium, auscultatio et publicorum secretorumque inquisitio et multarum rerum scientia, quae nec tuto narrantur nec tuto audiuntur.

1   13. Hoc secutum puto Democritum ita coepisse : " Qui tranquille volet vivere, nec privatim agat multa nec publice," ad supervacua scilicet referentem. Nam si necessaria sunt, et privatim et publice non tantum multa sed innumerabilia agenda sunt ; ubi

---

the funeral of a man they do not know, or the trial of someone who is always having a suit, or the betrothal of some woman who is always getting married, and, having attached themselves to some litter, have in some places even carried it. Afterwards, when they are returning home wearied to no purpose, they swear that they themselves do not know why they left home, or where they have been, and on the next day they will wander over the selfsame track. And so let all your effort be directed toward some object, let it keep some object in view! It is not activity that makes men restless, but false conceptions of things render them mad. For even madmen do not become agitated without some hope; they are excited by the mere appearance of some object, the falsity of which is not apparent to their afflicted mind. In the same way every one of those who go forth to swell the throng is led around the city by worthless and trivial reasons; dawn drives a man forth though he has no task to do, and, after he has been crushed in many men's door-ways, all in vain, and has saluted their nomenclators one after another, and has been shut out by many, he finds that, of them all, not one is more difficult to catch at home than himself. From this evil is derived that most disgusting vice of eavesdropping and prying into public and secret matters and learning of many things that it is neither safe to tell nor safe to listen to.

I fancy that Democritus [a] was thinking of this when he began: "If a man shall wish to live tranquilly, let him not engage in many affairs either public or private," referring of course to useless affairs. For if necessity demands, we must engage in many, even countless, affairs both public and private; but when

265

vero nullum officium sollemne nos citat, inhibendae
2 actiones. Nam qui multa agit, saepe fortunae
potestatem sui facit, quam tutissimum est raro
experiri, ceterum semper de illa cogitare et nihil sibi
de fide eius promittere. " Navigabo, nisi si quid
inciderit " et " Praetor fiam, nisi si quid obstiterit "
et " Negotiatio mihi respondebit, nisi si quid inter-
3 venerit." Hoc est quare sapienti nihil contra
opinionem dicamus accidere : non illum casibus
hominum excerpimus sed erroribus, nec illi omnia ut
voluit cedunt, sed ut cogitavit ; imprimis autem
cogitavit aliquid posse propositis suis resistere.
Necesse est autem levius ad animum pervenire
destitutae cupiditatis dolorem, cui successum non
utique promiseris.

1 14. Faciles etiam nos facere debemus, ne nimis
destinatis rebus indulgeamus, transeamusque in ea,
in quae nos ˙casus deduxerit, nec mutationem aut
consili aut status pertimescamus, dummodo nos
levitas, inimicissimum quieti vitium, non excipiat.
Nam et pertinacia necesse est anxia et misera sit,
cui fortuna saepe aliquid extorquet, et levitas multo
gravior nusquam se continens. Utrumque infestum
est tranquillitati, et nihil mutare posse et nihil pati.
2 Utique animus ab omnibus externis in se revocandus
est. Sibi confidat, se gaudeat, sua suspiciat, recedat
quantum potest ab alienis et se sibi adplicet, damna

there is no call from sacred duty, we must restrain our
activities. For if a man engages in many affairs, he
often puts himself in the power of Fortune, while his
safest course is rarely to tempt her, always to be
mindful of her, and never to put any trust in her
promises. Say, " I will set sail unless something
happens," and " I shall become praetor unless something hinders me," and " My enterprise will be
successful unless something interferes." This is why
we say that nothing happens to a wise man contrary
to his expectations—we release him, not from the
accidents, but from the blunders of mankind, nor do
all things turn out as he has wished, but as he has
thought ; but his first thought has been that something might obstruct his plans. Then, too, the
suffering that comes to the mind from the abandonment of desire must necessarily be much lighter if
you have not certainly promised it success.

   We ought also to make ourselves adaptable lest we
become too fond of the plans we have formed, and we
should pass readily to the condition to which chance
has led us, and not dread shifting either purpose or
positions—provided that fickleness, a vice most hostile
to repose, does not get hold of us. For obstinacy, from
which Fortune often wrests some concession, must
needs be anxious and unhappy, and much more
grievous must be a fickleness that nowhere shows
self-restraint. Both are foes to tranquillity—both
the inability to change and the inability to endure.
Most of all, the mind must be withdrawn from
external interests into itself. Let it have confidence
in itself, rejoice in itself, let it admire its own things,
let it retire as far as possible from the things of others
and devote itself to itself, let it not feel losses, let it

non sentiat, etiam adversa benigne interpretetur.
3 Nuntiato naufragio Zenon noster, cum omnia sua
audiret submersa : " Iubet," inquit, " me fortuna
expeditius philosophari." Minabatur Theodoro
philosopho tyrannus mortem et quidem insepultam :
" Habes," inquit, " cur tibi placeas, hemina sanguinis
in tua potestate est ; nam quod ad sepulturam pertinet, o te ineptum, si putas mea interesse, supra
4 terram an infra putrescam." Canus Iulius, vir imprimis magnus, cuius admirationi ne hoc quidem
obstat, quod nostro saeculo natus est, cum Gaio
diu altercatus, postquam abeunti Phalaris ille dixit :
" Ne forte inepta spe tibi blandiaris, duci te iussi,"
5 " Gratias," inquit, " ago, optime princeps." Quid
senserit dubito, multa enim mihi occurrunt. Contu-
meliosus esse voluit et ostendere, quanta crudelitas
esset, in qua mors beneficium erat ? An exprobravit
illi cotidianam dementiam ? (agebant enim gratias
et quorum liberi occisi et quorum bona ablata erant)
an tamquam libertatem libenter accepit ? Quic-
6 quid est, magno animo respondit. Dicet aliquis :
" Potuit post hoc iubere illum Gaius vivere." Non
timuit hoc Canus ; nota erat Gai in talibus imperiis
fides ! Credisne illum decem medios usque ad
supplicium dies sine ulla sollicitudine exegisse ?
Verisimile non est, quae vir ille dixerit, quae fecerit,

---

[a] *i.e.*, Caligula.

interpret kindly even adversities. Zeno, our master, when he received news of a shipwreck and heard that all his property had been sunk, said : " Fortune bids me to follow philosophy with fewer encumbrances." A tyrant was threatening the philosopher Theodorus with death and even with lack of burial: " You have the right," he replied, " to please yourself, you have within your power only a half pint of my blood ; for as to burial, you are a fool if you think it makes any difference to me whether I rot above ground or beneath it." Julius Canus, a rarely great man, whom even the fact that he was born in our own age does not prevent our admiring, had had a long dispute with Gaius,[a] and when, as he was leaving, Phalaris said to him : " That you may not by any chance comfort yourself with a foolish hope, I have ordered you to be executed," he replied : " Most excellent prince, I tender you my thanks." I am not sure what he meant, for many explanations occur to me. Did he wish to be insulting and show him how great his cruelty must be if it made death a kindness ? Or was he taunting him with the every-day proofs of insanity ?—for those whose children had been murdered and whose property had been confiscated used to thank him—or was it that he accepted death as a happy escape ? However it may be, it was a high-souled reply. But someone will say : " There was a possibility that after this Gaius might order him to live." Canus had no fear of that ; it was well known that in orders of this sort Gaius was a man of his word ! Will you believe that Canus spent the ten intervening days before his execution in no anxiety of any sort ? What the man said, what he did, how tranquil he was, passes all credence.

7 quam in tranquillo fuerit. Ludebat latrunculis, cum
centurio agmen periturorum trahens illum quoque
excitari iuberet. Vocatus numeravit calculos et
sodali suo: "Vide," inquit, "ne post mortem meam
mentiaris te vicisse"; tum annuens centurioni:
"Testis," inquit, "eris uno me antecedere." Lusisse
tu Canum illa tabula putas? Inlusit! Tristes erant
8 amici talem amissuri virum: "Quid maesti," inquit,
"estis? Vos quaeritis an immortales animae sint;
ego iam sciam." Nec desiit veritatem in ipso fine
9 scrutari et ex morte sua quaestionem habere. Prosequebatur. illum philosophus suus nec iam procul
erat tumulus, in quo Caesari deo nostro fiebat cotidianum sacrum; is: "Quid," inquit, "Cane, nunc
cogitas? Aut quae tibi mens est?" "Observare,"
inquit Canus, "proposui illo velocissimo momento an
sensurus sit animus exire se" promisitque, si quid
explorasset, circumiturum amicos et indicaturum,
10 quis esset animarum status. Ecce in media tempestate tranquillitas, ecce animus aeternitate dignus, qui
fatum suum in argumentum veri vocat, qui in ultimo
illo gradu positus exeuntem animam percontatur
nec usque ad mortem tantum sed aliquid etiam ex
ipsa morte discit. Nemo diutius philosophatus est.
Non raptim relinquetur magnus vir et cum cura

He was playing chess when the centurion who was dragging off a whole company of victims to death ordered that he also be summoned. Having been called, he counted the pawns and said to his partner : " See that after my death you do not claim falsely that you won " ; then nodding to the centurion, he said : " You will bear witness that I am one pawn ahead." Do you think that at that board Canus was playing a game ? Nay, he was making game ! His friends were sad at the thought of losing such a man ; but " Why," said he, " are you sorrowful? You are wondering whether our souls are immortal ; but I shall soon know." Nor up to the very end did he cease to search for truth and to make his own death a subject for debate. His own teacher of philosophy was accompanying him, and, when they were not far from the low hill on which the daily sacrifice to Caesar, our god, was made, said : " What are you thinking of now, Canus, or what state of mind are you in ? " And Canus said : " I have determined to watch whether the spirit will be conscious that it is leaving the body when that fleetest of moments comes," and he promised that, if he discovered anything, he would make the round of his friends, and reveal to them what the state of the soul really is. Here is tranquillity in the very midst of the storm, here is a mind worthy of immortality—a spirit that summons its own fate to the proof of truth, that, in the very act of taking that one last step, questions the departing soul, and learns, not merely up to the point of death, but seeks to learn something even from death itself. No one has ever played the philosopher longer. Not hastily shall so great a man be abandoned, and he must be spoken of with

dicendus. Dabimus te in omnem memoriam, clarissimum caput, Gaianae cladis magna portio !

1 15. Sed nihil prodest privatae tristitiae causas abiecisse ; occupat enim nonnumquam odium generis humani. Cum cogitaveris, quam sit rara simplicitas et quam ignota innocentia et vix umquam, nisi cum expedit, fides, et occurrit tot scelerum felicium turba[1] et libidinis lucra damnaque pariter invisa et ambitio usque eo iam se suis non continens terminis, ut per turpitudinem splendeat : agitur animus in noctem et velut eversis virtutibus, quas nec sperare licet nec

2 habere prodest, tenebrae oboriuntur. In hoc itaque flectendi sumus, ut omnia vulgi vitia non invisa nobis sed ridicula videantur et Democritum potius imitemur quam Heraclitum. Hic enim, quotiens in publicum processerat, flebat, ille ridebat ; huic omnia quae agimus miseriae, illi ineptiae videbantur. Elevanda ergo omnia et facili animo ferenda ; humanius est[a]

3 deridere vitam quam deplorare. Adice quod de humano quoque genere melius meretur qui ridet illud quam qui luget ; ille ei spei bonae aliquid relinquit, hic autem stulte deflet quae corrigi posse desperat. Et universa contemplanti maioris animi est qui risum non tenet quam qui lacrimas, quando lenissimum adfectum animi movet et nihil magnum, nihil

---

[1] et occurrit tot scelerum felicium turba *transposed by Hermes after Koch from a position after* generis humani.

---

[a] *i.e.*, better befits a man.

respect. O most glorious soul, chief victim of the murders of Gaius, to the memory of all time will I consign thee!

But it does no good to have got rid of the causes of individual sorrow; for one is sometimes seized by hatred of the whole human race. When you reflect how rare is simplicity, how unknown is innocence, and how good faith scarcely exists, except when it is profitable, and when you think of all the throng of successful crimes and of the gains and losses of lust, both equally hateful, and of ambition that, so far from restraining itself within its own bounds, now gets glory from baseness—when we remember these things, the mind is plunged into night, and as though the virtues, which it is now neither possible to expect nor profitable to possess, had been overthrown, there comes overwhelming gloom. We ought, therefore, to bring ourselves to believe that all the vices of the crowd are, not hateful, but ridiculous, and to imitate Democritus rather than Heraclitus. For the latter, whenever he went forth into public, used to weep, the former to laugh; to the one all human doings seemed to be miseries, to the other follies. And so we ought to adopt a lighter view of things, and put up with them in an indulgent spirit; it is more human[a] to laugh at life than to lament over it. Add, too, that he deserves better of the human race also who laughs at it than he who bemoans it; for the one allows it some measure of good hope, while the other foolishly weeps over things that he despairs of seeing corrected. And, considering everything, he shows a greater mind who does not restrain his laughter than he who does not restrain his tears, since the laugher gives expression to the mildest of the emotions, and

severum, ne miserum quidem ex tanto paratu putat.
4 Singula propter quae laeti ac tristes sumus sibi
quisque proponat et sciet verum esse quod Bion dixit :
omnia hominum negotia simillima initiis esse nec
vitam illorum magis sanctam aut severam esse quam
5 conceptum, in nihilum recidere de[1] nihilo natos.   Sed
satius est publicos mores et humana vitia placide
accipere nec in risum nec in lacrimas excidentem ;
nam alienis malis torqueri aeterna miseria est, alienis
delectari malis voluptas inhumana, sicut illa inutilis
humanitas flere, quia aliquis filium efferat, et frontem
6 suam fingere.   In suis quoque malis ita gerere se
oportet, ut dolori tantum des, quantum natura[2]
poscit, non quantum consuetudo ; plerique enim
lacrimas fundunt, ut ostendant, et totiens siccos
oculos habent, quotiens spectator defuit, turpe
iudicantes non flere, cum omnes faciant.   Adeo
penitus hoc se malum fixit, ex aliena opinione pendere,
ut in simulationem etiam res simplicissima, dolor,
veniat.
1   16. Sequitur pars, quae solet non immerito con-
tristare et in sollicitudinem adducere.   Ubi bonorum
exitus mali sunt, ubi Socrates cogitur in carcere mori,
Rutilius in exilio vivere, Pompeius et Cicero clientibus
suis praebere cervicem, Cato ille, virtutum viva
imago, incumbens gladio simul de se actum esse[3]
ac de re publica palam facere, necesse est torqueri

---

[1] in nihilum recidere de *added by Buecheler.*
[2] natura *added by Gertz.*
[3] actum esse *added by v. d. Vliet after* republica.

deems that there is nothing important, nothing serious, nor wretched either, in the whole outfit of life. Let a man set before himself the causes, one by one, that give rise to joy and sadness, and he will learn that what Bion said is true, that all the doings of men are just like their beginnings, and that their life is no more respectable or serious than their conception, that born from nothingness they go back to nothingness. Yet it is better to accept calmly the ways of the public and the vices of man, and be thrown neither into laughter nor into tears ; for it is unending misery to be worried by the misfortunes of others, and unhuman pleasure to take delight in the misfortunes of others, just as it is a useless show of humanity to weep and pull a long face because someone is burying a son. In the matter of one's own misfortunes, too, the right way to act is to bestow on them the measure of sorrow that Nature, not custom, demands ; for many shed tears in order to make a show of them, and, whenever a spectator is lacking, their eyes are dry, though they judge it disgraceful not to weep when everyone is doing it. This evil of depending on the opinion of others has become so deeply implanted that even grief, the most natural thing in the world, becomes now a matter of pretence.

I come now to a class of cases which is wont with good cause to sadden and bring us concern. When good men come to bad ends, when Socrates is forced to die in prison, Rutilius to live in exile, Pompey and Cicero to offer their necks to their own clients, and great Cato, the living image of all the virtues, by falling upon his sword to show that the end had come for himself and for the state at the same time, we needs must be distressed that Fortune pays her re-

tam iniqua praemia fortunam persolvere. Et quid
sibi quisque tunc speret, cum videat pessima optimos
2 pati ? Quid ergo est ? Vide quomodo quisque
illorum tulerit, et si fortes fuerunt, ipsorum illos
animo desidera, si muliebriter et ignave perierunt,
nihil perît ; aut digni sunt, quorum virtus tibi placeat,
aut indigni, quorum desideretur ignavia. Quid enim
est turpius quam si maximi viri timidos fortiter
3 moriendo faciunt ? Laudemus totiens dignum laudibus et dicamus : " Tanto fortior, tanto felicior !
Omnes effugisti casus, livorem, morbum ; existi ex
custodia ; non tu dignus mala fortuna dis visus es,
sed indignus, in quem iam aliquid fortuna posset."
Subducentibus vero se et in ipsa morte ad vitam
4 respectantibus manus iniciendae sunt ! Neminem
flebo laetum, neminem flentem ; ille lacrimas meas
ipse abstersit, hic suis lacrimis effecit, ne ullis dignus
sit. Ego Herculem fleam, quod vivus uritur, aut
Regulum, quod tot clavis configitur, aut Catonem,
quod vulnera vulnerat[1] sua ? Omnes isti levi temporis impensa invenerunt, quomodo aeterni fierent,
et ad immortalitatem moriendo venerunt.

1   17. Est et illa sollicitudinum non mediocris materia,
si te anxie componas nec ullis simpliciter ostendas,
qualis multorum vita est, ficta, ostentationi parata ;
torquet enim adsidua observatio sui et deprendi

---

[1] vulnerat *added by Rossbach.*

[a] *Cf.* Seneca, *Epistles*, lxvii. 13 : "adspice M. Catonem
sacro illi pectori purissimas manus admoventem et vulnera
parum alte demissa laxantem."

wards so unjustly. And what hope can anyone then have for himself when he sees that the best men suffer the worst fate ? What then is the answer ? See the manner in which each one of them bore his fate, and if they were brave, desire with your heart hearts like theirs, if they perished like a woman and a coward, then nothing perished ; either they deserve that you should admire their virtue, or they do not deserve that you should desire their cowardice. For if the greatest men by dying bravely make others cowards, what could be more shameful ? Let us praise those deserving of praise over and over and say : " The braver a man is, the happier he is ! You have escaped from all accident, jealousy, and sickness ; you have gone forth from prison ; it was not that you seemed to the gods to be worthy of evil fortune, but unworthy of being subject any longer to the power of Fortune." But those who draw back and on the very threshold of death look back toward life— there is need to lay hands on these ! I shall weep for no one who is happy, for no one who weeps ; the one with his own hand has wiped away my tears, the other by his tears has made himself unworthy of having any of mine. Should I weep for Hercules because he was burned alive ? or for Regulus because he was pierced by so many nails ? or for Cato because he wounded his own wounds [a] ? All these by a slight sacrifice of time found out how they might become eternal, and by dying reached immortality.

And this, too, affords no small occasion for anxieties—if you are bent on assuming a pose and never reveal yourself to anyone frankly, in the fashion of many who live a false life that is all made up for show ; for it is torturous to be constantly watching

aliter ac solet metuit. Nec umquam cura solvimur,
ubi totiens nos aestimari putamus quotiens aspici ;
nam et multa incidunt, quae invitos denudent, et,
ut bene cedat tanta sui diligentia, non tamen iucunda
vita aut secura est semper sub persona viventium.

2 At illa quantum habet voluptatis sincera et per se
inornata[1] simplicitas, nihil obtendens moribus suis !
Subit tamen et haec vita contemptus periculum, si
omnia omnibus patent ; sunt enim qui fastidiant
quicquid propius adierunt. Sed nec virtuti periculum
est, ne admota oculis revilescat, et satius est simplici-
tate contemni quam perpetua simulatione torqueri.
Modum tamen rei adhibeamus ; multum interest,
simpliciter vivas an neglegenter.

3 Multum et in se recedendum est ; conversatio
enim dissimilium bene composita disturbat et renovat
adfectus et quicquid imbecillum in animo nec per-
curatum est exulcerat. Miscenda tamen ista et alter-
nanda sunt, solitudo et frequentia. Illa nobis faciet
hominum desiderium, haec nostri, et erit altera
alterius remedium ; odium turbae sanabit solitudo,
taedium solitudinis turba.

4 Nec in eadem intentione aequaliter retinenda
mens est, sed ad iocos devocanda. Cum puerulis
Socrates ludere non erubescebat, et Cato vino laxabat
animum curis publicis fatigatum, et Scipio triumphale

---

[1] per se inornata *A* : prorsus inornata *Gertz* : per se
ornata *inferior mss.*

oneself and be fearful of being caught out of our
usual rôle. And we are never free from concern if
we think that every time anyone looks at us he is
always taking our measure ; for many things happen
that strip off our pretence against our will, and,
though all this attention to self is successful, yet
the life of those who live under a mask cannot
be happy and without anxiety. But how much
pleasure there is in simplicity that is pure, in itself
unadorned, and veils no part of its character ! Yet
even such a life as this does run some risk of scorn, if
everything lies open to everybody ; for there are
those who disdain whatever has become too familiar.
But neither does virtue run any risk of being despised
when she is brought close to the eyes, and it is better
to be scorned by reason of simplicity than tortured
by perpetual pretence. Yet we should employ
moderation in the matter ; there is much difference
between living naturally and living carelessly.

Moreover, we ought to retire into ourselves very
often ; for intercourse with those of dissimilar natures
disturbs our settled calm, and rouses the passions
anew, and aggravates any weakness in the mind that
has not been thoroughly healed. Nevertheless the
two things must be combined and resorted to alter-
nately—solitude and the crowd. The one will make
us long for men, the other for ourselves, and the one
will relieve the other ; solitude will cure our aversion
to the throng, the throng our weariness of solitude.

And the mind must not be kept invariably at the
same tension, but must be diverted to amusements.
Socrates did not blush to play with little children,
and Cato, when he was wearied by the cares of state,
would relax his mind with wine, and Scipio would

illud ac militare corpus movebat ad numeros, non
molliter se infringens, ut nunc mos est etiam incessu
ipso ultra muliebrem mollitiam fluentibus, sed ut
antiqui illi viri solebant inter lusum ac festa tempora
virilem in modum tripudiare, non facturi detrimentum,
5 etiam si ab hostibus suis spectarentur. Danda est
animis remissio; meliores acrioresque requieti
surgent. Ut fertilibus agris non est imperandum—
cito enim illos exhauriet numquam intermissa
fecunditas,—ita animorum impetus adsiduus labor
franget, vires recipient paulum resoluti et remissi;
nascitur ex assiduitate laborum animorum hebetatio
quaedam et languor.
6 Nec ad hoc tanta hominum cupiditas tenderet,
nisi naturalem quandam voluptatem haberet lusus
iocusque, quorum frequens usus omne animis pondus
omnemque vim eripiet; nam et somnus refectioni
necessarius est, hunc tamen si per diem noctemque
continues, mors erit. Multum interest, remittas ali-
7 quid an solvas! Legum conditores festos instituerunt
dies, ut ad hilaritatem homines publice cogerentur,
tamquam necessarium laboribus interponentes temperamentum; et magni, ut dixi, viri quidam sibi
menstruas certis diebus ferias dabant, quidam nullum
non diem inter otium et curas dividebant. Qualem
Pollionem Asinium oratorem magnum meminimus,
quem nulla res ultra decumam detinuit; ne epistulas
quidem post eam horam legebat, ne quid novae

---

^a Since the Romans divided the period between sunrise
and sunset into twelve hours, his labours ceased two hours
before sunset.

disport his triumphal and soldierly person to the sound of music, moving not with the voluptuous contortions that are now the fashion, when men even in walking squirm with more than a woman's voluptuousness, but in the manly style in which men in the days of old were wont to dance during the times of sport and festival, risking no loss of dignity even if their own enemies looked on. The mind must be given relaxation; it will arise better and keener after resting. As rich fields must not be forced—for their productiveness, if they have no rest, will quickly exhaust them—so constant labour will break the vigour of the mind, but if it is released and relaxed a little while, it will recover its powers; continuous mental toil breeds in the mind a certain dullness and languor.

Nor would the desire of men tend so much in this direction unless sport and amusement brought a sort of pleasure that was natural, but the frequent use of these will steal all weight and all force from the mind; for sleep also is necessary for refreshment, nevertheless if you prolong it throughout the day and night, it will be death. There is a great difference between slackening and removing your bond! The founders of our laws appointed days of festival in order that men might be forced by the state into merry-making, thinking that it was necessary to modify their toil by some interruption of their tasks; and among great men, as I have remarked, some used to set aside fixed days every month for a holiday, some divided every day into play-time and work-time. Asinius Pollio, the great orator, I remember, had such a rule, and never worked at anything beyond the tenth hour [a]; he would not even read letters after that hour for fear something new might arise

curae nasceretur, sed totius diei lassitudinem duabus
illis horis ponebat. Quidam medio die interiunxerunt
et in postmeridianas horas aliquid levioris operae
distulerunt. Maiores quoque nostri novam relationem post horam decumam in senatu fieri vetabant.
Miles vigilias dividit, et nox immunis est ab expe
8 ditione redeuntium. Indulgendum est animo dandumque subinde otium, quod alimenti ac virium loco
sit.

Et in ambulationibus apertis vagandum, ut caelo
libero et multo spiritu augeat attollatque se animus ;
aliquando vectatio iterque et mutata regio vigorem
dabunt convictusque et liberalior potio. Non numquam et usque ad ebrietatem veniendum, non ut
mergat nos, sed ut deprimat ; eluit enim curas et
ab imo animum movet et ut morbis quibusdam
ita tristitiae medetur ; Liberque non ob licentiam
linguae dictus est inventor vini, sed quia liberat
servitio curarum animum et adserit vegetatque et
9 audaciorem in omnis conatus facit. Sed ut libertatis
ita vini salubris moderatio est. Solonem Arcesilanque
indulsisse vino credunt, Catoni ebrietas obiecta est ;
facilius efficiet, quisquis obiecit ei, crimen honestum
quam turpem Catonem. Sed nec saepe faciendum est,
ne animus malam consuetudinem ducat, et aliquando
tamen in exultationem libertatemque extrahendus

---

^a Liber (Bacchus) is here the equivalent of Greek Lyaeus
(λύω " to loose ").

that needed attention, but in those two hours laid aside the weariness of the whole long day. Some break off in the middle of the day, and reserve some task that requires lighter effort for the afternoon hours. Our ancestors, too, forbade any new motion to be made in the senate after the tenth hour. The soldier divides his watches, and those who have just returned from an expedition have the whole night free. We must be indulgent to the mind, and from time to time must grant it the leisure that serves as its food and strength.

And, too, we ought to take walks out-of-doors in order that the mind may be strengthened and refreshed by the open air and much breathing ; sometimes it will get new vigour from a journey by carriage and a change of place and festive company and generous drinking. At times we ought to reach the point even of intoxication, not drowning ourselves in drink, yet succumbing to it ; for it washes away troubles, and stirs the mind from its very depths and heals its sorrow just as it does certain ills of the body ; and the inventor of wine is not called the Releaser[a] on account of the licence it gives to the tongue, but because it frees the mind from bondage to cares and emancipates it and gives it new life and makes it bolder in all that it attempts. But, as in freedom, so in wine there is a wholesome moderation. It is believed that Solon and Arcesilaus were fond of wine, and Cato has been reproached for drunkenness ; but whoever reproaches that man will more easily make reproach honourable than Cato base. Yet we ought not to do this often, for fear that the mind may contract an evil habit, nevertheless there are times when it must be drawn into rejoicing and freedom, and

283

10 tristisque sobrietas removenda paulisper. Nam sive Graeco poetae credimus ' aliquando et insanire iucundum est,' sive Platoni ' frustra poeticas fores compos sui pepulit,' sive Aristoteli ' nullum magnum ingenium sine mixtura dementiae fuit ' : non potest grande aliquid et super ceteros loqui nisi mota mens.

11 Cum vulgaria et solita contempsit instinctuque sacro surrexit excelsior, tunc demum aliquid cecinit grandius ore mortali. Non potest sublime quicquam et in arduo positum contingere, quam diu apud se est; desciscat oportet a solito et efferatur et mordeat frenos et rectorem rapiat suum eoque ferat, quo per se timuisset escendere.

12 Habes, Serene carissime, quae possint tranquillitatem tueri, quae restituere, quae subrepentibus vitiis resistant. Illud tamen scito, nihil horum satis esse validum rem imbecillam servantibus, nisi intenta et adsidua cura circumit animum labentem.

ᵃ The Greek sentiment, which survives in Menander's συμμανῆναι δ' ἔνια δεῖ (*Frag.* 421 Kock), reappears in Horace's "dulce est desipere in loco" (*Carm.* iv. 12. 28).

ᵇ The idea is an ancient commonplace; *cf.* Plato, *Phaedrus*, 245 ᴀ : Aristotle, *Problemata*, 30. 1.

gloomy sobriety must be banished for a while. For whether we believe with the Greek poet[a] that " sometimes it is a pleasure also to rave," or with Plato that " the sane mind knocks in vain at the door of poetry," or with Aristotle that " no great genius has ever existed without some touch of madness "[b] —be that as it may, the lofty utterance that rises above the attempts of others is impossible unless the mind is excited. When it has scorned the vulgar and the commonplace, and has soared far aloft fired by divine inspiration, then alone it chants a strain too lofty for mortal lips. So long as it is left to itself, it is impossible for it to reach any sublime and difficult height ; it must forsake the common track and be driven to frenzy and champ the bit and run away with its rider and rush to a height that it would have feared to climb by itself.

Here are the rules, my dearest Serenus, by which you may preserve tranquillity, by which you may restore it, by which you may resist the vices that steal upon it unawares. Yet be sure of this—none of them is strong enough to guard a thing so frail unless we surround the wavering mind with earnest and unceasing care.

LIBER X

AD PAVLINVM

DE BREVITATE VITAE

1 1. Maior pars mortalium, Pauline, de naturae malignitate conqueritur, quod in exiguum aevi gignamur, quod haec tam velociter, tam rapide dati nobis temporis spatia decurrant, adeo ut exceptis admodum paucis ceteros in ipso vitae apparatu vita destituat. Nec huic publico, ut opinantur, malo turba tantum et imprudens[1] volgus ingemuit; clarorum quoque virorum hic affectus querellas evocavit. Inde illa maximi medicorum exclamatio est: ' vitam brevem 2 esse, longam artem '; inde Aristotelis cum rerum natura exigentis minime conveniens sapienti viro lis : ' aetatis illam animalibus tantum indulsisse, ut

---

[1] imprudens *inferior mss.* : impudens *A.*

---

[a] It is clear from chapters 18 and 19 that, when this essay was written (in or about A.D. 49), Paulinus was *praefectus annonae*, the official who superintended the grain supply of Rome, and was, therefore, a man of importance. He was, believably, a near relative of Seneca's wife, Pompeia Paulina, and is usually identified with the father of a certain Pompeius Paulinus, who held high public posts under Nero (Pliny, *Nat. Hist.* xxxiii. 143; Tacitus, *Annals*, xiii. 53. 2; xv. 18. 4).

BOOK X

ON THE SHORTNESS OF LIFE

THE majority of mortals, Paulinus,[a] complain bitterly of the spitefulness of Nature, because we are born for a brief span of life, because even this space that has been granted to us rushes by so speedily and so swiftly that all save a very few find life at an end just when they are getting ready to live. Nor is it merely the common herd and the unthinking crowd that bemoan what is, as men deem it, an universal ill; the same feeling has called forth complaint also from men who were famous. It was this that made the greatest of physicians exclaim that " life is short, art is long; "[b] it was this that led Aristotle,[c] while expostulating with Nature, to enter an indictment most unbecoming to a wise man—that, in point of age, she has shown such favour to animals that they

[b] The famous aphorism of Hippocrates of Cos: ὁ βίος βραχύς, ἡ δὲ τέχνη μακρή.

[c] An error for Theophrastus, as shown by Cicero, *Tusc. Disp.* iii. 69: "Theophrastus autem moriens accusasse naturam dicitur, quod cervis et cornicibus vitam diuturnam, quorum id nihil interesset, hominibus, quorum maxime interfuisset, tam exiguam vitam dedisset; quorum si aetas potuisset esse longinquior, futurum fuisse ut omnibus perfectis artibus omni doctrina hominum vita erudiretur."

287

quina aut dena saecula educerent, homini in tam
multa ac magna genito tanto citeriorem terminum
3 stare.' Non exiguum temporis habemus, sed multum perdimus. Satis longa vita et in maximarum
rerum consummationem large data est, si tota bene
collocaretur ; sed ubi per luxum ac neglegentiam
diffluit, ubi nulli bonae rei impenditur, ultima demum
necessitate cogente quam ire non intelleximus
4 transisse sentimus. Ita est : non accipimus brevem
vitam, sed facimus, nec inopes eius sed prodigi sumus.
Sicut amplae et regiae opes, ubi ad malum dominum
pervenerunt, momento dissipantur, at quamvis
modicae, si bono custodi traditae sunt, usu crescunt,
ita aetas nostra bene disponenti multum patet.

1 2. Quid de rerum natura querimur ? Illa se
benigne gessit ; vita, si uti scias, longa est. At[1]
alium insatiabilis tenet avaritia, alium in supervacuis
laboribus operosa sedulitas ; alius vino madet, alius
inertia torpet ; alium defatigat ex alienis iudiciis
suspensa semper ambitio, alium mercandi praeceps
cupiditas circa omnis terras, omnia maria spe lucri
ducit ; quosdam torquet cupido militiae numquam
non aut alienis periculis intentos aut suis anxios ;
sunt quos ingratus superiorum cultus voluntaria
2 servitute consumat ; multos aut affectatio alienae
fortunae aut suae querella[2] detinuit ; plerosque

---

[1] at *supplied by Pauly.*
[2] querella *Madvig* : qua *A* : cura *Haase.*

---

* *i.e.,* of man. *Cf.* Hesiod, *Frag.* 183 (Rzach):

Ἐννέα τοι ζώει γενεὰς λακέρυζα κορώνη
ἀνδρῶν γηράντων· ἔλαφος δέ τε τετρακόρωνος.

drag out five or ten lifetimes,[a] but that a much shorter limit is fixed for man, though he is born for so many and such great achievements. It is not that we have a short space of time, but that we waste much of it. Life is long enough, and it has been given in sufficiently generous measure to allow the accomplishment of the very greatest things if the whole of it is well invested. But when it is squandered in luxury and carelessness, when it is devoted to no good end, forced at last by the ultimate necessity we perceive that it has passed away before we were aware that it was passing. So it is—the life we receive is not short, but we make it so, nor do we have any lack of it, but are wasteful of it. Just as great and princely wealth is scattered in a moment when it comes into the hands of a bad owner, while wealth however limited, if it is entrusted to a good guardian, increases by use, so our life is amply long for him who orders it properly.

Why do we complain of Nature ? She has shown herself kindly ; life, if you know how to use it, is long. But one man is possessed by an avarice that is insatiable, another by a toilsome devotion to tasks that are useless ; one man is besotted with wine, another is paralyzed by sloth ; one man is exhausted by an ambition that always hangs upon the decision of others, another, driven on by the greed of the trader, is led over all lands and all seas by the hope of gain ; some are tormented by a passion for war and are always either bent upon inflicting danger upon others or concerned about their own ; some there are who are worn out by voluntary servitude in a thankless attendance upon the great ; many are kept busy either in the pursuit of other men's fortune or in complaining of their own ; many, following no fixed aim, shifting

nihil certum sequentis vaga et inconstans et sibi
displicens levitas per nova consilia iactavit ; quibusdam nihil, quo cursum derigant, placet, sed mar-
centis oscitantisque fata deprendunt, adeo ut quod
apud maximum poetarum more oraculi dictum est,[a]
verum esse non dubitem : " Exigua pars est vitae,
qua vivimus." Ceterum quidem omne spatium non
3 vita sed tempus est. Urgent et circumstant vitia
undique nec resurgere aut in dispectum veri attollere
oculos sinunt, sed immersos et in cupiditatem infixos
premunt. Numquam illis recurrere ad se licet ; si
quando aliqua fortuito quies contigit, velut profundum mare, in quo post ventum quoque volutatio est,
fluctuantur nec umquam illis a cupiditatibus suis
4 otium stat. De istis me putas dicere, quorum in
confesso mala sunt ? Aspice illos, ad quorum
felicitatem concurritur ; bonis suis offocantur. Quam
multis divitiae graves sunt ! Quam multorum eloquentia et cotidiana[1] ostentandi ingenii sollicitatio[2]
sanguinem educit ! Quam multi continuis voluptatibus pallent ! Quam multis nihil liberi relinquit
circumfusus clientium populus ! Omnis denique
istos ab infimis usque ad summos pererra : hic advocat,[b]
hic adest, ille periclitatur, ille defendit, ille iudicat,
nemo se sibi vindicat, alius in alium consumitur.
Interroga de istis, quorum nomina ediscuntur, his
illos dinosci videbis notis : ille illius cultor est,

---

[1] eloquentia et (?) cotidiana *apparently* A^1.
[2] sollicitatio *Bourgery* : spatio A : occupatio *Gertz.*

---

[a] A prose rendering of an unknown poet. *Cf.* the epitaph
quoted by Cassius Dio, lxix. 19 : Σίμιλις ἐνταῦθα κεῖται βιοὺς
μὲν ἔτη τόσα, ζήσας δὲ ἔτη ἑπτά.
[b] Not one who undertook the actual defence, but one who
by his presence and advice lent support in court.

and inconstant and dissatisfied, are plunged by their fickleness into plans that are ever new; some have no fixed principle by which to direct their course, but Fate takes them unawares while they loll and yawn—so surely does it happen that I cannot doubt the truth of that utterance which the greatest of poets delivered with all the seeming of an oracle: "The part of life we really live is small." [a] For all the rest of existence is not life, but merely time. Vices beset us and surround us on every side, and they do not permit us to rise anew and lift up our eyes for the discernment of truth, but they keep us down when once they have overwhelmed us and we are chained to lust. Their victims are never allowed to return to their true selves; if ever they chance to find some release, like the waters of the deep sea which continue to heave even after the storm is past, they are tossed about and no rest from their lusts abides. Think you that I am speaking of the wretches whose evils are admitted? Look at those whose prosperity men flock to behold; they are smothered by their blessings. To how many are riches a burden! From how many do eloquence and the daily straining to display their powers draw forth blood! How many are pale from constant pleasures! To how many does the throng of clients that crowd about them leave no freedom! In short, run through the list of all these men from the lowest to the highest—this man desires an advocate,[b] this one answers the call, that one is on trial, that one defends him, that one gives sentence; no one asserts his claim to himself, everyone is wasted for the sake of another. Ask about the men whose names are known by heart, and you will see that these are the marks that distinguish them: A cultivates B and B

5 hic illius; suus nemo est. Deinde dementissima quorundam indignatio est : queruntur de superiorum fastidio, quod ipsis adire volentibus non vacaverint ! Audet quisquam de alterius superbia queri, qui sibi ipse numquam vacat ? Ille tamen te, quisquis es, insolenti quidem vultu sed aliquando respexit, ille aures suas ad tua verba demisit, ille te ad latus suum recepit ; tu non inspicere te umquam, non audire dignatus es. Non est itaque, quod ista officia cuiquam imputes, quoniam quidem, cum illa faceres, non esse cum alio volebas, sed tecum esse non poteras.

1 3. Omnia licet, quae umquam ingenia fulserunt, in hoc unum consentiant, numquam satis hanc humanarum mentium caliginem mirabuntur. Praedia sua occupari a nullo patiuntur et, si exigua contentio est de modo finium, ad lapides et arma discurrunt ; in vitam suam incedere alios sinunt, immo vero ipsi etiam possessores eius futuros inducunt. Nemo invenitur, qui pecuniam suam dividere velit ; vitam unusquisque quam multis distribuit ! Adstricti sunt in continendo patrimonio, simul ad iacturam temporis ventum est, profusissimi in eo, cuius unius honesta 2 avaritia est. Libet itaque ex seniorum turba comprendere aliquem : " Pervenisse te ad ultimum aetatis humanae videmus, centesimus tibi vel supra

cultivates C ; no one is his own master. And then certain men show the most senseless indignation— they complain of the insolence of their superiors, because they were too busy to see them when they wished an audience ! But can anyone have the hardihood to complain of the pride of another when he himself has no time to attend to himself ? After all, no matter who you are, the great man does sometimes look toward you even if his face is insolent, he does sometimes condescend to listen to your words, he permits you to appear at his side ; but you never deign to look upon yourself, to give ear to yourself. There is no reason, therefore, to count anyone in debt for such services, seeing that, when you performed them, you had no wish for another's company, but could not endure your own.

Though all the brilliant intellects of the ages were to concentrate upon this one theme, never could they adequately express their wonder at this dense darkness of the human mind. Men do not suffer anyone to seize their estates, and they rush to stones and arms if there is even the slightest dispute about the limit of their lands, yet they allow others to trespass upon their life—nay, they themselves even lead in those who will eventually possess it. No one is to be found who is willing to distribute his money, yet among how many does each one of us distribute his life ! In guarding their fortune men are often closefisted, yet, when it comes to the matter of wasting time, in the case of the one thing in which it is right to be miserly, they show themselves most prodigal. And so I should like to lay hold upon someone from the company of older men and say : " I see that you have reached the farthest limit of human life, you are

293

premitur annus ; agedum, ad computationem aetatem tuam revoca. Duc, quantum ex isto tempore
creditor, quantum amica, quantum rex, quantum
cliens abstulerit, quantum lis uxoria, quantum
servorum coercitio, quantum officiosa per urbem
discursatio. Adice morbos, quos manu fecimus,
adice et quod sine usu iacuit ; videbis te pauciores
3 annos habere quam numeras. Repete memoria
tecum, quando certus consilii fueris, quotus quisque
dies ut destinaveras processerit, quando tibi usus tui
fuerit, quando in statu suo vultus, quando animus
intrepidus, quid tibi in tam longo aevo facti operis
sit, quam multi vitam tuam diripuerint te non
sentiente quid perderes, quantum vanus dolor, stulta
laetitia, avida cupiditas, blanda conversatio abstulerit,
quam exiguum tibi de tuo relictum sit ; intelleges
te immaturum mori." Quid ergo est in causa ?
4 Tamquam semper victuri vivitis, numquam vobis
fragilitas vestra succurrit, non observatis, quantum
iam temporis transierit ; velut ex pleno et abundanti
perditis, cum interim fortasse ille ipse qui alicui[1] vel
homini vel rei donatur dies ultimus sit. Omnia
tamquam mortales timetis, omnia tamquam im-
5 mortales concupiscitis. Audies plerosque dicentes :
" A quinquagesimo anno in otium secedam, sexagesi-
mus me annus ab officiis dimittet." Et quem tandem
longioris vitae praedem accipis ? Quis ista sicut disponis

---

[1] alicui A^5 : aliquo A^1 : aliquoi *Gertz, Hermes.*

---

[a] Literally, " unripe." At 100 he should " come to his
grave in a full age, like as a shock of corn cometh in in
his season " (Job v. 26) ; but he is still unripe.

pressing hard upon your hundredth year, or are even beyond it; come now, recall your life and make a reckoning. Consider how much of your time was taken up with a moneylender, how much with a mistress, how much with a patron, how much with a client, how much in wrangling with your wife, how much in punishing your slaves, how much in rushing about the city on social duties. Add the diseases which we have caused by our own acts, add, too, the time that has lain idle and unused; you will see that you have fewer years to your credit than you count. Look back in memory and consider when you ever had a fixed plan, how few days have passed as you had intended, when you were ever at your own disposal, when your face ever wore its natural expression, when your mind was ever unperturbed, what work you have achieved in so long a life, how many have robbed you of life when you were not aware of what you were losing, how much was taken up in useless sorrow, in foolish joy, in greedy desire, in the allurements of society, how little of yourself was left to you; you will perceive that you are dying before your season!"[a] What, then, is the reason of this? You live as if you were destined to live forever, no thought of your frailty ever enters your head, of how much time has already gone by you take no heed. You squander time as if you drew from a full and abundant supply, though all the while that day which you bestow on some person or thing is perhaps your last. You have all the fears of mortals and all the desires of immortals. You will hear many men saying: "After my fiftieth year I shall retire into leisure, my sixtieth year shall release me from public duties." And what guarantee, pray, have you that your life will last longer? Who will

ire patietur? Non pudet te reliquias vitae tibi reservare et id solum tempus bonae menti destinare, quod in nullam rem conferri possit? Quam serum est tunc vivere incipere, cum desinendum est! Quae tam stulta mortalitatis oblivio in quinquagesimum et sexagesimum annum differre sana consilia et inde velle vitam inchoare, quo pauci perduxerunt!

1 4. Potentissimis et in altum sublatis hominibus excidere voces videbis, quibus otium optent, laudent, omnibus bonis suis praeferant. Cupiunt interim ex illo fastigio suo, si tuto liceat, descendere; nam ut nihil extra lacessat aut quatiat, in se ipsa fortuna ruit.

2 Divus Augustus, cui dii plura quam ulli praestiterunt, non desît quietem sibi precari et vacationem a re publica petere; omnis eius sermo ad hoc semper revolutus est, ut speraret otium. Hoc labores suos, etiam si falso, dulci tamen oblectabat solacio, ali-
3 quando se victurum sibi. In quadam ad senatum missa epistula, cum requiem suam non vacuam fore dignitatis nec a priore gloria discrepantem pollicitus esset, haec verba inveni: "Sed ista fieri speciosius quam promitti possunt. Me tamen cupido temporis optatissimi mihi provexit, ut quoniam rerum laetitia moratur adhuc, praeciperem aliquid voluptatis ex
4 verborum dulcedine." Tanta visa est res otium, ut illam, quia usu non poterat, cogitatione praesumeret. Qui omnia videbat ex se uno pendentia,

---

[a] The idea is that greatness sinks beneath its own weight. *Cf.* Seneca, *Agamemnon*, 88 *sq.*:

> Sidunt ipso pondere magna
> ceditque oneri Fortuna suo.

suffer your course to be just as you plan it ? Are you
not ashamed to reserve for yourself only the remnant
of life, and to set apart for wisdom only that time
which cannot be devoted to any business ? How
late it is to begin to live just when we must cease to
live ! What foolish forgetfulness of mortality to
postpone wholesome plans to the fiftieth and sixtieth
year, and to intend to begin life at a point to which
few have attained !

You will see that the most powerful and highly
placed men let drop remarks in which they long for
leisure, acclaim it, and prefer it to all their blessings.
They desire at times, if it could be with safety, to
descend from their high pinnacle ; for, though nothing from without should assail or shatter, Fortune
of its very self comes crashing down.[a]

The deified Augustus, to whom the gods vouchsafed
more than to any other man, did not cease to pray for
rest and to seek release from public affairs ; all his
conversation ever reverted to this subject—his hope
of leisure. This was the sweet, even if vain, consolation with which he would gladden his labours—that
he would one day live for himself. In a letter addressed to the senate, in which he had promised that
his rest would not be devoid of dignity nor inconsistent with his former glory, I find these words :
" But these matters can be shown better by deeds
than by promises. Nevertheless, since the joyful
reality is still far distant, my desire for that time most
earnestly prayed for has led me to forestall some of
its delight by the pleasure of words." So desirable a
thing did leisure seem that he anticipated it in thought
because he could not attain it in reality. He who saw
everything depending upon himself alone, who deter-

qui hominibus gentibusque fortunam dabat, illum
diem laetissimus cogitabat, quo magnitudinem suam
exueret. Expertus erat, quantum illa bona per
omnis terras fulgentia sudoris exprimerent, quantum
5 occultarum sollicitudinum tegerent. Cum civibus
primum, deinde cum collegis, novissime cum adfinibus
coactus armis decernere mari terraque sanguinem
fudit.

Per Macedoniam, Siciliam, Aegyptum, Syriam
Asiamque et omnis prope oras bello circumactus
Romana caede lassos exercitus ad externa bella
convertit. Dum Alpes pacat[1] immixtosque mediae
paci et imperio hostes perdomat, dum vel ultra
Rhenum et Euphraten et Danuvium terminos movet,
in ipsa urbe Murenae, Caepionis, Lepidi, Egnati,
aliorum in eum mucrones acuebantur. Nondum
horum effugerat insidias : filia et tot nobiles iuvenes
adulterio velut sacramento adacti iam infractam
aetatem territabant Paulusque[2] et iterum timenda
cum Antonio mulier. Haec ulcera cum ipsis membris
absciderat : alia subnascebantur ; velut grave multo
sanguine corpus parte semper aliqua rumpebatur.
Itaque otium optabat, in huius spe et cogitatione
labores eius residebant, hoc votum erat eius, qui voti
compotes facere poterat.

[1] pacat *inferior mss.* : placat *A*.
[2] Paullusque *Ruben* : plusque *A* : Iullusque *Bourgery
after Waltz.*

[a] The notorious Julia, who was banished by Augustus to
the island of Pandataria.

[b] In 31 B.C. Augustus had been pitted against Mark
Antony and Cleopatra; in 2 B.C. Iullus Antonius, younger
son of the triumvir, was sentenced to death by reason of his
intrigue with the elder Julia.

[c] The language is reminiscent of Augustus's own charac-

mined the fortune of individuals and of nations, thought most happily of that future day on which he should lay aside his greatness. He had discovered how much sweat those blessings that shone throughout all lands drew forth, how many secret worries they concealed. Forced to pit arms first against his countrymen, then against his colleagues, and lastly against his relatives, he shed blood on land and sea.

Through Macedonia, Sicily, Egypt, Syria, and Asia, and almost all countries he followed the path of battle, and when his troops were weary of shedding Roman blood, he turned them to foreign wars. While he was pacifying the Alpine regions, and subduing the enemies planted in the midst of a peaceful empire, while he was extending its bounds even beyond the Rhine and the Euphrates and the Danube, in Rome itself the swords of Murena, Caepio, Lepidus, Egnatius, and others were being whetted to slay him. Not yet had he escaped their plots, when his daughter [a] and all the noble youths who were bound to her by adultery as by a sacred oath, oft alarmed his failing years—and there was Paulus, and a second time the need to fear a woman in league with an Antony.[b] When he had cut away these ulcers [c] together with the limbs themselves, others would grow in their place; just as in a body that was overburdened with blood, there was always a rupture somewhere. And so he longed for leisure, in the hope and thought of which he found relief for his labours. This was the prayer of one who was able to answer the prayers of mankind.

terization of Julia and his two grandchildren in Suetonius (*Aug.* 65. 5): " nec (solebat) aliter eos appellare quam tris vomicas ac tria carcinomata sua " (" his trio of boils and trio of ulcers ").

1   5. M. Cicero inter Catilinas, Clodios iactatus Pompeiosque et Crassos, partim manifestos inimicos, partim dubios amicos, dum fluctuatur cum re publica et illam pessum euntem tenet, novissime abductus, nec secundis rebus quietus nec adversarum patiens, quotiens illum ipsum consulatum suum non sine 2 causa sed sine fine laudatum detestatur! Quam flebiles voces exprimit in quadam ad Atticum epistula iam victo patre Pompeio, adhuc filio in Hispania fracta arma refovente! " Quid agam," inquit, " hic, quaeris? Moror in Tusculano meo semiliber." Alia deinceps adicit, quibus et priorem aetatem complorat 3 et de praesenti queritur et de futura desperat. Semiliberum se dixit Cicero. At me hercules numquam sapiens in tam humile nomen procedet, numquam semiliber erit, integrae semper libertatis et solidae, solutus et sui iuris et altior ceteris. Quid enim supra eum potest esse, qui supra fortunam est?

1   6. Livius Drusus, vir acer et vehemens, cum leges novas et mala Gracchana movisset stipatus ingenti totius Italiae coetu, exitum rerum non pervidens, quas nec agere licebat nec iam liberum erat semel incohatas relinquere, execratus inquietam a primordiis vitam dicitur dixisse uni sibi ne puero quidem umquam ferias contigisse. Ausus est enim et

---

    a Not extant.
    b As tribune in 91 B.C. he proposed a corn law and the granting of citizenship to the Italians.

Marcus Cicero, long flung among men like Catiline and Clodius and Pompey and Crassus, some open enemies, others doubtful friends, as he is tossed to and fro along with the state and seeks to keep it from destruction, to be at last swept away, unable as he was to be restful in prosperity or patient in adversity—how many times does he curse that very consulship of his, which he had lauded without end, though not without reason! How tearful the words he uses in a letter [a] written to Atticus, when Pompey the elder had been conquered, and the son was still trying to restore his shattered arms in Spain! "Do you ask," he said, "what I am doing here? I am lingering in my Tusculan villa half a prisoner." He then proceeds to other statements, in which he bewails his former life and complains of the present and despairs of the future. Cicero said that he was "half a prisoner." But, in very truth, never will the wise man resort to so lowly a term, never will he be half a prisoner —he who always possesses an undiminished and stable liberty, being free and his own master and towering over all others. For what can possibly be above him who is above Fortune?

When Livius Drusus,[b] a bold and energetic man, had with the support of a huge crowd drawn from all Italy proposed new laws and the evil measures of the Gracchi, seeing no way out for his policy, which he could neither carry through nor abandon when once started on, he is said to have complained bitterly against the life of unrest he had had from the cradle, and to have exclaimed that he was the only person who had never had a holiday even as a boy. For, while he

pupillus adhuc et praetextatus iudicibus reos commendare et gratiam suam foro interponere tam
efficaciter quidem, ut quaedam iudicia constet ab
2 illo rapta. Quo non erumperet tam immatura
ambitio? Scires in malum ingens et privatum et
publicum evasuram tam praecoquem audaciam.
Sero itaque querebatur nullas sibi ferias contigisse
a puero seditiosus et foro gravis. Disputatur, an
ipse sibi manus attulerit; subito enim vulnere per
inguen accepto conlapsus est, aliquo dubitante, an
mors eius voluntaria esset, nullo, an tempestiva.

3 Supervacuum est commemorare plures, qui cum
aliis felicissimi viderentur, ipsi in se verum testimonium dixerunt perosi omnem actum annorum
suorum; sed his querellis nec alios mutaverunt nec
se ipsos. Nam cum verba eruperunt, adfectus ad
4 consuetudinem relabuntur. Vestra me hercules
vita, licet supra mille annos exeat, in artissimum
contrahetur; ista vitia nullum non saeculum de-
vorabunt. Hoc vero spatium quod, quamvis natura
currit, ratio dilatat, cito vos effugiat necesse est;
non enim adprenditis nec retinetis nec velocissimae
omnium rei moram facitis, sed abire ut rem supervacuam ac reparabilem sinitis.

was still a ward and wearing the dress of a boy, he had had the courage to commend to the favour of a jury those who were accused, and to make his influence felt in the law-courts, so powerfully, indeed, that it is very well known that in certain trials he forced a favourable verdict. To what lengths was not such premature ambition destined to go ? One might have known that such precocious hardihood would result in great personal and public misfortune. And so it was too late for him to complain that he had never had a holiday when from boyhood he had been a trouble-maker and a nuisance in the forum. It is a question whether he died by his own hand ; for he fell from a sudden wound received in his groin, some doubting whether his death was voluntary, no one, whether it was timely.

It would be superfluous to mention more who, though others deemed them the happiest of men, have expressed their loathing for every act of their years, and with their own lips have given true testimony against themselves ; but by these complaints they changed neither themselves nor others. For when they have vented their feelings in words, they fall back into their usual round. Heaven knows ! such lives as yours, though they should pass the limit of a thousand years, will shrink into the merest span ; your vices will swallow up any amount of time. The space you have, which reason can prolong, although it naturally hurries away, of necessity escapes from you quickly ; for you do not seize it, you neither hold it back, nor impose delay upon the swiftest thing in the world, but you allow it to slip away as if it were something superfluous and that could be replaced.

1 **7.** In primis autem et illos numero, qui nulli
rei nisi vino ac libidini vacant ; nulli enim turpius
occupati sunt. Ceteri etiam si vana gloriae imagine
teneantur, speciose tamen errant ; licet avaros mihi,
licet iracundos enumeres vel odia exercentes iniusta
vel bella, omnes isti virilius peccant ; in ventrem ac
2 libidinem proiectorum inhonesta labes est. Omnia
istorum tempora excute, aspice quam diu computent,
quam diu insidientur, quam diu timeant, quam diu
colant, quam diu colantur, quantum vadimonia sua
atque aliena occupent, quantum convivia, quae iam
ipsa officia sunt : videbis, quemadmodum illos
respirare non sinant vel mala sua vel bona.

3 Denique inter omnes convenit nullam rem bene
exerceri posse ab homine occupato, non eloquentiam,
non liberales disciplinas, quando districtus animus
nihil altius recipit, sed omnia velut inculcata respuit.
Nihil minus est hominis occupati quam vivere ; nullius
rei difficilior scientia est. Professores aliarum artium
volgo multique sunt, quasdam vero ex his pueri admodum ita percepisse visi sunt, ut etiam praecipere
possent. Vivere tota vita discendum est et, quod
magis fortasse miraberis, tota vita discendum est
4 mori. Tot maximi viri relictis omnibus impedi-

---

a Throughout the essay *occupati*, "the engrossed," is a
technical term designating those who are so absorbed in the
interests of life that they take no time for philosophy.

b i.e., the various types of *occupati* that have been
sketchily presented. The looseness of the structure has led
some editors to doubt the integrity of the passage.

But among the worst I count also those who have time for nothing but wine and lust; for none have more shameful engrossments.[a] The others, even if they are possessed by the empty dream of glory, nevertheless go astray in a seemly manner; though you should cite to me the men who are avaricious, the men who are wrathful, whether busied with unjust hatreds or with unjust wars, these all sin in more manly fashion. But those who are plunged into the pleasures of the belly and into lust bear a stain that is dishonourable. Search into the hours of all these people,[b] see how much time they give to accounts, how much to laying snares, how much to fearing them, how much to paying court, how much to being courted, how much is taken up in giving or receiving bail, how much by banquets—for even these have now become a matter of business—, and you will see how their interests, whether you call them evil or good, do not allow them time to breathe.

Finally, everybody agrees that no one pursuit can be successfully followed by a man who is busied with many things—eloquence cannot, nor the liberal studies—since the mind, when its interests are divided, takes in nothing very deeply, but rejects everything that is, as it were, crammed into it. There is nothing the busy man is less busied with than living; there is nothing that is harder to learn. Of the other arts there are many teachers everywhere; some of them we have seen that mere boys have mastered so thoroughly that they could even play the master. It takes the whole of life to learn how to live, and—what will perhaps make you wonder more—it takes the whole of life to learn how to die. Many very great men, having laid aside all

mentis, cum divitiis officiis voluptatibus renuntiassent,
hoc unum in extremam usque aetatem egerunt, ut
vivere scirent ; plures tamen ex his nondum se scire
5 confessi vita abierunt, nedum ut isti sciant. Magni,
mihi crede, et supra humanos errores eminentis viri
est nihil ex suo tempore delibari sinere, et ideo eius
vita longissima est, quia, quantumcumque patuit,
totum ipsi vacavit. Nihil inde incultum otiosumque
iacuit, nihil sub alio fuit, neque enim quicquam
repperit dignum quod cum tempore suo permutaret
custos eius parcissimus. Itaque satis illi fuit ; iis
vero necesse est defuisse, ex quorum vita multum
populus tulit.

6　Nec est quod putes non illos aliquando intellegere
damnum suum. Plerosque certe audies ex iis, quos
magna felicitas gravat, inter clientium greges aut
causarum actiones aut ceteras honestas miserias
exclamare interdum : " Vivere mihi non licet."
7 Quidni non liceat ? Omnes illi, qui te sibi advocant,
tibi abducunt. Ille reus quot dies abstulit ? Quot
ille candidatus ? Quot illa anus efferendis heredibus
lassa ? Quot ille ad irritandam avaritiam captantium
simulatus aeger ? Quot ille potentior amicus, qui
vos non in amicitiam, sed in apparatu[1] habet ? Dis-
punge, inquam, et recense vitae tuae dies ; videbis

---

[1] inamicitiã sed inapparatu *A*: in amicitiam sed in
apparatum *inferior* MSS.: in amicitia *Hermes*.

---

[a] *i.e.*, she has become the prey of legacy-hunters.

their encumbrances, having renounced riches, business, and pleasures, have made it their one aim up to the very end of life to know how to live ; yet the greater number of them have departed from life confessing that they did not yet know—still less do those others know. Believe me, it takes a great man and one who has risen far above human weaknesses not to allow any of his time to be filched from him, and it follows that the life of such a man is very long because he has devoted wholly to himself whatever time he has had. None of it lay neglected and idle ; none of it was under the control of another, for, guarding it most grudgingly, he found nothing that was worthy to be taken in exchange for his time. And so that man had time enough ; but those who have been robbed of much of their life by the public, have necessarily had too little of it.

And there is no reason for you to suppose that these people are not sometimes aware of their loss. Indeed, you will hear many of those who are burdened by great prosperity cry out at times in the midst of their throngs of clients, or their pleadings in court, or their other glorious miseries : " I have no chance to live." Of course you have no chance ! All those who summon you to themselves, turn you away from your own self. Of how many days has that defendant robbed you ? Of how many that candidate ? Of how many that old woman wearied with burying her heirs ? [a] Of how many that man who is shamming sickness for the purpose of exciting the greed of the legacy-hunters ? Of how many that very powerful friend who has you and your like on the list, not of his friends, but of his retinue ? Check off, I say, and review the days of your life ; you will see that very

8 paucos admodum et reiculos apud te resedisse. Adsecutus ille quos optaverat fasces cupit ponere et subinde dicit : " Quando hic annus praeteribit ? " Facit ille ludos, quorum sortem sibi optingere magno aestimavit : " Quando," inquit, " istos effugiam ? " Diripitur ille toto foro patronus et magno concursu omnia ultra, quam audiri potest, complet : " Quando," inquit, " res proferentur ? " Praecipitat quisque vitam suam et futuri desiderio laborat, praesentium **9** taedio. At ille qui nullum non tempus in usus suos confert, qui omnem diem tamquam ultimum[1] ordinat, nec optat crastinum nec timet. Quid enim est, quod iam ulla hora novae voluptatis possit adferre ? Omnia nota, omnia ad satietatem percepta sunt. De cetero fors fortuna, ut volet, ordinet ; vita iam in tuto est. Huic adici potest, detrahi nihil, et adici sic, quemadmodum saturo iam ac pleno aliquid cibi, quod nec desiderat et[2] **10** capit. Non est itaque quod quemquam propter canos aut rugas putes diu vixisse ; non ille diu vixit, sed diu fuit. Quid enim si illum multum putes navigasse, quem saeva tempestas a portu exceptum huc et illuc tulit ac vicibus ventorum ex diverso furentium per eadem spatia in orbem egit ? Non ille multum navigavit, sed multum iactatus est.

1 8. Mirari soleo, cum video aliquos tempus

[1] ultimum *Gertz after Bentley, Hermes* : vitam *A, Bourgery.*
[2] et *supplied by Madvig.*

----

[a] The rods that were the symbol of high office.
[b] At this time the management of the public games was committed to the praetors.

few, and those the refuse, have been left for you. That man who had prayed for the *fasces*,[a] when he attains them, desires to lay them aside and says over and over : " When will this year be over ! " That man gives games,[b] and, after setting great value on gaining the chance to give them, now says : " When shall I be rid of them ? " That advocate is lionized throughout the whole forum, and fills all the place with a great crowd that stretches farther than he can be heard, yet he says : " When will vacation-time come ? " Everyone hurries his life on and suffers from a yearning for the future and a weariness of the present. But he who bestows all of his time on his own needs, who plans out every day as if it were his last, neither longs for nor fears the morrow. For what new pleasure is there that any hour can now bring ? They are all known, all have been enjoyed to the full. Mistress Fortune may deal out the rest as she likes ; his life has already found safety. Something may be added to it, but nothing taken from it, and he will take any addition as the man who is satisfied and filled takes the food which he does not desire and yet can hold. And so there is no reason for you to think that any man has lived long because he has grey hairs or wrinkles ; he has not lived long —he has existed long. For what if you should think that that man had had a long voyage who had been caught by a fierce storm as soon as he left harbour, and, swept hither and thither by a succession of winds that raged from different quarters, had been driven in a circle around the same course ? Not much voyaging did he have, but much tossing about.

I am often filled with wonder when I see some men demanding the time of others and those from whom

petentes et eos, qui rogantur, facillimos. Illud
uterque spectat, propter quod tempus petitum est,
ipsum quidem neuter; quasi nihil petitur, quasi
nihil datur. Re omnium pretiosissima luditur; fallit
autem illos, quia res incorporalis est, quia sub oculos
non venit, ideoque vilissima aestimatur, immo paene
2 nullum eius pretium est. Annua, congiaria homines
carissime accipiunt et illis aut laborem aut operam
aut diligentiam suam locant. Nemo aestimat tempus; utuntur illo laxius quasi gratuito. At eosdem
aegros vide, si mortis periculum propius admotum
est, medicorum genua tangentes, si metuunt capitale
supplicium, omnia sua, ut vivant, paratos impendere!
3 Tanta in illis discordia adfectuum est. Quodsi posset
quemadmodum praeteritorum annorum cuiusque
numerus proponi, sic futurorum, quomodo illi, qui
paucos viderent superesse, trepidarent, quomodo
illis parcerent! Atqui facile est quamvis exiguum
dispensare, quod certum est; id debet servari diligentius, quod nescias quando deficiat.

4 Nec est tamen, quod putes illos ignorare, quam
cara res sit; dicere solent eis, quos valdissime diligunt, paratos se partem annorum suorum dare. Dant
nec intellegunt; dant autem ita, ut sine illorum in-
cremento sibi detrahant. Sed hoc ipsum, an de-

they ask it most indulgent. Both of them fix their eyes on the object of the request for time, neither of them on the time itself; just as if what is asked were nothing, what is given, nothing. Men trifle with the most precious thing in the world; but they are blind to it because it is an incorporeal thing, because it does not come beneath the sight of the eyes, and for this reason it is counted a very cheap thing—nay, of almost no value at all. Men set very great store by pensions and doles, and for these they hire out their labour or service or effort. But no one sets a value on time; all use it lavishly as if it cost nothing. But see how these same people clasp the knees of physicians if they fall ill and the danger of death draws nearer, see how ready they are, if threatened with capital punishment, to spend all their possessions in order to live! So great is the inconsistency of their feelings. But if each one could have the number of his future years set before him as is possible in the case of the years that have passed, how alarmed those would be who saw only a few remaining, how sparing of them would they be! And yet it is easy to dispense an amount that is assured, no matter how small it may be; but that must be guarded more carefully which will fail you know not when.

Yet there is no reason for you to suppose that these people do not know how precious a thing time is; for to those whom they love most devotedly they have a habit of saying that they are ready to give them a part of their own years. And they do give it, without realizing it; but the result of their giving is that they themselves suffer loss without adding to the years of their dear ones. But the very thing

trahant,[1] nesciunt; ideo tolerabilis est illis iactura
5 detrimenti latentis. Nemo restituet annos, nemo
iterum te tibi reddet. Ibit, qua coepit aetas, nec
cursum suum aut revocabit aut supprimet; nihil
tumultuabitur, nihil admonebit velocitatis suae.
Tacita labetur; non illa se regis imperio, non favore
populi longius proferet. Sicut missa est a primo
die, curret; nusquam devertetur, nusquam remo-
rabitur. Quid fiet? Tu occupatus es, vita festinat;
mors interim aderit, cui, velis nolis, vacandum est.

1 **9.** Potestne quicquam stultius esse quam quorundam[2] sensus, hominum eorum dico qui prudentiam
iactant? Operosius occupati sunt, ut melius possint
vivere; impendio vitae vitam instruunt! Cogitationes suas in longum ordinant; maxima porro vitae
iactura dilatio est; illa primum quemque extrahit
diem, illa eripit praesentia, dum ulteriora promittit.
Maximum vivendi impedimentum est expectatio, quae
pendet ex crastino, perdit hodiernum. Quod in manu
fortunae positum est, disponis, quod in tua, dimittis.
Quo spectas? Quo te extendis? Omnia quae ven-
2 tura sunt in incerto iacent; protinus vive! Clamat
ecce maximus vates et velut divino ore instinctus[3]
salutare carmen canit:

[1] andetraant *A*[2]: unde detrahant *Madvig, Hermes.*
[2] stultius esse quam quorundam *supplied by Bourgery*:
alii alia.
[3] ore instinctus *A*: ore instinctu *Hermes*: furore instinctus *Muretus*: ore et instinctu *Gertz*: horrore instinctus
Bourgery.

they do not know is whether they are suffering loss ; therefore the removal of something that is lost without being noticed they find is bearable. Yet no one will bring back the years, no one will bestow you once more on yourself. Life will follow the path it started upon, and will neither reverse nor check its course ; it will make no noise, it will not remind you of its swiftness. Silent it will glide on ; it will not prolong itself at the command of a king, or at the applause of the populace. Just as it was started on its first day, so it will run ; nowhere will it turn aside, nowhere will it delay. And what will be the result ? You have been engrossed, life hastens by ; meanwhile death will be at hand, for which, willy nilly, you must find leisure.

Can anything be sillier than the point of view of certain people—I mean those who boast of their foresight ? They keep themselves very busily engaged in order that they may be able to live better ; they spend life in making ready to live ! They form their purposes with a view to the distant future ; yet postponement is the greatest waste of life ; it deprives them of each day as it comes, it snatches from them the present by promising something hereafter. The greatest hindrance to living is expectancy, which depends upon the morrow and wastes to-day. You dispose of that which lies in the hands of Fortune, you let go that which lies in your own. Whither do you look ? At what goal do you aim ? All things that are still to come lie in uncertainty ; live straightway ! See how the greatest of bards cries out, and, as if inspired with divine utterance, sings the saving strain :

Optima quaeque dies miseris mortalibus **aevi**
prima fugit.

" Quid cunctaris ? " inquit, " Quid cessas ? Nisi
occupas, fugit." Et cum occupaveris, tamen fugiet ;
itaque cum celeritate temporis utendi velocitate
certandum est et velut ex torrenti rapido nec semper
3 ituro cito hauriendum. Hoc quoque pulcherrime
ad exprobrandam infinitam cunctationem,[1] quod non
optimam quamque aetatem sed diem dicit. Quid
securus et in tanta temporum fuga lentus menses
tibi et annos in longam seriem, utcumque aviditati
tuae visum est, exporrigis ? De die tecum loquitur
4 et de hoc ipso fugiente. Num dubium est ergo, quin
optima quaeque prima dies fugiat mortalibus miseris,
id est occupatis ? Quorum puerilis adhuc animos
senectus opprimit, ad quam imparati inermesque
perveniunt, nihil enim provisum est ; subito in illam
necopinantes inciderunt, accedere eam cotidie non
5 sentiebant. Quemadmodum aut sermo aut lectio
aut aliqua intentior cogitatio iter facientis decipit et
pervenisse ante sentiunt quam adpropinquasse, sic
hoc iter vitae adsiduum et citatissimum, quod vigi-
lantes dormientesque eodem gradu facimus, occupatis
non apparet nisi in fine.
1 **10.** Quod proposui si in partes velim et argumenta
diducere, multa mihi occurrent, per quae probem
brevissimam esse occupatorum vitam. Solebat dicere

[1] cunctationem *Hermes after Gertz* : cognationem *A* :
cogitationem *some inferior* MSS., *Bourgery, Duff.*

---

[a] Virgil, *Georgics*, iii. 66 *sq.*
[b] A much admired teacher of Seneca.

> The fairest day in hapless mortals' life
> Is ever first to flee.[a]

" Why do you delay," says he, " Why are you idle ?
Unless you seize the day, it flees." Even though you
seize it, it still will flee ; therefore you must vie with
time's swiftness in the speed of using it, and, as from a
torrent that rushes by and will not always flow, you
must drink quickly. And, too, the utterance of the
bard is most admirably worded to cast censure upon
infinite delay, in that he says, not " the fairest age,"
but " the fairest day." Why, to whatever length your
greed inclines, do you stretch before yourself months
and years in long array, unconcerned and slow though
time flies so fast ? The poet speaks to you about the
day, and about this very day that is flying. Is there,
then, any doubt that for hapless mortals, that is, for
men who are engrossed, the fairest day is ever the
first to flee ? Old age surprises them while their
minds are still childish, and they come to it unpre-
pared and unarmed, for they have made no provision
for it ; they have stumbled upon it suddenly and unexpectedly, they did not notice that it was drawing
nearer day by day. Even as conversation or reading
or deep meditation on some subject beguiles the
traveller, and he finds that he has reached the
end of his journey before he was aware that he was
approaching it, just so with this unceasing and most
swift journey of life, which we make at the same
pace whether waking or sleeping ; those who are
engrossed become aware of it only at the end.

Should I choose to divide my subject into heads
with their separate proofs, many arguments will
occur to me by which I could prove that busy men find
life very short. But Fabianus,[b] who was none of your

Fabianus, non ex his cathedraris philosophis, sed **ex** veris et antiquis: 'contra adfectus impetu, non suptilitate pugnandum, nec minutis vulneribus sed incursu avertendam aciem; non probam cavillationem esse, nam contundi debere, non vellicari.' Tamen ut illis error exprobretur suus, docendi, non tantum deplorandi sunt.

2 In tria tempora vita dividitur: quod fuit, quod est, quod futurum est. Ex iis quod agimus breve est, quod acturi sumus dubium, quod egimus certum. Hoc est enim, in quod fortuna ius perdidit, quod in nullius arbitrium reduci potest. Hoc amittunt occupati; nec enim illis vacat praeterita respicere, et si vacet, iniucunda est paenitendae rei recordatio.

3 Inviti itaque ad tempora male exacta animum revocant nec audent ea retemptare, quorum vitia, etiam quae aliquo praesentis voluptatis lenocinio surripiebantur, retractando patescunt. Nemo, nisi quoi[1] omnia acta sunt sub censura sua, quae numquam fallitur, libenter se in praeteritum retorquet;

4 ille qui multa ambitiose concupiit, superbe contempsit, impotenter vicit, insidiose decepit, avare rapuit, prodige effudit, necesse est memoriam suam timeat. Atqui haec est pars temporis nostri sacra ac dedicata, omnis humanos casus supergressa, extra regnum fortunae

---

[1] quoi *Gruter* : quo *A.*

lecture-room philosophers of to-day, but one of the genuine and old-fashioned kind, used to say that we must fight against the passions with main force, not with artifice, and that the battle-line must be turned by a bold attack, not by inflicting pinpricks ; that sophistry is not serviceable, for the passions must be, not nipped, but crushed. Yet, in order that the victims of them may be censured, each for his own particular fault, I say that they must be instructed, not merely wept over.

Life is divided into three periods—that which has been, that which is, that which will be. Of these the present time is short, the future is doubtful, the past is certain. For the last is the one over which Fortune has lost control, is the one which cannot be brought back under any man's power. But men who are engrossed lose this ; for they have no time to look back upon the past, and even if they should have, it is not pleasant to recall something they must view with regret. They are, therefore, unwilling to direct their thoughts backward to ill-spent hours, and those whose vices become obvious if they review the past, even the vices which were disguised under some allurement of momentary pleasure, do not have the courage to revert to those hours. No one willingly turns his thought back to the past, unless all his acts have been submitted to the censorship of his conscience, which is never deceived ; he who has ambitiously coveted, proudly scorned, recklessly conquered, treacherously betrayed, greedily seized, or lavishly squandered, must needs fear his own memory. And yet this is the part of our time that is sacred and set apart, put beyond the reach of all human mishaps, and removed from the dominion of Fortune, the part which is disquieted by

subducta, quam non inopia, non metus, non morborum
incursus exagitet ; haec nec turbari nec eripi potest :
perpetua eius et intrepida possessio est. Singuli
tantum dies, et hi per momenta, praesentes sunt ;
at praeteriti temporis omnes, cum iusseritis, aderunt,
ad arbitrium tuum inspici se ac detineri patientur,
5 quod facere occupatis non vacat. Securae et quietae
mentis est in omnes vitae suae partes discurrere ;
occupatorum animi, velut sub iugo sint, flectere se
ac respicere non possunt. Abit igitur vita eorum in
profundum ; et ut nihil prodest, licet quantumlibet
ingeras, si non subest quod excipiat ac servet, sic,
nihil refert quantum temporis detur, si non est ubi
subsidat, per quassos foratosque animos transmittitur.
6 Praesens tempus brevissimum est, adeo quidem, ut
quibusdam nullum videatur ; in cursu enim semper
est, fluit et praecipitatur ; ante desinit esse quam
venit, nec magis moram patitur quam mundus aut
sidera, quorum inrequieta semper agitatio numquam
in eodem vestigio manet. Solum igitur ad occupatos
praesens pertinet tempus, quod tam breve est, ut
arripi non possit, et id ipsum illis districtis in multa
subducitur.

1 11. Denique vis scire quam non diu vivant? Vide
quam cupiant diu vivere. Decrepiti senes paucorum
annorum accessionem votis mendicant ; minores
natu se ipsos esse fingunt ; mendacio sibi blandiuntur
et tam libenter se fallunt quam si una fata decipiant.

---

a An allusion to the fate of the Danaids, who in Hades
forever poured water into a vessel with a perforated bottom.

no want, by no fear, by no attacks of disease ; this can neither be troubled nor be snatched away—it is an everlasting and unanxious possession. The present offers only one day at a time, and each by minutes ; but all the days of past time will appear when you bid them, they will suffer you to behold them and keep them at your will—a thing which those who are engrossed have no time to do. The mind that is untroubled and tranquil has the power to roam into all the parts of its life ; but the minds of the engrossed, just as if weighted by a yoke, cannot turn and look behind. And so their life vanishes into an abyss ; and as it does no good, no matter how much water you pour into a vessel, if there is no bottom ^a to receive and hold it, so with time—it makes no difference how much is given ; if there is nothing for it to settle upon, it passes out through the chinks and holes of the mind. Present time is very brief, so brief, indeed, that to some there seems to be none ; for it is always in motion, it ever flows and hurries on ; it ceases to be before it has come, and can no more brook delay than the firmament or the stars, whose ever unresting movement never lets them abide in the same track. The engrossed, therefore, are concerned with present time alone, and it is so brief that it cannot be grasped, and even this is filched away from them, distracted as they are among many things.

In a word, do you want to know how they do not " live long " ? See how eager they are to live long ! Decrepit old men beg in their prayers for the addition of a few more years ; they pretend that they are younger than they are ; they comfort themselves with a falsehood, and are as pleased to deceive themselves as if they deceived Fate at the same time. But

Iam vero cum illos aliqua imbecillitas mortalitatis admonuit, quemadmodum paventes moriuntur, non tamquam exeant de vita, sed tamquam extrahantur. Stultos se fuisse, qui non vixerint, clamitant et, si modo evaserint ex illa valitudine, in otio victuros ; tunc quam frustra paraverint, quibus non fruerentur,

2 quam in cassum omnis ceciderit labor, cogitant. At quibus vita procul ab omni negotio agitur, quidni spatiosa sit ? Nihil ex illa delegatur, nihil alio atque alio spargitur, nihil inde fortunae traditur, nihil neglegentia interit, nihil largitione detrahitur, nihil supervacuum est ; tota, ut ita dicam, in reditu est. Quantulacumque itaque abunde sufficit, et ideo, quandoque ultimus dies venerit, non cunctabitur sapiens ire ad mortem certo gradu.

1 12. Quaeris fortasse, quos occupatos vocem ? Non est quod me solos putes dicere, quos a basilica immissi demum canes eiciunt, quos aut in sua vides turba speciosius elidi aut in aliena contemptius, quos officia domibus suis evocant, ut alienis foribus inlidant, aut[1] hasta praetoris infami lucro et quandoque sup-

2 puraturo exercet. Quorundam otium occupatum est; in villa aut in lecto suo, in media solitudine, quamvis ab omnibus recesserint, sibi ipsi molesti sunt ; quorum non otiosa vita dicenda· est, sed desidiosa occupatio.

---

[1] aut *added by Madvig.*

---

when at last some infirmity has reminded them of their mortality, in what terror do they die, feeling that they are being dragged out of life, and not merely leaving it. They cry out that they have been fools because they have not really lived, and that they will live henceforth in leisure if only they escape from this illness; then at last they reflect how uselessly they have striven for things which they did not enjoy, and how all their toil has gone for nothing. But for those whose life is passed remote from all business, why should it not be ample? None of it is assigned to another, none of it is scattered in this direction and that, none of it is committed to Fortune, none of it perishes from neglect, none is subtracted by wasteful giving, none of it is unused; the whole of it, so to speak, yields income. And so, however small the amount of it, it is abundantly sufficient, and therefore, whenever his last day shall come, the wise man will not hesitate to go to meet death with steady step.

Perhaps you ask whom I would call " the engrossed " ? There is no reason for you to suppose that I mean only those whom the dogs[a] that have at length been let in drive out from the law-court, those whom you see either gloriously crushed in their own crowd of followers, or scornfully in someone else's, those whom social duties call forth from their own homes to bump them against someone else's doors, or whom the praetor's hammer[b] keeps busy in seeking gain that is disreputable and that will one day fester. Even the leisure of some men is engrossed; in their villa or on their couch, in the midst of solitude, although they have withdrawn from all others, they are themselves the source of their own worry; we should say that these are living, not in leisure, but in busy

Illum tu otiosum vocas qui Corinthia, paucorum furore pretiosa, anxia suptilitate concinnat et maiorem dierum partem in aeruginosis lamellis consumit? Qui in ceromate (nam, pro facinus! ne Romanis quidem vitiis laboramus) spectator puerorum rixantium sedet? Qui iumentorum suorum greges in 3 aetatium et colorum paria diducit? Qui athletas novissimos[1] pascit? Quid? illos otiosos vocas, quibus apud tonsorem multae horae transmittuntur, dum decerpitur, si quid proxima nocte subcrevit, dum de singulis capillis in consilium itur, dum aut disiecta coma restituitur aut deficiens hinc atque illinc in frontem compellitur? Quomodo irascuntur, si tonsor paulo neglegentior fuit, tamquam virum tonderet! Quomodo excandescunt, si quid ex iuba sua decisum est, si quid extra ordinem iacuit, nisi omnia in anulos suos reciderunt! Quis est istorum qui non malit rem publicam turbari quam comam suam[2]? Qui non sollicitior sit de capitis sui decore quam de salute? Qui non comptior esse malit quam honestior? Hos tu otiosos vocas inter pectinem speculumque occu- 4 patos? Quid illi, qui in componendis, audiendis, discendis canticis operati sunt, dum vocem, cuius rectum cursum natura et optimum et simplicissimum fecit, in flexus modulationis inertissimae torquent, quorum digiti aliquod intra se carmen metientes semper sonant, quorum, cum ad res serias, etiam

---

[1] novissimos *A*: novis cibis *Madvig, Duff*: novissimo more *Gertz*.

[2] suam *Muretus transfers from a place after* publicam.

---

[a] *Cf.* Pliny, *Epistles*, i. 9. 8 : " satius est enim, ut Atilius noster eruditissime simul et facetissime dixit, otiosum esse quam nihil agere."

idleness.[a] Would you say that that man is at leisure [b] who arranges with finical care his Corinthian bronzes, that the mania of a few makes costly, and spends the greater part of each day upon rusty bits of copper? Who sits in a public wrestling-place (for, to our shame! we labour with vices that are not even Roman) watching the wrangling of lads? Who sorts out the herds of his pack-mules into pairs of the same age and colour? Who feeds all the newest athletes? Tell me, would you say that those men are at leisure who pass many hours at the barber's while they are being stripped of whatever grew out the night before? while a solemn debate is held over each separate hair? while either disarranged locks are restored to their place or thinning ones drawn from this side and that toward the forehead? How angry they get if the barber has been a bit too careless, just as if he were shearing a real man! How they flare up if any of their mane is lopped off, if any of it lies out of order, if it does not all fall into its proper ringlets! Who of these would not rather have the state disordered than his hair? Who is not more concerned to have his head trim rather than safe? Who would not rather be well barbered than upright? Would you say that these are at leisure who are occupied with the comb and the mirror? And what of those who are engaged in composing, hearing, and learning songs, while they twist the voice, whose best and simplest movement Nature designed to be straightforward, into the meanderings of some indolent tune, who are always snapping their fingers as they beat time to some song they have in their head, who are overheard humming

[b] For the technical meaning of *otiosi*, "the leisured," see Seneca's definition at the beginning of chap. 14.

saepe tristes adhibiti sunt, exauditur tacita modu-
latio ? Non habent isti otium, sed iners negotium.
5 Convivia me hercules horum ·non posuerim inter
vacantia tempora, cum videam, quam solliciti argentum ordinent, quam diligenter exoletorum suorum
tunicas succingant, quam suspensi sint, quomodo
aper a coco exeat, qua celeritate signo dato glabri
ad ministeria discurrant, quanta arte scindantur aves
in frusta non enormia, quam curiose infelices pueruli
ebriorum sputa detergeant. Ex his elegantiae lauti-
tiaeque fama captatur et usque eo in omnes vitae
secessus mala sua illos secuntur, ut nec bibant sine am-
6 bitione nec edant. Ne illos quidem inter otiosos nume-
raverim, qui sella se et lectica huc et illuc ferunt et ad
gestationum suarum, quasi deserere illas non liceat,
horas occurrunt, quos quando lavari debeant, quando
natare, quando cenare, alius admonet ; usque[1] eo
nimio delicati animi languore solvuntur, ut per se scire
7 non possint, an esuriant! Audio quendam ex delica-
tis—si modo deliciae vocandae sunt vitam et consuetudinem humanam dediscere—, cum ex balneo inter
manus elatus et in sella positus esset, dixisse inter-
rogando : " Iam sedeo ? " Hunc tu ignorantem, an
sedeat, putas scire an vivat, an videat, an otiosus sit ?
Non facile dixerim, utrum magis miserear, si hoc

[1] usque *Gertz* : et usque *A.*

a tune when they have been summoned to serious, often even melancholy, matters? These have not leisure, but idle occupation. And their banquets, Heaven knows! I cannot reckon among their unoccupied hours, since I see how anxiously they set out their silver plate, how diligently they tie up the tunics of their pretty slave-boys, how breathlessly they watch to see in what style the wild boar issues from the hands of the cook, with what speed at a given signal smooth-faced boys hurry to perform their duties, with what skill the birds are carved into portions all according to rule, how carefully unhappy little lads wipe up the spittle of drunkards. By such means they seek the reputation of being fastidious and elegant, and to such an extent do their evils follow them into all the privacies of life that they can neither eat nor drink without ostentation. And I would not count these among the leisured class either—the men who have themselves borne hither and thither in a sedan-chair and a litter, and are punctual at the hours for their rides as if it were unlawful to omit them, who are reminded by someone else when they must bathe, when they must swim, when they must dine; so enfeebled are they by the excessive lassitude of a pampered mind that they cannot find out by themselves whether they are hungry! I hear that one of these pampered people—provided that you can call it pampering to unlearn the habits of human life—when he had been lifted by hands from the bath and placed in his sedan-chair, said questioningly: " Am I now seated ? " Do you think that this man, who does not know whether he is sitting, knows whether he is alive, whether he sees, whether he is at leisure ? I find it hard to say whether I pity him

8 ignoravit, an si ignorare se finxit. Multarum quidem
rerum oblivionem sentiunt, sed multarum et imitantur. Quaedam vitia illos quasi felicitatis argumenta delectant ; nimis humilis et contempti hominis
videtur scire quid facias. I nunc et mimos multa
mentiri ad exprobrandam luxuriam puta. Plura me
hercules praetereunt quam fingunt et tanta incredi-
bilium vitiorum copia ingenioso in hoc unum saeculo
processit, ut iam mimorum arguere possimus neglegentiam. Esse aliquem, qui usque eo deliciis interierit
9 ut an sedeat alteri credat ! Non est ergo hic otiosus,
aliud illi nomen imponas; aeger est, immo mortuus
est ; ille otiosus est, cui otii sui et sensus est. Hic
vero semivivus, cui ad intellegendos corporis sui habitus indice opus est, quomodo potest hic ullius temporis dominus esse ?

1 13. Persequi singulos longum est, quorum aut
latrunculi aut pila aut excoquendi in sole corporis cura
consumpsere vitam. Non sunt otiosi, quorum voluptates multum negotii habent. Nam de illis nemo
dubitabit, quin operose nihil agant, qui litterarum in-
utilium studiis detinentur, quae iam apud Romanos
2 quoque magna manus est. Graecorum iste morbus
fuit quaerere, quem numerum Ulixes remigum habuis-
set, prior scripta esset Ilias an Odyssia, praeterea
an eiusdem essent auctoris, alia deinceps huius notae,

---

a Actors in the popular mimes, or low farces, that were
often censured for their indecencies.

more if he really did not know, or if he pretended
not to know this. They really are subject to forgetfulness of many things, but they also pretend forgetfulness of many. Some vices delight them as being
proofs of their prosperity ; it seems the part of a man
who is very lowly and despicable to know what he
is doing. After this imagine that the mimes[a] fabri-
cate many things to make a mock of luxury ! In
very truth, they pass over more than they invent, and
such a multitude of unbelievable vices has come forth
in this age, so clever in this one direction, that by now
we can charge the mimes with neglect. To think that
there is anyone who is so lost in luxury that he takes
another's word as to whether he is sitting down !
This man, then, is not at leisure, you must apply to
him a different term—he is sick, nay, he is dead ;
that man is at leisure, who has also a perception of
his leisure. But this other who is half alive, who, in
order that he may know the postures of his own body,
needs someone to tell him—how can he be the master
of any of his time ?

It would be tedious to mention all the different
men who have spent the whole of their life over chess
or ball or the practice of baking their bodies in the
sun. They are not unoccupied whose pleasures are
made a busy occupation. For instance, no one will
have any doubt that those are laborious triflers who
spend their time on useless literary problems, of whom
even among the Romans there is now a great number.
It was once a foible confined to the Greeks to inquire
into what number of rowers Ulysses had, whether
the *Iliad* or the *Odyssey* was written first, whether
moreover they belong to the same author, and various
other matters of this stamp, which, if you keep them

quae sive contineas, nihil tacitam conscientiam iuvant
3 sive proferas, non doctior videaris sed molestior. Ecce
Romanos quoque invasit inane studium supervacua
discendi. His diebus audii quendam referentem,
quae primus quisque ex Romanis ducibus fecisset;
primus navali proelio Duilius vicit, primus Curius
Dentatus in triumpho duxit elephantos. Etiamnunc
ista, etsi ad veram gloriam non tendunt, circa civilium
tamen operum exempla versantur ; non est pro-
futura talis scientia, est tamen quae nos speciosa
4 rerum vanitate detineat. Hoc quoque quaerentibus
remittamus, quis Romanis primus persuaserit navem
conscendere. Claudius is fuit, Caudex ob hoc ipsum
appellatus, quia plurium tabularum contextus caudex
apud antiquos vocatur, unde publicae tabulae codices
dicuntur et naves nunc quoque ex antiqua consuetudine, quae commeatus per Tiberim subvehunt, codi-
5 cariae vocantur. Sane et hoc ad rem pertineat, quod
Valerius Corvinus primus Messanam vicit et primus
ex familia Valeriorum urbis captae in se translato
nomine Messana appellatus est paulatimque vulgo
6 permutante litteras Messala dictus. Num et hoc
cuiquam curare permittes, quod primus L. Sulla in
circo leones solutos dedit, cum alioquin alligati
darentur, ad conficiendos eos missis a rege Boccho
iaculatoribus ? Et hoc sane remittatur : num et

---

^a The ancient codex was made of tablets of wood fastened
together.

to yourself, in no way pleasure your secret soul, and, if you publish them, make you seem more of a bore than a scholar. But now this vain passion for learning useless things has assailed the Romans also. In the last few days I heard someone telling who was the first Roman general to do this or that; Duilius was the first who won a naval battle, Curius Dentatus was the first who had elephants led in his triumph. Still, these matters, even if they add nothing to real glory, are nevertheless concerned with signal services to the state; there will be no profit in such knowledge, nevertheless it wins our attention by reason of the attractiveness of an empty subject. We may excuse also those who inquire into this—who first induced the Romans to go on board ship. It was Claudius, and this was the very reason he was surnamed Caudex, because among the ancients a structure formed by joining together several boards was called a *caudex*, whence also the Tables of the Law are called *codices*,[a] and, in the ancient fashion, boats that carry provisions up the Tiber are even to-day called *codicariae*. Doubtless this too may have some point—the fact that Valerius Corvinus was the first to conquer Messana, and was the first of the family of the Valerii to bear the surname Messana because he had transferred the name of the conquered city to himself, and was later called Messala after the gradual corruption of the name in the popular speech. Perhaps you will permit someone to be interested also in this—the fact that Lucius Sulla was the first to exhibit loosed lions in the Circus, though at other times they were exhibited in chains, and that javelin-throwers were sent by King Bocchus to despatch them? And, doubtless, this too may find some excuse—but does

Pompeium primum in circo elephantorum duodе-
viginti pugnam edidisse commissis more proeli noxiis[1]
hominibus ad ullam rem bonam pertinet? Princeps
civitatis et inter antiquos principes, ut fama tradidit,
bonitatis eximiae memorabile putavit spectaculi
genus novo more perdere homines. Depugnant?
Parum est. Lancinantur? Parum est: ingenti
7 mole animalium exterantur! Satius erat ista in
oblivionem ire, ne quis postea potens disceret in-
videretque rei minime humanae. O quantum cali-
ginis mentibus nostris obicit magna felicitas! Ille se
supra rerum naturam esse tunc credidit, cum tot
miserorum hominum catervas sub alio caelo natis
beluis obiceret, cum bellum inter tam disparia animalia
committeret, cum in conspectum populi Romani
multum sanguinis funderet mox plus ipsum fundere
coacturus. At idem postea Alexandrina perfidia
deceptus ultimo mancipio transfodiendum se praebuit, tum demum intellecta inani iactatione cogno-
minis sui.
8 Sed ut illo revertar, unde decessi, et in eadem
materia ostendam supervacuam quorumdam diligentiam : idem narrabat Metellum victis in Sicilia Poenis
triumphantem unum omnium Romanorum ante
currum centum et viginti captivos elephantos duxisse ;

[1] *Text uncertain: others read* innoxis.

[a] Such, doubtless, as Marius, Sulla, Caesar, Crassus.
[b] Pliny (*Nat. Hist.* viii. 21) reports that the people were so
moved by pity that they rose in a body and called down
curses upon Pompey. Cicero's impressions of the occasion
are recorded in *Ad Fam.* vii. 1. 3 : "extremus elephantorum
dies fuit, in quo admiratio magna vulgi atque turbae,
delectatio nulla exstitit; quin etiam misericordia quaedam
consecuta est atque opinio eiusmodi, esse quandam illi
beluae cum genere humana societatem."

it serve any useful purpose to know that Pompey was the first to exhibit the slaughter of eighteen elephants in the Circus, pitting criminals against them in a mimic battle? He, a leader of the state and one who, according to report, was conspicuous among the leaders[a] of old for the kindness of his heart, thought it a notable kind of spectacle to kill human beings after a new fashion. Do they fight to the death? That is not enough! Are they torn to pieces? That is not enough! Let them be crushed by animals of monstrous bulk! Better would it be that these things pass into oblivion lest hereafter some all-powerful man should learn them and be jealous of an act that was nowise human.[b] O, what blindness does great prosperity cast upon our minds! When he was casting so many troops of wretched human beings to wild beasts born under a different sky, when he was proclaiming war between creatures so ill matched, when he was shedding so much blood before the eyes of the Roman people, who itself was soon to be forced to shed more, he then believed that he was beyond the power of Nature. But later this same man, betrayed by Alexandrine treachery, offered himself to the dagger of the vilest slave, and then at last discovered what an empty boast his surname[c] was.

But to return to the point from which I have digressed, and to show that some people bestow useless pains upon these same matters—the man I mentioned related that Metellus, when he triumphed after his victory over the Carthaginians in Sicily, was the only one of all the Romans who had caused a hundred and twenty captured elephants to be led

a i.e., Magnus.

Sullam ultimum Romanorum protulisse pomerium,
quod numquam provinciali, sed Italico agro adquisito
proferre moris apud antiquos fuit. Hoc scire magis
prodest, quam Aventinum montem extra pomerium
esse, ut ille adfirmabat, propter alteram ex duabus
causis, aut quod plebs eo secessisset, aut quod Remo
auspicante illo loco aves non addixissent, alia deinceps
innumerabilia, quae aut farta[1] sunt mendaciis aut
9 similia? Nam ut concedas omnia eos fide bona
dicere, ut ad praestationem scribant, tamen cuius
ista errores minuent? Cuius cupiditates prement?
Quem fortiorem, quem iustiorem, quem liberaliorem
facient? Dubitare se interim Fabianus noster
aiebat, an satius esset nullis studiis admoveri quam
his implicari.

1   14. Soli omnium otiosi sunt qui sapientiae vacant,
soli vivunt; nec enim suam tantum aetatem bene
tuentur. Omne aevum suo adiciunt; quidquid
annorum ante illos actum est, illis adquisitum est.
Nisi ingratissimi sumus, illi clarissimi sacrarum
opinionum conditores nobis nati sunt, nobis vitam
praeparaverunt. Ad res pulcherrimas ex tenebris
ad lucem erutas alieno labore deducimur; nullo
nobis saeculo interdictum est, in omnia admittimur
et, si magnitudine animi egredi humanae imbecil-

---

[1] farta *A* : paria *Haase.*

---

[a] A name applied to a consecrated space kept vacant
within and (according to Livy, i. 44) without the city wall.
The right of extending it belonged originally to the king
who had added territory to Rome.

before his car; that Sulla was the last of the Romans who extended the *pomerium*,[a] which in old times it was customary to extend after the acquisition of Italian, but never of provincial, territory. Is it more profitable to know this than that Mount Aventine, according to him, is outside the *pomerium* for one of two reasons, either because that was the place to which the plebeians had seceded, or because the birds had not been favourable when Remus took his auspices on that spot—and, in turn, countless other reports that are either crammed with falsehood or are of the same sort? For though you grant that they tell these things in good faith, though they pledge themselves for the truth of what they write, still whose mistakes will be made fewer by such stories? Whose passions will they restrain? Whom will they make more brave, whom more just, whom more noble-minded? My friend Fabianus used to say that at times he was doubtful whether it was not better not to apply oneself to any studies than to become entangled in these.

Of all men they alone are at leisure who take time for philosophy, they alone really live; for they are not content to be good guardians of their own lifetime only. They annex every age to their own; all the years that have gone before them are an addition to their store. Unless we are most ungrateful, all those men, glorious fashioners of holy thoughts, were born for us; for us they have prepared a way of life. By other men's labours we are led to the sight of things most beautiful that have been wrested from darkness and brought into light; from no age are we shut out, we have access to all ages, and if it is our wish, by greatness of mind, to pass beyond the

litatis angustias libet, multum, per quod spatiemur,
2 temporis est. Disputare cum Socrate licet, dubitare
cum Carneade, cum Epicuro quiescere, hominis
naturam cum Stoicis vincere, cum Cynicis excedere.
Cum rerum natura in consortium omnis aevi patiatur
incedere, quidni ab hoc exiguo et caduco temporis
transitu in illa toto nos demus animo, quae immensa,
quae aeterna sunt, quae cum melioribus communia ?
3   Isti, qui per officia discursant, qui se aliosque in-
quietant, cum bene insanierint, cum omnium limina
cotidie perambulaverint nec⁻ ullas apertas fores
praeterierint, cum per diversissimas domos meri-
toriam salutationem circumtulerint, quotum quemque
ex tam immensa et variis cupiditatibus districta urbe
4 poterunt videre ? Quam multi erunt, quorum illos
aut somnus aut luxuria aut inhumanitas summoveat !
Quam multi qui illos, cum diu torserint, simulata
festinatione transcurrant ! Quam multi per refertum
clientibus atrium prodire vitabunt et per obscuros
aedium aditus profugient, quasi non inhumanius sit
decipere quam excludere ! Quam multi hesterna
crapula semisomnes et graves illis miseris suum
somnum rumpentibus ut alienum expectent, vix
adlevatis labris insusurratum miliens nomen oscita-
tione superbissima reddent !
5   Hos in veris officiis morari licet dicamus, qui

ᵃ The New Academy taught that certainty of knowledge
was unattainable.
ᵇ The *salutatio* was held in the early morning.

narrow limits of human weakness, there is a great
stretch of time through which we may roam. We may
argue with Socrates, we may doubt *a* with Carneades,
find peace with Epicurus, overcome human nature
with the Stoics, exceed it with the Cynics. Since
Nature allows us to enter into fellowship with every
age, why should we not turn from this paltry and
fleeting span of time and surrender ourselves with all
our soul to the past, which is boundless, which is
eternal, which we share with our betters ?

Those who rush about in the performance of social
duties, who give themselves and others no rest, when
they have fully indulged their madness, when they
have every day crossed everybody's threshold, and
have left no open door unvisited, when they have
carried around their venal greeting to houses that
are very far apart—out of a city so huge and torn by
such varied desires, how few will they be able to
see ? How many will there be who either from
sleep or self-indulgence or rudeness will keep them
out ! How many who, when they have tortured
them with long waiting, will rush by, pretending to
be in a hurry ! How many will avoid passing out
through a hall that is crowded with clients, and will
make their escape through some concealed door—
as if it were not more discourteous to deceive than to
exclude. How many, still half asleep and sluggish from
last night's debauch, scarcely lifting their lips in the
midst of a most insolent yawn, manage to bestow on
yonder poor wretches, who break their own slumber *b*
in order to wait on that of another, the right name
only after it has been whispered to them a thousand
times !

But we may fairly say that they alone are engaged

Zenonem, qui Pythagoran cotidie et Democritum
ceterosque antistites bonarum artium, qui Aristo-
telen et Theophrastum volent habere quam familia-
rissimos. Nemo horum non vacabit, nemo non
venientem ad se beatiorem, amantiorem sui dimittet,
nemo quemquam vacuis a se manibus abire patietur ;
nocte conveniri, interdiu ab omnibus mortalibus
possunt.

1 15. Horum te mori nemo coget, omnes docebunt ;
horum nemo annos tuos conteret, suos tibi contribuet ;
nullius ex his sermo periculosus erit, nullius amicitia
capitalis, nullius sumptuosa observatio. Feres ex
illis, quidquid voles ; per illos non stabit, quominus

2 quantum plurimum cupieris[1] haurias. Quae illum
felicitas, quam pulchra senectus manet, qui se in
horum clientelam contulit ! Habebit, cum quibus
de minimis maximisque rebus deliberet, quos de se
cotidie consulat, a quibus audiat verum sine contumelia, laudetur sine adulatione, ad quorum se
similitudinem effingat.

3 Solemus dicere non fuisse in nostra potestate, quos
sortiremur parentes, forte hominibus datos ; nobis
vero ad nostrum arbitrium nasci licet. Nobilissi-
morum ingeniorum familiae sunt ; elige in quam
adscisci velis ; non in nomen tantum adoptaberis,
sed in ipsa bona, quae non erunt sordide nec maligne

4 custodienda ; maiora fient, quo illa pluribus diviseris.

---

[1] quantum plurimum cupieris *Muretus* : plurimum quantum ceperis *A* : cum coeperis *Hermes after Vahlen.*

in the true duties of life who shall wish to have Zeno, Pythagoras, Democritus, and all the other high priests of liberal studies, and Aristotle and Theophrastus, as their most intimate friends every day. No one of these will be " not at home," no one of these will fail to have his visitor leave more happy and more devoted to himself than when he came, no one of these will allow anyone to leave him with empty hands ; all mortals can meet with them by night or by day.

No one of these will force you to die, but all will teach you how to die ; no one of these will wear out your years, but each will add his own years to yours ; conversations with no one of these will bring you peril, the friendship of none will endanger your life, the courting of none will tax your purse. From them you will take whatever you wish ; it will be no fault of theirs if you do not draw the utmost that you can desire. What happiness, what a fair old age awaits him who has offered himself as a client to these ! He will have friends from whom he may seek counsel on matters great and small, whom he may consult every day about himself, from whom he may hear truth without insult, praise without flattery, and after whose likeness he may fashion himself.

We are wont to say that it was not in our power to choose the parents who fell to our lot, that they have been given to men by chance ; yet *we* may be the sons of whomsoever we will. Households there are of noblest intellects ; choose the one into which you wish to be adopted ; you will inherit not merely their name, but even their property, which there will be no need to guard in a mean or niggardly spirit ; the more persons you share it with, the greater it will become.

Ĥi tibi dabunt ad aeternitatem iter et te in illum
locum, ex quo nemo deicitur, sublevabunt. Haec una
ratio est extendendae mortalitatis, immo in[1] immortalitatem vertendae. Honores, monimenta, quidquid
aut decretis ambitio iussit aut operibus extruxit, cito
subruitur ; nihil non longa demolitur vetustas et
movet. At iis, quae consecravit sapientia, nocere
non potest ; nulla abolebit aetas, nulla deminuet ;
sequens ac deinde semper ulterior aliquid ad venerationem conferet, quoniam quidem in vicino versatur
5 invidia, simplicius longe posita miramur. Sapientis
ergo multum patet vita, non idem illum qui ceteros terminus cludit. Solus generis humani legibus solvitur ;
omnia illi saecula ut deo serviunt. Transît tempus
aliquod ? Hoc recordatione comprendit. Instat ?
Hoc utitur. Venturum est ? Hoc praecipit. Longam illi vitam facit omnium temporum in unum
conlatio.

1 16. Illorum brevissima ac sollicitissima aetas est,
qui praeteritorum obliviscuntur, praesentia necle-
gunt, de futuro timent ; cum ad extrema venerunt,
sero intellegunt miseri, tam diu se, dum nihil agunt,
2 occupatos fuisse. Nec est, quod hoc argumento pro-
bari putes longam illos agere vitam, quia interdum
mortem invocant. Vexat illos imprudentia incertis
adfectibus et incurrentibus in ipsa, quae metuunt ;
3 mortem saepe ideo optant, quia timent. Illud quoque
argumentum non est quod putes diu viventium, quod
saepe illis longus videtur dies, quod, dum veniat con-

---

[1] in *commonly added.*

These will open to you the path to immortality, and will raise you to a height from which no one is cast down. This is the only way of prolonging mortality—nay, of turning it into immortality. Honours, monuments, all that ambition has commanded by decrees or reared in works of stone, quickly sink to ruin ; there is nothing that the lapse of time does not tear down and remove. But the works which philosophy has consecrated cannot be harmed ; no age will destroy them, no age reduce them ; the following and each succeeding age will but increase the reverence for them, since envy works upon what is close at hand, and things that are far off we are more free to admire. The life of the philosopher, therefore, has wide range, and he is not confined by the same bounds that shut others in. He alone is freed from the limitations of the human race ; all ages serve him as if a god. Has some time passed by ? This he embraces by recollection. Is time present ? This he uses. Is it still to come ? This he anticipates. He makes his life long by combining all times into one.

But those who forget the past, neglect the present, and fear for the future have a life that is very brief and troubled ; when they have reached the end of it, the poor wretches perceive too late that for such a long while they have been busied in doing nothing. Nor because they sometimes invoke death, have you any reason to think it any proof that they find life long. In their folly they are harassed by shifting emotions which rush them into the very things they dread ; they often pray for death because they fear it. And, too, you have no reason to think that this is any proof that they are living a long time—the fact that the day often seems to them long, the fact

dictum tempus cenae, tarde ire horas queruntur;
nam si quando illos deseruerunt occupationes, in otio
relicti aestuant, nec quomodo id disponant aut extra-
hant sciunt. Itaque ad occupationem aliquam tendunt
et quod interiacet omne tempus grave est; tam me
hercules, quam cum dies muneris gladiatorii edictus
est, aut cum alicuius alterius vel spectaculi vel voluptatis expectatur constitutum, transilire medios dies
volunt. Omnis illis speratae rei longa dilatio est.
4 At illud tempus, quod amant,[1] breve est et praeceps
breviusque multo suo fit[2] vitio; aliunde enim alio
transfugiunt et consistere in una cupiditate non possunt. Non sunt illis longi dies, sed invisi; at contra
quam exiguae noctes videntur, quas in complexu
5 scortorum aut vino exigunt! Inde etiam poetarum
furor fabulis humanos errores alentium, quibus visus
est Iuppiter voluptate concubitus delenitus duplicasse
noctem. Quid aliud est vitia nostra incendere quam
auctores illis inscribere deos et dare morbo exemplo
divinitatis excusatam licentiam? Possunt istis non
brevissimae videri noctes, quas tam care mercantur?
Diem noctis expectatione perdunt, noctem lucis metu.
1 17. Ipsae voluptates eorum trepidae et variis terroribus inquietae sunt subitque cum maxime ex-
sultantis sollicita cogitatio: " Haec quam diu?"

---

[1] amant *Muretus* : amanti *A.*
[2] fit *added by Erasmus before* suo.

that they complain that the hours pass slowly until the time set for dinner arrives ; for, whenever their engrossments fail them, they are restless because they are left with nothing to do, and they do not know how to dispose of their leisure or to drag out the time. And so they strive for something else to occupy them, and all the intervening time is irksome ; exactly as they do when a gladiatorial exhibition has been announced, or when they are waiting for the appointed time of some other show or amusement, they want to skip over the days that lie between. All postponement of something they hope for seems long to them. Yet the time which they enjoy is short and swift, and it is made much shorter by their own fault ; for they flee from one pleasure to another and cannot remain fixed in one desire. Their days are not long to them, but hateful ; yet, on the other hand, how scanty seem the nights which they spend in the arms of a harlot or in wine ! It is this also that accounts for the madness of poets in fostering human frailties by the tales in which they represent that Jupiter under the enticement of the pleasures of a lover doubled the length of the night. For what is it but to inflame our vices to inscribe the name of the gods as their sponsors, and to present the excused indulgence of divinity as an example to our own weakness ? Can the nights which they pay for so dearly fail to seem all too short to these men ? They lose the day in expectation of the night, and the night in fear of the dawn.

The very pleasures of such men are uneasy and disquieted by alarms of various sorts, and at the very moment of rejoicing the anxious thought comes over them : "How long will these things last ? " This

Ab hoc affectu reges suam flevere potentiam, nec illos magnitudo fortunae suae delectavit, sed venturus aliquando finis exterruit. Cum per magna camporum spatia porrigeret exercitum nec numerum eius sed mensuram conprenderet Persarum rex insolentissimus, lacrimas profudit, quod intra centum annos nemo ex tanta iuventute superfuturus esset.
2 At illis admoturus erat fatum ipse qui flebat perditurusque alios in mari, alios in terra, alios proelio, alios fuga et intra exiguum tempus consumpturus
3 illos, quibus centesimum annum timebat. Quid, quod gaudia quoque eorum trepida sunt? Non enim solidis causis innituntur, sed eadem qua oriuntur vanitate turbantur. Qualia autem putas esse tempora etiam ipsorum confessione misera, cum haec quoque, quibus se attollunt et super hominem efferunt,
4 parum sincera sint? Maxima quaeque bona sollicita sunt nec ulli fortunae minus bene quam optimae creditur; alia felicitate ad tuendam felicitatem opus est et pro ipsis quae successere votis vota facienda sunt. Omne enim quod fortuito obvenit instabile est, quoque altius surrexerit, opportunius est in occasum. Neminem porro casura delectant; miserrimam ergo necesse est, non tantum brevissimam, vitam esse eorum, qui magno parant labore, quod maiore possideant. Operose adsecuntur quae volunt, anxii tenent quae
5 adsecuti sunt; nulla interim numquam amplius redi-

---

^a Xerxes, who invaded Greece in 480 B.C.
^b On the plain of Doriscus in Thrace the huge land force was estimated by counting the number of times a space capable of holding 10,000 men was filled (Herodotus, vii. 60).
^c Herodotus, vii. 45, 46 tells the story.

feeling has led kings to weep over the power they possessed, and they have not so much delighted in the greatness of their fortune, as they have viewed with terror the end to which it must some time come. When the King of Persia,[a] in all the insolence of his pride, spread his army over the vast plains and could not grasp its number but simply its measure,[b] he shed copious tears because inside of a hundred years not a man of such a mighty army would be alive.[c] But he who wept was to bring upon them their fate, was to give some to their doom on the sea, some on the land, some in battle, some in flight, and within a short time was to destroy all those for whose hundredth year he had such fear. And why is it that even their joys are uneasy from fear? Because they do not rest on stable causes, but are perturbed as groundlessly as they are born. But of what sort do you think those times are which even by their own confession are wretched, since even the joys by which they are exalted and lifted above mankind are by no means pure? All the greatest blessings are a source of anxiety, and at no time is fortune less wisely trusted than when it is best; to maintain prosperity there is need of other prosperity, and in behalf of the prayers that have turned out well we must make still other prayers. For everything that comes to us from chance is unstable, and the higher it rises, the more liable it is to fall. Moreover, what is doomed to perish brings pleasure to no one; very wretched, therefore, and not merely short, must the life of those be who work hard to gain what they must work harder to keep. By great toil they attain what they wish, and with anxiety hold what they have attained; meanwhile they take no account of time that will never more

turi temporis ratio est. Novae occupationes veteribus
substituuntur, spes spem excitat, ambitionem ambitio.
Miseriarum non finis quaeritur, sed materia mutatur.
Nostri nos honores torserunt ? Plus temporis alieni
auferunt. Candidati laborare desîmus ? Suffraga-
tores incipimus. Accusandi deposimus molestiam ?
Iudicandi nanciscimur. Iudex desît esse ? Quaesitor
est. Alienorum bonorum mercennaria procuratione
6 consenuit ? Suis opibus distinetur. Marium caliga
dimisit ? Consulatus exercet. Quintius dictaturam
properat pervadere ? Ab aratro revocabitur. Ibit[1]
in Poenos nondum tantae maturus rei Scipio ; victor
Hannibalis, victor Antiochi, sui consulatus decus,
fraterni sponsor, ni per ipsum mora esset, cum Iove
reponeretur ; civiles servatorem agitabunt seditiones
et post fastiditos a iuvene diis aequos honores iam
senem contumacis exili delectabit ambitio. Numquam derunt vel felices vel miserae sollicitudinis
causae ; per occupationes vita trudetur. Otium
numquam agetur, semper optabitur.

1   18. Excerpe itaque te volgo, Pauline carissime,
et in tranquilliorem portum non pro aetatis spatio
iactatus tandem recede. Cogita, quot fluctus subieris,
quot tempestates partim privatas sustinueris, partim

---

[1] ibit *A* : ivit *Haase* : ibat *Duff*.

---

[a] *Caliga*, the boot of the common soldier, is here synony-
mous with service in the army.
[b] His first appointment was announced to him while he
was ploughing his own fields.
[c] He did not allow his statue to be placed in the Capitol.
[d] Disgusted with politics, he died in exile at Liternum.

return. New engrossments take the place of the old, hope leads to new hope, ambition to new ambition. They do not seek an end of their wretchedness, but change the cause. Have we been tormented by our own public honours? Those of others take more of our time. Have we ceased to labour as candidates? We begin to canvass for others. Have we got rid of the troubles of a prosecutor? We find those of a judge. Has a man ceased to be a judge? He becomes president of a court. Has he become infirm in managing the property of others at a salary? He is perplexed by caring for his own wealth. Have the barracks ^a set Marius free? The consulship keeps him busy. Does Quintius ^b hasten to get to the end of his dictatorship? He will be called back to it from the plough. Scipio will go against the Carthaginians before he is ripe for so great an undertaking; victorious over Hannibal, victorious over Antiochus, the glory of his own consulship, the surety for his brother's, did he not stand in his own way, he would be set beside Jove ^c; but the discord of civilians will vex their preserver, and, when as a young man he had scorned honours that rivalled those of the gods, at length, when he is old, his ambition will take delight in stubborn exile.^d Reasons for anxiety will never be lacking, whether born of prosperity or of wretchedness; life pushes on in a succession of engrossments. We shall always pray for leisure, but never enjoy it.

And so, my dearest Paulinus, tear yourself away from the crowd, and, too much storm-tossed for the time you have lived, at length withdraw into a peaceful harbour. Think of how many waves you have encountered, how many storms, on the one hand, you have sustained in private life, how many, on the other,

publicas in te converteris ; satis iam per laboriosa et
inquieta documenta exhibita virtus est : experire,
quid in otio faciat. Maior pars aetatis, certe melior
rei publicae data sit ; aliquid temporis tui sume
2 etiam tibi. Nec te ad segnem aut inertem quietem
voco, non ut somno et caris turbae voluptatibus quidquid est in te indolis vividae mergas. Non est istud
adquiescere ; invenies maiora omnibus adhuc strenue
tractatis operibus, quae repositus et securus agites.
3 Tu quidem orbis terrarum rationes administras
tam abstinenter quam alienas, tam diligenter
quam tuas, tam religiose quam publicas. In
officio amorem consequeris, in quo odium vitare
difficile est ; sed tamen, mihi crede, satius est vitae
4 suae rationem quam frumenti publici nosse. Istum
animi vigorem rerum maximarum capacissimum a
ministerio honorifico quidem sed parum ad beatam
vitam apto revoca et cogita non id egisse te ab aetate
prima omni cultu studiorum liberalium, ut tibi multa
milia frumenti bene committerentur ; maius quiddam
et altius de te promiseras. Non derunt et frugalitatis
exactae homines et laboriosae operae ; tanto aptiora
portandis oneribus tarda iumenta sunt quam
nobiles equi, quorum generosam pernicitatem quis
5 umquam gravi sarcina pressit ? Cogita praeterea,
quantum sollicitudinis sit ad tantam te molem obicere ;

you have brought upon yourself in public life ; long enough has your virtue been displayed in laborious and unceasing proofs—try how it will behave in leisure. The greater part of your life, certainly the better part of it, has been given to the state ; take now some part of your time for yourself as well. And I do not summon you to slothful or idle inaction, or to drown all your native energy in slumbers and the pleasures that are dear to the crowd. That is not to rest ; you will find far greater works than all those you have hitherto performed so energetically, to occupy you in the midst of your release and retirement. You, I know, manage the accounts of the whole world as honestly as you would a stranger's, as carefully as you would your own, as conscientiously as you would the state's. You win love in an office in which it is difficult to avoid hatred ; but nevertheless, believe me, it is better to have knowledge of the ledger of one's own life than of the corn-market. Recall that keen mind of yours, which is most competent to cope with the greatest subjects, from a service that is indeed honourable but hardly adapted to the happy life, and reflect that in all your training in the liberal studies, extending from your earliest years, you were not aiming at this—that it might be safe to entrust many thousand pecks of corn to your charge ; you gave hope of something greater and more lofty. There will be no lack of men of tested worth and painstaking industry. But plodding oxen are much more suited to carrying heavy loads than thoroughbred horses, and who ever hampers the fleetness of such high-born creatures with a heavy pack ? Reflect, besides, how much worry you have in subjecting yourself to such a great burden ; your deal-

cum ventre tibi humano negotium est. Nec rationem
patitur nec aequitate mitigatur nec ulla prece flectitur
populus esuriens. Modo modo intra paucos illos dies,
quibus C. Caesar perît, si quis inferis sensus est, hoc
gravissime ferens, quod sciebat populo Romano superstiti[1] septem aut octo certe dierum cibaria superesse,
dum ille pontes navibus iungit et viribus imperi ludit,
aderat ultimum malorum obsessis quoque, alimen-
torum egestas ; exitio paene ac fame constitit et,
quae famem sequitur, rerum omnium ruina furiosi et
6 externi et infeliciter superbi regis imitatio. Quem
tunc animum habuerunt illi, quibus erat mandata
frumenti publici cura, saxa, ferrum, ignes, Gaium
excepturi ? Summa dissimulatione tantum inter
viscera latentis mali tegebant, cum ratione scilicet.
Quaedam enim ignorantibus aegris curanda sunt ;
causa multis moriendi fuit morbum suum nosse.

1 19. Recipe te ad haec tranquilliora, tutiora, maiora !
Simile tu putas esse, utrum cures, ut incorruptum et
a fraude advehentium et a neglegentia frumentum
transfundatur in horrea, ne concepto umore vitietur
et concalescat, ut ad mensuram pondusque respon-
deat, an ad haec sacra et sublimia accedas sciturus,

---

[1] *The text is very dubious :* quod sciebat populo Romano
superstiti *Hermes* : quod dicebat populo Romano super stite
A : quod populo Romano superstite, dicebant *Madvig.*

---

[a] Probably an allusion to the mad wish of Caligula :
" utinam populus Romanus unam cervicem haberet ! "
(Suetonius, *Calig.* 30), cited in *De Ira*, iii. 19. 2. The logic
of the whole passage suffers from the uncertainty of the text.

[b] Three and a half miles long, reaching from Baiae to the
mole of Puteoli (Suetonius, *Calig.* 19).

ings are with the belly of man. A hungry people neither listens to reason, nor is appeased by justice, nor is bent by any entreaty. Very recently within those few days after Gaius Caesar died—still grieving most deeply (if the dead have any feeling) because he knew that the Roman people were alive [a] and had enough food left for at any rate seven or eight days— while he was building his bridges of boats [b] and playing with the resources of the empire, we were threatened with the worst evil that can befall men even during a siege—the lack of provisions ; his imitation of a mad and foreign and misproud king [c] was very nearly at the cost of the city's destruction and famine and the general revolution that follows famine. What then must have been the feeling of those who had charge of the corn-market, and had to face stones, the sword, fire—and a Caligula ? By the greatest subterfuge they concealed the great evil that lurked in the vitals of the state—with good reason, you may be sure. For certain maladies must be treated while the patient is kept in ignorance ; knowledge of their disease has caused the death of many.

Do you retire to these quieter, safer, greater things ! Think you that it is just the same whether you are concerned in having corn from oversea poured into the granaries, unhurt either by the dishonesty or the neglect of those who transport it, in seeing that it does not become heated and spoiled by collecting moisture and tallies in weight and measure, or whether you enter upon these sacred and lofty studies with the purpose of discovering what substance, what

* Xerxes, who laid a bridge over the Hellespont.

quae materia sit dei, quae voluptas, quae condicio,
quae forma ; quis animum tuum casus expectet ;
ubi nos a corporibus dimissos natura componat ; quid
sit quod huius mundi gravissima quaeque in medio
sustineat, supra levia suspendat, in summum ignem
ferat, sidera vicibus suis excitet ; cetera deinceps in-
2 gentibus plena miraculis ? Vis tu relicto solo mente
ad ista respicere ! Nunc, dum calet sanguis, vigentibus[1] ad meliora eundum est. Expectat te in hoc
genere vitae multum bonarum artium, amor virtutium
atque usus, cupiditatium oblivio, vivendi ac moriendi
scientia, alta rerum quies.

3 Omnium quidem occupatorum condicio misera est,
eorum tamen miserrima, qui ne suis quidem laborant
occupationibus, ad alienum dormiunt somnum, ad
alienum ambulant gradum, amare et odisse, res omnium liberrimas, iubentur. Hi si volent scire quam
brevis ipsorum vita sit, cogitent ex quota parte sua
sit.

1 20. Cum videris itaque praetextam saepe iam
sumptam, cum celebre in foro nomen, ne invideris ;
ista vitae damno parantur. Ut unus ab illis nume-
retur annus, omnis annos suos conterent. Quosdam
antequam in summum ambitionis eniterentur, inter
prima luctantis aetas reliquit ; quosdam cum in consummationem dignitatis per mille indignitates erepsis-
sent, misera subît cogitatio laborasse ipsos in titulum

---

[1] vigentibus *A* : sensibus *added by Duff after Madvig.*

---

[a] The Roman year was dated by the names of the two
annual consuls.

pleasure, what mode of life, what shape God has ; what fate awaits your soul ; where Nature lays us to rest when we are freed from the body ; what the principle is that upholds all the heaviest matter in the centre of this world, suspends the light on high, carries fire to the topmost part, summons the stars to their proper changes—and other matters, in turn, full of mighty wonders ? You really must leave the ground and turn your mind's eye upon these things ! Now while the blood is hot, we must enter with brisk step upon the better course. In this kind of life there awaits much that is good to know—the love and practice of the virtues, forgetfulness of the passions, knowledge of living and dying, and a life of deep repose.

The condition of all who are engrossed is wretched, but most wretched is the condition of those who labour at engrossments that are not even their own, who regulate their sleep by that of another, their walk by the pace of another, who are under orders in case of the freest things in the world—loving and hating. If these wish to know how short their life is, let them reflect how small a part of it is their own.

And so when you see a man often wearing the robe of office, when you see one whose name is famous in the Forum, do not envy him ; those things are bought at the price of life. They will waste all their years, in order that they may have one year reckoned by their name.[a] Life has left some in the midst of their first struggles, before they could climb up to the height of their ambition ; some, when they have crawled up through a thousand indignities to the crowning dignity, have been possessed by the unhappy thought that they have but toiled for an inscription

sepulcri ; quorundam ultima senectus, dum in novas
spes ut iuventa disponitur, inter conatus magnos et
2 improbos invalida defecit. Foedus ille, quem in
iudicio pro ignotissimis litigatoribus grandem natu
et imperitae coronae assensiones captantem, spiritus
liquit ; turpis ille, qui vivendo lassus citius quam
laborando inter ipsa officia conlapsus est ; turpis,
quem accipiendis immorientem rationibus diu tractus
3 risit heres. Praeterire quod mihi occurrit exemplum
non possum. S. Turannius[1] fuit exactae diligentiae
senex, qui post annum nonagesimum, cum vacationem
procurationis ab C. Caesare ultro accepisset, componi
se in lecto et velut exanimem a circumstante familia
plangi iussit. Lugebat domus otium domini senis
nec finivit ante tristitiam, quam labor illi suus re-
4 stitutus est. Adeone iuvat occupatum mori ? Idem
plerisque animus est ; diutius cupiditas illis laboris
quam facultas est ; cum imbecillitate corporis pug-
nant, senectutem ipsam nullo alio nomine gravem
iudicant, quam quod illos seponit. Lex a quinquagesimo anno militem non legit, a sexagesimo
senatorem non citat ; difficilius homines a se otium
5 impetrant quam a lege. Interim dum rapiuntur
et rapiunt, dum alter alterius quietem rumpit, dum
mutuo miseri sunt, vita est sine fructu, sine voluptate,
sine ullo profectu animi. Nemo in conspicuo mortem

[1] S. Turannius *Gertz*: ſtyrannius *A.*

---

a *i.e.*, long kept out of his inheritance.
b Tacitus (*Annals*, i. 7) gives the *praenomen* as Gaius.

352

on a tomb ; some who have come to extreme old age, while they adjusted it to new hopes as if it were youth, have had it fail from sheer weakness in the midst of their great and shameless endeavours. Shameful is he whose breath leaves him in the midst of a trial when, advanced in years and still courting the applause of an ignorant circle, he is pleading for some litigant who is the veriest stranger ; disgraceful is he who, exhausted more quickly by his mode of living than by his labour, collapses in the very midst of his duties ; disgraceful is he who dies in the act of receiving payments on account, and draws a smile from his long delayed *a* heir. I cannot pass over an instance which occurs to me. Sextus *b* Turannius was an old man of long tested diligence, who, after his ninetieth year, having received release from the duties of his office by Gaius Caesar's own act, ordered himself to be laid out on his bed and to be mourned by the assembled household as if he were dead. The whole house bemoaned the leisure of its old master, and did not end its sorrow until his accustomed work was restored to him. Is it really such pleasure for a man to die in harness ? Yet very many have the same feeling ; their desire for their labour lasts longer than their ability ; they fight against the weakness of the body, they judge old age to be a hardship on no other score than because it puts them aside. The law does not draft a soldier after his fiftieth year, it does not call a senator after his sixtieth ; it is more difficult for men to obtain leisure from themselves than from the law. Meantime, while they rob and are being robbed, while they break up each other's repose, while they make each other wretched, their life is without profit, without pleasure, without any improvement

habet, nemo non procul spes intendit ; quidam vero
disponunt etiam illa, quae ultra vitam sunt, magnas
moles sepulcrorum et operum publicorum dedica-
tiones et ad rogum munera et ambitiosas exequias.
At me hercules istorum funera, tamquam minimum
vixerint, ad faces et cereos ducenda sunt.

---

a *i.e.*, as if they were children, whose funerals took place
by night (Servius, *Aeneid*, xi. 143).

of the mind. No one keeps death in view, no one refrains from far-reaching hopes ; some men, indeed, even arrange for things that lie beyond life—huge masses of tombs and dedications of public works and gifts for their funeral-pyres and ostentatious funerals. But, in very truth, the funerals of such men ought to be conducted by the light of torches and wax tapers,[a] as though they had lived but the tiniest span.

LIBER XI

DE CONSOLATIONE

1   1. Urbes ac monumenta saxo structa, si vitae[1]
nostrae compares, firma sunt ; si redigas ad condicionem naturae omnia destruentis et unde edidit
eodem revocantis, caduca sunt. Quid enim immortale manus mortales fecerunt ? Septem illa
miracula et si qua his multo mirabiliora sequentium
annorum extruxit ambitio aliquando solo aequata
visentur.   Ita est : nihil perpetuum, pauca diuturna
sunt ; aliud alio modo fragile est, rerum exitus
variantur, ceterum quicquid coepit et desinit.

2   Mundo quidam minantur interitum et hoc universum, quod omnia divina humanaque complectitur,
si fas putas credere, dies aliquis dissipabit et in con-
fusionem veterem tenebrasque demerget.   Eat nunc
aliquis et singulas comploret animas, Carthaginis ac
Numantiae Corinthique cinerem et si quid aliud altius

---

[1] urbes ac monumenta saxo structa, si vitae *supplied by
Gertz.*

---

[a] The essay begins abruptly after the loss of some part of
the text.   Polybius, to whom Seneca here proffers consolation upon the death of a brother, was a freedman who had
gained wealth and official importance under the emperor
Claudius.   He at one time was the emperor's secretary

BOOK XI

ON CONSOLATION

CITIES [a] and monuments made of stone, if you compare them with our life, are enduring; if you submit them to the standard of Nature's law they are perishable, since Nature brings all things to destruction and recalls them to the state from which they sprang. For what that mortal hands have made is ever immortal? The seven wonders of the world and all the works, far more wonderful than these, that the ambition of later years has reared, will some day be seen levelled to the ground. So it is—nothing is everlasting, few things are even long-lasting; one thing perishes in one way, another in another, though the manner of their passing varies, yet whatever has beginning has also an end.

Some there are who threaten even the world with destruction, and (if you think that piety admits the belief) this universe, which contains all the works of gods and men, will one day be scattered and plunged into the ancient chaos and darkness. What folly, then, for anyone to weep for the lives of individuals, to mourn over the ashes of Carthage and Numantia and Corinth and the fall of any other city, mayhap loftier

a studiis (Suet. *Claudius*, 28), and when this essay was written was holding the responsible post *a libellis* (ch. 6. 5).

cecidit lamentetur, cum etiam hoc quod non habet
quo cadat sit interiturum ; eat aliquis et fata tantum
aliquando nefas ausura sibi non pepercisse con-
3 queratur. Quis tam superbae impotentisque arro-
gantiae est, ut in hac naturae necessitate omnia ad
eundem finem revocantis se unum ac suos seponi velit
ruinaeque etiam ipsi mundo imminenti aliquam
4 domum subtrahat ? Maximum ergo solacium est
cogitare id sibi accidisse, quod omnes ante se passi
sunt omnesque passuri ; et ideo mihi videtur rerum
natura, quod gravissimum fecerat, commune fecisse,
ut crudelitatem fati consolaretur aequalitas.

1   2. Illud quoque te non minimum adiuverit, si
cogitaveris nihil profuturum dolorem tuum nec illi,
quem desideras, nec tibi ; noles enim longum esse,
quod irritum est. Nam si quicquam tristitia profec-
turi sumus, non recuso quicquid lacrimarum fortunae
meae superfuit tuae fundere ; inveniam etiamnunc
per hos exhaustos iam fletibus domesticis oculos quod
2 effluat, si modo id tibi futurum bono est. Quid
cessas ? Conqueramur, atque adeo ipse hanc litem
meam faciam : " Iniquissima omnium iudicio fortuna,
adhuc videbaris sinu eum hominem continuisse,[1] qui
munere tuo tantam venerationem receperat, ut, quod
raro ulli contigit, felicitas eius effugeret invidiam.
Ecce eum dolorem illi, quem salvo Caesare accipere

---

[1] sinu eum hominem continuisse *Joh. Müller* : eum
hominem continuisse *O, Ball* : in eo homine te continuisse
Duff after Madvig.

---

[a] Seneca writes from exile in Corsica, to which he was
banished under Claudius (A.D. 41).

than these, when even this universe will perish though it has no place into which it can fall ; what folly for anyone to complain that Fate, though she will some day dare so great a crime, has not spared even him ! Who is of such haughty and overweening presumption as to wish that he and his dear ones alone be excepted from this law of Nature that brings all things to their end, and to exempt some one household from the destruction that threatens even the world itself ? A man, therefore, will find the greatest comfort in the thought that what has befallen himself was suffered by all who were before him and will be suffered by all who come after him ; and Nature has, it seems to me, made universal what she had made hardest to bear in order that the uniformity of fate might console men for its cruelty.

And it will help you, too, not a little if you reflect that your grief can accomplish nothing either for him whose loss you mourn or for yourself ; for the suffering that is vain you will be unwilling to prolong. For if we are likely to accomplish anything by sorrow, I do not refuse to shed whatever tears my own fortune *a* has left me in regret for yours ; for I shall even yet find some that may flow from these eyes of mine, that have already been drained by my personal woes, if only thereby I may do you some good. Why do you hesitate ? Let us lament together, or rather I myself will bring forth this indictment as my own : " O Fortune, you who by the verdict of all men are most unjust, you seemed hitherto to have cherished this man in your bosom, for, thanks to you, he had by a rare accident won so much respect that his prosperity escaped envy. But now you have stamped upon him the greatest sorrow that, while Caesar

359

maximum poterat, impressisti, et cum bene illum
undique circuisses, intellexisti hac parte tantummodo
3 patere ictibus tuis. Quid enim illi aliud faceres?
Pecuniam eriperes? Numquam illi obnoxius fuit;
nunc quoque, quantum potest, illam a se abigit et
in tanta facilitate adquirendi nullum maiorem ex ea
4 fructum quam contemptum eius petit. Eriperes
illi amicos? Sciebas tam amabilem esse, ut facile
in locum amissorum posset alios substituere; unum
enim hunc ex eis, quos in principali domo potentes
vidi, cognovisse videor, quem omnibus amicum habere
5 cum expediat, magis tamen etiam libet. Eriperes
illi bonam opinionem? Solidior est haec apud eum,
quam ut a te quoque ipsa concuti possit. Eriperes
bonam valetudinem? Sciebas animum eius libera-
libus disciplinis, quibus non innutritus tantum sed
innatus est, sic esse fundatum, ut supra omnis
6 corporis dolores emineret. Eriperes spiritum?
Quantulum nocuisses! Longissimum illi ingeni
aevum fama promisit; id egit ipse, ut meliore sui
parte duraret et compositis eloquentiae praeclaris
operibus a mortalitate se vindicaret. Quam diu
fuerit ullus litteris honor, quam diu steterit aut
Latinae linguae potentia aut Graecae gratia, vigebit
cum maximis viris, quorum se ingeniis vel contulit
7 vel, si hoc verecundia eius recusat, applicuit. Hoc

lives, he could possibly have received, and, having
thoroughly reconnoitred him on every side, you discovered that from this direction only was he exposed
to your arrows. For what other harm could you have
dealt him ? Should you have snatched away his
money ? But he was never its slave ; even now he
thrusts it from him as much as he can, and, though
he has so many opportunities to acquire it, he seeks
from it no greater gain than the power to scorn it.
Should you have snatched away his friends ? But you
knew that, so lovable is he, he could easily substitute
others in place of those he had lost ; for of all those I
have seen holding high place in the imperial household,
I seem to have discovered in him the only one whom,
though it is to the interest of all, it is yet even more
their pleasure, to have as a friend. Should you have
snatched away his good reputation ? But in his case
this is too well-grounded for even you to be able
to shake it. Should you have snatched away good
health ? But you knew that his mind was so well-
grounded by liberal studies—for he had not merely
been bred, but born, among books—that it rose
superior to all pains of the body. Should you have
snatched away his life ? But how little you could
have harmed him ! Fame has promised him that
the life of his genius shall be very long ; and he
himself has made it his aim that he should endure,
in the better part of him, and by the composition of
glorious works of eloquence rescue himself from
mortality. So long as letters shall have any honour,
so long as the force of the Latin or the grace of the
Greek tongue shall survive, he shall flourish in the
company of those giants of whose genius he has made
himself a rival, or, if his modesty refuses so much, a

ergo unum excogitasti, quomodo maxime illi posses
nocere ; quo melior est enim quisque, hoc saepius
ferre te consuevit sine ullo dilectu furentem et inter
ipsa beneficia metuendam. Quantulum erat tibi
immunem ab hac iniuria praestare eum hominem,
in quem videbatur indulgentia tua ratione certa
pervenisse et non ex tuo more temere incidisse ! "

1   3. Adiciamus, si vis, ad has querellas ipsius adules-
centis interceptam inter prima incrementa indolem ;
dignus fuit ille te fratre. Tu certe eras dignissimus,
qui ne ex indigno quidem quicquam doleres fratre.
Redditur illi testimonium aequale omnium hominum ;
desideratur in tuum honorem, laudatur in suum.
2 Nihil in illo fuit, quod non libenter adgnosceres. Tu
quidem etiam minus bono fratri fuisses bonus, sed in
illo pietas tua idoneam nacta materiam multo se
liberius exercuit. Nemo potentiam eius iniuria sensit,
numquam ille te fratrem ulli minatus est. Ad exemplum se modestiae tuae formaverat cogitabatque,
quantum tu et ornamentum tuorum esses et onus ;
3 suffecit ille huic sarcinae. O dura fata et nullis aequa
virtutibus ! Antequam felicitatem suam nosset frater
tuus, exemptus est. Parum autem me indignari scio ;
nihil est enim difficilius quam magno dolori paria
verba reperire. Etiamnunc tamen, si quid proficere

----

a *i.e.*, if you must grieve for a brother, you highly deserve
that he should not be an undeserving one.

devotee. Consequently, Fortune, you have found out that this is the only way in which you could injure him very deeply ; for the better a man is, the more often is he wont to endure your assaults—you who vent your rage without discrimination, and are to be feared even in the midst of your kindnesses. How little it would have cost you to render him exempt from such an injury—a man to whom, it seemed, your favour had been extended on a fixed principle, and had not, after your usual fashion, fallen upon him at random."

Let us add, if you will, to these grounds of complaint the character of the youth himself, cut off in the midst of its first growth ; worthy was he to be your brother. You, at any rate, were most worthy that not even an unworthy brother should be to you any cause for grief.[a] All men alike bear witness to his character ; he is regretted in compliment to you, he is lauded in compliment to himself. There was nothing in him which you were not glad to recognize. You would indeed have been good even to a brother less good, but in his case your natural affection, having found a suitable object, displayed itself much more generously. No one was ever made to feel his power from an injury he did, he never threatened anyone with your being his brother. He had moulded himself after the pattern of your modesty, and remembered what a great ornament you were to your family, and what a responsibility ; but he was equal to this burden. O pitiless Fate, always unjust to virtue ! Before your brother could know his own happiness, he was taken from it. But I know that I express my indignation poorly ; for nothing is so difficult as to find words to match a great sorrow. Yet once again,

363

4 possumus, conqueramur : " Quid tibi voluisti, tam
iniusta et tam violenta fortuna ? Tam cito te indulgentiae tuae paenituit ? Quae ista crudelitas est, in
medios fratres impetum facere et tam cruenta rapina
concordissimam turbam imminuere ? Tam bene
stipatam optimorum adulescentium domum, in nullo
fratre degenerantem, turbare et sine ulla causa de-
5 libare voluisti[1] ? Nihil ergo prodest innocentia ad
omnem legem exacta, nihil antiqua frugalitas, nihil
felicitatis summae potentia summa conservata absti-
nentia, nihil sincerus et tutus litterarum amor, nihil ab
omni labe mens vacans ? Luget Polybius, et in uno
fratre quid de reliquis possit metuere admonitus
etiam de ipsis doloris sui solaciis timet. Facinus
indignum ! Luget Polybius et aliquid propitio dolet
Caesare ! Hoc sine dubio, impotens fortuna, captasti,
ut ostenderes neminem contra te ne a Caesare
quidem posse defendi."

1 4. Diutius accusare fata possumus, mutare non
possumus. Stant dura et inexorabilia ; nemo illa
convicio, nemo fletu, nemo causa movet ; nihil umquam ulli parcunt nec remittunt. Proinde parcamus
lacrimis nihil proficientibus ; facilius enim nos inferis
dolor iste adiciet quam illos nobis reducet. Qui si
nos torquet, non adiuvat, primo quoque tempore de-
ponendus est et ab inanibus solaciis atque amara
quadam libidine dolendi animus recipiendus est.

---

[1] est, in medios . . . delibare voluisti *O with punctuation
of Duff* : *Hermes after Gertz deletes* voluisti.

if words can be of any avail, let us complain together :
" What did you mean, O Fortune, by being so
unjust and so violent ? Did you repent so quickly
of your former kindness ? What cruelty is this,
to make your assault upon a company of brothers,
and by such cruel robbery to impoverish so loving
a group ? Did you mean to break up a household
of admirable young men so closely united, no one
of whom fell short of his brothers, and without
any reason to take one from their number? Does
blamelessness, then, avail nothing, though tested by
every principle ? old-fashioned simplicity, nothing ?
persistent self-restraint when there was unlimited
opportunity to gain unlimited wealth, nothing ? a
sincere and safe love of letters, nothing ? a mind
free from every taint of sin, nothing ? Polybius
mourns, and, warned by the fate of one brother
of what he may dread concerning the rest, he
fears for the very solaces of his sorrow. O the
shame ! Polybius mourns and suffers sorrow while
Caesar smiles upon him ! O unbridled Fortune,
clearly what you aimed at was this—to show that
no one can be protected against you—no, not even
by Caesar."

We can go on blaming Fate much longer, change it
we cannot. It stands harsh and inexorable ; no one
can move it by reproaches, no one by tears, no one
by his cause ; it never lets anyone off nor shows
mercy. Accordingly let us refrain from tears, that
profit nothing ; for sooner will this grief unite us
with the dead than bring them back to us. And if
grief tortures us and does not help us, we ought to
lay it aside as soon as possible, and recall the mind
from its empty consolations and a sort of morbid

2 Nam lacrimis nostris nisi ratio finem fecerit, fortuna non faciet.

Omnis agedum mortalis circumspice, larga ubique flendi et adsidua materia est. Alium ad cotidianum opus laboriosa egestas vocat, alium ambitio numquam quieta sollicitat, alius divitias, quas optaverat, metuit et voto laborat suo, alium solitudo torquet,[1] alium semper vestibulum obsidens turba ; hic habere se dolet liberos, hic perdidisse. Lacrimae nobis

3 deerunt ante quam causae dolendi. Non vides, qualem nobis vitam rerum natura promiserit, quae primum nascentium hominum fletum esse voluit ? Hoc principio edimur, huic omnis sequentium annorum ordo consentit. Sic vitam agimus, ideoque moderate id fieri debet a nobis, quod saepe faciendum est, et respicientes, quantum a tergo rerum tristium immineat, si non finire lacrimas, at certe reservare debemus. Nulli parcendum est rei magis quam huic, cuius tam frequens usus est.

1 5. Illud quoque te non minimum adiuverit, si cogitaveris nulli minus gratum esse dolorem tuum quam ei, cui praestari videtur ; torqueri ille te aut non vult aut non intellegit. Nulla itaque eius officii ratio est, quod ei, cui praestatur, si nihil sentit, super-

---

[1] solitudo torquet *Hermes after Haupt* : sollicitudo alium labor torquet *O.*

pleasure in grieving. For unless reason puts an end to our tears, fortune will not do so.

Come, look about you, survey all mortals—everywhere there is ample and constant reason for tears. Toilsome poverty summons one man to his daily task, never-resting ambition harasses another ; one fears the riches that he had prayed for, and suffers from the granting of his prayer ; his loneliness torments one, the throng that besieges his threshold, another ; this man mourns because he has children, this one because he has lost them. Tears will fail us sooner than the causes for weeping. Do you not see what sort of life Nature has promised us—she who decreed that the first act of man at birth should be to weep [a] ? With such a beginning are we brought forth, with such the whole series of later years accords. Thus we spend our lives, and therefore we ought to do in moderation this thing that we must do so often ; and as we look back upon the great mass of sorrows that threatens us behind, we ought, if not to end our tears, yet at any rate to keep guard over them. Nothing must be husbanded more carefully than that of which there is such frequent need.

And this also will give you no small help—if you reflect that there is no one who is less pleased by your grief than he to whom it seems to be offered ; for he either does not wish you to suffer, or does not know that you do. There is, therefore, no sense in this service, for if he to whom it is offered lacks

---

[a] Lucretius (v 222 *sqq.*) supplies a famous example of this ancient commonplace ; see p. 35, note [a]. *Cf.* Shakespeare, *King Lear*, iv. 6 :

　　When we are born, we cry that we are come
　　To this great stage of fools.

2 vacuum est, si sentit, ingratum est. Neminem esse
toto orbe terrarum, qui delectetur lacrimis tuis,
audacter dixerim. Quid ergo? Quem nemo adversus
te animum gerit, eum esse tu credis fratris tui, ut
cruciatu tui noceat tibi, ut te velit abducere ab
occupationibus tuis, id est a studio et a Caesare?
Non est hoc simile veri. Ille enim indulgentiam tibi
tamquam fratri praestitit, venerationem tamquam
parenti, cultum tamquam superiori; ille desiderio
tibi esse vult, tormento esse non vult. Quid itaque
iuvat dolori intabescere, quem, si quis defunctis
3 sensus est, finiri frater tuus cupit? De alio fratre,
cuius incerta posset voluntas videri, omnia haec in
dubio ponerem et dicerem : " Sive te torqueri lacrimis numquam desinentibus frater tuus cupit, indignus
hoc affectu tuo est; sive non vult, utrique vestrum
inhaerentem dolorem dimitte; nec impius frater sic
desiderari debet nec pius sic velit." In hoc vero,
cuius tam explorata pietas est, pro certo habendum
est nihil esse illi posse acerbius, quam si tibi hic
casus eius acerbus est, si te ullo modo torquet, si
oculos tuos, indignissimos hoc malo, sine ullo flendi
fine et conturbat idem et exhaurit.

4 Pietatem tamen tuam nihil aeque a lacrimis tam
inutilibus abducet, quam si cogitaveris fratribus te
tuis exemplo esse debere fortiter hanc fortunae in-

ᵃ The Epicureans taught that the soul perished along with
the body.

consciousness,^a it is useless, and, if he has consciousness, it is displeasing to him. I may say boldly that there is no one in the whole wide world who finds pleasure in your tears. And what then? Do you suppose that your brother has towards you the disposition that no one else displays—the desire that you should withdraw from your ordinary tasks—that is, from the serving of Caesar—in order to do harm to yourself by self-torture? This is not likely. For he always paid to you the love due to a brother, the respect due to a parent, and the court due to a superior; he wishes to be missed by you, not to cause you suffering. Why, therefore, do you choose to pine away with a sorrow which, if the dead have any consciousness, your brother desires to have ended? Were it any other brother, about whose goodwill there might seem to be some uncertainty, I should put all these things doubtfully, and say: "If your brother desires that you be tortured with tears that never cease, he is unworthy of this affection of yours; if he does not wish this, leave off the grief that is painful to both; an unloving brother ought not, and a loving brother would not want, to be mourned for in this way." But in his case his brotherly love has been so clearly proved that we must feel sure that nothing could be more bitter for him than seeing that this mishap of his is bitter for you, that it in any way causes you distress, that to those eyes of yours, which least deserve so great an ill, it, too, brings both trouble and exhaustion without any end of weeping.

Nothing, however, will so effectually restrain your love from such useless tears as the thought that you ought to give to your brothers an example by bearing

iuriam sustinendi. Quod duces magni faciunt rebus
affectis, ut hilaritatem de industria simulent et adversas res adumbrata laetitia abscondant, ne militum
animi, si fractam ducis sui mentem viderint, et ipsi
collabantur, id nunc tibi quoque faciendum est.
5 Indue dissimilem animo tuo vultum et, si potes,
proice omnem ex toto dolorem, si minus, introrsus
abde et contine, ne appareat, et da operam, ut fratres
tui te imitentur, qui honestum putabunt, quod-
cumque te facientem viderint, animumque ex vultu
tuo sument.   Et solacium debes esse illorum et
consolator ; non poteris autem horum maerori obstare,
si tuo indulseris.

1   6. Potest et illa res a luctu te prohibere nimio, si
tibi ipse renuntiaveris nihil horum, quae facis, posse
subduci.   Magnam tibi personam hominum consensus imposuit ; haec tibi tuenda est.   Circumstat te
omnis ista consolantium frequentia et in animum
tuum inquirit ac perspicit quantum roboris ille adversus dolorem habeat et utrumne tu tantum rebus
secundis uti dextere scias, an et adversas possis viri-
2 liter ferre.   Observantur oculi tui.   Liberiora sunt
omnia iis, quorum affectus tegi possunt ; tibi nullum
secretum liberum est.   In multa luce fortuna te
posuit ; omnes scient, quomodo te in isto tuo gesseris
vulnere, utrumne statim percussus arma summiseris
an in gradu steteris.   Olim te in altiorem ordinem et
amor Caesaris extulit et tua studia eduxerunt.   Nihil
370

this injustice of Fortune bravely. This is the way great generals act in times of disaster—they purposely make pretence of cheerfulness, and conceal their misfortunes by feigning joy, lest the soldiers themselves should likewise grow faint-hearted if they saw the spirit of their leader broken. You also must now do the same. Assume an expression that belies your feeling, and, if you can, wholly cast out all your sorrow; if not, hide it in your heart, and keep it from showing, and make effort to have your brothers copy you, who will think whatever they see you doing to be right, and will take heart from your face. You ought to be to them both their comfort and their consoler; but you will not be able to check their sorrow if you indulge your own.

And it may be that this also will keep you from excessive grief—if you remind yourself that none of the things that you do can be kept secret. Public opinion has assigned to you an important rôle; this you must maintain. All yonder throng that offers you consolation stands about you, and it searches into your heart, and descries how much strength this has in the face of sorrow, and whether you only know how to use prosperity adroitly, or are able also to bear adversity with courage. They watch your eyes! Those have more liberty whose feelings are able to be concealed; you are not free to have any privacy. Fortune has placed you in the bright light; all people will know how you have behaved under this wound of yours—whether the moment you were struck you laid down your arms, or stood your ground. Long ago the love of Caesar lifted you to a higher rank, and your literary pursuits have elevated you. Nothing vulgar, nothing base

te plebeium decet, nihil humile. Quid autem tam humile ac muliebre est quam consumendum se dolori
3 committere ? Non idem tibi in luctu pari quod tuis fratribus licet ; multa tibi non permittit opinio de studiis ac moribus tuis recepta, multum a te homines exigunt, multum expectant. Si volebas tibi omnia licere, ne convertisses in te ora omnium ; nunc tantum tibi praestandum est, quantum promisisti. Omnes illi, qui opera ingenii tui laudant, qui describunt, quibus, cum fortuna tua opus non sit, ingenio opus est, custodes animi tui sunt. Nihil umquam ita potes indignum facere perfecti et eruditi viri professione, ut non multos admirationis de te
4 suae paeniteat. Non licet tibi flere immodice, nec hoc tantummodo non licet ; ne somnum quidem extendere in partem diei licet aut a tumultu rerum in otium ruris quieti confugere aut assidua laboriosi officii statione fatigatum corpus voluptaria peregrinatione recreare aut spectaculorum varietate animum detinere aut ex tuo arbitrio diem disponere. Multa tibi non licent, quae humillimis et in angulo
5 iacentibus licent. Magna servitus est magna fortuna ; non licet tibi quicquam arbitrio tuo facere. Audienda sunt tot hominum milia, tot disponendi libelli ; tantus rerum ex orbe toto coeuntium congestus, ut possit per ordinem suum principis maximi animo subici, exigendus est. Non licet tibi, inquam,

---

a In the duties of his office *a libellis* Polybius received the petitions and memorials addressed to the emperor and drew up replies for the imperial signature.

befits you. Yet what is so base and so womanish as to
give oneself over to be utterly consumed by sorrow?
Though you have equal grief, you do not have
the same liberty as your brothers; there are many
things that the opinion which others have formed of
your learning and your character does not permit
you to do—men demand much of you, expect much.
If you wished to be free to do everything, you should
not have turned all faces toward you; as it is, you
must make good all that of which you have given
promise. All those who praise the works of your genius,
who take copies of them, who, though they have no
need of your greatness, have need of your genius, keep
watch on your mind. And thus you can never do
anything unworthy of your claim to be a sage and a
scholar without making many repent of their admiration for you. You may not weep beyond measure,
nor is this the only thing you may not do; you may
not either prolong sleep into the hours of day, or flee
from the turmoil of business to the leisure of rural
repose, or refresh your body, wearied by its constant
guard at the post of toilsome duty, by a trip abroad
for pleasure, or engage your mind with a variety of
shows, or arrange your day according to your own
desire. Many things you may not do, which the
lowliest wretch that lies in his corner may do. A
great fortune is a great slavery; you may not do
anything according to your wish. You must give
audience to countless thousands of men, countless
petitions *a* must be disposed of; so great is the pile
of business, accumulated from every part of the world,
that must be carefully weighed in order that it may
be brought to the attention of a most illustrious prince
in the proper order. You, I say, are not allowed to

flere ; ut multos flentes audire possis, ut periclitantium et ad misericordiam mitissimi Caesaris pervenire cupientium lacrimas siccare,[1] lacrimae tibi tuae adsiccandae sunt.

1 7. Haec tamen etiamnunc levioribus te remediis adiuvabunt ; cum voles omnium rerum oblivisci, Caesarem cogita. Vide, quantam huius in te indulgentiae fidem, quantam industriam debeas ; intelleges non magis tibi incurvari licere quam illi, si quis modo est fabulis traditus,[2] cuius umeris mundus in-

2 nititur. Caesari quoque ipsi, cui omnia licent, propter hoc ipsum multa non licent. Omnium somnos illius vigilia defendit, omnium otium illius labor, omnium delicias illius industria, omnium vacationem illius occupatio. Ex quo se Caesar orbi terrarum dedicavit, sibi eripuit, et siderum modo, quae irrequieta semper cursus suos explicant, numquam illi licet subsistere

3 nec quicquam suum facere. Ad quendam itaque modum tibi quoque eadem necessitas iniungitur ; non licet tibi ad utilitates tuas, ad studia tua respicere. Caesare orbem terrarum possidente impertire te nec voluptati nec dolori nec ulli alii rei potes ; totum te

4 Caesari debes. Adice nunc quod, cum semper praedices cariorem tibi spiritu tuo Caesarem esse, fas tibi non est salvo Caesare de fortuna queri. Hoc incolumi salvi tibi sunt tui, nihil perdidisti ; non tantum siccos oculos tuos esse sed etiam laetos oportet ; in hoc tibi omnia sunt, hic pro omnibus est.

---

[1] lacrimas siccare *added by Hermes.*
[2] traditus *O :* tradito *Duff.*

---

a *i.e.,* Atlas.

weep ; in order that you may be able to listen to the many who weep—in order that you may dry the tears of those who are in peril and desire to obtain mercy from Caesar's clemency, it is your own tears that you must dry.

My suggestions, so far, deal with the milder remedies, nevertheless they will help you ; but when you shall wish to forget everything else—think of Caesar. Think what loyalty, what industry, you owe him in return for his imperial favour to you ; you will then understand that you may no more bend beneath the burden than he *a*—if there really is anyone such as myths tell of—whose shoulders uphold the sky. Even Caesar himself, who may do all things, may not do many things for the very same reason. His watchfulness guards all men's sleep, his toil all men's ease, his industry all men's dissipations, his work all men's vacation. On the day that Caesar dedicated himself to the wide world, he robbed himself of himself ; and even as the planets, which, unresting, ever pursue their courses, he may never halt or do anything for himself. And so, to a certain degree, the same necessity is enjoined upon you also ; you may not pay regard to your own interests or to your books. While Caesar owns the wide world, you can give no part of yourself either to pleasure or sorrow or anything else ; you owe the whole of yourself to Caesar. And besides, since you always declare that Caesar is dearer to you than your own life, it is not right for you to make complaint of Fortune while Caesar is alive. So long as he is alive, your dear ones are alive—you have lost nothing. Your eyes ought to be not only dry, but even happy ; in him you have all things, he takes the place of all. If you allow your-

Quod longe a sensibus tuis prudentissimis[1] piissimisque abest, adversus felicitatem tuam parum gratus es, si tibi quicquam hoc salvo flere permittis.

1   8. Monstrabo etiamnunc non quidem firmius remedium sed familiarius. Si quando te domum receperis, tunc erit tibi metuenda tristitia. Nam quam diu numen tuum intueberis, nullum illa ad te inveniet accessum, omnia in te Caesar tenebit ; cum ab illo discesseris, tunc velut occasione data insidiabitur solitudini tuae dolor et requiescenti animo tuo pau-

2 latim irrepet. Itaque non est quod ullum tempus vacare patiaris a studiis. Tunc tibi litterae tuae tam diu ac tam fideliter amatae gratiam referant, tunc te illae antistitem et cultorem suum vindicent, tunc Homerus et Vergilius tam bene de humano genere meriti, quam tu et de illis et de omnibus meruisti, quos pluribus notos esse voluisti quam scripserant, multum tecum morentur ; tutum id erit omne tempus, quod illis tuendum commiseris. Tunc Caesaris tui opera, ut per omnia saecula domestico narrentur praeconio, quantum potes, compone ; nam ipse tibi optime formandi condendique res gestas et materiam dabit et exemplum.

3   Non audeo te eo usque producere, ut fabellas quoque et Aesopeos logos, intemptatum Romanis ingeniis opus, solita tibi venustate conectas. Difficile est quidem, ut ad haec hilariora studia tam vehementer perculsus animus tam cito possit accedere ;

---

[1] prudentissimis *O* : pudentissimis *Hermes after Stangl.*

[a] As is shown in ch. 11. 5, Polybius had translated Homer into Latin and Virgil into Greek.

[b] Seneca ignores the fact that Phaedrus, who flourished under Tiberius, had turned Aesop's Fables into Latin verse.

self to weep for anything while he is alive, you lack
gratitude for your good fortune; but this is very
foreign to your sensible and loyal disposition.

Further, I shall prescribe a remedy that is not
indeed surer, but more private. Whenever you retire
to your home, then will be the time for you to dread
your sadness. For as long as your divinity is before
your eyes, that will find no access to you, Caesar will
possess all that is in you; but when you have left
him, then, having found, as it were, a good opportunity, sorrow will lie in wait for your loneliness, and
will little by little steal upon your mind when it is unoccupied. And so there is no reason why you should
allow any of your time to be without the interest of
literature. Then let your books, so long and so
faithfully loved, repay your favour, then let them
claim you for their high priest and worshipper, then
let Homer and Virgil, to whom the human race owes
as much as they and all men owe to you, whom you
wished to become known to a wider circle than that
for which they wrote,[a] be much in your company;
the time that you entrust to their safeguarding will
be safe indeed. Then, with your best powers, compile
an account of the deeds of your Caesar, so that, being
heralded by one of his own household, they may be
repeated throughout all ages; since, for the fashioning and writing of history, he himself will best supply
you with both matter and model.

I do not venture to push you to the point of putting
together also, with your characteristic charm, the
tales and fables of Aesop—a task that Roman talent
has not yet essayed.[b] It would be difficult indeed for
a mind so severely smitten to approach so quickly this
lighter kind of literature; nevertheless, if it shall be

hoc tamen argumentum habeto iam corroborati eius
et redditi sibi, si poterit a severioribus scriptis ad
4 haec solutiora procedere. In illis enim quamvis
aegrum eum adhuc et secum reluctantem avocabit
ipsa rerum, quas tractabit, austeritas ; haec, quae
remissa fronte commentanda sunt, non feret, nisi cum
iam sibi ab omni parte constiterit. Itaque debebis
eum severiore materia primum exercere, deinde
hilariore temperare.

1   9. Illud quoque magno tibi erit levamento, si saepe
te sic interrogaveris : " Utrumne meo nomine doleo
an eius qui decessit ? Si meo, perit indulgentiae iactatio et incipit dolor hoc uno excusatus, quod honestus
est, cum ad utilitatem respicit, a pietate desciscere ;
nihil autem minus bono viro convenit quam in fratris
2 luctu calculos ponere. Si illius nomine doleo, necesse
est alterutrum ex his duobus esse iudicem. Nam si
nullus defunctis sensus superest, evasit omnia frater
meus vitae incommoda et in eum restitutus est locum,
in quo fuerat antequam nasceretur, et expers omnis
mali nihil timet, nihil cupit, nihil patitur. Quis iste
furor est pro eo me numquam dolere desinere, qui
3 numquam doliturus est ? Si est aliquis defunctis
sensus, nunc animus fratris mei velut ex diutino
carcere emissus, tandem sui iuris et arbitrii, gestit et
rerum naturae spectaculo fruitur et humana omnia ex

able to pass from more serious compositions to these less exacting ones, you must count this as proof that it has now recovered its strength and is itself again. For in the case of the former, the very sternness of the subject which it treats will distract the mind although still suffering and struggling with itself; the latter, which must be pondered with a brow unbent, it will not endure until it has wholly recovered its native harmony. Your duty, therefore, will be first to give it hard work with a more serious subject, and then to modify its effort with a lighter.

It will also serve as a great relief, if you will often question yourself thus : " Am I grieving on my own account, or on account of him who has departed ? If on my own account, this parade of affection is idle, and my grief, the only excuse for which is that it is honourable, begins to show defection from brotherly love when it looks toward personal advantage ; but nothing is less becoming to a good man than to be calculating in his grief for a brother. If I grieve on his account, I must decide that one or the other of the two following views is true. For, if the dead retain no feeling whatever, my brother has escaped from all the ills of life, and has been restored to that state in which he had been before he was born, and, exempt from every ill, he fears nothing, desires nothing, suffers nothing. What madness this is—that I should never cease to grieve for one who will never grieve any more ! If, however, the dead do retain some feeling, at this moment my brother's soul, released, as it were, from its long imprisonment, exults to be at last its own lord and master, enjoys the spectacle of Nature, and from its higher place looks down upon all human things, while upon things

loco superiore despicit, divina vero, quorum rationem tam diu frustra quaesierat, propius intuetur. Quid itaque eius desiderio maceror, qui aut beatus aut nullus est? Beatum deflere invidia est, nullum dementia.''

4 An hoc te movet, quod videtur ingentibus et cum maxime circumfusis bonis caruisse? Cum cogitaveris multa esse, quae perdidit, cogita plura esse, quae non timet. Non ira eum torquebit, non morbus affliget, non suspicio lacesset, non edax et inimica semper alienis processibus invidia consectabitur, non metus sollicitabit, non levitas fortunae cito munera sua transferentis inquietabit. Si bene computes, plus illi 5 remissum quam ereptum est. Non opibus fruetur, non tua simul ac sua gratia; non accipiet beneficia, non dabit. Miserum putas, quod ista amisit, an beatum, quod non desiderat? Mihi crede, is beatior est, cui fortuna supervacua est, quam is, cui parata[1] est. Omnia ista bona, quae nos speciosa sed fallaci voluptate delectant, pecunia, dignitas, potentia aliaque complura, ad quae generis humani caeca cupiditas obstupescit, cum labore possidentur, cum invidia conspiciuntur, eos denique ipsos, quos exornant, et premunt; plus minantur quam prosunt. Lubrica et incerta sunt, numquam bene tenentur; nam ut nihil de tempore futuro timeatur, ipsa tamen magnae 6 felicitatis tutela sollicita est. Si velis credere altius

---

[1] parata *O* : parta *Pincianus*.

---

[a] In the teaching of many of the Stoics, the heavenly bodies were identified with the gods.

divine,[a] the explanation of which it had so long sought in vain, it gazes with a nearer vision. And so why should I pine away in yearning for him who either is happy or does not exist? But to weep for one who is happy is envy; for one who does not exist, madness."

Or is it this that moves you—the thought that he has been deprived of great blessings just when they were showered upon him? But when you reflect that there are many things which he has lost, reflect also that there are more which he no longer fears. He is not racked by anger, he is not smitten with disease, he is not worried by suspicion, he is not assailed by gnawing envy that is always hostile to other men's successes, he is not disquieted by fear, he is not alarmed by the fickleness of Fortune, who quickly shifts her favours. If you count carefully, he has been spared more than he has lost. He will not enjoy wealth, nor favour at court, his own together with yours; he will not receive benefits, he will not bestow them. Do you think that he is unhappy because he has lost these things, or happy because he does not miss them? Believe me, he is happier who does not need good fortune than he for whom it is in store. All those goods which delight us by their showy, but deceptive, charm—money, standing, power, and the many other things at the sight of which the human race, in its blind greed, is filled with awe—bring trouble to their possessor, stir jealousy in the beholder, and in the end also crush the very men that they adorn; they are more of a menace than a good. They are slippery and uncertain, and are never held happily; for though there should be no anxiety about the future, yet the mere preservation of great prosperity is full of worry. If we are to believe some who

veritatem intuentibus, omnis vita supplicium est.
In hoc profundum inquietumque proiecti mare, alternis aestibus reciprocum et modo allevans nos subitis
incrementis, modo maioribus damnis deferens assidue-
que iactans, numquam stabili consistimus loco, pendemus et fluctuamur et alter in alterum illidimur
et aliquando naufragium facimus, semper timemus;
7 in hoc tam procelloso et ad omnes tempestates
exposito mari navigantibus nullus portus nisi mortis
est. Ne itaque invideris fratri tuo; quiescit. Tandem
liber, tandem tutus, tandem aeternus est. Superstitem Caesarem omnemque eius prolem, superstitem
te cum communibus habet fratribus. Antequam
quicquam ex suo favore fortuna mutaret, stantem
adhuc illam et munera plena manu congerentem
8 reliquit. Fruitur nunc aperto et libero caelo, ex
humili atque depresso in eum emicuit locum, quisquis
ille est, qui solutas vinculis animas beato recipit sinu,
et nunc libere illic vagatur omniaque rerum naturae
bona cum summa voluptate perspicit. Erras: non
perdidit lucem frater tuus, sed sinceriorem sortitus
9 est. Omnibus illo nobis commune est iter. Quid
fata deflemus? Non reliquit ille nos sed antecessit.
Est, mihi crede, magna felicitas in ipsa necessitate
moriendi. Nihil ne in totum quidem diem certi est.
Quis in tam obscura et involuta veritate divinat,
utrumne fratri tuo mors inviderit an consuluerit?
1 10. Illud quoque, qua iustitia in omnibus rebus es,
necesse est te adiuvet cogitantem non iniuriam tibi

have a more profound insight into truth, all life is a torment. Plunged into this deep and restless sea, that ebbs and flows with changing tides, now uplifting us with sudden accessions of fortune, now sweeping us downward with greater losses and flinging us about incessantly, we never stay steadfast in one place, we dangle aloft, are tossed hither and thither, collide with each other, and sometimes suffer shipwreck, always fear it ; for those who sail upon this sea, so stormy and exposed to every gale, there is no harbour save death. And so do not grudge your brother this—he is at rest. At last he is free, at last safe, at last immortal. He leaves Caesar and all of Caesar's offspring still surviving, he leaves you surviving in company with the brothers of you both. While Fortune was still standing near him and bestowing her gifts with generous hand, he left her before she could make any change in her favour. He delights now in the open and boundless sky, from a low and sunken region he has darted aloft to that place (whatever it be) which receives in its happy embrace souls that are freed from their chains ; and he now roams there, and explores with supreme delight all the blessings of Nature. You are mistaken—your brother has not lost the light of day, but he has gained a purer light. The way thither is the same for us all. Why do we bemoan his fate ? He has not left us, but has gone before. Believe me, there is great happiness in the very necessity of dying. We can be sure of nothing—not even for the whole of one day. Where the truth is so dark and involved, who can divine whether Death had a grudge against your brother or sought his welfare ?

And, such is your justice in all things, this, too, must give you comfort—the thought that no wrong has

factam, quod talem fratrem amisisti, sed beneficium datum, quod tam diu tibi pietate eius uti fruique 2 licuit. Iniquus est, qui muneris sui arbitrium danti non relinquit, avidus, qui non lucri loco habet, quod accepit, sed damni, quod reddidit. Ingratus est, qui iniuriam vocat finem voluptatis, stultus, qui nullum fructum esse putat bonorum nisi praesentium, qui non et in praeteritis adquiescit et ea iudicat certiora, quae abierunt, quia de illis ne desinant non est 3 timendum. Nimis angustat gaudia sua, qui eis tantummodo, quae habet ac videt, frui se putat et habuisse eadem pro nihilo ducit; cito enim nos omnis voluptas relinquit, quae fluit et transit et paene ante quam veniat aufertur. Itaque in praeteritum tempus animus mittendus est et quicquid nos umquam delectavit reducendum ac frequenti cogitatione pertractandum est; longior fideliorque 4 est memoria voluptatum quam praesentia. Quod habuisti ergo optimum fratrem, in summis bonis pone! Non est quod cogites, quanto diutius habere potueris, sed quam diu habueris. Rerum natura illum tibi sicut ceteris fratres suos non mancipio dedit, sed commodavit; cum visum est deinde repetît nec tuam in 5 eo satietatem secuta est sed suam legem. Si quis pecuniam creditam solvisse se moleste ferat, eam

---

ᵃ Cf. Lucretius, iii. 971:

    Vitaque mancipio nulli datur omnibus usu.

been done you because you lost such a brother, but that a favour was shown you, because you were permitted to have and enjoy his affection so long. He who does not leave to the giver the power over his own gift is unfair, he who does not count whatever he receives as gain and yet counts whatever he gives back as loss, is greedy. He who calls the ending of pleasure an injustice is an ingrate ; he who thinks that there is no enjoyment from blessings unless they are present, who does not find comfort also in past blessings, and does not regard those that are gone as more certain because he need have no fear that they will cease—this man is a fool. He limits his pleasures too narrowly who thinks that he enjoys only those which he now has and sees, and counts his having had these same pleasures as nothing ; for every pleasure quickly leaves us—it flows on and passes by and is gone almost before it comes. And so our thoughts must be turned towards time that has passed, and whatever has once brought us pleasure must be recalled, and we must ruminate over it by frequent thought ; the remembrance of pleasures is more lasting and trustworthy than their reality. Count this, then, among your greatest blessings—the fact that you have had an excellent brother ! There is no reason for you to think of how much longer you might have had him—think, rather, of how long you did have him. Nature gave him to you, just as she gives to others their brothers, not as a permanent possession, but as a loan*a*; when it seemed best to her, then she took him back, nor was she guided by your having had your fill of him, but only by her own law. If anyone should be angry that he has had to pay back borrowed money—especially that of which

praesertim, cuius usum gratuitum acceperit, nonne
iniustus vir habeatur ? Dedit natura fratri tuo vitam,
dedit et tibi. Quae suo iure usa si a quo voluit
debitum suum citius exegit ; non illa in culpa est,
cuius nota erat condicio, sed mortalis animi spes
avida, quae subinde, quid rerum natura sit, oblivisci-
tur nec umquam sortis suae meminit, nisi cum
6 admonetur. Gaude itaque habuisse te tam bonum
fratrem et usum fructumque eius, quamvis brevior
voto tuo fuerit, boni consule. Cogita iucundissimum
esse, quod habuisti, humanum, quod perdidisti. Nec
enim quicquam minus inter se consentaneum est
quam aliquem moveri, quod sibi talis frater parum
diu contigerit, non gaudere, quod tamen contigerit.

1 11. "At inopinanti ereptus est." Sua quemque
credulitas decipit et in eis, quae diligit, voluntaria
mortalitatis oblivio. Natura nulli se necessitatis
suae gratiam facturam esse testata est. Cotidie
praeter oculos nostros transeunt notorum ignotorum-
que funera, nos tamen aliud agimus et subitum id
putamus esse, quod nobis tota vita denuntiatur
futurum. Non est itaque ista fatorum iniquitas, sed
mentis humanae pravitas insatiabilis rerum omnium,
quae indignatur inde excidere, quo admissa est
2 precario. Quanto ille iustior, qui nuntiata filii
morte dignam magno viro vocem emisit : " Ego
cum genui, tum moriturum scivi." Prorsus non

he had the use without paying interest—would he not be considered an unfair man ? Nature gave your brother his life, she has likewise given you yours. If she has required from him from whom she wanted it an earlier payment of her loan, she has but used her own right ; the fault is not with her, for her terms were known, but with the greedy hopes of mortal minds that often forget what Nature is, and never remember their own lot except when they are reminded. Rejoice, therefore, that you have had such a good brother, and have had the use and enjoyment of him ; though this was briefer than you wished, count it so much good. Reflect that to have had him is most delightful ; to have lost him, the human lot. For nothing is less consistent than for a man to grieve because he did not have long enough the blessing of such a brother, and not to rejoice because, after all, such a blessing had once been his.

"But," you say, "he was snatched from me unexpectedly." Every man is deceived by his own credulity, and in the case of those whom he loves he wilfully forgets mortality. Yet Nature has made it clear that she will exempt no man from her stern law. Every day the funerals of acquaintances and strangers pass by before our eyes, we, nevertheless, pay no heed, and we count that event as sudden of whose coming the whole of life has given us warning. This, therefore, is not the injustice of Fate, but the perversity of the human mind that, with its insatiable greed for all things, chafes at leaving a place to which it was admitted on sufferance. How much more righteous was he who, on the announcement of the death of his son, uttered the words, worthy of a great man: " When I begat him, I knew then that he would

387

mireris ex hoc natum esse, qui fortiter mori posset.
Non accepit tamquam novum nuntium filii mortem ;
quid enim est novi hominem mori, cuius tota vita
nihil aliud quam ad mortem iter est ? " Ego cum
3 genui, tum moriturum scivi." Deinde adiecit rem
maioris et prudentiae et animi : " Et huic rei sustuli."
Omnes huic rei tollimur ; quisquis ad vitam editur,
ad mortem destinatur. Gaudeamus ergo[1] eo, quod
dabitur, reddamusque id, cum reposcemur. Alium
alio tempore fata comprehendent, neminem praeter-
ibunt. In procinctu stet animus et id quod necesse
est numquam timeat, quod incertum est semper
expectet.

4 Quid dicam duces ducumque progeniem et multis
aut consulatibus conspicuos aut triumphis sorte
defunctos inexorabili ? Tota cum regibus regna
populique cum regentibus[2] tulere fatum suum ; omnes,
immo omnia in ultimum.diem spectant. Non idem
universis finis est ; alium in medio cursu vita deserit,
alium in ipso aditu relinquit, alium in extrema
senectute fatigatum iam et exire cupientem vix
emittit ; alio quidem atque alio tempore, omnes
tamen in eundem locum tendimus. Utrumne stultius sit nescio mortalitatis legem ignorare, an impu-
dentius recusare.

5 Agedum illa, quae multo ingenii tui labore cele-
brata sunt, in manus sume utriuslibet auctoris carmina, quae tu ita resolvisti, ut quamvis structura

---

[1] ergo *added by Erasmus.*
[2] regentibus *Haase*: gentibus O.

---

* This and the later quotation are drawn from the *Telamo*,
a tragedy of Ennius (Vahlen, p. 177). The reference is to
the dead Ajax, Telamon's son.

die."[a] We need not be at all surprised that the son
of such a man was one who was able to die bravely.
He did not receive the news of the death of his son as
a strange thing; for why is it surprising that man
should die when his whole life is nothing but a journey
towards death? " When I begat him, I knew then
that he would die," he said. And then he added some
words that show even greater wisdom and courage:
" And it was for this that I reared him." It is for this
that we all are reared; every man who is brought into
life is appointed to die. Let us rejoice, therefore, in
whatever shall be given us, and let us return it when
we are asked for it. The Fates will seize one at one
time, another at another; they will pass no man by.
Let the mind, then, stand in readiness, and let it never
fear whatever must be, let it always expect whatever
may be.

Why need I tell you of generals and the offspring of
generals, of men famous for their many consulships
or many triumphs, who have finished their appointed
lot? Whole kingdoms with their kings and peoples
with their rulers have met their fate; all men, nay,
all things, look toward their last day. They do not
all have the same end; life forsakes one in the middle
of his career, it leaves another at the very entrance,
and another it reluctantly releases in extreme old age
when he is now worn out and eager to depart; one
goes at one time, another at another, yet we are
all travelling toward the same place. I know not
whether it is more foolish to be ignorant of the law of
mortality, or more presumptuous to refuse to obey it.

Turn, now, to those poems which the efforts of your
genius have made famous and which you have turned
into prose with such skill that, though their form has

illorum recesserit, permaneat tamen gratia—sic
enim illa ex alia lingua in aliam transtulisti, ut,
quod difficillimum erat, omnes virtutes in alienam
te orationem secutae sint : — nullus erit in illis
scriptis liber, qui non plurima varietatis humanae
incertorumque casuum et lacrimarum ex alia atque
6 alia causa fluentium exempla tibi suggerat. Lege,
quanto spiritu ingentibus intonueris verbis ; pudebit
te subito deficere et ex tanta orationis magnitudine
desciscere. Ne commiseris, ut quisquis exemplaris
modo[1] scripta tua mirabatur quaerat quomodo tam
grandia tamque solida tam fragilis animus conceperit.
1   12. Potius ab istis te, quae torquent, ad haec
tot et tanta, quae consolantur, converte ac respice
optimos fratres, respice uxorem, filium respice ; pro
omnium horum salute hac tecum portione fortuna
decidit. Multos habes, in quibus adquiescas. Ab
hac te infamia vindica, ne videatur omnibus plus apud
te valere unus dolor quam haec tam multa solacia.
2 Omnis istos una tecum perculsos vides nec posse tibi
subvenire, immo etiam ultro expectare, ut a te sub-
leventur, intellegis ; et ideo quanto minus in illis doc-
trinae minusque ingenii est, tanto magis obsistere te
necesse est communi malo. Est autem hoc ipsum
solacii loco, inter multos dolorem suum dividere ;
qui quia dispensatur inter plures, exigua debet apud
te parte subsidere.

---

[1] exemplaris modo *Hermes after Schultess* : exemplo ac
modo *BGV* : exempto modo *Duff after Madvig*.

disappeared, they, nevertheless, retain all their charm (for you have so performed the most difficult task of transferring them from one language to another that all their merits have followed them into the foreign speech) —take into your hands whichever of the two authors you please, and you will find that there is not a single book of their writings which does not supply numberless examples of the vicissitudes of human life, of unexpected misfortunes, and of tears that for one reason or another have been made to flow. Read with what great vigour you have thundered in mighty words; suddenly to break down and fall short of such grandeur of utterance will make you blush. Let it not happen that every one who admired your writings as a model should wonder how a spirit so easily broken produced such mighty and substantial works.

Do you turn, rather, from the thoughts that torture you to the many and great sources of consolation you have, and look upon your admirable brothers, look upon your wife, look upon your son ; it is for all their lives that Fortune has settled with you for this partial payment. You have many on whose affection to rest. Save yourself from the shame of having everybody think that your grief for one counts for more than these many sources of comfort. You see that they all have been smitten along with you, and you know that they are not able to come to your rescue—nay, even that they on their part are expecting to be rescued by you; and, therefore, the less their learning, the less their ability than yours, the more necessary it is for you to withstand the common misfortune. Moreover, to share one's grief with many is in itself a kind of consolation ; because, if it is distributed among many, the part that is left behind with you must be small.

3 Non desinam totiens tibi offerre Caesarem. Illo
moderante terras et ostendente quanto melius bene-
ficiis imperium custodiatur quam armis, illo rebus
humanis praesidente[1] non est periculum, ne quid
perdidisse te sentias ; in hoc uno tibi satis praesidi,
solaci est. Attolle te et, quotiens lacrimae sub-
oriuntur oculis tuis, totiens illos in Caesarem derige ;
siccabuntur maximi et clarissimi conspectu numinis ;
fulgor eius illos, ut nihil aliud possint aspicere, prae-
4 stringet et in se haerentes detinebit. Hic tibi, quem
tu diebus intueris ac noctibus, a quo numquam deicis
animum, cogitandus est, hic contra fortunam ad-
vocandus. Nec dubito, cum tanta illi adversus omnes
suos sit mansuetudo tantaque indulgentia, quin iam
multis solaciis tuum istud vulnus obduxerit, iam
multa, quae dolori obstarent tuo, congesserit. Quid
porro ? Ut nihil horum fecerit, nonne protinus
ipse conspectus per se tantummodo cogitatusque
5 Caesar maximo solacio tibi est ? Dii illum deaeque
terris diu commodent ! Acta hic divi Augusti
aequet, annos vincat ! Quam diu inter mortales
erit, nihil ex domo sua mortale esse sentiat ! Rectorem Romano imperio filium longa fide approbet
et ante illum[2] consortem patris quam successorem
aspiciat ! Sera et nepotibus demum nostris dies
nota sit, qua illum gens sua caelo asserat !
1 13. Abstine ab hoc manus tuas, fortuna, nec in
isto potentiam tuam nisi ea parte, qua prodes,

---

[1] praesidente *Erasmus* : praeside *C.*
[2] illum *O* : illud *Hermes after Schultess.*

---

[a] The reference is to Britannicus, son of Messalina.
Claudius's actual successor was Nero, his stepson.

I shall not cease to confront you over and over again with Caesar. While he governs the earth, while he shows how much better it is to safeguard the empire by benefits than by arms, while he presides over human affairs, there is no danger of your feeling that you have suffered any loss; in this one source you have ample protection, ample consolation. Lift yourself up, and every time that tears well up in your eyes, fix these upon Caesar; at the sight of the exceeding greatness and splendour of his divinity they will be dried; his brilliance will dazzle them so that they will be able to see nothing else, and will keep them fastened upon himself. He, whom you behold day and night, from whom you never lower your thoughts, must fill your mind, he must be summoned to your help against Fortune. And, so great is his kindness, so great is his gracious favour toward all followers, I do not doubt that he has already covered over this wound of yours with many balms, that he has already supplied many things to stay your sorrow. Besides, even though he has done none of these things, are not the very sight and merely the thought of Caesar, in themselves, forthwith to you the very greatest comfort ? May gods and goddesses lend him long to earth ! May he rival the achievements, may he surpass the years, of the deified Augustus ! So long as he shall linger among mortals, may he not learn that aught of his house is mortal ! By long proof may he commend his son [a] as ruler to the Roman Empire and see him his father's consort ere that he is his successor ! Late be the day and known only to our grandchildren on which his kindred claim him for the skies !

From him, O Fortune, refrain thy hands, and in his case display not thy power save in that part where thou

ostenderis! Patere illum generi humano iam diu
aegro et affecto mederi, patere quicquid prioris
principis furor concussit in suum locum restituere ac
reponere! Sidus hoc, quod praecipitato in profundum et demerso in tenebras orbi refulsit, semper
2 luceat! Hic Germaniam pacet, Britanniam aperiat,
et patrios triumphos ducat et novos; quorum me
quoque spectatorem futurum, quae ex virtutibus
eius primum optinet locum, promittit clementia.
Nec enim sic me deiecit, ut nollet erigere, immo ne
deiecit quidem, sed impulsum a fortuna et cadentem
sustinuit et in praeceps euntem leniter divinae manus
usus moderatione deposuit; deprecatus est pro me
senatum et vitam mihi non tantum dedit sed etiam
3 petît. Viderit: qualem volet esse, existimet cau-
sam meam. Vel iustitia eius bonam perspiciat vel
clementia faciat bonam; utrumque in aequo mihi
eius beneficium erit, sive innocentem me scierit esse,
sive voluerit. Interim magnum miseriarum mearum
solacium est videre misericordiam eius totum orbem
pervagantem; quae cum ex ipso angulo, in quo ego
defixus sum, complures multorum iam annorum ruina
obrutos effoderit et in lucem reduxerit, non vereor
ne me unum transeat. Ipse autem optime novit
tempus, quo cuique debeat succurrere; ego omnem
4 operam dabo, ne pervenire ad me erubescat. O

---

^a The mad Caligula.

^b The chief glory of Claudius's reign was the conquest of
Britain (A.D. 43).

^c These details of Seneca's mishap are not known from
any other source. The cause of his banishment was a
reputed intrigue with Julia, the notorious sister of Caligula
(Cassius Dio, lx. 8. 5).

dost benefit. Suffer him to heal the human race, that has long been sick and in evil case, suffer him to restore and return all things to their place out of the havoc the madness of the preceding prince *a* has wrought! May this sun, which has shed its light upon a world that had plunged into the abyss and was sunk in darkness, ever shine! May he bring peace to Germany, open up Britain,*b* and celebrate again both his father's triumphs and new ones! And his mercy, which in the list of his virtues holds the chief place, raises the hope that of these I also shall not fail to be a spectator. For he has not cast me down with no thought of ever lifting me up—nay, he has not even cast me down, but when I had been smitten by Fortune and was falling, he checked my fall, and, using the mitigating power of his divine hand, he let me down gently when I was plunging to destruction; he besought the senate in my behalf, and not only gave me my life, but even begged it.*c* Be his the care—howsoever he shall wish, such let him account my case. Let either his justice discern that it is good, or his mercy make it good; whether he shall discern that I am innocent, or shall wish me to be so—either, in my eyes, will equally show his kindness. Meanwhile, the great consolation of my own wretchedness is to see his compassion spreading over the whole world; and since even in this remote corner, in which I am planted, his mercy has unearthed many who were buried under a downfall that came long years ago, and has restored them to light, I do not fear that I shall be the only one it will pass by. But he himself knows best the time at which he ought to come to each man's rescue; I, for my part, shall strive that he should not blush to come to mine. O how blessed is your mercy,

felicem clementiam tuam, Caesar, quae efficit, ut
quietiorem sub te agant vitam exules, quam nuper
sub Gaio egere principes ! Non trepidant nec per
singulas horas gladium expectant nec ad omnem
navium conspectum pavent ; per te habent ut fortunae saevientis modum ita spem quoque melioris
eiusdem ac praesentis quietem. Scias licet ea demum
fulmina esse iustissima, quae etiam percussi colunt.

1   14. Hic itaque princeps, qui publicum omnium
hominum solacium est, aut me omnia fallunt aut iam
recreavit animum tuum et tam magno vulneri maiora
adhibuit remedia. Iam te omni confirmavit modo,
iam omnia exempla, quibus ad animi aequitatem
compellereris, tenacissima memoria rettulit, iam
omnium praecepta sapientum assueta sibi facundia
2 explicuit. Nullus itaque melius has adloquendi partes
occupaverit. Aliud habebunt hoc dicente pondus
verba velut ab oraculo missa ; omnem vim doloris tui
divina eius contundet auctoritas. Hunc itaque tibi
puta dicere : " Non te solum fortuna desumpsit sibi,
quem tam gravi afficeret iniuria ; nulla domus in toto
orbe terrarum aut est aut fuit sine aliqua complora-
tione. Transibo exempla vulgaria, quae etiam si
minora, tamen innumera sunt, ad fastus te et annales
3 perducam publicos. Vides omnes has imagines, quae
implevere Caesarum atrium ? Nulla non harum aliquo
suorum incommodo insignis est ; nemo non ex istis

ª The records of high officials of successive years such as
the *Fasti Consulares.*

Caesar, which makes exiles live more peacefully under your rule than did princes recently under the rule of Gaius ! They are not uneasy, nor do they expect the sword hour by hour, nor cower at the sight of every ship ; through you they possess not only a limit to the cruelty of Fortune, but also the hope of her being more kindly and peace even as she is. One may know that those thunderbolts are indeed most just which even those they have smitten worship.

And so this prince, who is the universal consolation of all mankind, has already, if I am not altogether mistaken, revived your spirit and applied the more potent remedies to a wound so serious. He has already strengthened you in every way ; by reason of his most retentive memory he has already presented to you all the examples which could bring your mind to a state of equanimity ; with his habitual eloquence he has already set before you the precepts of all the sages. There is no one, therefore, who could better have appropriated these rôles of the comforter. Words, when he speaks, have, as if the utterances of an oracle, a different weight ; his divine authority will dull all the sharpness of your grief. Think, then, that he speaks to you in these words : " You are not the only one whom Fortune has picked out to afflict with an injury so grievous ; there is no family in all the earth, nor has there ever been one, that has no one to mourn for. I will pass over examples from the masses, which, while they have less weight, are nevertheless countless—I will direct you to the Calendar ^a and the State Chronicles. See you all these portrait busts that fill the hall of the Caesars ? Every one of these men is marked by some ill that befell their dear ones ; every one, too, of those men

in ornamentum saeculorum refulgentibus viris aut
desiderio suorum tortus est aut a suis cum maximo
animi cruciatu desideratus est.

4   " Quid tibi referam Scipionem Africanum, cui mors
fratris in exilio nuntiata est ? Is frater, qui eripuit
fratrem carceri, non potuit eripere fato. Et quam
impatiens iuris aequi pietas Africani fuerit, cunctis
apparuit ; eodem enim die Scipio Africanus, quo
viatoris manibus fratrem abstulerat, tribuno quoque
plebis privatus intercessit. Tam magno tamen fra-
5 trem desideravit hic animo, quam defenderat. Quid
referam Aemilianum Scipionem, qui uno paene
eodemque tempore spectavit patris triumphum duo-
rumque fratrum funera ? Adulescentulus tamen ac
propemodum puer tanto animo tulit illam familiae
suae super ipsum Pauli triumphum concidentis
subitam vastitatem, quanto debuit ferre vir in hoc
natus, ne urbi Romanae aut Scipio deesset aut
Carthago superesset.

1   15. " Quid referam duorum Lucullorum diremptam
morte concordiam ? Quid Pompeios ? quibus ne
hoc quidem saeviens reliquit fortuna, ut una eademque conciderent ruina. Vixit Sextus Pompeius primum sorori superstes, cuius morte optime cohaerentis
Romanae pacis vincula resoluta sunt, idemque hic

ᵃ L. Cornelius Scipio Asiaticus, who after his victory over
Antiochus of Syria in 190 B.C. was accused of having received
bribes from the king and of the misappropriation of money
paid to the state.
    ᵇ *i.e.*, the republican form of government.
    ᶜ A Scipio by adoption, but by birth a son of Aemilius
Paulus, who triumphed over Perseus of Macedonia in
167 B.C. Of his two younger sons, one died a few days
before the triumph, the other a few days after it. This

whose glory lights up the ages was either tortured with yearning for dear ones, or was yearned for by dear ones with bitterest torture of mind.

" Why need I remind you of Scipio Africanus, who learned of the death of his brother while he himself was in exile ? The brother who snatched his brother[a] from prison was not able to snatch him from Fate. And Africanus's brotherly love made it clear to all how impatient he was of equal rights[b] ; for on the same day on which he had rescued his brother from the hands of a court-summoner, he also, though he held no office, interfered with the acts of a tribune of the people. Yet he showed as much greatness of spirit in his grief for his brother as he had shown in his defence. Why need I remind you of Scipio Aemilianus,[c] who viewed the triumph of his father and the funerals of his two brothers at almost the same time ? Nevertheless, a mere youth and hardly more than a boy, he bore that sudden desolation, which befell his own family close upon the triumph of Paulus, with all the courage that became a *man*, born to the end that a Scipio might not fail, or Carthage outlive, the city of Rome.

" Why need I remind you of the two Luculli, whose concord was broken only by death ? Or of the Pompeys, to whom cruel Fortune did not even grant that they should perish together in the same disaster ? Sextus Pompeius, in the first place, survived his sister,[d] by whose death the closely knit bonds of peace between the Romans were broken, and he

Scipio, better known as Africanus the younger, destroyed Carthage in 146 B.C.
[d] From what follows Seneca seems to have confused Pompeia, sister of Sextus, with Julia, daughter of Caesar and wife of the elder Pompey.

vixit superstes optimo fratri, quem fortuna in hoc
evexerat, ne minus alte eum deiceret, quam patrem
deiecerat; et post hunc tamen casum Sextus Pompeius non tantum dolori, sed etiam bello suffecit.
2 Innumerabilia undique exempla separatorum morte
fratrum succurrunt, immo contra vix ulla umquam
horum paria conspecta sunt una senescentia. Sed
contentus nostrae domus exemplis ero; nemo enim
tam expers erit sensus ac sanitatis, ut fortunam ulli
queratur luctum intulisse, quam sciet etiam Caesarum
lacrimas concupisse.
3 " Divus Augustus amisit Octaviam sororem caris-
simam et ne ei quidem rerum natura lugendi neces-
sitatem abstulit, cui caelum destinaverat, immo vero
idem omni genere orbitatis vexatus sororis filium
successioni praeparatum suae perdidit; denique ne
singulos eius luctus enumerem, et generos ille amisit
et liberos et nepotes, ac nemo magis ex omnibus
mortalibus hominem esse se, dum inter homines erat,
sensit. Tamen tot tantosque luctus cepit rerum
omnium capacissimum eius pectus victorque divus
Augustus non gentium tantummodo externarum, sed
etiam dolorum fuit.
4 " Gaius Caesar, divi Augusti, avunculi mei magni
nepos, circa primos iuventae suae annos Lucium
fratrem carissimum sibi princeps iuventutis principem
eiusdem iuventutis amisit in apparatu Parthici belli

ᵃ First Marcellus and then M. Agrippa, husbands of Julia.
ᵇ An honorary title conferred upon these youths by the
knights; *cf. Monumentum Ancyranum,* 14: "equites autem
Romani universi principem iuventutis utrumque eorum
parmis et hastis argenteis donatum appellaverunt."

likewise survived his excellent brother, whom
Fortune had raised aloft for the very purpose of hurl-
ing him down from a pinnacle not less high than
that from which she had hurled his father; and yet,
even after this misfortune, Sextus Pompeius sustained
the burden, not only of grief, but also of war. The
examples that are supplied from every side of
brothers who were separated by death are innumer-
able—nay, almost never have pairs of brothers been
seen who were growing old together. But I shall be
content with examples from my own family; for no
one will be so devoid of feeling and good sense as to
complain that Fortune has brought grief upon any
man when he knows that she has coveted the tears
of even the Caesars.

" The deified Augustus lost his darling sister
Octavia, and not even was he, whom Nature had
destined for heaven, made exempt from the necessity
of mourning—nay, he was harassed by every sort of
bereavement, and, when he had planned to make his
sister's son his own successor, he lost him. In fine,
not to mention his sorrows one by one, he lost his
sons-in-law [a] and his children and his grandchildren,
and, while he lingered among men, no one of all
mortals had clearer evidence that he was a man.
Nevertheless, his heart that was able to bear all
things bore bravely these many deep afflictions, and
the deified Augustus rose victor, not only over foreign
nations, but also over sorrows.

" Gaius Caesar, grandson of the deified Augustus,
my great-uncle, when he was in the early years of
manhood, lost his beloved brother Lucius; Prince of
the Roman Youth,[b] he lost a 'Prince' of that same
youth in the very midst of his preparation for the

et graviore multo animi vulnere quam postea corporis
ictus est ; quod utrumque et piissime idem et fortis-
sime tulit.

5   " Ti.[1] Caesar patruus meus Drusum Germanicum
patrem meum, minorem natu quam ipse erat fratrem,
intima Germaniae recludentem et gentes ferocissimas
Romano subicientem imperio in complexu et in
osculis suis amisit. Modum tamen lugendi non sibi
tantum sed etiam aliis fecit ac totum exercitum non
solum maestum sed etiam attonitum corpus Drusi sui
sibi vindicantem ad morem Romani luctus redegit
iudicavitque non militandi tantum disciplinam esse
servandam sed etiam dolendi. Non potuisset ille
lacrimas alienas compescere, nisi prius pressisset suas.

1   16. " M. Antonius avus meus, nullo minor nisi eo
a quo victus est, tunc cum rem publicam consti-
tueret et triumvirali potestate praeditus nihil supra
se videret, exceptis vero duobus collegis omnia infra
2 se cerneret, fratrem interfectum audivit. Fortuna
impotens, quales ex humanis malis tibi ipsa ludos
facis ! Eo ipso tempore, quo M. Antonius civium
suorum vitae sedebat mortisque arbiter, M. Antonii
frater duci iubebatur ad supplicium ! Tulit hoc tamen
tam triste vulnus eadem magnitudine animi M.
Antonius, qua omnia alia adversa toleraverat, et hoc
fuit eius lugere viginti legionum sanguine fratri
parentare.

[1] Ti. *added by Lipsius.*

---

[a] The coalition formed by Octavius, Antony, and Lepidus
in 43 B.C.
[b] *i.e.,* the republican army under Brutus and Cassius at
Philippi (42 B.C.).

Parthian War, and he suffered much more deeply from this wound of the mind than he did later from the wound of his body; yet he bore both most righteously and bravely.

"Tiberius Caesar, my uncle, lost his younger brother Drusus Germanicus, my father, just when he was opening up the remote parts of Germany, and was bringing the fiercest tribes under the power of Rome, and, holding him in his arms, he gave him a last kiss. Yet, not only for himself but for others, he set a limit upon mourning, and when the whole army was not only disconsolate but even distraught, and claimed the body of the loved Drusus for itself, he forced it to return to the Roman fashion of mourning, and ruled that discipline must be maintained, not only in fighting, but also in grieving. But he would not have been able to check the tears of others if he had not first repressed his own.

"Mark Antony, my grandfather, second to none save his conqueror, received the news of his brother's execution just at the time when he was setting the state in order, and when, as a member of the triumvirate,[a] he beheld no man above him—nay, with the exception of his two colleagues, saw all men beneath him. O unbridled Fortune, what sport dost thou make for thyself out of human ills! At the very time at which Mark Antony sat enthroned with the power of life and death over his own countrymen, the brother of Mark Antony was being ordered to execution! Yet such a bitter wound was borne by Mark Antony with the same loftiness of spirit with which he had endured all his other adversities, and this was his mourning— to give sacrifice to the shade of his brother with the blood of twenty legions [b]!

3 " Sed ut omnia alia exempla praeteream, ut in me
quoque ipso alia taceam funera, bis me fraterno luctu
aggressa fortuna est, bis intellexit laedi me posse,
vinci non posse. Amisi[1] Germanicum fratrem, quem
quomodo amaverim, intellegit profecto quisquis cogitat, quomodo suos fratres pii fratres ament ; sic
tamen affectum meum rexi, ut nec relinquerem
quicquam, quod exigi deberet a bono fratre, nec
facerem, quod reprehendi posset in principe."

4 Haec ergo puta tibi parentem publicum referre
exempla, eundem ostendere, quam nihil sacrum in-
tactumque sit fortunae, quae ex eis penatibus ausa est
funera ducere, ex quibus erat deos petitura. Nemo
itaque miretur aliquid ab illa aut crudeliter fieri aut
inique ; potest enim haec adversus privatas domos
ullam aequitatem nosse aut ullam modestiam, cuius
implacabilis saevitia totiens ipsa funestavit pulvi-
5 naria ? Faciamus licet illi convicium non nostro
tantum ore sed etiam publico, non tamen mutabitur ;
adversus omnis se preces omnisque querimonias
exiget. Hoc fuit in rebus humanis fortuna, hoc erit.
Nihil inausum sibi reliquit, nihil intactum relinquet ;
ibit violentior per omnia, sicut solita est semper, eas
quoque domos ausa iniuriae causa intrare, in quas
per templa aditur, et atram laureatis foribus induet
6 vestem. Hoc unum obtineamus ab illa votis ac
precibus publicis, si nondum illi genus humanum

---

[1] *Duff adds* amisi sororem *before* amisi.

---

[a] Probably an allusion to the fact that the imperial palace
on the Palatine was flanked by temples.

" But to pass over all other examples, to be silent concerning the other deaths, even in my own case also twice has Fortune assailed me through my grief as a brother, twice has she learned that I might be injured, but that I could not be conquered. I lost my brother Germanicus, and how much I loved him all those assuredly understand who consider how brothers, who have true affection, love their brothers ; yet I so ruled my feelings that I neither left any-thing undone that ought to have been required of a loving brother, nor did anything that a prince could have been censured for doing."

Consider, therefore, that these are the examples the Father of the State cites for you, and that he also shows how nothing is sacred and inviolable to For-tune, who has dared to lead funerals from those house-holds whence she was to seek gods. And so let no man be surprised at any cruel or unjust act of hers ; for is it possible that she, whose insatiate cruelty has so often desolated the very seats of the gods, should know any justice or self-restraint in her dealings with private families ? Though we heap reproach upon her, voicing not merely our own protest, but that of all men, she will not be changed ; she will work her will despite all entreaties, despite all complaints. Such has Fortune ever been in human affairs, such will she ever be. Nothing has she ever left undared, nothing will she ever leave untried ; in violent rage will she range through all places just as has always been her wont, she who, on injury bent, has dared to enter even those houses whose entrance lies through the temples of the gods,[a] and she will drape the laurelled doors with the garb of mourning. If she has not yet resolved to destroy utterly the human race,

placuit consumere, si Romanum adhuc nomen propitia
respicit : hunc principem lapsis hominum rebus
datum, sicut omnibus mortalibus, sibi esse sacratum
velit ! Discat ab illo clementiam fiatque mitissimo
omnium principum mitis !

1   17. Debes itaque eos intueri omnes, quos paulo
ante rettuli, aut adscitos caelo aut proximos, et ferre
aequo animo fortunam ad te quoque porrigentem
manus, quas ne ab eis quidem, per quos iuramus,
abstinet ; debes illorum imitari firmitatem in per-
ferendis et evincendis doloribus, in quantum modo
2 homini fas est per divina ire vestigia. Quamvis sint[1]
in aliis rebus dignitatum ac nobilitatum magna dis-
crimina, virtus in medio posita est ; neminem dedignatur, qui modo dignum se illa iudicat. Optime certe
illos imitaberis, qui cum indignari possent non esse
ipsos exsortes huius mali, tamen in hoc uno se ceteris
exaequari hominibus non iniuriam sed ius mortalitatis
iudicaverunt tuleruntque nec nimis acerbe et aspere,
quod acciderat, nec molliter et effeminate ; nam et
non sentire mala sua non est hominis et non ferre
non est viri.

3   Non possum tamen, cum omnes circumierim Caesares, quibus fortuna fratres sororesque eripuit, hunc
praeterire ex omni Caesarum numero excerpendum,
quem rerum natura in exitium opprobriumque humani

---

[1] sint *added by Gertz.*

if she still looks with favour upon the name of Roman, may we by public vows and prayers obtain from her this one concession—that this prince, who has been granted to the fallen estate of mankind, should be held as sacred by her as he is by all mortal men ! Let her learn mercy from him, and to the kindest of all princes let her become kind !

And so you ought to turn your eyes upon all these —those whom I have just mentioned as either enrolled in the skies or soon so to be—and submit calmly to Fortune, who now lays also upon you the hands that she does not withhold even from those by whose names we swear ; you must imitate the firmness of these in enduring and conquering sorrows, so far as it is permissible for a man to follow in the footsteps of the gods. Although in other matters there are great distinctions of rank and birth, virtue is accessible to all ; she deems no man unworthy if only he deems himself worthy of her. Surely you cannot do better than imitate those who, though they might have been indignant that even they were not exempt from this evil, yet decided that it was not injustice, but the law of mortality, that in this one respect put them on a level with the rest of mankind, and endured what had befallen them neither with too much bitterness and wrath, nor in a weak and womanly fashion ; for it is not human not to feel misfortunes, and it is not manly not to bear them.

And yet, since I have run through the roll of all the Caesars from whom Fortune snatched brothers and sisters, I cannot pass by the one whose name ought to be torn from every list of the Caesars, whom Nature produced to be the ruin and the shame of the human race, who utterly wasted and wrecked the

generis edidit, a quo imperium adustum atque eversum funditus principis mitissimi recreat clementia.

4 C. Caesar amissa sorore Drusilla, is homo, qui non magis dolere quam gaudere principaliter posset, conspectum conversationemque civium suorum profugit, exsequis sororis suae non interfuit, iusta sorori non praestitit, sed in Albano suo tesseris ac foro et pervolgatis[1] huiusmodi aliis occupationibus acerbissimi funeris elevabat mala. Pro pudor imperii! Principis Romani lugentis sororem alea solacium fuit!

5 Idem ille Gaius furiosa inconstantia modo barbam capillumque summittens modo tondens[2] Italiae ac Siciliae oras errabundus permetiens et numquam satis certus, utrum lugeri vellet an coli sororem, eodem omni tempore, quo templa illi constituebat ac pulvinaria, eos qui parum maesti fuerant, crudelissima adficiebat animadversione; eadem enim intemperie animi adversarum rerum ictus ferebat, qua secundarum elatus eventu super humanum in-

6 tumescebat modum. Procul istud exemplum ab omni Romano sit viro, luctum suum aut intempestivis sevocare lusibus aut sordium ac squaloris foeditate irritare aut alienis malis oblectare minime humano solacio.

1 18. Tibi vero nihil ex consuetudine mutandum est tua, quoniam quidem ea instituisti amare studia, quae et optime felicitatem extollunt et facillime minuunt calamitatem eademque et ornamenta

---

[1] et pervolgatis *Haase* : & puocatis et *ADHB* : et pyrgo talisque *Gertz*.   [2] tondens *added by Wesenberg.*

---

[a] Literally, "cushion couches," on which the images of the gods were displayed.

[b] *i.e.*, they had accepted the idea of her deification, and had not mourned for her as a mortal.

empire that is now being restored by the mercy of the kindliest of princes. Having lost his sister Drusilla, Gaius Caesar, a man who could no more indulge his grief than his pleasure in princely fashion, fled the sight and society of his fellow-men, did not attend the funeral of his sister, did not pay to his sister the ordinary tributes, but in his villa at Alba he tried to relieve his distress at her deeply regretted death with dice and gaming-board and other common engrossments of this sort. What a disgrace to the empire! Gambling was the solace of a Roman prince mourning for his sister! And this same Gaius with mad caprice, sometimes allowing his beard and hair to grow, sometimes shearing them close, wandering aimlessly along the coast of Italy and Sicily, and never quite sure whether he wished his sister to be lamented or worshipped, during the whole time that he was rearing temples and shrines *a* to her memory would inflict the most cruel punishment upon those who had not shown sufficient sorrow *b*; for he was bearing the blows of adversity with the same lack of self-restraint from which, when puffed up by prosperity, he was swollen with pride beyond all human decency. Far be it from every manly Roman to follow such an example—either to divert his sorrow by untimely amusements, or to encourage it by disgraceful neglect and squalor, or to seek relief by that most inhuman of consolations, the causing of suffering to others.

You, however, need make no change in your habits, since, indeed, you have taught yourself to love those studies which most fittingly exalt prosperity and most easily lessen calamity, and are at the same time both the greatest adornments and the greatest comforts

maxima homini sunt et solacia. Nunc itaque te
studiis tuis immerge altius, nunc illa tibi velut munimenta animi circumda, ne ex ulla tui parte inveniat
2 introitum dolor. Fratris quoque tui produc memoriam
aliquo scriptorum monimento tuorum ; hoc enim
unum est in[1] rebus humanis opus, cui nulla tempestas
noceat, quod nulla consumat vetustas. Cetera, quae
per constructionem lapidum et marmoreas moles aut
terrenos tumulos in magnam eductos altitudinem
constant, non propagant longam diem, quippe et
ipsa intereunt ; immortalis est ingeni memoria.
Hanc tu fratri tuo largire, in hac eum conloca ; melius
illum duraturo semper consecrabis ingenio quam
irrito dolore lugebis.

3　Quod ad ipsam fortunam pertinet, etiam si nunc
agi apud te causa eius non potest—omnia enim illa,
quae nobis dedit, ob hoc ipsum, quod aliquid eripuit,
invisa sunt,—tunc tamen erit agenda, cum primum
aequiorem te illi iudicem dies fecerit ; tunc enim
poteris in gratiam cum illa redire. Nam multa
providit, quibus hanc emendaret iniuriam, multa
etiamnunc dabit, quibus redimat ; denique ipsum
4 hoc, quod abstulit, ipsa dederat tibi. Noli ergo
contra te ingenio uti tuo, noli adesse dolori tuo.
Potest quidem eloquentia tua quae parva sunt
approbare pro magnis, rursus magna attenuare et ad
minima deducere ; sed alio istas vires servet suas,

---

[1] in *added by Wesenberg.*

for man. Now, therefore, bury yourself more deeply in your studies, now encircle yourself with them as bulwarks for your mind in order that sorrow may find no point that will give entrance to you. And, too, prolong the remembrance of your brother by some memorial in your writings ; for among human achievements this is the only work that no storm can harm, nor length of time destroy. All others, those that are formed by piling up stones and masses of marble, or rearing on high huge mounds of earth, do not secure a long remembrance, for they themselves will also perish ; but the fame of genius is immortal. Do you lavish such upon your brother, in such embalm his name. It will be better for you to immortalize him by your genius that will live forever than mourn for him with a sorrow that is futile.

So far as concerns Fortune herself, even if it is impossible just now to plead her case before you—for everything that she has given us is hateful to you merely for the reason that she has snatched one thing from you—yet there will be need to plead her case as soon as lapse of time shall have made you a more impartial judge ; for then you will be able to restore her to favour. For she has provided many things to offset this injustice ; she will still give you many things to make atonement for it ; indeed this very thing that she has now withdrawn she had herself given. Refuse, therefore, to employ your talent against yourself, refuse to give support to your sorrow. For it is possible for your eloquence to make things that are really small seem important, and, on the other hand, to minimize important things and reduce them to merest trifles ; but let it keep the former kind of power for another occasion—just

nunc tota se in solacium tuum conferat. Et tamen
dispice, ne hoc iam quoque ipsum sit supervacuum ;
aliquid enim a nobis natura exigit, plus vanitate
5 contrahitur. Numquam autem ego a te, ne ex toto
maereas, exigam. Et scio inveniri quosdam durae
magis quam fortis prudentiae viros, qui negent doliturum esse sapientem. Hi non videntur mihi unquam
in eiusmodi casum incidisse, alioquin excussisset illis
fortuna superbam sapientiam et ad confessionem
6 eos veri etiam invitos compulisset. Satis praestiterit
ratio, si id unum ex dolore, quod et superest et abundat, exciderit ; ut quidem nullum omnino esse eum
patiatur, nec sperandum ulli nec concupiscendum est.
Hunc potius modum servet, qui nec impietatem imi-
tetur nec insaniam et nos in eo teneat habitu, qui et
piae mentis est nec motae. Fluant lacrimae, sed
eaedem et desinant, trahantur ex imo gemitus pectore,
sed idem et finiantur ; sic rege animum tuum, ut et
7 sapientibus te adprobare possis et fratribus. Effice,
ut frequenter fratris tui memoriam tibi velis occurrere,
ut illum et sermonibus celebres et adsidua recordatione repraesentes tibi, quod ita demum consequi
poteris, si tibi memoriam eius iucundam magis quam
flebilem feceris ; naturale est enim, ut semper
animus ab eo refugiat, ad quod cum tristitia rever-
8 titur. Cogita modestiam eius, cogita in rebus agendis
sollertiam, in exsequendis industriam, in promissis

---

* Such was the teaching of the stricter Stoics.

now let it direct all its effort toward giving you comfort. And yet consider whether even this be not by this time superfluous ; for Nature requires from us some sorrow, while more than this is the result of vanity. But never will I demand of you that you should not grieve at all. And I well know that some men are to be found whose wisdom is harsh rather than brave, who deny that the wise man will ever grieve.[a] But these, it seems to me, can never have fallen upon this sort of mishap ; if they had, Fortune would have knocked their proud philosophy out of them, and, even against their will, have forced them to admit the truth. Reason will have accomplished enough if only she removes from grief whatever is excessive and superfluous ; it is not for anyone to hope or to desire that she should suffer us to feel no sorrow at all. Rather let her maintain a mean which will copy neither indifference nor madness, and will keep us in the state that is the mark of an affectionate, and not an unbalanced, mind. Let your tears flow, but let them also cease, let deepest sighs be drawn from your breast, but let them also find an end ; so rule your mind that you may win approval both from wise men and from brothers. Make yourself willing to encounter oft the memory of your brother, both to speak of him frequently in your conversation, and to picture him to yourself by constant remembrance, all of which you will be able to accomplish only if you make the thought of him more pleasant than tearful ; for it is only natural that the mind should always shrink from a subject to which it reverts with sadness. Think of his modesty, think of his alertness in the activities of life, of his diligence in performing them, of his stead-

constantiam. Omnia dicta eius ac facta et aliis
expone et tibimet ipse commemora. Qualis fuerit
cogita qualisque sperari potuerit. Quid enim de illo
non tuto sponderi fratre posset ?

9 Haec, utcumque potui, longo iam situ obsoleto et
hebetato animo composui. Quae si aut parum
respondere ingenio tuo aut parum mederi dolori
videbuntur, cogita, quam non possit is alienae vacare
consolationi, quem sua mala occupatum tenent, et
quam non facile latina ei homini verba succurrant,
quem barbarorum inconditus et barbaris quoque
humanioribus gravis fremitus circumsonat.

fastness to promises. Set forth all his words and deeds to others, and do you yourself recall them to mind. Think what he was, and what he might have been expected to become. For what guarantee could not have been safely given concerning such a brother?

I have put these things together, as best I could, with a mind now weakened and dulled by long rusting. If they shall seem to you to be ill suited to your intelligence, or to ill supply the healing of your sorrow, reflect how he who is held fast in the grip of his own misfortunes is not at leisure to comfort others, and how Latin words do not suggest themselves readily to one in whose ears the uncouth jargon of barbarians is ever ringing, distressing even to the more civilized barbarians.

LIBER XII

DE CONSOLATIONE

1   1. Saepe iam, mater optima, impetum cepi consolandi te, saepe continui. Ut auderem, multa me
impellebant. Primum vi.ebar depositurus omnia
incommoda, cum lacrimas tuas, etiam si supprimere
non potuissem, interim certe abstersissem; deinde
plus habiturum me auctoritatis non dubitabam ad
excitandam te, si prior ipse consurrexissem; praeterea timebam, ne a me victa fortuna aliquem
meorum vinceret. Itaque utcumque conabar manu
super plagam meam imposita ad obliganda vulnera
2 vestra reptare. Hoc propositum meum erant rursus
quae retardarent. Dolori tuo, dum recens saeviret,
sciebam occurrendum non esse, ne illum ipsa solacia
irritarent et accenderent; nam in morbis quoque
nihil est perniciosius quam immatura medicina.
Expectabam itaque, dum ipse vires suas frangeret

---

* Writing in philosophic serenity from his place of exile,
Seneca seeks to allay his mother's grief at the mishap that
has befallen him. After her widowhood she seems to have
lived with her father in Spain (ch. 18. 9), but had, ap-

416

BOOK XII

ON CONSOLATION

OFTEN, my best of mothers, I have felt the impulse to send you consolation,ᵃ and as often I have checked it. The motives that urged me to be so bold were many. In the first place, I thought that I should lay aside all my troubles when, even though I could not stop your weeping, I had meanwhile at least wiped away your tears; again, I felt sure that I should have more power to raise you up, if I had first arisen from my own grief; besides, I was afraid that Fortune, though vanquished by me, might still vanquish someone dear to me. And so, placing my hand over my own gash, I was trying as best I could to creep forward to bind up your wounds. On the other hand, there were reasons which made me delay as regards my purpose. I knew that I ought not to intrude upon your grief while its violence was fresh, lest my very condolences should irritate and inflame it; for in bodily ills also nothing is more harmful than an untimely use of medicine. I was waiting, therefore, until your grief should of itself subdue its violence, and its soreness, soothed by time

parently, visited Rome shortly before her son's banishment (ch. 15. 3).

et ad sustinenda remedia mora mitigatus tangi se
ac tractari pateretur. Praeterea cum omnia claris-
simorum ingeniorum monimenta ad compescendos
moderandosque luctus composita evolverem, non
inveniebam exemplum eius, qui consolatus suos
3 esset, cum ipse ab illis comploraretur. Ita in re
nova haesitabam verebarque, ne haec non consolatio
esset, sed exulceratio. Quid, quod novis verbis nec
ex vulgari et cotidiana sumptis adlocutione opus
erat homini ad consolandos suos ex ipso rogo caput
adlevanti ? Omnis autem magnitudo doloris modum
excedentis necesse est dilectum verborum eripiat,
4 cum saepe vocem quoque ipsam intercludat. Utcumque conitar non fiducia ingenii, sed quia possum
instar efficacissimae consolationis esse ipse consolator.
Cui nihil negares, huic hoc utique te non esse nega-
turam, licet omnis maeror contumax sit, spero, ut
desiderio tuo velis a me modum statui.

1   2. Vide quantum de indulgentia tua promiserim
mihi. Potentiorem me futurum apud te non dubito
quam dolorem tuum, quo nihil est apud miseros po-
tentius. Itaque ne statim cum eo concurram, adero
prius illi et quibus excitetur ingeram ; omnia pro-
2 feram et rescindam, quae iam obducta sunt. Dicet
aliquis : " Quod hoc genus est consolandi, obliterata
mala revocare et animum in omnium aerumnarum

---

a Such as Crantor's treatise Περὶ πένθους, which Cicero calls
a "libellus non magnus, verum aureolus" (*Acad.* ii. 135),
and Cicero's own *Consolatio*. The reference is to an ancient
and well established literary *genre* (*cf.* Introd. p. vii).

to tolerate remedies, should submit to being touched and handled. Moreover, although I unrolled all the works[a] that the most famous writers had composed for the purpose of repressing and controlling sorrow, not one instance did I find of a man who had offered consolation to his dear ones when he himself was bewailed by them; thus, in a novel situation I faltered, and I feared that my words might supply, not consolation, but an aggravation. And besides, a man who was lifting his head from the very bier to comfort his dear ones—what need he would have of words that were new and not drawn from the common and everyday forms of condolence! But the very greatness of every grief that passes bounds must necessarily snatch away the power of choosing words, since often it chokes even the voice itself. Yet I shall try as best I can, not because I have confidence in my eloquence, but because the mere fact that I myself am able to act as comforter may amount to most effective comfort. You who could refuse me nothing, will surely not, I hope, refuse me—although all sorrow is stubborn—your consent to my setting bounds to your grieving.

See how great a thing I have promised to myself from your indulgence. I do not doubt that I shall have more power over you than your grief, though there is nothing that has more power over the wretched. And so, that I may not join battle with it immediately, I shall first uphold it, and be lavish with what will encourage it; I shall expose and tear open all the wounds that have already closed over. But someone will say : "What sort of consolation is this, to recall ills that are blotted out and to set the mind, when it is scarcely able to bear one sorrow, in full

suarum conspectu conlocare vix unius patientem ? "
Sed is cogitet, quaecumque usque eo perniciosa sunt,
ut contra remedium convaluerint, plerumque con-
trariis curari. Omnis itaque luctus illi suos, omnia
lugubria admovebo ; hoc erit non molli via mederi,
sed urere ac secare. Quid consequar ? Ut pudeat
animum tot miseriarum victorem aegre ferre unum
3 vulnus in corpore tam cicatricoso. Fleant itaque
diutius et gemant, quorum delicatas mentes ener-
vavit longa felicitas, et ad levissimarum iniuriarum
motus conlabantur ; at quorum omnes anni per
calamitates transierunt, gravissima quoque forti et
immobili constantia perferant. Unum habet adsidua
infelicitas bonum, quod quos semper vexat, novissime
indurat.

4 Nullam tibi fortuna vacationem dedit a gravissimis
luctibus ; ne natalem quidem tuum excepit. Amisisti
matrem statim nata, immo dum nasceris, et ad vitam
quodammodo exposita es. Crevisti sub noverca,
quam tu quidem omni obsequio et pietate, quanta
vel in filia conspici potest, matrem fieri coegisti ;
nulli tamen non magno constitit etiam bona noverca.
Avunculum indulgentissimum, optimum ac fortissi-
mum virum, cum adventum eius expectares, amisisti,
et ne saevitiam suam fortuna leviorem diducendo
faceret, intra tricensimum diem carissimum virum,
5 ex quo mater trium liberorum eras, extulisti. Lugenti

ᵃ A reference to the Roman custom by which a new-born
babe, unless acknowledged by its father, was exposed to die.
ᵇ Whether Helvia's or Seneca's uncle is not clear, but it
seems natural to associate the incident with that related in
ch. 19. 4.

view of all its sorrows ? " But let him reflect that
whenever diseases become so malignant that they
grow strong in spite of treatment they are then
commonly treated by opposite methods. And so to
the stricken mind I shall exhibit all its distresses, all
its garbs of woe ; my purpose will be not to heal
by gentle measures, but to cauterize and cut. And
what shall I gain ? I shall cause a heart that has been
victorious over so many afflictions to be ashamed to
bewail one wound the more upon a body so marked
with scars. Let those, therefore, whose pampered
minds have been weakened by long happiness, weep
and moan continuously, and faint away at the threat of
the slightest injury ; but let those whose years have
all been passed in a succession of calamities endure
even the heaviest blows with strong and unwaver-
ing resolution. Constant misfortune brings this one
blessing, that those whom it always assails, it at last
fortifies.

To you Fortune has never given any respite from
the heaviest woes ; she did not except even the day
of your birth. You lost your mother as soon as you
had been born, nay, while you were being born, and
entering life you became, as it were, an outcast.[a]
You grew up under a stepmother, but by your complete obedience and devotion as great as can be seen
even in a daughter you forced her to become a true
mother; nevertheless every child has paid a great
price even for a good stepmother. My most loving
uncle,[b] an excellent and very brave man, you lost
just when you were awaiting his arrival, and, lest
Fortune by dividing her cruelty should make it
lighter, within thirty days you buried your dearest
husband, who had made you the proud mother of

tibi luctus nuntiatus est omnibus quidem absentibus
liberis, quasi de industria in id tempus coniectis
malis tuis, ut nihil esset, ubi se dolor tuus reclinaret.
Transeo tot pericula, tot metus, quos sine intervallo
in te incursantis pertulisti. Modo modo in eundem
sinum, ex quo tres nepotes emiseras, ossa trium
nepotum recepisti ; intra vicesimum diem, quam
filium meum in manibus et in osculis tuis mortuum
funeraveras, raptum me audisti. Hoc adhuc defuerat tibi, lugere vivos.

1   3. Gravissimum est ex omnibus, quae umquam
in corpus tuum descenderunt, recens vulnus, fateor ;
non summam cutem rupit, pectus et viscera ipsa divisit. Sed quemadmodum tirones leviter saucii tamen
vociferantur et manus medicorum magis quam ferrum
horrent, at veterani, quamvis confossi, patienter ac
sine gemitu velut aliena corpora exsaniari patiuntur,
ita tu nunc debes fortiter praebere te curationi.

2 Lamentationes quidem et heiulatus et alia, per
quae fere muliebris dolor tumultuatur, amove ;
perdidisti enim tot mala, si nondum misera esse
didicisti. Ecquid videor non timide tecum egisse ?
Nihil tibi subduxi ex malis tuis, sed omnia coacervata
ante te posui.

1   4. Magno id animo feci ; constitui enim vincere
dolorem tuum, non circumscribere. Vincam autem,

three children. This blow was announced when you were already mourning, when, too, all of your children were absent, just as if your misfortunes had been concentrated into that period purposely in order that your grief might find nothing to rest upon. I pass over the countless dangers, the countless fears which you have endured, though they assailed you without cessation. But lately into the self-same lap from which you had let three grandchildren go, you took back the bones of three grandchildren. Less than twenty days after you had buried my son, who died in your arms and amid your kisses, you heard that I had been snatched from you. This misfortune you had still lacked—to mourn the living.

Of all the wounds that have ever gone deep into your body, this latest one, I admit, is the most serious; it has not merely torn the outer skin, but pierced your very breast and vitals. But just as raw recruits cry out even when they are slightly wounded, and shudder more at the hands of surgeons than they do at the sword, while veterans, though deeply wounded, submit patiently and without a groan to the cleansing of their festered bodies just as if these were not their own, so now you ought to offer yourself bravely to be healed. But away with lamentations and outcries and the other demonstrations by means of which women usually vent their noisy grief ; for you have missed the lesson of so many ills if you have not yet learned how to be wretched. Do I seem to have dealt with you now without fear ? Not a single one of your misfortunes have I hidden away ; I have placed them all before you in a heap.

In a heroic spirit have I done this ; for I have determined to conquer your grief, not to dupe it. And

puto, primum **si** ostendero nihil me pati, propter
quod ipse dici possim miser, nedum propter quod
miseros etiam quos contingo faciam, deinde si ad te
transiero et probavero ne tuam quidem gravem esse
fortunam, quae tota ex mea pendet.

2 Hoc prius adgrediar, quod pietas tua audire gestit,
nihil mihi mali esse. Si potuero, ipsas res, quibus
me putat premi, non esse intolerabiles faciam manifestum ; sin id credi non potuerit, at ego mihi ipse
magis placebo, quod inter eas res beatus ero, quae
3 miseros solent facere. Non est, quod de me aliis
credas ; ipse tibi, ne quid incertis opinionibus per-
turberis, indico me non esse miserum. Adiciam,
quo securior sis, ne fieri quidem me posse miserum.

1 5. Bona condicione geniti sumus, si eam non
deseruerimus. Id egit rerum natura, ut ad bene **vi**-
vendum non magno apparatu opus esset ; unusquisque facere se beatum potest. Leve momentum
in adventiciis rebus est et quod in neutram partem
magnas vires habeat. Nec secunda sapientem
evehunt nec adversa demittunt ; laboravit enim
semper, ut in se plurimum poneret, ut a **se** omne
2 gaudium peteret. Quid ergo ? Sapientem esse me
dico ? Minime ; nam id quidem si profiteri possem,
non tantum negarem miserum esse me, sed omnium
fortunatissimum et in vicinum deo perductum prae-

too I shall conquer it, I think, if, in the first place, I show that there is nothing in my condition that could cause anyone to call me wretched, still less cause those also to whom I am related to be wretched on my account ; and, secondly, if I turn next to you, and prove that your fortune also, which depends wholly upon mine, is not a painful one.

First of all, I shall proceed to prove what your love is eager to hear—that I am suffering no ill. If I can, I shall make it clear that those very circumstances, which your love fancies weigh me down, are not intolerable ; but if it will be impossible for you to believe this, I, at any rate, shall be better pleased with myself if I show that I am happy under circumstances that usually make others wretched. You are not asked to believe the report of others about me ; that you may not be at all disturbed by ungrounded suppositions, I myself inform you that I am not unhappy. That you may be the more assured, I will add, too, that I cannot even be made unhappy.

We are born under conditions that would be favourable if only we did not abandon them. Nature intended that we should need no great equipment for living happily ; each one of us is able to make his own happiness. External things are of slight importance, and can have no great influence in either direction. Prosperity does not exalt the wise man, nor does adversity cast him down ; for he has always endeavoured to rely entirely upon himself, to derive all of his joy from himself. What, then ? Do I say that I am a wise man ? By no means ; for if I could make that claim, I should thereby not only deny that I am unhappy, but should also declare that I am the most fortunate of all men and had been brought into

dicarem. Nunc, quod satis est ad omnis miserias leniendas, sapientibus me viris dedi et nondum in auxilium mei validus in aliena castra confugi, eorum 3 scilicet, qui facile se ac suos tuentur. Illi me iusserunt stare adsidue velut in praesidio positum et omnis conatus fortunae, omnis impetus prospicere multo ante quam incurrant. Illis gravis est, quibus repentina est ; facile eam sustinet, qui semper expectat. Nam et hostium adventus eos prosternit, quos inopinantis occupavit ; at qui futuro se bello ante bellum paraverunt, compositi et aptati primum, qui tumul- 4 tuosissimus est, ictum facile excipiunt. Numquam ego fortunae credidi, etiam cum videretur pacem agere ; omnia illa, quae in me indulgentissime conferebat, pecuniam, honores, gratiam, eo loco posui, unde posset sine motu meo repetere. Intervallum inter illa et me magnum habui ; itaque abstulit illa, non avulsit. Neminem adversa fortuna comminuit, 5 nisi quem secunda decepit. Illi qui munera eius velut sua et perpetua amaverunt, qui se suspici propter illa voluerunt, iacent et maerent, cum vanos et pueriles animos, omnis solidae voluptatis ignaros, falsa et mobilia oblectamenta destituunt ; at ille, qui se laetis rebus non inflavit, nec mutatis contrahit. Adversus utrumque statum invictum animum tenet exploratae iam firmitatis ; nam in ipsa felicitate, quid contra infelicitatem valeret, expertus est. 6 Itaque ego in illis, quae omnes optant, existimavi

---

nearness with God. As it is, fleeing to that which is able to lighten all sorrows, I have surrendered myself to wise men and, not yet being strong enough to give aid to myself, I have taken refuge in the camp *a* of others—of those, clearly, who can easily defend themselves and their followers. They have ordered me to stand ever watching, like a soldier placed on guard, and to anticipate all the attempts and all the assaults of Fortune long before she strikes. Her attack falls heavy only when it is sudden; he easily withstands her who always expects her. For the arrival too of the enemy lays low only those whom it catches off guard; but those who have made ready for the coming war before it arrives, fully formed and ready armed, easily sustain the first impact, which is always the most violent. Never have I trusted Fortune, even when she seemed to be offering peace; the blessings she most fondly bestowed upon me—money, office, and influence—I stored all of them in a place from which she could take them back without disturbing me. Between them and me I have kept a wide space; and so she has merely taken them, not torn them, from me. No man is crushed by hostile Fortune who is not first deceived by her smiles. Those who love her gifts as if they were their very own and lasting, who desire to be esteemed on account of them, grovel and mourn when the false and fickle delights forsake their empty, childish minds, that are ignorant of every stable pleasure; but he who is not puffed up by happy fortune does not collapse when it is reversed. The man of long-tested constancy, when faced with either condition, keeps his mind unconquered; for in the very midst of prosperity he proves his strength to meet adversity. Consequently, I have always be-

427

semper nihil veri boni inesse, tum inania et specioso
ac deceptorio fuco circumlita inveni, intra nihil
habentia fronti suae simile. Nunc in his, quae mala
vocantur, nihil tam terribile ac durum invenio quam
opinio volgi minabatur. Verbum quidem ipsum persuasione quadam et consensu iam asperius ad aures
venit et audientis tamquam triste et execrabile
ferit. Ita enim populus iussit ; sed populi scita ex
magna parte sapientes abrogant.

1 6. Remoto ergo iudicio plurium, quos prima
rerum species, utcumque credita est, aufert, videamus,
quid sit exilium. Nempe loci commutatio. Ne angu-
stare videar vim eius et quidquid pessimum in se
habet subtrahere, hanc commutationem loci sequuntur incommoda : paupertas, ignominia, contemptus.
Adversus ista postea confligam ; interim primum
illud intueri volo, quid acerbi adferat ipsa loci commutatio.

2 " Carere patria intolerabile est." Aspice agedum
hanc frequentiam, cui vix urbis immensae tecta
sufficiunt ; maxima pars istius turbae patria caret.
Ex municipiis et coloniis suis, ex toto denique orbe
terrarum confluxerunt. Alios adduxit ambitio, alios
necessitas officii publici, alios imposita legatio, alios
luxuria opportunum et opulentum vitiis locum
428

lieved that there was no real good in the things that
most men pray for ; besides, I have always found
that they were empty and, though painted over with
showy and deceptive colours, have nothing within
to match their outward show. Even now in the
midst of these so-called evils I find nothing so fearful
and harsh as the fancy of everyone foreboded. The
very name of exile, by reason of a sort of persuasion
and general consent, falls by now upon the ears very
harshly, and strikes the hearer as something gloomy
and accursed. For so the people have decreed, but
decrees of the people wise men in large measure
annul.

Therefore, putting aside the verdict of the majority
who are swept away by the first appearance of things,
no matter what ground they have to trust it, let us
see what exile is. It is a change of place. That I may
not seem to narrow its force and to subtract the worst
it holds, I will admit that this changing of place is
attended by disadvantages—by poverty, disgrace,
and scorn. These matters I shall cope with later ;
meanwhile, the first question that I wish to consider
is what unpleasantness the mere changing of place
brings with it.

" To be deprived of one's country is intolerable,"
you say. But come now, behold this concourse of
men, for whom the houses of huge Rome scarcely
suffice ; most of this throng are now deprived of their
country. From their towns and colonies, from the
whole world, in fact, hither have they flocked. Some
have been brought by ambition, some by the obligation of a public trust, some by an envoy's duty having
been laid upon them, some, seeking a convenient and
rich field for vice, by luxury, some by a desire for the

quaerens, alios liberalium studiorum cupiditas, alios
spectacula ; quosdam traxit amicitia, quosdam industria laxam ostendendae virtuti nancta materiam;
quidam venalem formam attulerunt, quidam venalem
3 eloquentiam—nullum non hominum genus concu-
currit in urbem et virtutibus et vitiis magna pretia
ponentem. Iube istos omnes ad nomen citari et
" unde domo " quisque sit quaere. Videbis maiorem
partem esse, quae relictis sedibus suis venerit in
maximam quidem ac pulcherrimam urbem, non
4 tamen suam. Deinde ab hac civitate discede, quae
veluti communis potest dici, omnes urbes circumi ;
nulla non magnam partem peregrinae multitudinis
habet. Transi ab iis, quarum amoena positio et
opportunitas regionis plures adlicit ; deserta loca et
asperrimas insulas, Sciathum et Seriphum, Gyarum et
Cossuran,[1] percense ; nullum invenies exilium, in quo
5 non aliquis animi causa moretur. Quid tam nudum
inveniri potest, quid tam abruptum undique quam
hoc saxum ? Quid ad copias respicienti ieiunius ?
Quid ad homines inmansuetius ? Quid ad ipsum
loci situm horridius ? Quid ad caeli naturam intem-
perantius ? Plures tamen hic peregrini quam cives
consistunt. Usque eo ergo commutatio ipsa locorum
gravis non est, ut hic quoque locus a patria quosdam
6 abduxerit. Invenio qui dicant inesse naturalem
quandam irritationem animis commutandi sedes et
transferendi domicilia ; mobilis enim et inquieta
homini mens data est, nusquam se tenet, spargitur

---

[1] Cossuran *Gertz*: Corsican *A*.

---

[a] A small island near Malta; the others mentioned are
small, isolated islands in the Aegean Sea.
[b] The island of Corsica, Seneca's place of exile.

higher studies, some by the public spectacles; some have been drawn by friendship, some, seeing the ample opportunity for displaying energy, by the chance to work; some have presented their beauty for sale, some their eloquence for sale—every class of person has swarmed into the city that offers high prizes for both virtues and vices. Have all of them summoned by name and ask of each: " Whence do you hail ? " You will find that there are more than half who have left their homes and come to this city, which is truly a very great and a very beautiful one, but not their own. Then leave this city, which in a sense may be said to belong to all, and travel from one city to another; everyone will have a large proportion of foreign population. Pass from the cities that entice very many by their delightful situation and an advantageous position; survey the desert places and the rockiest islands—Sciathus and Seriphus, Gyarus and Cossura *a*; you will find no place of exile where someone does not linger of his own desire. What can be found so barren, what so precipitous on every side as this rock *b* ? If its resources are viewed, what is more starved ? if its people, what is more uncivilized ? if the very topography of the place, what is more rugged ? if the character of its climate, what is more intemperate ? Yet here reside more foreigners than natives. So far, therefore, is the mere changing of places from being a hardship that even this place has tempted some from their native land. I find some who say that nature has planted in the human breast a certain restlessness that makes man seek to change his abode and find a new home; for to him has been given a mind that is fickle and restless, it lingers nowhere; it ranges to and fro, and

et cogitationes suas in omnia nota atque ignota dimittit, vaga et quietis impatiens et novitate rerum 7 laetissima. Quod non miraberis, si primam eius originem aspexeris. Non est ex terreno et gravi concreta corpore, ex illo caelesti spiritu descendit; caelestium autem natura semper in motu est, fugit et velocissimo cursu agitur. Aspice sidera mundum inlustrantia; nullum eorum perstat. Sol[1] labitur adsidue et locum ex loco mutat-et, quamvis cum universo vertatur, in contrarium nihilo minus ipsi mundo refertur, per omnis signorum partes discurrit, numquam resistit; perpetua eius agitatio et aliunde alio 8 commigratio est. Omnia volvuntur semper et in transitu sunt; ut lex et naturae necessitas ordinavit, aliunde alio deferuntur; cum per certa annorum spatia orbes suos explicuerint, iterum ibunt per quae venerant. I nunc et humanum animum ex isdem, quibus divina constant, seminibus compositum moleste ferre transitum ac migrationem puta, cum dei natura adsidua et citatissima commutatione vel delectet se vel conservet.

1 7. A caelestibus agedum te ad humana converte; videbis gentes populosque universos mutasse sedem. Quid sibi volunt in mediis barbarorum regionibus Graecae urbes? quid inter Indos Persasque Macedonicus sermo? Scythia et totus ille ferarum indomitarumque gentium tractus civitates Achaiae

---

[1] sol *added by Michaëlis.*

sends forth its thoughts to all places, known and unknown—a rover, impatient of repose and happiest in
the midst of new scenes. And this will not make you
wonder if you consider its earliest origin. It was not
formed from heavy and terrestrial matter, it came
down from yonder spirit in the sky; but celestial things
by their very nature are always in motion, they ever
flee and are driven on in swiftest course. Behold the
planets that light the world; no one of them stands
still. The sun glides onward ceaselessly and changes
from place to place, and although it revolves with the
universe, it moves none the less in a direction contrary
to that of the world itself, it runs through all the signs
of the zodiac and never halts; its movement is in-
cessant and it shifts from one position to another.
All the planets are ever whirling on and passing by;
as the inviolable law of Nature has decreed, they are
swept from one position to another; when in the
course of fixed periods of years they have rounded
out their circuits, they will enter again upon the paths
by which they came. What folly, then, to think that
the human mind, which has been formed from the
self-same elements as these divine beings, is troubled
by journeying and changing its home, while God's
nature finds delight or, if you will, its preservation
in continuous and most speedy movement!

Come now, turn your attention from things divine
to the affairs of men; you will see that whole tribes
and nations have changed their abodes. Why do we
find Greek cities in the very heart of barbarian
countries? why the Macedonian tongue among the
Indians and the Persians? Scythia and all that
great stretch which is peopled with fierce and unconquered tribes show Achaean towns planted on

Ponticis impositas litoribus ostentat ; non perpetuae
hiemis saevitia, non hominum ingenia ad similitudinem caeli sui horrentia transferentibus domos suas
2 obstiterunt. Atheniensis in Asia turba est ; Miletus
quinque et septuaginta urbium populum in diversa
effudit ; totum Italiae latus, quod infero mari adluitur,
maior Graecia fuit.   Tuscos Asia sibi vindicat ;
Tyrii Africam incolunt, Hispaniam Poeni ; Graeci
se in Galliam immiserunt, in Graeciam Galli ; Pyre-
3 naeus Germanorum transitus non inhibuit—per invia,
per incognita versavit se humana levitas. Liberos con-
iugesque et graves senio parentes traxerunt. Alii
longo errore iactati non iudicio elegerunt locum, sed
lassitudine proximum occupaverunt, alii armis sibi
ius in aliena terra fecerunt ; quasdam gentes, cum
ignota peterent, mare hausit, quaedam ibi consederunt, ubi illas rerum omnium inopia deposuit.
4   Nec omnibus eadem causa relinquendi quaerendi-
que patriam fuit.   Alios excidia urbium suarum
hostilibus armis elapsos in aliena spoliatos suis ex-
pulerunt ; alios domestica seditio summovit ; alios
nimia superfluentis populi frequentia ad exonerandas
vires[1] emisit ; alios pestilentia aut frequentes
terrarum hiatus aut aliqua intoleranda infelicis soli

----

[1] vires A : urbes *Pincianus.*

----

[a] Such as Abydos, Tomi, Cyzicus, Odessus on or near
the Black Sea, and Naucratis in Egypt.
   [b] It was commonly believed that the Etruscans came from
Lydia (Herodotus, i. 94).
   [c] An allusion to the Phocaeans, mentioned below.
   [d] Really Gallograecia or Galatia in Asia Minor, in which
the Gauls were settled after their various invasions in the
third century B.C.
   [e] Seneca seems to have confused these with the Celti-

the shores of the Pontic Sea; not by the fierceness of eternal winter, not by the temper of the inhabitants, as savage as their climate, were men deterred from seeking there new homes. A host of Athenians dwell in Asia; Miletus has poured forth in divers directions enough people to fill seventy-five cities *a*; the whole coast of Italy which is washed by the Lower Sea became a greater Greece; Asia claims the Tuscans *b* as her own; Tyrians live in Africa, Carthaginians in Spain; the Greeks *c* thrust themselves into Gaul, the Gauls into Greece *d*; the Pyrenees did not stay the passage of the Germans *e*—through pathless, through unknown regions restless man has made his way. Wives and children and elders burdened with age trailed along. Some have not settled upon a place from choice, but, tossed about in long wandering, from very weariness have seized upon the nearest; others have established their right in a foreign land by the sword; some tribes, seeking unknown regions, were swallowed up by the sea; some settled in the spot in which a lack of supplies had stranded them.

And not all have had the same reason for leaving their country and seeking a new one. Some, having escaped the destruction of their cities by the forces of the enemy, have been thrust into strange lands when stripped of their own; some have been cast out by civil discord; some have gone forth in order to relieve the pressure from over-crowding caused by an excess of population; some have been driven out by pestilence or repeated earthquakes or certain unbearable defects of an unproductive soil; some

berians, who crossed from Gaul into Spain at an early period.

vitia eiecerunt; quosdam fertilis orae et in maius
laudatae fama corrupit. Alios alia causa excivit
5 domibus suis; illud utique manifestum est, nihil
eodem loco mansisse, quo genitum est. Adsiduus
generis humani discursus est; cotidie aliquid in tam
magno orbe mutatur. Nova urbium fundamenta
iaciuntur, nova gentium nomina extinctis prioribus
aut in accessionem validioris conversis oriuntur.
Omnes autem istae populorum transportationes quid
aliud quam publica exilia sunt? Quid te tam longo
6 circumitu traho? Quid interest enumerare Ante-
norem Patavi conditorem et Euandrum in ripa
Tiberis regna Arcadum conlocantem? Quid Dio-
meden aliosque, quos Troianum bellum victos simul
7 victoresque per alienas terras dissipavit? Romanum
imperium nempe auctorem exulem respicit, quem
profugum capta patria, exiguas reliquias trahentem
necessitas et victoris metus longinqua quaerentem
in Italiam detulit. Hic deinde populus quot colonias
in omnem provinciam misit! Ubicumque vicit
Romanus, habitat. Ad hanc commutationem locorum
libentes nomina dabant et relictis aris suis trans
8 maria sequebatur colonos senex.[1] Res quidem non
desiderat plurium enumerationem; unum tamen
adiciam, quod in oculos se ingerit. Haec ipsa insula
saepe iam cultores mutavit. Ut antiquiora, quae
vetustas obduxit, transeam, Phocide relicta Graii,
qui nunc Massiliam incolunt, prius in hac insula

---

[1] colonos senex *A* : colonus vexillum *Madvig* : *alii alia.*

---

[a] The settlers of Massilia were from Phocaea (*cf.* Herod.
i. 165 *sqq.*) in Asia Minor, not from Phocis in Greece.

have been beguiled by the fame of a fertile shore that was too highly praised. Different peoples have been impelled by different reasons to leave their homes. But at least this is clear—none has stayed in the place where it was born. The human race is constantly rushing to and fro ; in this vast world some change takes place every day. The foundations of new cities are laid, the names of new nations arise, while former ones are blotted out or lost by annexation with a stronger. But all these transmigrations of peoples—what are they but wholesale banishments ? Why should I drag you through the whole long circle ? What need to cite Antenor, founder of Patavium, and Evander, who planted the authority of the Arcadians on the banks of the Tiber ? Why mention Diomedes and the others, victors and vanquished alike, who were scattered throughout strange lands by the Trojan War ? The Roman Empire itself, in fact, looks back to an exile as its founder—a refugee from his captured city, who, taking along a small remnant of his people and driven by fear of the victor to seek a distant land, was brought by destiny into Italy. This people, in turn—how many colonies has it sent to every province ! Wherever the Roman conquers, there he dwells. With a view to this change of country, volunteers would gladly give in their names, and the old man, leaving his altars, would follow the colonists overseas. The matter does not require a listing of more instances ; yet I shall add one which thrusts itself before the eyes. This very island has ofttimes changed its dwellers. To say nothing of older matters, which antiquity has veiled, the Greeks who now inhabit Marseilles, after leaving Phocis,[a]

consederunt, ex qua quid eos fugaverit, incertum est,
utrum caeli gravitas an praepotentis Italiae conspectus
an natura importuosi maris ; nam in causa non
fuisse feritatem accolarum eo apparet, quod maxime
tunc trucibus et inconditis Galliae populis se inter-
9 posuerunt. Transierunt deinde Ligures in eam,
transierunt et Hispani, quod ex similitudine ritus[1]
apparet ; eadem enim tegmenta capitum idemque
genus calciamenti quod Cantabris est, et verba
quaedam ; nam totus sermo conversatione Graecorum Ligurumque a patrio descivit. Deductae
deinde sunt duae civium Romanorum coloniae, altera
a Mario, altera a Sulla ; totiens huius aridi et spinosi
10 saxi mutatus est populus ! Vix denique invenies
ullam terram, quam etiamnunc indigenae colant ;
permixta omnia et insiticia sunt. Alius alii successit ;
hic concupivit, quod illi fastidio fuit ; ille unde
expulerat, eiectus est. Ita fato placuit, nullius rei
eodem semper loco stare fortunam.

1 8. Adversus ipsam commutationem locorum detractis ceteris incommodis, quae exilio adhaerent,
satis hoc remedii putat Varro, doctissimus Romanorum, quod, quocumque venimus, eadem rerum
natura utendum est. M. Brutus satis hoc putat,
quod licet in exilium euntibus virtutes suas secum
2 ferre. Haec etiam si quis singula parum iudicat

---

[1] ex similitudine ritus *A* : ex similitudinibus *Gertz.*

first settled on this island, and it is doubtful what drove them from it—whether the harshness of the climate, or the near sight of all-powerful Italy, or the harbourless character of the sea ; for that the fierceness of the natives was not the cause is clear from the fact that they established themselves in the midst of what were then the most savage and uncivilized peoples of Gaul. Later the Ligurians crossed into the island, and the Spaniards also came, as the similarity of customs shows ; for the islanders wear the same head-coverings and the same kind of foot-gear as the Cantabrians, and certain of their words are the same ; but only a few, for from intercourse with the Greeks and Ligurians their language as a whole has lost its native character. Still later two colonies of Roman citizens were transported to the island, one by Marius, the other by Sulla ; so many times has the population of this barren and thorny rock been changed! In short, you will scarcely find any land in which there dwells to this day a native population ; everywhere the inhabitants are of mongrel and ingrafted stock. One people has followed upon another ; what one scorned, the other coveted ; one that drove another from its land, has been in turn expelled. Thus Fate has decreed that nothing should stand always upon the same plane of fortune. Varro, the most learned of the Romans, holds that, barring all the other ills of exile, the mere changing of place is offset by this ample compensation—the fact that wherever we come, we must still find there the same order of Nature. Marcus Brutus thinks that this is enough—the fact that those who go into exile may take along with them their virtues. Even though one may

efficacia ad consolandum exulem, utraque in unum
conlata fatebitur plurimum posse. Quantulum enim
est, quod perdidimus ! Duo quae pulcherrima sunt,
quocumque nos moverimus, sequentur : natura
3 communis et propria virtus. Id actum est, mihi
crede, ab illo, quisquis formator universi fuit, sive
ille deus est potens omnium, sive incorporalis ratio
ingentium operum artifex, sive divinus spiritus per
omnia maxima ac minima aequali intentione diffusus,
sive fatum et immutabilis causarum inter se cohaeren-
tium series—id, inquam, actum est, ut in alienum
arbitrium nisi vilissima quaeque non caderent.
4 Quidquid optimum homini est, id extra humanam
potentiam iacet, nec dari nec eripi potest. Mundus
hic, quo nihil neque maius neque ornatius rerum
natura genuit, et[1] animus contemplator admira-
torque mundi, pars eius magnificentissima, propria
nobis et perpetua et tam diu nobiscum mansura sunt,
5 quam diu ipsi manebimus. Alacres itaque et erecti,
quocumque res tulerit, intrepido gradu properemus,
emetiamur quascumque terras. Nullum inveniri
exilium intra mundum potest ; nihil enim, quod intra
mundum[2] est, alienum homini est. Undecumque
ex aequo ad caelum erigitur acies, paribus intervallis omnia divina ab omnibus humanis distant.
6 Proinde, dum oculi mei ab illo spectaculo, cuius
insatiabiles sunt, non abducantur, dum mihi solem
lunamque intueri liceat, dum ceteris inhaerere

[1] et *added by Gertz.*
[2] potest ; nihil enim, quod intra mundum *added by
Vahlen.*

[a] As has been shown in ch. 6. 7.
[b] The Stoic dogma of the City of the World; *cf.* Seneca,
De Otio, 4. 1.

decide that these considerations taken singly do not
suffice to give full consolation to the exile, yet he will
admit that they are all-powerful when they are
combined. For how little it is that we have lost!
Wherever we betake ourselves, two things that are
most admirable will go with us—universal Nature
and our own virtue. Believe me, this was the intention of the great creator of the universe, whoever he
may be, whether an all-powerful God, or incorporeal
Reason contriving vast works, or divine Spirit per-
vading all things from the smallest to the greatest
with uniform energy, or Fate and an unalterable
sequence of causes clinging one to the other—this, I
say, was his intention, that only the most worthless
of our possessions should fall under the control of
another. All that is best for a man lies beyond the
power of other men, who can neither give it nor take
it away. This firmament, than which Nature has
created naught greater and more beautiful, and the
most glorious part of it, the human mind[a] that surveys
and wonders at the firmament, are our own everlasting
possessions, destined to remain with us so long
as we ourselves shall remain. Eager, therefore,
and erect, let us hasten with dauntless step
wherever circumstance directs, let us traverse any
lands whatsoever. Inside the world there can be
found no place of exile ; for nothing that is inside
the world is foreign to mankind.[b] No matter where
you lift your gaze from earth to heaven, the realms
of God and man are separated by an unalterable
distance. Accordingly, so long as my eyes are not
deprived of that spectacle with which they are never
sated, so long as I may behold the sun and the moon,
so long as I may fix my gaze upon the other planets,

sideribus, dum ortus eorum occasusque et intervalla
et causas investigare vel ocius meandi vel tardius,
spectare tot per noctem stellas micantis et alias
immobiles, alias non in magnum spatium exeuntis
sed intra suum se circumagentis vestigium, quasdam
subito erumpentis, quasdam igne fuso praestringentes
aciem, quasi decidant, vel longo tractu cum luce
multa praetervolantes, dum cum his sim et caelestibus,
qua homini fas est, immiscear, dum animum ad
cognatarum rerum conspectum tendentem in sublimi
semper habeam—quantum refert mea, quid calcem?

1 9. "At non est haec terra frugiferarum aut
laetarum arborum ferax; non magnis nec naviga-
bilibus fluminum alveis irrigatur; nihil gignit, quod
aliae gentes petant, vix ad tutelam incolentium
fertilis; non pretiosus hic lapis caeditur, non auri
2 argentique venae eruuntur." Angustus animus est,
quem terrena delectant; ad illa abducendus est,
quae ubique aeque apparent, ubique aeque splendent.
Et hoc cogitandum est, ista veris bonis per falsa et
prave credita obstare. Quo longiores porticus ex-
pedierint, quo altius turres sustulerint, quo latius
vicos porrexerint, quo depressius aestivos specus
foderint, quo maiori mole fastigia cenationum sub-
duxerint, hoc plus erit, quod illis caelum abscondat.
3 In eam te regionem casus eiecit, in qua lautissimum
receptaculum casa est; ne tu pusilli animi es et

so long as I may trace out their risings and settings,
their periods, and the reasons for the swiftness or
the slowness of their wandering, behold the countless stars that gleam throughout the night—some at
rest, while others do not enter upon a great course,
but circle around within their own field, some
suddenly shooting forth, some blinding the eyes with
scattered fire as if they were falling, or flying by
with a long trail of lingering light—so long as I may
be with these, and, in so far as it is permitted to a
man, commune with celestial beings, so long as I may
keep my mind directed ever to the sight of kindred
things on high, what difference does it make to me
what soil I tread upon?

"But," you say, "this land yields no fruitful or
pleasing trees; it is watered by the channels of no
great or navigable rivers; it produces nothing that
other nations desire, it scarcely bears enough to
support its own inhabitants; no costly marble is
quarried here, no veins of gold and silver are unearthed." But it is a narrow mind that finds its
pleasure in earthly things; it should turn from these
to those above, which everywhere appear just the
same, everywhere are just as bright. This, too, we
must bear in mind, that earthly things because of
false and wrongly accepted values cut off the sight of
these true goods. The longer the rich man extends
his colonnades, the higher he lifts his towers, the
wider he stretches out his mansions, the deeper he
digs his caverns for summer, the huger loom the roofs
of the banquet-halls he rears, so much the more there
will be to hide heaven from his sight. Has misfortune
cast you into a country where the most sumptuous
shelter is a hut? Truly you show a paltry spirit and

sordide se consolantis, si ideo id fortiter pateris,
quia Romuli casam nosti. Dic illud potius : " Istud
humile tugurium nempe virtutes recipit ? Iam
omnibus templis formosius erit, cum illic iustitia conspecta fuerit, cum continentia, cum prudentia, pietas,
omnium officiorum recte dispensandorum ratio,
humanorum divinorumque scientia. Nullus angustus
est locus, qui hanc tam magnarum virtutium turbam
capit ; nullum exilium grave est, in quod licet cum
hoc ire comitatu."

4   Brutus in eo libro, quem de virtute composuit,
ait se Marcellum vidisse Mytilenis exulantem et,
quantum modo natura hominis pateretur, beatissime
viventem neque umquam cupidiorem bonarum
artium quam illo tempore. Itaque adicit visum sibi
se magis in exilium ire, qui sine illo rediturus esset,
5 quam illum in exilio relinqui. O fortunatiorem
Marcellum eo tempore, quo exilium suum Bruto
adprobavit, quam quo rei publicae consulatum !
Quantus ille vir fuit, qui effecit, ut aliquis exul sibi
videretur, quod ab exule recederet ! Quantus vir
fuit, qui in admirationem sui adduxit hominem etiam
6 Catoni suo mirandum ! Idem Brutus ait C. Caesarem
Mytilenas praetervectum, quia non sustineret videre
deformatum virum. Illi quidem reditum impetravit
senatus publicis precibus tam sollicitus ac maestus,
ut omnes illo die Bruti habere animum viderentur
et non pro Marcello sed pro se deprecari, ne exules
essent, si sine illo fuissent ; sed plus multo consecutus

ª It was dedicated to Cicero (*De Finibus*, i. 3. 8).
ᵇ The bitter enemy of Caesar, who after Pompey's defeat at
Pharsalus retired to Mytilene. He had been consul in 51 B.C.
ᶜ In 46 B.C., but Marcellus was murdered at the Piraeus
on his way home.

take to yourself mean comfort if you bear this bravely only because you know the hut of Romulus. Say, rather, this: "This lowly hovel, I suppose, gives entrance to the virtues? When justice, when temperance, when wisdom and righteousness and understanding of the proper apportionment of all duties and the knowledge of God and man are seen therein, it will straightway become more stately than any temple. No place that can hold this concourse of such great virtues is narrow ; no exile can be irksome to which one may go in such company as this."

Brutus, in the book [a] he wrote on virtue, says that he saw Marcellus [b] in exile at Mytilene, living as happily as the limitations of human nature permit, and that he had never been more interested in liberal studies than he was at that time. And so he adds that, when he was about to return to Rome without him, he felt that he himself was going into exile instead of leaving him behind in exile. How much more favoured was Marcellus at that time when as an exile he won the approval of Brutus than when as consul he won the approval of the state ! What a man he must have been to have made any one feel that he himself was an exile because he was parting from an exile ! What a man he must have been to have drawn to himself the admiration of one whom Cato, his kinsman, had to admire ! Brutus says, too, that Gaius Caesar had sailed past Mytilene because he could not bear to see a hero in disgrace. The senate did indeed by public petitions secure his recall, [c] being meanwhile so anxious and sad that all its members on that day seemed to feel as Brutus did and to be pleading, not for Marcellus, but for themselves, lest they should be exiles if they should be left without him; but

est, quo die illum exulem Brutus relinquere non potuit, Caesar videre. Contigit enim illi testimonium utriusque : Brutus sine Marcello reverti se doluit, 7 Caesar erubuit. Num dubitas, quin se ille Marcellus tantus vir sic ad tolerandum aequo animo exilium saepe adhortatus sit : " Quod patria cares, non est miserum. Ita te disciplinis imbuisti, ut scires omnem locum sapienti viro patriam esse. Quid porro ? Hic, qui te expulit, non ipse per annos decem continuos patria caruit ? Propagandi sine dubio 8 imperii causa ; sed nempe caruit. Nunc ecce trahit illum ad se Africa resurgentis belli minis plena, trahit Hispania, quae fractas et adflictas partes refovet, trahit Aegyptus infida, totus denique orbis, qui ad occasionem concussi imperii intentus est. Cui primum rei occurret ? Cui parti se opponet ? Aget illum per omnes terras victoria sua. Illum suspiciant et colant gentes ; tu vive Bruto miratore contentus ! "

1 ·10. Bene ergo exilium tulit Marcellus nec quicquam in animo eius mutavit loci mutatio, quamvis eam paupertas sequeretur. In qua nihil mali esse, quisquis modo nondum pervenit in insaniam omnia subvertentis avaritiae atque luxuriae, intellegit. Quantulum enim est, quod in tutelam hominis necessarium sit ! Et cui deesse hoc potest ullam 2 modo virtutem habenti ? Quod ad me quidem pertinet, intellego me non opes sed occupationes

446

he attained far more on that day when Brutus could not bear to leave him, and Caesar to see him as an exile! For he was so fortunate as to have testimony from both—Brutus grieved to return without Marcellus, but Caesar blushed! Can you doubt that Marcellus, great hero that he was, often encouraged himself by such thoughts as these to bear his exile with patience? "The mere loss of your country is not unhappiness. You have so steeped yourself in studies as to know that to the wise man every place is his country. And, besides, the very man who drove you forth—was he not absent from his country through ten successive years? His reason was, it is true, the extension of the empire, but for all that he was away from his country. See! now he is drawn toward Africa, which is rife with menace as war again lifts up its head; he is drawn toward Spain, which is nursing back the strength of crushed and shattered forces; he is drawn toward faithless Egypt—in short, toward the whole world, waiting for a chance to strike the stricken empire. Which matter shall he cope with first? Toward what quarter set his face? Throughout all lands shall he be driven, a victim of his own victory. Him let the nations reverence and worship, but do you live content to have Brutus an admirer!"

Nobly, then, did Marcellus endure his exile, and his change of place made no change at all in his mind, although poverty went with him. But everyone who has not yet attained to insanity of greed and luxury, which upset everything, knows that there is no calamity in that. For how small a sum is needed to support a man! And who can fail to have this little if he possesses any merit whatsoever? So far as concerns myself, I know that I have lost, not wealth,

perdidisse. Corporis exigua desideria sunt. Frigus
summoveri vult, alimentis famem ac sitim extinguere;
quidquid extra concupiscitur, vitiis, non usibus
laboratur. Non est necesse omne perscrutari profundum nec strage animalium ventrem onerare nec
conchylia ultimi maris ex ignoto litore eruere ; dii
istos deaeque perdant, quorum luxuria tam invidiosi
3 imperii fines transcendit ! Ultra Phasin capi volunt,
quod ambitiosam popinam instruat, nec piget a
Parthis, a quibus nondum poenas repetîmus, aves
petere. Undique convehunt omnia, nota ignota,[1]
fastidienti gulae ; quod dissolutus deliciis stomachus
vix admittat, ab ultimo portatur oceano ; vomunt
ut edant, edunt ut vomant, et epulas, quas toto orbe
conquirunt, nec concoquere dignantur. Ista si quis
despicit, quid illi paupertas nocet ? Si quis con-
cupiscit, illi paupertas etiam prodest ; invitus enim
sanatur et, si remedia ne coactus quidem recipit,
interim certe, dum non potest, illa[2] nolenti similis
4 est. C. Caesar, quem mihi videtur rerum natura
edidisse, ut ostenderet, quid summa vitia in summa
fortuna possent, centiens sestertio cenavit uno die ;
et in hoc omnium adiutus ingenio vix tamen invenit,
quomodo trium provinciarum tributum una cena
5 fieret. O miserabiles, quorum palatum nisi ad

---

[1] ignota *added by Hermes after Gertz.*
[2] illa *A with punctuation of Duff*: velle *Hermes after
Madvig.*

---

but my "engrossments."[a] The wants of the body are trifling. It requires protection from the cold and the quenching of hunger and thirst by food and drink; if we covet anything beyond, we toil to serve, not our needs, but our vices. We have no need to scour the depths of every sea, to load the belly with the carnage of dumb creatures, to wrest shell-fish from the distant shore of farthest sea—curses of gods and goddesses upon the wretches whose luxury overleaps the bounds of an empire that already stirs too much envy! They want game that is caught beyond the Phasis to supply their pretentious kitchens, and from the Parthians, from whom Rome has not yet got vengeance, they do not blush to get—birds! From every quarter they gather together every known and unknown thing to tickle a fastidious palate; the food which their stomachs, weakened by indulgence, can scarcely retain is fetched from farthest ocean; they vomit that they may eat, they eat that they may vomit, and they do not deign even to digest the feasts for which they ransack the whole world. If a man despises such things, what harm can poverty do him? If a man covets them, poverty becomes even a benefit to him; for he is made whole in spite of himself, and, if even under compulsion he will not take his medicine, for a time at least, while he cannot get them, he is as though he did not want them. Gaius Caesar, whom, as it seems to me, Nature produced merely to show how far supreme vice, when combined with supreme power, could go, dined one day at a cost of ten million sesterces; and though everybody used their ingenuity to help him, yet he could hardly discover how to spend the tribute-money from three provinces on one dinner! How unhappy those whose

pretiosos cibos non excitatur! Pretiosos autem non eximius sapor aut aliqua faucium dulcedo sed raritas et difficultas parandi facit. Alioqui, si ad sanam illis mentem placeat reverti, quid opus est tot artibus ventri servientibus? Quid mercaturis? Quid vastatione silvarum? Quid profundi perscrutatione? Passim iacent alimenta, quae rerum natura omnibus locis disposuit, sed haec velut caeci transeunt et omnes regiones pervagantur, maria traiciunt et, cum famem exiguo possint sedare, magno irritant.

6 Libet dicere: "Quid deducitis naves? Quid manus et adversus feras et adversus homines armatis? Quid tanto tumultu discurritis? Quid opes opibus adgeritis? Non vultis cogitare, quam parva vobis corpora sint? Nonne furor et ultimus mentium error est, cum tam exiguum capias, cupere multum? Licet itaque augeatis census, promoveatis fines; numquam tamen corpora vestra laxabitis. Cum bene cesserit negotiatio, multum militia rettulerit, cum indagati undique cibi coierint, non habebitis, ubi 7 istos apparatus vestros conlocetis. Quid tam multa conquiritis? Scilicet maiores nostri, quorum virtus etiamnunc vitia nostra sustentat, infelices erant, qui sibi manu sua parabant cibum, quibus terra cubile erat, quorum tecta nondum auro fulgebant, quorum templa nondum gemmis nitebant. Itaque tunc per fictiles deos religiose iurabatur; qui illos invocaverant,

---

^a Typical of primitive simplicity; cf. Juvenal, xi. 115 sq.:
Hanc rebus Latiis curam praestare solebat
fictilis et nullo violatus Iuppiter auro.

appetite is stirred at the sight of none but costly foods! And it is not their choice flavour or some delight to the palate that makes them costly, but their rarity and the difficulty of getting them. Otherwise, if men should be willing to return to sanity of mind, what is the need of so many arts that minister to the belly? What need of commerce? What need of ravaging the forests? What need of ransacking the deep? The foods which Nature has placed in every region lie all about us, but men, just as if blind, pass these by and roam through every region, they cross the seas and at great cost excite their hunger when at little cost they might allay it. One would like to say: "Why do you launch your ships? Why do you arm your bands both against man and against wild beasts? Why do you rush to and fro in such wild confusion? Why do you pile riches on riches? You really should remember how small your bodies are! Is it not madness and the wildest lunacy to desire so much when you can hold so little? And so you may swell your incomes, and extend your boundaries; yet you will never enlarge the capacity of your bellies. Though your business may prosper, though warfare may profit you much, though you may bring together foods hunted from every quarter, yet you will have no place in which to store your hoards. Why do you search for so many things? Our ancestors, of course, were unhappy—they whose virtue even to this day props up our vices, who by their own hands provided themselves with food, whose couch was the earth, whose ceilings did not yet glitter with gold, whose temples were not yet shining with precious stones. And so in those days they would solemnly take oath by gods of clay,[a] and those who had invoked them

451

8 ad hostem morituri, ne fallerent, redibant. Scilicet
minus beate vivebat dictator noster, qui Samnitium
legatos audît, cum vilissimum cibum in foco ipse
manu sua versaret, illa, qua iam saepe hostem per-
cusserat laureamque in Capitolini Iovis gremio
reposuerat, quam Apicius nostra memoria vixit, qui
in ea urbe, ex qua aliquando philosophi velut corrup-
tores iuventutis abire iussi sunt, scientiam popinae
professus disciplina sua saeculum infecit.'' Cuius
9 exitum nosse operae pretium est. Cum sestertium
milliens in culinam coniecisset, cum tot congiaria
principum et ingens Capitolii vectigal singulis comi-
sationibus exsorpsisset, aere alieno oppressus rationes
suas tunc primum coactus inspexit. Superfuturum
sibi sestertium centiens computavit et velut in
ultima fame victurus, si in sestertio centiens vixisset,
10 veneno vitam finivit. Quanta luxuria erat, cui
centiens sestertium egestas fuit! I nunc et puta
pecuniae modum ad rem pertinere, non animi.
Sestertium centiens aliquis extimuit et, quod alii
voto petunt, veneno fugit! Illi vero tam pravae
mentis homini ultima potio saluberrima fuit. Tunc
venena edebat bibebatque, cum immensis epulis
non delectaretur tantum, sed gloriaretur, cum vitia
sua ostentaret, cum civitatem in luxuriam suam con-
verteret, cum iuventutem ad imitationem sui sollici-

---

a An allusion to Regulus, hero of the First Punic War,
who, keeping faith with the Carthaginians, returned to
captivity and death.

b Manius Curius, famous for his triumphs over the
Samnites, Sabines, and Pyrrhus.

c As was the privilege of the *triumphator.*

d See p. 126, note *b.*

e In 161 B.C.

would go back to the enemy,[a] preferring to die rather
than break faith. And our dictator,[b] he who, while he
gave audience to the envoys of the Samnites, was busy
at his hearth, cooking with his own hand the cheapest
sort of food, with that hand that had often smitten
the enemy before and had placed a laurel wreath[c]
upon the lap of Capitoline Jove—this man, of course,
was living less happily than did Apicius[d] within
our own memory, who in this very city, which at
one time the philosophers were ordered to leave[e] as
being 'corruptors of youth,' as a professor of the
science of the cook-shop defiled the age with his
teaching." It is worth our while to learn his end.
After he had squandered a hundred million sesterces
upon his kitchen, after he had drunk up at every one
of his revels the equivalent of the many largesses of
the emperors and the huge revenue of the Capitol,
then for the first time, when overwhelmed with debt
and actually forced, he began to examine his accounts.
He calculated that he would have ten million sesterces left, and considering that he would be living
in extreme starvation if he lived on ten million sesterces, he ended his life by poison. But how great
was his luxury if ten millions counted as poverty!
What folly then to think that it is the amount of
money and not the state of mind that matters! Ten
million sesterces made one man shudder, and a sum
that others seek by prayer he escaped from by poison!
For a man so perverted in desire, his last draught was
really the most wholesome. When he not only enjoyed, but boasted of his enormous banquets, when
he flaunted his vices, when he attracted the attention
of the community to his wantonness, when he enticed
the young to imitate his own course, who even without

taret etiam sine malis exemplis per se docilem.
11 Haec accidunt divitias non ad rationem revocantibus,
cuius certi fines sunt, sed ad vitiosam consuetudinem,
cuius immensum et incomprensibile arbitrium est.
Cupiditati nihil satis est, naturae satis est etiam
parum. Nullum ergo paupertas exulis incommodum
habet; nullum enim tam inops exilium est, quod
non alendo homini abunde fertile sit.

1 11. "At vestem ac domum desideraturus est
exsul." Haec[1] quoque ad usum tantum desiderabit:
neque tectum ei deerit neque velamentum; aeque
enim exiguo tegitur corpus quam alitur. Nihil
homini natura, quod necessarium faciebat, fecit
2 operosum. Sed desiderat saturatam multo conchylio
purpuram, intextam auro variisque et coloribus
distinctam et artibus: non fortunae iste vitio, sed
suo pauper est. Etiam si illi quidquid amisit re-
stitueris, nihil ages; plus enim restituendo[2] deerit ex
eo, quod cupit, quam exsuli ex eo, quod habuit.
3 Sed desiderat aureis fulgentem vasis supellectilem
et antiquis nominibus artificum argentum nobile, aes
paucorum insania pretiosum et servorum turbam,
quae quamvis magnam domum angustet, iumentorum
corpora differta et coacta pinguescere et nationum
omnium lapides: ista congerantur licet, numquam
explebunt inexplebilem animum, non magis quam
ullus sufficiet umor ad satiandum eum, cuius deside-

[1] haec *A* : si haec *inferior mss.*, *Duff.*
[2] restituendo *A* : restituto *Muretus*, *Duff.*

---

[a] *i.e.*, to his native land.
[b] *Cf. De Brevitate Vitae*, 12. 2.

bad examples are quick enough to learn of themselves, it was then that he was eating and drinking
poisons. Such are the pitfalls of those who measure
riches, not by the standard of reason, which has its
bounds fixed, but by the standard of a mode of living
that is vicious, and yet has boundless and illimitable
desire. Nothing will satisfy greed, but even scant
measure is enough for Nature's need. Therefore the
poverty of an exile holds no hardship; for no place
of exile is so barren as not to yield ample support
for a man.

" But," you say, " the exile is likely to miss his
raiment and his house." Will he desire these also
merely to the extent of his need? Then he will
lack neither shelter nor covering; for it takes just
as little to shield as to feed the body. Nature has
made nothing difficult which at the same time she
made necessary for man. But if he desires cloth of
purple steeped in rich dye, threaded with gold,
and damasked with various colours and patterns, it is
not Nature's fault but his own if he is poor. Even
if you restore to him whatever he has lost, it will do
no good; for he who will need to be restored[a] will
still lack more of all that he covets than as an exile
he lacked of all that he once had. But if he desires
tables that gleam with vessels of gold, and silver
plate that boasts the names of ancient artists, bronze[b]
made costly by the crazy fad of a few, and a throng
of slaves that would hamper a house however large,
beasts of burden with bodies over-stuffed and forced
to grow fat, and the marbles of every nation—though
he should amass all these, they will no more be able
to satisfy his insatiable soul than any amount of
drink will ever suffice to quench the thirst of a man

rium non ex inopia, sed ex aestu ardentium viscerum
4 oritur ; non enim sitis illa, sed morbus est.   Nec hoc
in pecunia tantum aut alimentis evenit.   Eadem
natura est in omni desiderio, quod modo non ex
inopia, sed ex vitio nascitur ; quidquid illi congesseris,
non finis erit cupiditatis, sed gradus.   Qui continebit
itaque se intra naturalem modum, paupertatem non
sentiet ; qui naturalem modum excedet, eum in
summis quoque opibus paupertas sequetur.   Neces-
sariis rebus et exilia sufficiunt, supervacuis nec regna.
5 Animus est, qui divites facit ; hic in exilia sequitur
et in solitudinibus asperrimis, cum quantum satis est
sustinendo corpori invenit, ipse bonis suis abundat
et fruitur.   Pecunia ad animum nihil pertinet, non
magis quam ad deos immortalis.   Omnia ista, quae
6 imperita ingenia et nimis corporibus suis addicta
suspiciunt, lapides, aurum, argentum et magni
levatique mensarum orbes terrena sunt pondera,
quae non potest amare sincerus animus ac naturae
suae memor, levis ipse, expeditus et, quandoque
emissus fuerit, ad summa emicaturus ; interim
quantum per moras membrorum et hanc circumfusam
gravem sarcinam licet, celeri et volucri cogitatione
7 divina perlustrat.   Ideoque nec exulare umquam
potest, liber et deis cognatus et omni mundo omnique
aevo par ; nam cogitatio eius circa omne caelum it,
in omne praeteritum futurumque tempus immittitur.
Corpusculum hoc, custodia et vinculum animi, huc

whose desire arises, not from need, but from the fire that burns in his vitals ; for this is not thirst, but disease. Nor is this true only in respect to money or food. Every want that springs, not from any need, but from vice is of a like character ; however much you gather for it will serve, not to end, but to advance desire. He, therefore, who keeps himself within the bounds of nature will not feel poverty ; but he who exceeds the bounds of nature will be pursued by poverty even though he has unbounded wealth. Even places of exile will provide necessaries, but not even kingdoms superfluities. It is the mind that makes us rich ; this goes with us into exile, and in the wildest wilderness, having found there all that the body needs for its sustenance, it itself overflows in the enjoyment of its own goods. The mind has no concern with money—no whit more than have the immortal gods. Those things that men's untutored hearts revere, sunk in the bondage of their bodies—jewels, gold, silver, and polished tables, huge and round—all these are earthly dross, for which the untainted spirit, conscious of its own nature, can have no love, since it is itself light and uncumbered, waiting only to be released from the body before it soars to highest heaven. Meanwhile, hampered by mortal limbs and encompassed by the heavy burden of the flesh, it surveys, as best it can, the things of heaven in swift and winged thought. And so the mind can never suffer exile, since it is free, kindred to the gods, and at home in every world and every age ; for its thought ranges over all heaven and projects itself into all past and future time. This poor body, the prison and fetter of the soul, is tossed hither and thither ;

atque illuc iactatur ; in hoc supplicia, in hoc latrocinia, in hoc morbi exercentur. Animus quidem ipse
sacer et aeternus est et cui non possit inici manus.

1   12. Ne me putes ad elevanda incommoda paupertatis, quam nemo gravem sentit, nisi qui putat,
uti tantum praeceptis sapientium, primum aspice,
quanto maior pars sit pauperum, quos nihilo notabis
tristiores sollicitioresque divitibus ; immo nescio an
eo laetiores sint, quo animus illorum in pauciora
2 distringitur. Transeamus opes paene inopes, veniamus[1] ad locupletes. Quam multa tempora sunt,
quibus pauperibus similes sint ! Circumcisae sunt
peregrinantium sarcinae et quotiens festinationem
necessitas itineris exegit, comitum turba dimittitur.
Militantes quotam partem rerum suarum secum
habent, cum omnem apparatum castrensis disciplina
3 summoveat ? Nec tantum condicio illos temporum
aut locorum inopia pauperibus exaequat ; sumunt
quosdam dies, cum iam illos divitiarum taedium cepit,
quibus humi cenent et remoto auro argentoque
fictilibus utantur. Dementes ! hoc quod aliquando
concupiscunt, semper timent. O quanta illos caligo
mentium, quanta ignorantia veritatis excaecat, quos
timor paupertatis[2] exercet, quam voluptatis causa
4 imitantur ! Me quidem, quotiens ad antiqua exempla
respexi, paupertatis uti solaciis pudet, quoniam
quidem eo temporum luxuria prolapsa est, ut maius

---

[1] opes paene inopes, veniamus *Madvig* : ape spe non
obveniamus *A*.

[2] excaecat, quos timor paupertatis *added by Vahlen.*

458

upon it punishments, upon it robberies, upon it diseases work their will. But the soul itself is sacred and eternal, and upon it no hand can be laid.

But, that you may not think that I am using merely the precepts of philosophers for the purpose of belittling the ills of poverty, which no man feels to be burdensome unless he thinks it so, consider, in the first place, how much larger is the proportion of poor men, and yet you will observe that they are not a whit sadder or more anxious than the rich ; nay, I am inclined to think that they are happier because they have fewer things to harass their minds. Let us pass over the wealth that is almost poverty, let us come to the really rich. How many are the occasions on which they are just like the poor ! If they go abroad, they must cut down their baggage, and whenever the pressure of the journey requires haste, they dismiss their train of attendants. And those who are in the army—how small a part of their possessions do they have with them since camp discipline prohibits every luxury ! And not only does the necessity of certain times and places put them on a level with the poor in actual want, but, when a weariness of riches happens to seize them, they even choose certain days on which to dine on the ground and use earthen vessels, refraining from gold and silver plate. Madmen !—this state which they always dread, they sometimes even covet. O what darkness of mind, what ignorance of truth blinds those who, harassed by the fear of poverty, for pleasure's sake simulate poverty ! As for myself, whenever I look back upon the great examples of antiquity, I am ashamed to seek any consolations for poverty, since in these times luxury has

viaticum exulum sit, quam olim patrimonium principum fuit. Unum fuisse Homero servum, tres Platoni,
nullum Zenoni, a quo coepit Stoicorum rigida ac
virilis sapientia, satis constat. Num ergo quisquam
eos misere vixisse dicet, ut non ipse miserrimus ob
5 hoc omnibus videatur ? Menenius Agrippa, qui inter
patres ac plebem publicae gratiae sequester fuit, aere
conlato funeratus est. Atilius Regulus, cum Poenos
in Africa funderet, ad senatum scripsit mercennarium
suum discessisse et ab eo desertum esse rus, quod
senatui publice curari, dum abesset Regulus, placuit.
Fuitne tanti servum non habere, ut colonus eius
6 populus Romanus esset ? Scipionis filiae ex aerario
dotem acceperunt, quia nihil illis reliquerat pater.
Aequum me hercules erat populum Romanum tributum Scipioni semel conferre, cum a Carthagine
semper exigeret. O felices viros puellarum, quibus
populus Romanus loco soceri fuit ! Beatioresne istos
putas, quorum pantomimae deciens sestertio nubunt,
quam Scipionem, cuius liberi a senatu, tutore suo, in
7 dotem aes grave acceperunt ? Dedignatur aliquis
paupertatem, cuius tam clarae imagines sunt ?
Indignatur exsul aliquid sibi deesse, cum defuerit
Scipioni dos, Regulo mercennarius, Menenio funus,
cum omnibus illis quod deerat ideo honestius supple-

---

[a] In the early exchange the unit of value was a pound of
copper.

reached such a pitch that the allowance of exiles is larger than the inheritance of the chief men of old. It is well known that Homer had one slave, Plato three, that Zeno, the founder of the strict and virile school of Stoic philosophy, had none. Will any one say, therefore, that these men lived poorly without seeming from his very words to be the poorest wretch alive? Menenius Agrippa, who acting as mediator between the patricians and plebeians brought harmony to the state, was buried by public subscription. Atilius Regulus, when he was engaged in routing the Carthaginians in Africa, wrote to the senate that his hired-hand had absconded and left the farm abandoned; whereupon the senate decreed that, as long as Regulus was away, his farm was to be managed by the state. Was it not worth his while to have no slave in order that the Roman people might become his labourer? Scipio's daughters received their dowry from the public treasury because their father had left them nothing. Heaven knows! it was only fair for the Roman people to bestow tribute on Scipio just once since he was always exacting it from Carthage. O happy the maidens' husbands in having the Roman people as their father-in-law! Think you that those whose daughters dance upon the stage and wed with a dowry of a million sesterces are happier than Scipio, whose children had the senate as their guardian and received from it a weight of copper[a] for their dowry? Can any one scorn Poverty when she has a pedigree so illustrious? Can an exile chafe at suffering any need when Scipio had need of a dowry, Regulus of a hireling, Menenius of a funeral? when in the case of all of these what they needed was supplied to their

tum sit, quia defuerat? His ergo advocatis non tantum tuta est, sed etiam gratiosa paupertas.

1 13. Responderi potest: " Quid artificiose ista diducis, quae singula sustineri possunt, conlata non possunt? Commutatio loci tolerabilis est, si tantum locum mutes; paupertas tolerabilis est, si ignominia 2 absit, quae vel sola opprimere animos solet." Adversus hunc, quisquis me malorum turba terrebit, his verbis utendum erit: " Si contra unam quamlibet partem fortunae satis tibi roboris est, idem adversus omnis erit. Cum semel animum virtus induravit, undique invulnerabilem praestat. Si avaritia dimisit, vehementissima generis humani pestis, moram tibi ambitio non faciet; si ultimum diem non quasi poenam, sed quasi naturae legem aspicis, ex quo pectore metum mortis eieceris, in id nullius rei timor 3 audebit intrare; si cogitas libidinem non voluptatis causa homini datam, sed propagandi generis, quem non violaverit hoc secretum et infixum visceribus ipsis exitium, omnis alia cupiditas intactum praeteribit. Non singula vitia ratio sed pariter omnia 4 prosternit; in universum semel vincitur." Ignominia tu putas quemquam sapientem moveri posse, qui omnia in se reposuit, qui ab opinionibus vulgi secessit? Plus etiam quam ignominia est mors ignominiosa. Socrates tamen eodem illo vultu, quo

greater honour for the very reason that they had had the need? With such defenders, therefore, as these the cause of poverty becomes not only safe, but greatly favoured.

To this one may reply: "Why do you artfully divide things which, if taken separately, can be endured; if combined, cannot? Change of place is tolerable if you change merely your place; poverty is tolerable if it be without disgrace, which even alone is wont to crush the spirit." In reply to this man, the one who tries to frighten me with an aggregation of ills, I shall have to use such words as these: "If you have enough strength to cope with any one phase of fortune, you will have enough to cope with all. When virtue has once steeled your mind, it guarantees to make it invulnerable from every quarter. If greed, the mightiest curse of the human race, has relaxed its hold, ambition will not detain you; if you regard the end of your days, not as a punishment, but as an ordinance of nature, when once you have cast from your breast the fear of death, the fear of no other thing will dare to enter in; if you consider sexual desire to have been given to man, not for the gratification of pleasure, but for the continuance of the human race, when once you have escaped the violence of this secret destruction implanted in your very vitals, every other desire will pass you by unharmed. Reason lays low the vices not one by one, but all together; the victory is gained once for all." Think you that any wise man can be moved by disgrace—a man who relies wholly upon himself, who draws aloof from the opinions of the common herd? Worse even than disgrace is a disgraceful death. And yet Socrates, wearing the same aspect wherewith he had once all

triginta tyrannos solus aliquando in ordinem redegerat, carcerem intravit ignominiam ipsi loco
detracturus ; neque enim poterat carcer videri in
5 quo Socrates erat. Quis usque eo ad conspiciendam
veritatem excaecatus est, ut ignominiam putet
Marci Catonis fuisse duplicem in petitione praeturae
et consulatus repulsam ? Ignominia illa praeturae
et consulatus fuit, quibus ex Catone honor habebatur.
6 Nemo ab alio contemnitur, nisi a se ante contemptus
est. Humilis et proiectus animus sit isti contumeliae
opportunus ; qui vero adversus saevissimos casus se
extollit et ea mala, quibus alii opprimuntur, evertit,
ipsas miserias infularum loco habet, quando ita
adfecti sumus, ut nihil aeque magnam apud nos
admirationem occupet quam homo fortiter miser.
7 Ducebatur Athenis ad supplicium Aristides, cui
quisquis occurrerat deiciebat oculos et ingemescebat,
non tamquam in hominem iustum sed tamquam in
ipsam iustitiam animadverteretur ; inventus est
tamen, qui in faciem eius inspueret. Poterat ob hoc
moleste ferre, quod sciebat neminem id ausurum
puri oris ; at ille abstersit faciem et subridens ait
comitanti se magistratui : " Admone istum, ne
postea tam improbe oscitet." Hoc fuit contumeliam
8 ipsi contumeliae facere. Scio quosdam dicere contemptu nihil esse gravius, mortem ipsis potiorem
videri. His ego respondebo et' exilium saepe con-
temptione omni carere. Si magnus vir cecidit,
magnus iacuit, non magis illum contemni, quam

---

^a For the incident see Plato, *Apology*, 32 c or Xenophon,
Memorabilia, i. 2. 32.
^b Apparently an error for Phocion (Plutarch, *Phoc.* 36).
^c For, as Seneca says (*De Cons. Sap.* 11. 2), " contumelia
a *contemptu* dicta **est.**"

alone put the Thirty Tyrants in their place,[a] entered prison, and so was to rob even prison of all disgrace; for no place that held Socrates could possibly seem a prison. Who has become so blind to the perception of truth as to think that the twofold defeat of Marcus Cato in his candidacy for the praetorship and the consulship was to him a disgrace? It was the praetorship and the consulship, on which Cato was conferring honour, that suffered the disgrace. No one is despised by another unless he is first despised by himself. An abject and grovelling mind may be liable to such insult; but a man who rises up to face the most cruel of misfortunes, and overthrows the evils by which others are crushed—this man's very sorrows crown him, as it were, with a halo, since we are so constituted that nothing stirs our admiration so much as a man who is brave in adversity.

At Athens, when Aristides[b] was being led to death, everyone who met him would cast down his eyes and groan, feeling that it was not merely a just man, but Justice herself who was being doomed to die; yet one man was found who spat into his face. He might have resented this for the simple reason that he knew well that no clean-mouthed man would have dared to do it. But he wiped his face and smiled, saying to the officer that attended him: " Remind that fellow not to open his mouth so offensively another time." This was to put insult[c] upon insult itself. I know that there are some who say that nothing is harder to bear than scorn, that death itself seems more desirable to them. To these I will reply that even exile is often free from any mark of scorn. If a great man falls, though prostrate, he is still great— men no more scorn him, I say, than they tread upon

465

aedium sacrarum ruinae calcantur, quas religiosi
aeque ac stantis adorant.

1 14. Quoniam meo nomine nihil habes, mater
carissima, quod te in infinitas lacrimas agat, sequitur
ut causae tuae te stimulent. Sunt autem duae ; nam
aut illud te movet, quod praesidium aliquod videris
amisisse, aut illud, quod desiderium ipsum per se
pati non potes.

2 Prior pars mihi leviter perstringenda est ; novi
enim animum tuum nihil in suis praeter ipsos aman-
tem. Viderint illae matres, quae potentiam liberorum
muliebri impotentia exercent, quae, quia feminis
honores non licet gerere, per illos ambitiosae sunt,
quae patrimonia filiorum et exhauriunt et captant,

3 quae eloquentiam commodando aliis fatigant. Tu
liberorum tuorum bonis plurimum gavisa es, minimum
usa ; tu liberalitati nostrae semper imposuisti modum,
cum tuae non imponeres ; tu filia familiae locupletibus
filiis ultro contulisti ; tu patrimonia nostra sic ad-
ministrasti, ut tamquam in tuis laborares, tamquam
alienis abstineres ; tu gratiae nostrae, tamquam
alienis rebus utereris, pepercisti et ex honoribus
nostris nihil ad te nisi voluptas et impensa pertinuit.
Numquam indulgentia ad utilitatem respexit ; non
potes itaque.ea in erepto filio desiderare, quae in[1]
incolumi numquam ad te pertinere duxisti.

1 15. Illo omnis consolatio mihi vertenda est, unde

---

[1] in *added by Haase.*

---

[a] The legal phraseology (*filia familiae*) shows that Helvia
had, as was customary under the Empire, married *sine
conventione*, and thus remained under the rule of her
father (*in patria potestate*), who was still alive (ch. 18. 9).
The point here is that she had not yet inherited wealth.

the fallen walls of a temple, which the devout still revere as deeply as when they were standing.

Since you have no reason, my dearest mother, to be forced to endless tears on my own account, it follows that you are goaded to them by reasons of your own. Now there are two possibilities. For what moves you is either the thought that you have lost some protection, or the mere longing for me is more than you can endure.

The first consideration I must touch upon very lightly; for I well know that your heart values nothing in your dear ones except themselves. Let other mothers look to that—the mothers who make use of a son's power with a woman's lack of self-control, who, because they cannot hold office, seek power through their sons, who both spend their sons' inheritances and hope to be their heirs, who wear out their eloquence in lending it to others. But you have always had the greatest joy in the blessings of your children, yet you have used them not at all; you have always set bounds to our generosity, though you set none to your own; you, though a daughter in your father's household,[a] actually made presents to your wealthy sons; you managed our inheritances with such care that they might have been your own, with such scrupulousness that they might have been a stranger's; you were as sparing in the use of our influence as if you were using a stranger's property, and from our elections to office nothing accrued to you except your pleasure and the expense. Never did your fondness look to self-interest. You cannot, therefore, in the loss of a son miss what you never considered your own concern while he was still safe.

So I must direct all my effort at consolation upon

467

vera vis materni doloris oritur : " Ergo complexu fili
carissimi careo ; non conspectu eius, non sermone
possum frui ! Ubi est ille, quo viso tristem vultum
relaxavi, in quo omnes sollicitudines meas deposui ?
Ubi conloquia, quorum inexplebilis eram ? Ubi
studia, quibus libentius quam femina, familiarius
quam mater intereram ? Ubi ille occursus ? Ubi
2 matre visa semper puerilis hilaritas ? " Adicis istis loca
ipsa gratulationum et convictuum et, ut necesse est,
efficacissimas ad vexandos animos recentis conversa-
tionis notas. Nam hoc quoque adversus te crudeliter
fortuna molita est, quod te ante tertium demum diem
quam perculsus sum, securam nec quicquam tale
3 metuentem digredi voluit. Bene nos longinquitas
locorum diviserat, bene aliquot annorum absentia
huic te malo praeparaverat. Redisti, non ut voluptatem ex filio perciperes, sed ut consuetudinem
desiderii perderes. Si multo ante afuisses, fortius
tulisses ipso intervallo desiderium molliente ; si non
recessisses, ultimum certe fructum biduo diutius
videndi filium tulisses. Nunc crudele fatum ita composuit, ut nec fortunae meae interesses nec absentiae
4 adsuesceres. Sed quanto ista duriora sunt, tanto
maior tibi virtus advocanda est et velut cum hoste

the second point—the true source of the power of a mother's grief. " I am deprived," you say, " of the embraces of my dearest son ; I may no longer enjoy the pleasure of seeing him, the pleasure of his conversation ! Where is he the very sight of whom would smooth my troubled brow, upon whom I unloaded all my anxieties ? Where are the talks, of which I could never have enough ? Where are the studies, which I shared with more than a woman's pleasure, with more than a mother's intimacy ? Where the fond meeting ? Where the boyish glee that was always stirred by the sight of his mother ? " You add to all this the actual scenes of our rejoicings and intercourse and the reminders of our recent association, which are, necessarily, the most potent causes of mental distress. For Fortune cruelly contrived to deal you even this blow—she willed that you should part from me only two days before I was struck down, and you had no reason for concern nor any fear of such a disaster. It is well that we had been separated before by a great distance, it is well that an absence of several years had prepared you for this misfortune. By returning to Rome, you failed to gain the pleasure of seeing your son, and lost the habit of doing without him. Had you been absent long before, you could have borne my misfortune more bravely, since separation itself lessens our longing ; had you not gone away, you would have at least gained the final pleasure of seeing your son two days longer. As it was, cruel Fate contrived that you should neither be with me in the midst of disaster, nor have grown accustomed to my absence. But the harder these circumstances are, the more courage must you summon, and you must engage with For-

noto ac saepe iam victo acrius congrediendum. Non ex intacto corpore tuo sanguis hic fluxit; per ipsas cicatrices percussa es.

1   16. Non est quod utaris excusatione muliebris nominis, cui paene concessum est immoderatum in lacrimas ius, non immensum tamen; et ideo maiores decem mensum spatium lugentibus viros dederunt, ut cum pertinacia muliebris maeroris publica constitutione deciderent. Non prohibuerunt luctus, sed finierunt; nam et infinito dolore, cum aliquem ex carissimis amiseris, adfici stulta indulgentia est, et nullo inhumana duritia. Optimum inter pietatem et rationem temperamentum est et sentire desiderium 2 et opprimere. Non est quod ad quasdam feminas respicias, quarum tristitiam semel sumptam mors finivit (nosti quasdam, quae amissis filiis imposita lugubria numquam exuerunt). A te plus exigit vita ab initio fortior; non potest muliebris excusatio contingere ei, a qua omnia muliebria vitia afuerunt.

3   Non te maximum saeculi malum, impudicitia, in numerum plurium adduxit; non gemmae te, non margaritae flexerunt; non tibi divitiae velut maximum generis humani bonum refulserunt; non te, bene in antiqua et severa institutam domo, periculosa etiam probis peiorum detorsit imitatio; numquam te fecunditatis tuae, quasi exprobraret aetatem, puduit,

470

tune the more fiercely, as with an enemy well known
and often conquered before. It is not from an un-
scathed body that your blood has now flowed ; you
have been struck in the very scars of old wounds.

It is not for you to avail yourself of the excuse of
being a woman, who, in a way, has been granted
the right to inordinate, yet not unlimited, tears.
And so our ancestors, seeking to compromise with the
stubbornness of a woman's grief by a public ordinance, granted the space of ten months as the limit
of mourning for a husband. They did not forbid
their mourning, but limited it ; for when you lose
one who is most dear, to be filled with endless sorrow
is foolish fondness, and to feel none is inhuman hardness. The best course is the mean between affection and reason—both to have a sense of loss and to
crush it. There is no need for you to regard certain
women, whose sorrow once assumed ended only
with their death — some you know, who, having
put on mourning for sons they had lost, never laid the
garb aside. From you life, that was sterner from
the start, requires more ; the excuse of being a
woman can be of no avail to one who has always
lacked all the weaknesses of a woman.

Unchastity, the greatest evil of our time, has never
classed you with the great majority of women;
jewels have not moved you, nor pearls ; to your
eyes the glitter of riches has not seemed the greatest
boon of the human race ; you, who were soundly
trained in an old-fashioned and strict household,
have not been perverted by the imitation of worse
women that leads even the virtuous into pitfalls ;
you have never blushed for the number of your children,
as if it taunted you with your years, never have

numquam more aliarum, quibus omnis commendatio
ex forma petitur, tumescentem uterum abscondisti
quasi indecens onus, nec intra viscera tua conceptas
4 spes liberorum elisisti ; non faciem coloribus ac leno-
ciniis polluisti ; numquam tibi placuit vestis, quae
nihil amplius nudaret, cum poneretur.   Unicum
tibi ornamentum, pulcherrima et nulli obnoxia aetati
5 forma, maximum decus visa est pudicitia.   Non potes
itaque ad obtinendum dolorem muliebre nomen
praetendere, ex quo te virtutes tuae seduxerunt ;
tantum debes a feminarum lacrimis abesse, quantum
vitiis.   Ne feminae quidem te sinent intabescere
volneri tuo, sed leviorem[1] necessario maerore cito
defunctam iubebunt exsurgere, si modo illas intueri
voles feminas, quas conspecta virtus inter magnos
viros posuit.
6   Corneliam ex duodecim liberis ad duos fortuna
redegerat ; si numerare funera Corneliae velles,
amiserat decem, si aestimare, amiserat Gracchos.
Flentibus tamen circa se et fatum eius execrantibus
interdixit, ne fortunam accusarent, quae sibi filios
Gracchos dedisset.   Ex hac femina debuit nasci, qui
diceret in contione : "Tu matri meae male dicas,
quae me peperit ? "   Multo mihi vox matris videtur
animosior ; filius magno aestimavit Gracchorum
natales, mater et funera.

---

[1] leviorem *fortasse* = laetiorem *Basore* : levior necessario
A : vel pio necessarioque *Gertz* : leviore et necessario *Ellis* :
alii alia.

---

[a] An allusion to the gauzy stuffs from Cos affected by
some women.   *Cf.* Propertius, i. 2. 1 *sq.* :

Quid iuvat ornato procedere, vita, capillo
et tenuis Coa veste movere sinus ?

you, in the manner of other women whose only recommendation lies in their beauty, tried to conceal your pregnancy as if an unseemly burden, nor have you ever crushed the hope of children that were being nurtured in your body ; you have not defiled your face with paints and cosmetics ; never have you fancied the kind of dress *a* that exposed no greater nakedness by being removed. In you has been seen that peerless ornament, that fairest beauty on which time lays no hand, that chiefest glory which is modesty. You cannot, therefore, allege your womanhood as an excuse for persistent grief, for your very virtues set you apart ; you must be as far removed from woman's tears as from her vices. But even women will not allow you to pine away from your wound, but will bid you finish quickly with necessary sorrow, and then rise with lighter heart—I mean, if you are willing to turn your gaze upon the women whose conspicuous bravery has placed them in the rank of mighty heroes.

Cornelia bore twelve children, but Fortune had reduced their number to two ; if you wished to count Cornelia's losses, she had lost ten, if to appraise them, she had lost the two Gracchi. Nevertheless, when her friends were weeping around her and cursing her fate, she forbade them to make any indictment against Fortune, since it was Fortune who had allowed the Gracchi to be her sons. Such a woman had right to be the mother of him who exclaimed in the public assembly : " Do you dare to revile the mother who gave birth to me ? " But to me his mother's utterance seems more spirited by far ; the son set great value on the birthdays of the Gracchi, but the mother on their funerals as well.

7 Rutilia Cottam filium secuta est in exilium et usque
eo fuit indulgentia constricta, ut mallet exilium pati
quam desiderium, nec ante in patriam quam cum filio
rediit. Eundem iam reducem et in republica floren-
tem tam fortiter amisit quam secuta est, nec quisquam lacrimas eius post elatum filium notavit. In
expulso virtutem ostendit, in amisso prudentiam;
nam et nihil illam a pietate deterruit et nihil in
tristitia supervacua stultaque detinuit. Cum his te
numerari feminis volo. Quarum vitam semper imi-
tata es, earum in coercenda comprimendaque aegri-
tudine optime sequeris exemplum.

1 17. Scio rem non esse in nostra potestate nec
ullum adfectum servire, minime vero eum, qui ex
dolore nascitur; ferox enim et adversus omne remedium contumax est. Volumus interim illum
obruere et devorare gemitus; per ipsum tamen
compositum fictumque vultum lacrimae profunduntur.
Ludis interim aut gladiatoribus animum occupamus;
at illum inter ipsa, quibus avocatur, spectacula levis
2 aliqua desiderii nota subruit. Ideo melius est vincere illum quam fallere; nam qui delusus et voluptatibus aut occupationibus abductus est, resurgit et
ipsa quiete impetum ad saeviendum conligit. At
quisquis rationi cessit, in perpetuum componitur.
Non sum itaque tibi illa monstraturus, quibus usos

---

[a] C. Aurelius Cotta was driven into exile in 91 B.C. by reason
of his sympathy with Italian insurgents, and returned in
82 B.C.

Rutilia followed her son Cotta^a into exile, and was so wrapped up in her love for him that she preferred exile to losing him ; and only her son's return brought her back to her native land. But when, after he had been restored and now had risen to honour in the state, he died, she let him go just as bravely as she had clung to him ; and after her son was buried no one saw her shed any tears. When he was exiled, she showed courage, when she lost him, wisdom ; for in the one case she did not desist from her devotion, and in the other did not persist in useless and foolish sorrow. In the number of such women as these I wish you to be counted. In your effort to restrain and suppress your sorrow your best course will be to follow the example of those women whose life you have always copied.

I know well that this is a matter that is not in our own power, and that no emotion is submissive, least of all that which is born from sorrow ; for it is wild and stubbornly resists every remedy. Sometimes we will to crush it and to swallow down our cries, yet tears pour down our faces even when we have framed the countenance to deceive. Sometimes we occupy the mind with public games or the bouts of gladiators, but amid the very spectacles that divert the mind it is crushed by some slight reminder of its loss. Therefore it is better to subdue our sorrow than to cheat it ; for when it has withdrawn and has been beguiled by pleasures or engrossments, it rises up again, and from its very rest gathers new strength for its fury. But the grief that has submitted to reason is allayed for ever. And so I am not going to point you to the expedients that I know many have used, suggesting that you distract

esse multos scio, ut peregrinatione te vel longa detineas vel amoena delectes, ut rationum accipiendarum diligentia, patrimonii administratione multum occupes temporis, ut semper novo te aliquo negotio implices. Omnia ista ad exiguum momentum prosunt nec remedia doloris sed impedimenta sunt; 3 ego autem malo illum desinere quam decipi. Itaque illo te duco, quo omnibus, qui fortunam fugiunt, confugiendum est, ad liberalia studia. Illa sanabunt vulnus tuum, illa omnem tristitiam tibi evellent. His etiam si numquam adsuesses, nunc utendum erat; sed quantum tibi patris mei antiquus rigor permisit, omnes bonas artes non quidem comprendisti, attigisti tamen. Utinam quidem virorum 4 optimus, pater meus, minus maiorum consuetudini deditus voluisset te praeceptis sapientiae erudiri potius quam imbui! Non parandum tibi nunc esset auxilium contra fortunam sed proferendum; propter istas, quae litteris non ad sapientiam utuntur sed ad luxuriam instruuntur, minus te indulgere studiis passus est. Beneficio tamen rapacis ingenii plus quam pro tempore hausisti; iacta sunt disciplinarum omnium fundamenta. Nunc ad illas re-5 vertere; tutam te praestabunt. Illae consolabuntur, illae delectabunt, illae si bona fide in animum tuum intraverint, numquam amplius intrabit dolor, numquam sollicitudo, numquam adflictationis

or cheer your mind by travel, whether to distant
or pleasant places, that you employ much time in
diligent examination of your accounts and in the
management of your estate, that you should always
be involved in some new tasks. All such things
avail for a brief space only, and are not the remedies
but the hindrances of sorrow; but I would rather
end it than beguile it. And so I guide you to that
in which all who fly from Fortune must take refuge
—to philosophic studies. They will heal your wound,
they will uproot all your sadness. Even if you had not
been acquainted with them before, you would need
to use them now; but, so far as the old-fashioned
strictness of my father permitted you, though you
have not indeed fully grasped all the liberal arts,
still you have had some dealings with them.
Would that my father, truly the best of men, had
surrendered less to the practice of his forefathers,
and had been willing to have you acquire a thorough
knowledge of the teachings of philosophy instead
of a mere smattering! In that case you would now
have, not to devise, but merely to display, your
protection against Fortune. But he did not suffer
you to pursue your studies because of those women
who do not employ learning as a means to wisdom,
but equip themselves with it for the purpose of
display. Yet, thanks to your acquiring mind, you
imbibed more than might have been expected in the
time you had; the foundations of all systematic
knowledge have been laid. Do you return now to
these studies; they will render you safe. They will
comfort you, they will cheer you; if in earnest they
gain entrance to your mind, nevermore will sorrow
enter there, nevermore anxiety, nevermore the use-

irritae supervacua vexatio. Nulli horum patebit
pectus tuum ; nam ceteris vitiis iam pridem clusum
est. Haec quidem certissima praesidia su..t et
quae sola te fortunae eripere possint.

1 18. Sed quia, dum in illum portum, quem tibi
studia promittunt, pervenis, adminiculis quibus
innitaris opus est, volo interim solacia tibi tua
ostendere. Respice fratres meos, quibus salvis
2 fas tibi non est accusare fortunam. In utroque
habes, quod te diversa virtute delectet. Alter
honores industria consecutus est, alter sapienter
contempsit. Adquiesce alterius fili dignitate, alterius quiete, utriusque pietate! Novi fratrum meorum intimos adfectus. Alter in hoc dignitatem
excolit, ut tibi ornamento sit, alter in hoc se ad
tranquillam quietamque vitam recepit, ut tibi
3 vacet. Bene liberos tuos et in auxilium et in oblec-
tamentum fortuna disposuit ; potes alterius dignitate
defendi, alterius otio frui. Certabunt in te officiis
et unius desiderium duorum pietate supplebitur ;
audacter possum promittere : nihil tibi deerit
praeter numerum.

4 Ab his ad nepotes quoque respice—Marcum
blandissimum puerum, ad cuius conspectum nulla
potest durare tristitia ; nihil tam magnum, nihil
tam recens in cuiusquam pectore furit, quod non
5 circumfusus ille permulceat. Cuius non lacrimas
illius hilaritas supprimat ? Cuius non contractum

---

a Conjecturally Marcus Annaeus Lucanus, Seneca's precocious nephew, who achieved great fame as the author of
the *Pharsalia*, and died miserably at the age of twenty-six,
a victim of the Pisonian conspiracy.

less distress of futile suffering. To none of these will your heart be open ; for to all other weaknesses it has long been closed. Philosophy is your most unfailing safeguard, and she alone can rescue you from the power of Fortune.

But because you have need of something to lean upon until you can reach that haven which philosophy promises to you, I wish meanwhile to point out the consolations you still have. Turn your eyes upon my brothers ; while they live, you have no right to complain of Fortune. Different as their merits are, you have reason to rejoice in both. The one by his energy has attained public honours ; the other with wisdom has scorned them. Find comfort in the prestige of one son, in the retirement of the other—in the devotion of both! The secret motives of my brothers I well know. The one fosters his prestige for the real purpose of shedding lustre upon you ; the other retired to a life of tranquillity and repose for the real purpose of using his leisure for you. It was kind of Fortune so to arrange the lives of your children that they would bring help and pleasure to you ; you can both be protected by the position of the one, and enjoy the leisure of the other. They will vie in their services to you, and the blank that one has caused will be filled by the devotion of two. I can make a confident promise—you will lack nothing except the full number.

From these turn your eyes, too, upon your grandchildren—to Marcus,[a] a most winsome lad, the sight of whom no sorrow can possibly withstand ; no one's heart can hold a sorrow so great or so fresh that his embrace will not soothe it. Whose tears would his merriment not stay ? Whose heart contracted

sollicitudine animum illius argutiae solvant? Quem
non in iocos evocabit illa lascivia? Quem non in se
convertet et abducet infixum cogitationibus illa
6 neminem satiatura garrulitas? Deos oro, contingat
hunc habere nobis superstitem! In me omnis
fatorum crudelitas lassata consistat; quidquid
matri dolendum fuit, in me transierit, quidquid
aviae, in me. Floreat reliqua in suo statu turba.
Nihil de orbitate, nihil de condicione mea querar,
fuerim tantum nihil amplius doliturae domus pia-
mentum.

7　Tene in gremio cito tibi daturam pronepotes
Novatillam, quam sic in me transtuleram, sic mihi
adscripseram, ut posset videri, quod me amisit,
quamvis salvo patre pupilla; hanc et pro me dilige!
Abstulit illi nuper fortuna matrem; tua potest
efficere pietas, ut perdidisse se matrem doleat
8 tantum, non et sentiat. Nunc mores eius compone,
nunc forma; altius praecepta descendunt, quae
teneris imprimuntur aetatibus. Tuis adsuescat sermonibus, ad tuum fingatur arbitrium; multum
illi dabis, etiam si nihil dederis praeter exemplum.
Hoc tibi tam sollemne officium pro remedio erit;
non potest enim animum pie dolentem a sollicitudine
avertere nisi aut ratio aut honesta occupatio.

9　Numerarem inter magna solacia patrem quoque
tuum, nisi abesset; nunc tamen ex adfectu tuo,
480

by pain will his lively prattle not release? Whom will his playfulness not provoke to mirth? Whom intent upon his own thoughts will he not attract to himself and divert by the chatter that no one will weary of? I pray the gods that we may have the good fortune to die before he does! May all the cruelty of Fate be exhausted and stop at me; whatever grief you are doomed to suffer as a mother, whatever as a grandmother—may it all be shifted to me! May all the rest of my band be blest with no change in their lot. I make no complaint of my childlessness, none of my present fortune; only let me be a scapegoat for the family, and know that it will have no more sorrow.

Hold to your bosom Novatilla, who so soon will present you with great-grandchildren, whom I had so transferred to myself, had so adopted as my own, that in losing me she may well seem to be an orphan although her father is still living; do you cherish her for me also! Fortune recently snatched from her her mother, but you by your affection can see to it that she shall but mourn, and not really know, her mother's loss. Now is the time to order her character, now is the time to shape it; instruction that is stamped upon the plastic years leaves a deeper mark. Let her become accustomed to your conversation, let her be moulded to your pleasure; you will give her much even if you give her nothing but your example. Such a sacred duty as this will bring to you relief; for only philosophy or an honourable occupation can turn from its distress the heart that sorrows from affection.

Among your great comforts I would count your father also, were he not now absent. As it is, never-

qui illius in te sit cogita; intelleges, quanto iustius
sit te illi servari quam mihi impendi. Quotiens te
immodica vis doloris invaserit et sequi se iubebit,
patrem cogita! Cui tu quidem tot nepotes pronepotesque dando effecisti, ne unica esses; con-
summatio tamen aetatis actae feliciter in te vertitur. Illo vivo nefas est te, quod vixeris, queri.

1 19. Maximum adhuc solacium tuum tacueram,
sororem tuam, illud fidelissimum tibi pectus, in quod
omnes curae tuae pro indiviso transferuntur, illum
animum omnibus nobis maternum. Cum hac tu
lacrimas tuas miscuisti, in huius primum respirasti
2 sinu. Illa quidem adfectus tuos semper sequitur;
in mea tamen persona non tantum pro te dolet.
Illius manibus in urbem perlatus sum, illius pio
maternoque nutricio per longum tempus aeger
convalui; illa pro quaestura mea gratiam suam
extendit et, quae ne sermonis quidem aut clarae
salutationis sustinuit audaciam, pro me vicit indulgentia verecundiam. Nihil illi seductum vitae
genus, nihil modestia in tanta feminarum petulantia
rustica, nihil quies, nihil secreti et ad otium repositi
mores obstiterunt, quo minus pro me etiam ambi-
3 tiosa fieret. Hoc est, mater carissima, solacium quo
reficiaris. Illi te, quantum potes, iunge, illius

---

[a] Perhaps a sister-in-law, since in § 4 she appears to be the
wife of Seneca's uncle, a mother's brother (*avunculus*). Or
avunculus below may mean the husband of a mother's sister.
482

theless, let your love for him make you think of what his is for you, and you will understand how much more just it is that you should be preserved for him than sacrificed for me. Whenever excessive grief assails you with its power and bids you submit, do you think of your father ! It is true that, by giving to him so many grandchildren and great-grand-children, you have saved yourself from being his sole treasure ; nevertheless the crowning pleasure of his happy life depends on you. While he lives, it is wrong to complain because you have lived.

Of your greatest source of comfort I have thus far said nothing—your sister,[a] that heart most loyal to you, upon which without reserve you unload all your cares, who for all of us has the feeling of a mother. With her tears you have mingled yours, and in her arms you first learned to breathe again. While she closely shares all your feelings, yet in my case it is not for your sake only that she grieves. It was in her arms that I was carried to Rome, it was by her devoted and motherly nursing that I re-covered from a lengthened illness ; she it was who, when I was standing for the quaestorship, gave me generous support—she, who lacked the courage even for conversation or a loud greeting, in order to help me, conquered her shyness by her love. Neither her retired mode of life, nor her modesty, so old-fashioned amid the great boldness of present women, nor her quietness, nor her habits of seclusion and devotion to leisure prevented her at all from becoming even ambitious in order to help me. She, my dearest mother, is the source of comfort from which you will gain new strength. To her attach yourself as closely as you can, in her embraces

483

artissimis amplexibus alliga. Solent maerentes ea,
quae maxime diligunt, fugere et libertatem dolori
suo quaerere. Tu ad illam te, quidquid cogitaveris, confer ; sive servare istum habitum voles sive
deponere, apud illam invenies vel finem doloris tui
4 vel comitem. Sed si prudentiam perfectissimae
feminae novi, non patietur te nihil profuturo maerore
consumi et exemplum tibi suum, cuius ego etiam
spectator fui, narrabit.

Carissimum virum amiserat, avunculum nostrum,
cui virgo nupserat, in ipsa quidem navigatione ; tulit
tamen eodem tempore et luctum et metum evictisque
5 tempestatibus corpus eius naufraga evexit. O
quam multarum egregia opera in obscuro iacent !
Si huic illa simplex admirandis virtutibus contigisset antiquitas, quanto ingeniorum certamine
celebraretur uxor, quae, oblita imbecillitatis, oblita metuendi etiam firmissimis maris, caput suum
periculis pro sepultura obiecit et, dum cogitat de
viri funere, nihil de suo timuit ! Nobilitatur carminibus omnium, quae se pro coniuge vicariam dedit.
Hoc amplius est, discrimine vitae sepulcrum viro
quaerere ; maior est amor, qui pari periculo minus
redimit.

6   Post hoc nemo miratur, quod per sedecim annos,

---

enfold yourself most closely. Those who are in grief are prone to avoid the ones they love most dearly, and to seek liberty for the indulgence of their sorrow. Do you, however, share with her your every thought; whether you wish to retain or to lay aside your mood, you will find in her either the end of your sorrow or a comrade in it. But if I know rightly the wisdom of this most perfect woman, she will not suffer you to be consumed by a grief that will profit you nothing, and she will recount to you an experience of her own, which I myself also witnessed.

In the very midst of a voyage she lost her dearly beloved husband, my uncle, whom she had married when a maiden; nevertheless, she bore up bravely, enduring at the same time both grief and fear, and, overmastering the storm, bore his body safe to land amid the shipwreck. O how many noble deeds of women are unknown to fame! If she had had the good fortune to live in the days of old when men were frank in admiration of heroic deeds, with what rivalry of genius would her praise be sung— a wife who forgetful of her own weakness, forgetful of the sea, which even the stoutest hearts must dread, exposed her own life to peril to give another burial, and, while she planned her husband's funeral, had no fear at all about her own! She[a] who gave herself to death in place of her husband has fame from the songs of all poets. But for a wife to seek burial for her husband at the risk of her own life is far more; for she who, enduring equal danger, has smaller recompense shows greater love.

After this no one can be surprised that throughout the sixteen years during which her husband was

quibus Aegyptum maritus eius optinuit, numquam
in publico conspecta est, neminem provincialem
domum suam admisit, nihil a viro petît, nihil a se
peti passa est. Itaque loquax et in contumelias
praefectorum ingeniosa provincia, in qua etiam
qui vitaverunt culpam non effugerunt infamiam,
velut unicum sanctitatis exemplum suspexit et,
quod illi difficillimum est, cui etiam periculosi sales
placent, omnem verborum licentiam continuit et
hodie similem illi, quamvis numquam speret, semper
optat. Multum erat, si per XVI annos illam pro-
7 vincia probasset; plus est, quod ignoravit. Haec
non ideo refero, ut laudes eius exsequar, quas circumscribere est tam parce transcurrere, sed ut intellegas
magni animi esse feminam, quam non ambitio, non
avaritia, comites omnis potentiae et pestes, vicerunt, non metus mortis iam exarmata nave naufragium suum spectantem deterruit, quo minus
exanimi viro haerens non quaereret, quemadmodum inde exiret, sed quemadmodum efferret.
Huic parem virtutem exhibeas oportet et animum
a luctu recipias et id agas, ne quis te putet partus
tui paenitere.
1   20. Ceterum quia necesse est, cum omnia
feceris, cogitationes tamen tuas subinde ad me
recurrere nec quemquam nunc ex liberis tuis fre-
quentius tibi obversari, non quia illi minus cari
sunt, sed quia naturale est manum saepius ad id
referre, quod doleat, qualem me cogites accipe:

governor of Egypt she was never seen in public, never admitted a native to her house, sought no favour from her husband, nor suffered any to be sought from herself. And so a province that was gossipy and ingenious in devising insults for its rulers, one in which even those who shunned wrongdoing did not escape ill fame, respected her as a singular example of blamelessness, restrained altogether the licence of their tongues—a most difficult thing for a people who take pleasure in even dangerous witticisms—and to-day ever hopes, although it never expects, to see one like her. It would be much to her credit if she had won the approval of the province for sixteen years ; that she escaped its notice is still more. I do not cite these things for the purpose of recounting her praises —for to list them so scantily is to do them injustice —but in order that you may understand the high-mindedness of a woman who has submitted neither to the love of power nor to the love of money—those attendants and curses of all authority—who, with ship disabled and now viewing her own shipwreck, was not deterred by the fear of death from clinging to her lifeless husband and seeking, not how she might escape from the ship, but how she might take him with her. You must show a courage to match hers, must recall your mind from grief, and strive that no one may think that you regret your motherhood.

But because, though you have done everything, your thoughts must necessarily revert at times to me, and it must be that under the circumstances no one of your children engages your mind so often—not that the others are less dear, but that it is natural to lay the hand more often on the part that hurts—hear now how you must think of me. I am as happy and

laetum et alacrem velut optimis rebus. Sunt
enim optimae, quoniam animus omnis occupationis
expers operibus suis vacat et modo se levioribus
studiis oblectat, modo ad considerandam suam
2 universique naturam veri avidus insurgit. Terras
primum situmque earum quaerit, deinde condicionem circumfusi maris cursusque eius alternos et
recursus. Tunc quidquid inter caelum terrasque
plenum formidinis interiacet perspicit et hoc toni-
tribus, fulminibus, ventorum flatibus ac nimborum
nivisque et grandinis iactu tumultuosum spatium.
Tum peragratis humilioribus ad summa perrumpit
et pulcherrimo divinorum spectaculo fruitur, aeterni-
tatis suae memor in omne quod fuit futurumque
est vadit omnibus saeculis.

cheerful as when circumstances were best. Indeed, they are now best, since my mind, free from all other engrossment, has leisure for its own tasks, and now finds joy in lighter studies, now, being eager for the truth, mounts to the consideration of its own nature and the nature of the universe. It seeks knowledge, first, of the lands and where they lie, then of the laws that govern the encompassing sea with its alternations of ebb and flow. Then it takes ken of all the expanse, charged with terrors, that lies between heaven and earth—this nearer space, disturbed by thunder, lightning, blasts of winds, and the downfall of rain and snow and hail. Finally, having traversed the lower spaces, it bursts through to the heights above, and there enjoys the noblest spectacle of things divine, and, mindful of its own immortality, it proceeds to all that has been and will ever be throughout the ages of all time.

INDEX OF NAMES

(The references are to the pages of the English translation.)

491

INDEX OF NAMES

492

INDEX OF NAMES

493

INDEX OF NAMES

INDEX OF NAMES

INDEX OF NAMES

Printed in Great Britain by R. & R. CLARK, LIMITED, *Edinburgh*

THE LOEB CLASSICAL LIBRARY

VOLUMES ALREADY PUBLISHED

LATIN AUTHORS

AMMIANUS MARCELLINUS. J. C. Rolfe. 3 Vols.

APULEIUS : THE GOLDEN ASS (METAMORPHOSES). W. Adlington (1566). Revised by S. Gaselee.

ST. AUGUSTINE : CITY OF GOD. 7 Vols. Vol. I. G. E. McCracken. Vol. II. W. M. Green. Vol. III. D. Wiesen. Vol. IV. P. Levine. Vol. V. E. M. Sanford and W. M. Green. Vol. VI. W. C. Greene. Vol. VII. W. M. Green.

ST. AUGUSTINE, CONFESSIONS OF. W. Watts (1631). 2 Vols.

ST. AUGUSTINE : SELECT LETTERS. J. H. Baxter.

AUSONIUS. H. G. Evelyn White. 2 Vols.

BEDE. J. E. King. 2 Vols.

BOETHIUS : TRACTS AND DE CONSOLATIONE PHILOSOPHIAE. Rev. H. F. Stewart and E. K. Rand. Revised by S. J. Tester.

CAESAR : ALEXANDRIAN, AFRICAN AND SPANISH WARS. A. G. Way.

CAESAR : CIVIL WARS. A. G. Peskett.

CAESAR : GALLIC WAR. H. J. Edwards.

CATO AND VARRO : DE RE RUSTICA. H. B. Ash and W. D. Hooper.

CATULLUS. F. W. Cornish ; TIBULLUS. J. B. Postgate ; and PERVIGILIUM VENERIS. J. W. Mackail.

CELSUS : DE MEDICINA. W. G. Spencer. 3 Vols.

CICERO : BRUTUS AND ORATOR. G. L. Hendrickson and H. M. Hubbell.

CICERO : DE FINIBUS. H. Rackham.

CICERO : DE INVENTIONE, etc. H. M. Hubbell.

CICERO : DE NATURA DEORUM AND ACADEMICA. H. Rackham.

CICERO : DE OFFICIIS. Walter Miller.

CICERO : DE ORATORE, etc. 2 Vols. Vol. I : DE ORATORE, Books I and II. E. W. Sutton and H. Rackham. Vol. II : DE ORATORE, Book III ; DE FATO ; PARADOXA STOICORUM ; DE PARTITIONE ORATORIA. H. Rackham.

CICERO : DE REPUBLICA, DE LEGIBUS. Clinton W. Keyes.

THE LOEB CLASSICAL LIBRARY

Cicero: De Senectute, De Amicitia, De Divinatione. W. A. Falconer.

Cicero: In Catilinam, Pro Murena, Pro Sulla, Pro Flacco. New version by C. Macdonald.

Cicero: Letters to Atticus. E. O. Winstedt. 3 Vols.

Cicero: Letters to his Friends. W. Glynn Williams, M. Cary, M. Henderson. 4 Vols.

Cicero: Philippics. W. C. A. Ker.

Cicero: Pro Archia, Post Reditum, De Domo, De Haruspicum Responsis, Pro Plancio. N. H. Watts.

Cicero: Pro Caecina, Pro Lege Manilia, Pro Cluentio, Pro Rabirio. H. Grose Hodge.

Cicero: Pro Caelio, De Provinciis Consularibus, Pro Balbo. R. Gardner.

Cicero: Pro Milone, In Pisonem, Pro Scauro, Pro Fonteio, Pro Rabirio Postumo, Pro Marcello, Pro Ligario, Pro Rege Deiotaro. N. H. Watts.

Cicero: Pro Quinctio, Pro Roscio Amerino, Pro Roscio Comoedo, Contra Rullum. J. H. Freese.

Cicero: Pro Sestio, In Vatinium. R. Gardner.

[Cicero]: Rhetorica ad Herennium. H. Caplan.

Cicero: Tusculan Disputations. J. E. King.

Cicero: Verrine Orations. L. H. G. Greenwood. 2 Vols.

Claudian. M. Platnauer. 2 Vols.

Columella: De Re Rustica, De Arboribus. H. B. Ash, E. S. Forster, E. Heffner. 3 Vols.

Curtius, Q.: History of Alexander. J. C. Rolfe. 2 Vols.

Florus. E. S. Forster; and Cornelius Nepos. J. C. Rolfe.

Frontinus: Stratagems and Aqueducts. C. E. Bennett and M. B. McElwain.

Fronto: Correspondence. C. R. Haines. 2 Vols.

Gellius. J. C. Rolfe. 3 Vols.

Horace: Odes and Epodes. C. E. Bennett.

Horace: Satires, Epistles, Ars Poetica. H. R. Fairclough.

Jerome: Select Letters. F. A. Wright.

Juvenal and Persius. G. G. Ramsay.

Livy. B. O. Foster, F. G. Moore, Evan T. Sage, A. C. Schlesinger and R. M. Geer (General Index). 14 Vols.

Lucan. J. D. Duff.

Lucretius. W. H. D. Rouse. Revised by M. F. Smith.

Manilius. G. P. Goold.

Martial. W. C. A. Ker. 2 Vols. Revised by E. H. Warmington.

Minor Latin Poets: from Publilius Syrus to Rutilius Namatianus, including Grattius, Calpurnius Siculus,

2

THE LOEB CLASSICAL LIBRARY

THE LOEB CLASSICAL LIBRARY

Varro: De Lingua Latina. R. G. Kent. 2 Vols.
Velleius Paterculus and Res Gestae Divi Augusti.
F. W. Shipley.
Virgil. H. R. Fairclough. 2 Vols.
Vitruvius: De Architectura. F. Granger. 2 Vols.

GREEK AUTHORS

Achilles Tatius. S. Gaselee.
Aelian: On the Nature of Animals. A. F. Scholfield.
3 Vols.
Aeneas Tacticus, Asclepiodotus and Onasander. The
Illinois Greek Club.
Aeschines. C. D. Adams.
Aeschylus. H. Weir Smyth. 2 Vols.
Alciphron, Aelian and Philostratus: Letters. A. R.
Benner and F. H. Fobes.
Apollodorus. Sir James G. Frazer. 2 Vols.
Apollonius Rhodius. R. C. Seaton.
The Apostolic Fathers. Kirsopp Lake. 2 Vols.
Appian: Roman History. Horace White. 4 Vols.
Aratus. Cf. Callimachus: Hymns and Epigrams.
Aristides. C. A. Behr. 4 Vols. Vol. I.
Aristophanes. Benjamin Bickley Rogers. 3 Vols. Verse
trans.
Aristotle: Art of Rhetoric. J. H. Freese.
Aristotle: Athenian Constitution, Eudemian Ethics.
Virtues and Vices. H. Rackham.
Aristotle: The Categories. On Interpretation. H. P.
Cooke; Prior Analytics. H. Tredennick.
Aristotle: Generation of Animals. A. L. Peck.
Aristotle: Historia Animalium. A. L. Peck. 3 Vols.
Vols. I and II.
Aristotle: Metaphysics. H. Tredennick. 2 Vols.
Aristotle: Meteorologica. H. D. P. Lee.
Aristotle: Minor Works. W. S. Hett. "On Colours,"
"On Things Heard," "Physiognomics," "On Plants,"
"On Marvellous Things Heard," "Mechanical Prob-
lems," "On Invisible Lines," "Situations and Names of
Winds," "On Melissus, Xenophanes, and Gorgias."
Aristotle: Nicomachean Ethics. H. Rackham.
Aristotle: Oeconomica and Magna Moralia. G. C.
Armstrong. (With Metaphysics, Vol. II.)
Aristotle: On the Heavens. W. K. C. Guthrie.

4

THE LOEB CLASSICAL LIBRARY

ARISTOTLE: ON THE SOUL, PARVA NATURALIA, ON BREATH.
W. S. Hett.

ARISTOTLE: PARTS OF ANIMALS. A. L. Peck: MOVEMENT
AND PROGRESSION OF ANIMALS. E. S. Forster.

ARISTOTLE: PHYSICS. Rev. P. Wicksteed and F. M. Corn-
ford. 2 Vols.

ARISTOTLE: POETICS; LONGINUS ON THE SUBLIME. W. Ham-
ilton Fyfe; DEMETRIUS ON STYLE. W. Rhys Roberts.

ARISTOTLE: POLITICS. H. Rackham.

ARISTOTLE: POSTERIOR ANALYTICS. H. Tredennick; TOPICS.
E. S. Forster.

ARISTOTLE: PROBLEMS. W. S. Hett. 2 Vols.

ARISTOTLE: RHETORICA AD ALEXANDRUM. H. Rackham.
(With PROBLEMS, Vol. II.)

ARISTOTLE: SOPHISTICAL REFUTATIONS. COMING-TO-BE AND
PASSING-AWAY. E. S. Forster; ON THE COSMOS. D. J.
Furley.

ARRIAN: HISTORY OF ALEXANDER AND INDICA. 2 Vols.
Vol. I. P. Brunt. Vol. II. Rev. E. Iliffe Robson.

ATHENAEUS: DEIPNOSOPHISTAE. C. B. Gulick. 7 Vols.

BABRIUS AND PHAEDRUS (Latin). B. E. Perry.

ST. BASIL: LETTERS. R. J. Deferrari. 4 Vols.

CALLIMACHUS: FRAGMENTS. C. A. Trypanis; MUSAEUS:
HERO AND LEANDER. T. Gelzer and C. Whitman.

CALLIMACHUS: HYMNS AND EPIGRAMS, AND LYCOPHRON.
A. W. Mair; ARATUS. G. R. Mair.

CLEMENT OF ALEXANDRIA. Rev. G. W. Butterworth.

COLLUTHUS. Cf. OPPIAN.

DAPHNIS AND CHLOE. Cf. LONGUS.

DEMOSTHENES I: OLYNTHIACS, PHILIPPICS AND MINOR
ORATIONS: I-XVII AND XX. J. H. Vince.

DEMOSTHENES II: DE CORONA AND DE FALSA LEGATIONE.
C. A. and J. H. Vince.

DEMOSTHENES III: MEIDIAS, ANDROTION, ARISTOCRATES,
TIMOCRATES, ARISTOGEITON. J. H. Vince.

DEMOSTHENES IV-VI: PRIVATE ORATIONS AND IN NEAERAM.
A. T. Murray.

DEMOSTHENES VII: FUNERAL SPEECH, EROTIC ESSAY, EX-
ORDIA AND LETTERS. N. W. and N. J. DeWitt.

DIO CASSIUS: ROMAN HISTORY. E. Cary. 9 Vols.

DIO CHRYSOSTOM. 5 Vols. Vols. I and II. J. W. Cohoon.
Vol. III. J. W. Cohoon and H. Lamar Crosby. Vols. IV
and V. H. Lamar Crosby.

DIODORUS SICULUS. 12 Vols. Vols. I-VI. C. H. Oldfather.
Vol. VII. C. L. Sherman. Vol. VIII. C. B. Welles. Vols.

THE LOEB CLASSICAL LIBRARY

IX and X. Russel M. Geer. Vols. XI and XII. F. R. Walton. General Index. Russel M. Geer.

DIOGENES LAERTIUS. R. D. Hicks. 2 Vols. New Introduction by H. S. Long.

DIONYSIUS OF HALICARNASSUS : CRITICAL ESSAYS. S. Usher. 2 Vols.

DIONYSIUS OF HALICARNASSUS : ROMAN ANTIQUITIES. Spelman's translation revised by E. Cary. 7 Vols.

EPICTETUS. W. A. Oldfather. 2 Vols.

EURIPIDES. A. S. Way. 4 Vols. Verse trans.

EUSEBIUS : ECCLESIASTICAL HISTORY. Kirsopp Lake and J. E. L. Oulton. 2 Vols.

GALEN : ON THE NATURAL FACULTIES. A. J. Brock.

THE GREEK ANTHOLOGY. W. R. Paton. 5 Vols.

THE GREEK BUCOLIC POETS (THEOCRITUS, BION, MOSCHUS). J. M. Edmonds.

GREEK ELEGY AND IAMBUS WITH THE ANACREONTEA. J. M. Edmonds. 2 Vols.

GREEK MATHEMATICAL WORKS. Ivor Thomas. 2 Vols.

HERODES. Cf. THEOPHRASTUS : CHARACTERS.

HERODIAN. C. R. Whittaker. 2 Vols.

HERODOTUS. A. D. Godley. 4 Vols.

HESIOD AND THE HOMERIC HYMNS. H. G. Evelyn White.

HIPPOCRATES AND THE FRAGMENTS OF HERACLEITUS. W. H. S. Jones and E. T. Withington. 4 Vols.

HOMER : ILIAD. A. T. Murray. 2 Vols.

HOMER : ODYSSEY. A. T. Murray. 2 Vols.

ISAEUS. E. S. Forster.

ISOCRATES. George Norlin and LaRue Van Hook. 3 Vols.

[ST. JOHN DAMASCENE]: BARLAAM AND IOASAPH. Rev. G. R. Woodward, Harold Mattingly and D. M. Lang.

JOSEPHUS. 9 Vols. Vols. I-IV. H. St. J. Thackeray. Vol. V. H. St. J. Thackeray and Ralph Marcus. Vols. VI and VII. Ralph Marcus. Vol. VIII. Ralph Marcus and Allen Wikgren. Vol. IX. L. H. Feldman.

JULIAN. Wilmer Cave Wright. 3 Vols.

LIBANIUS : SELECTED WORKS. A. F. Norman. 3 Vols. Vols. I and II.

LONGUS : DAPHNIS AND CHLOE. Thornley's translation revised by J. M. Edmonds ; and PARTHENIUS. S. Gaselee.

LUCIAN. 8 Vols. Vols. I-V. A. M. Harmon. Vol. VI. K. Kilburn. Vols. VII and VIII. M. D. Macleod.

LYCOPHRON. Cf. CALLIMACHUS : HYMNS AND EPIGRAMS.

LYRA GRAECA. J. M. Edmonds. 3 Vols.

LYSIAS. W. R. M. Lamb.

THE LOEB CLASSICAL LIBRARY

MANETHO. W. G. Waddell; PTOLEMY: TETRABIBLOS. F. E. Robbins.

MARCUS AURELIUS. C. R. Haines.

MENANDER I. New edition by W. G. Arnott.

MINOR ATTIC ORATORS. 2 Vols. K. J. Maidment and J. O. Burtt.

MUSAEUS: HERO AND LEANDER. *Cf.* CALLIMACHUS: FRAGMENTS.

NONNOS: DIONYSIACA. W. H. D. Rouse. 3 Vols.

OPPIAN, COLLUTHUS, TRYPHIODORUS. A. W. Mair.

PAPYRI. NON-LITERARY SELECTIONS. A. S. Hunt and C. C. Edgar. 2 Vols. LITERARY SELECTIONS (Poetry). D. L. Page.

PARTHENIUS. *Cf.* LONGUS.

PAUSANIAS: DESCRIPTION OF GREECE. W. H. S. Jones. 4 Vols. and Companion Vol. arranged by R. E. Wycherley.

PHILO. 10 Vols. Vols. I-V. F. H. Colson and Rev. G. H. Whitaker. Vols. VI-X. F. H. Colson. General Index. Rev. J. W. Earp.
Two Supplementary Vols. Translation only from an Armenian Text. Ralph Marcus.

PHILOSTRATUS: THE LIFE OF APOLLONIUS OF TYANA. F. C. Conybeare. 2 Vols.

PHILOSTRATUS: IMAGINES; CALLISTRATUS: DESCRIPTIONS. A. Fairbanks.

PHILOSTRATUS AND EUNAPIUS: LIVES OF THE SOPHISTS. Wilmer Cave Wright.

PINDAR. Sir J. E. Sandys.

PLATO: CHARMIDES, ALCIBIADES, HIPPARCHUS, THE LOVERS, THEAGES, MINOS AND EPINOMIS. W. R. M. Lamb.

PLATO: CRATYLUS, PARMENIDES, GREATER HIPPIAS, LESSER HIPPIAS. H. N. Fowler.

PLATO: EUTHYPHRO, APOLOGY, CRITO, PHAEDO, PHAEDRUS. H. N. Fowler.

PLATO: LACHES, PROTAGORAS, MENO, EUTHYDEMUS. W. R. M. Lamb.

PLATO: LAWS. Rev. R. G. Bury. 2 Vols.

PLATO: LYSIS, SYMPOSIUM, GORGIAS. W. R. M. Lamb.

PLATO: REPUBLIC. Paul Shorey. 2 Vols.

PLATO: STATESMAN, PHILEBUS. H. N. Fowler; ION. W. R. M. Lamb.

PLATO: THEAETETUS AND SOPHIST. H. N. Fowler.

PLATO: TIMAEUS, CRITIAS, CLITOPHO, MENEXENUS, EPISTULAE. Rev. R. G. Bury.

PLOTINUS. A. H. Armstrong. 6 Vols. Vols. I-III.

THE LOEB CLASSICAL LIBRARY

PLUTARCH : MORALIA. 16 Vols. Vols. I-V. F. C. Babbitt.
Vol. VI. W. C. Helmbold. Vol. VII. P. H. De Lacy and
B. Einarson. Vol. VIII. P. A. Clement, H. B. Hoffleit.
Vol. IX. E. L. Minar, Jr., F. H. Sandbach, W. C.
Helmbold. Vol. X. H. N. Fowler. Vol. XI. L. Pearson,
F. H. Sandbach. Vol. XII. H. Cherniss, W. C. Helmbold.
Vol. XIII, Parts 1 and 2. H. Cherniss. Vol. XIV. P. H.
De Lacy and B. Einarson. Vol. XV. F. H. Sandbach.

PLUTARCH : THE PARALLEL LIVES. B. Perrin. 11 Vols.

POLYBIUS. W. R. Paton. 6 Vols.

PROCOPIUS : HISTORY OF THE WARS. H. B. Dewing. 7 Vols.

PTOLEMY : TETRABIBLOS. *Cf.* MANETHO.

QUINTUS SMYRNAEUS. A. S. Way. Verse trans.

SEXTUS EMPIRICUS. Rev. R. G. Bury. 4 Vols.

SOPHOCLES. F. Storr. 2 Vols. Verse trans.

STRABO : GEOGRAPHY. Horace L. Jones. 8 Vols.

THEOPHRASTUS : CHARACTERS. J. M. Edmonds ; HERODES,
etc. A. D. Knox.

THEOPHRASTUS : DE CAUSIS PLANTARUM. G. K. K. Link and
B. Einarson. 3 Vols. Vol. I.

THEOPHRASTUS : ENQUIRY INTO PLANTS. Sir Arthur Hort.
2 Vols.

THUCYDIDES. C. F. Smith. 4 Vols.

TRYPHIODORUS. *Cf.* OPPIAN.

XENOPHON : ANABASIS. C. L. Brownson.

XENOPHON : CYROPAEDIA. Walter Miller. 2 Vols.

XENOPHON : HELLENICA. C. L. Brownson.

XENOPHON : MEMORABILIA AND OECONOMICUS. E. C. Marchant ; SYMPOSIUM AND APOLOGY. O. J. Todd.

XENOPHON : SCRIPTA MINORA. E. C. Marchant and G. W.
Bowersock.

DESCRIPTIVE PROSPECTUS ON APPLICATION

CAMBRIDGE, MASS.   LONDON

HARVARD UNIV. PRESS   WILLIAM HEINEMANN LTD